Mathematical Fuzzy Logic in the Emerging Fields of Engineering, Finance, and Computer Sciences

Mathematical Fuzzy Logic in the Emerging Fields of Engineering, Finance, and Computer Sciences

Editor

Amit K. Shukla

MDPI • Basel • Beijing • Wuhan • Barcelona • Belgrade • Manchester • Tokyo • Cluj • Tianjin

Editor
Amit K. Shukla
Faculty of Information Technology
University of Jyväskylä
Jyväskylä
Finland

Editorial Office
MDPI
St. Alban-Anlage 66
4052 Basel, Switzerland

This is a reprint of articles from the Special Issue published online in the open access journal *Axioms* (ISSN 2075-1680) (available at: www.mdpi.com/journal/axioms/special_issues/Fuzzy_Logic_in_Engineering_Finance_Computer_Sciences).

For citation purposes, cite each article independently as indicated on the article page online and as indicated below:

LastName, A.A.; LastName, B.B.; LastName, C.C. Article Title. *Journal Name* **Year**, *Volume Number*, Page Range.

ISBN 978-3-0365-5936-0 (Hbk)
ISBN 978-3-0365-5935-3 (PDF)

© 2023 by the authors. Articles in this book are Open Access and distributed under the Creative Commons Attribution (CC BY) license, which allows users to download, copy and build upon published articles, as long as the author and publisher are properly credited, which ensures maximum dissemination and a wider impact of our publications.

The book as a whole is distributed by MDPI under the terms and conditions of the Creative Commons license CC BY-NC-ND.

Contents

About the Editor vii

Preface to "Mathematical Fuzzy Logic in the Emerging Fields of Engineering, Finance, and Computer Sciences" ix

Amit K. Shukla
Mathematical Fuzzy Logic in the Emerging Fields of Engineering, Finance, and Computer Sciences
Reprinted from: *Axioms* **2022**, *11*, 615, doi:10.3390/axioms11110615 1

Songsong Dai, Lei Du, Haifeng Song and Yingying Xu
On the Composition of Overlap and Grouping Functions
Reprinted from: *Axioms* **2021**, *10*, 272, doi:10.3390/axioms10040272 5

Eunsuk Yang
Basic Core Fuzzy Logics and Algebraic Routley–Meyer-Style Semantics
Reprinted from: *Axioms* **2021**, *10*, 273, doi:10.3390/axioms10040273 15

Yadan Jiang and Dong Qiu
The Relationships among Three Kinds of Divisions of Type-1 Fuzzy Numbers
Reprinted from: *Axioms* **2022**, *11*, 77, doi:10.3390/axioms11020077 31

Nguyen Van Thanh and Nguyen Thi Kim Lan
A New Hybrid Triple Bottom Line Metrics and Fuzzy MCDM Model: Sustainable Supplier Selection in the Food-Processing Industry
Reprinted from: *Axioms* **2022**, *11*, 57, doi:10.3390/axioms11020057 41

Chia-Nan Wang, Nhat-Luong Nhieu, Kim-Phong Tran and Yen-Hui Wang
Sustainable Integrated Fuzzy Optimization for Multimodal Petroleum Supply Chain Design with Pipeline System: The Case Study of Vietnam
Reprinted from: *Axioms* **2022**, *11*, 60, doi:10.3390/axioms11020060 55

Juan Carlos Martin, Natalia Soledad Bustamante-Sánchez and Alessandro Indelicato
Analyzing the Main Determinants for Being an Immigrant in Cuenca (Ecuador) Based on a Fuzzy Clustering Approach
Reprinted from: *Axioms* **2022**, *11*, 74, doi:10.3390/axioms11020074 81

Dušan J. Simjanović, Nemanja Zdravković and Nenad O. Vesić
On the Factors of Successful e-Commerce Platform Design during and after COVID-19 Pandemic Using Extended Fuzzy AHP Method
Reprinted from: *Axioms* **2022**, *11*, 105, doi:10.3390/axioms11030105 103

Oscar Castillo, Juan R. Castro and Patricia Melin
Interval Type-3 Fuzzy Aggregation of Neural Networks for Multiple Time Series Prediction: The Case of Financial Forecasting
Reprinted from: *Axioms* **2022**, *11*, 251, doi:10.3390/axioms11060251 121

Alessandro Indelicato, Juan Carlos Martín and Raffaele Scuderi
Comparing Regional Attitudes toward Immigrants in Six European Countries
Reprinted from: *Axioms* **2022**, *11*, 345, doi:10.3390/axioms11070345 135

Dillip Ranjan Nayak, Neelamadhab Padhy, Pradeep Kumar Mallick, Mikhail Zymbler and Sachin Kumar
Brain Tumor Classification Using Dense Efficient-Net
Reprinted from: *Axioms* **2022**, *11*, 34, doi:10.3390/axioms11010034 . . . . **151**

Daniel Doz, Darjo Felda and Mara Cotič
Combining Students' Grades and Achievements on the National Assessment of Knowledge: A Fuzzy Logic Approach
Reprinted from: *Axioms* **2022**, *11*, 359, doi:10.3390/axioms11080359 . . . . **165**

Sunny Mishra, Amit K. Shukla and Pranab K. Muhuri
Explainable Fuzzy AI Challenge 2022: Winner's Approach to a Computationally Efficient and Explainable Solution
Reprinted from: *Axioms* **2022**, *11*, 489, doi:10.3390/axioms11100489 . . . . **185**

Fernando Castelló-Sirvent and Carlos Meneses-Eraso
Research Agenda on Multiple-Criteria Decision-Making: New Academic Debates in Business and Management
Reprinted from: *Axioms* **2022**, *11*, 515, doi:10.3390/axioms11100515 . . . . **201**

About the Editor

Amit K. Shukla

Dr. Amit K. Shukla is currently working at the Faculty of Information Technology, University of Jyvaskyla, Finland. He received his Ph.D. in Computer Science from South Asian University, New Delhi, India, for which he acquired a prestigious INSPIRE fellowship from the Department of Science and Technology, Government of India. Amit was awarded the gold medal for his Master's degree (2013) from the same university. He chaired the ACM chapter of South Asian University in 2011-2012 and is currently an IEEE Young Professional and an active member of societies such as the IEEE Computational Intelligence Society, EUSFLAT, and the Finnish Artificial Intelligence Society.

Amit has been the editorial board member of MDPI's *Axioms* journal since July 2021. He is a regular reviewer of journals such as *Engineering Applications of Artificial Intelligence, Applied Soft Computing, IEEE Transactions on Fuzzy Systems, Neural Computing and Applications,* and *Journal of Advanced Research.* His research areas include fuzzy sets and systems, Industry 4.0, explainable artificial intelligence, anomaly detection, transfer learning, machine learning, and soft-computing approaches.

As a young researcher, he has a h-index of 20 on Google Scholar and 40 publications in reputed SCI journals and CORE A/B-ranked International Conferences. He has chaired and co-chaired several sessions at WCCI 2020 and 2022. In the recently concluded WCCI 2022, Amit was the FUZZ-IEEE mentoring program co-lead. He also has two years of industrial experience as a software engineer, working on projects from companies such as NOKIA and SONY.

Preface to "Mathematical Fuzzy Logic in the Emerging Fields of Engineering, Finance, and Computer Sciences"

Mathematical fuzzy logic (MFL) specifically targets many-valued logic and has significantly contributed to the logical foundations of fuzzy set theory (FST). It explores the computational and philosophical rationale behind uncertainties due to imprecision in the backdrop of traditional mathematical logic. Since uncertainty is present in almost every real-world application, it is essential to develop novel approaches and tools for efficient processing.

This book is the collection of the publications in the Special Issue "Mathematical Fuzzy Logic in the Emerging Fields of Engineering, Finance, and Computer Sciences", which aims to cover theoretical and practical aspects of MFL. The research works cover the contributions of MFL (and FST) to the emerging fields of engineering, finance, and computer sciences. Specifically, this book addresses several problems, such as:
- Industrial optimization problems
- Multi-criteria decision-making
- Financial forecasting problems
- Image processing
- Educational data mining
- Explainable artificial intelligence, etc.

This Special Issue received a significant number of publications for the publications; however, only a few could be selected. The editor would like to thank all the authors for contributing to this book. We sincerely hope this book will encourage and inspire researchers to explore this exciting area of mathematical fuzzy logic. From the wide range of application areas already covered in this book, we believe that it will motivate researchers to utilize MFL and FST in other emerging areas.

Amit K. Shukla
Editor

Editorial

Mathematical Fuzzy Logic in the Emerging Fields of Engineering, Finance, and Computer Sciences

Amit K. Shukla

Faculty of Information Technology, University of Jyvaskyla, P.O. Box 35 (Agora), 40014 Jyvaskyla, Finland; amit.k.shukla@jyu.fi

With more than 50 years of literature, fuzzy logic has gradually progressed from an emerging field to a developed research domain, incorporating the sub-domain of mathematical fuzzy logic (MFL). Primarily, MFL's objective is to formulate a mathematical tool to model uncertainty due to vagueness in real-world scenarios. It specifically targets many-valued logic and has significantly contributed to the logical foundations of fuzzy set theory (FST).

Through the efforts and substantial interest of researchers, the literature on the theory and modeling of MFL has expanded rapidly, improving our understanding of this domain. However, more attention is required from the research community, especially in the current context where data-driven information retrieval and explainability are of great concern with the growth of never-ending data resources. Moving forward, MFL aims to target a wide range of complex problems in many applicative contexts ranging from the medical sciences to finance, commerce, engineering, and computer sciences. Further, it also holds significance when applied to the applications of artificial intelligence and deep learning.

This book presents papers on the cutting-edge contributions of MFL to the emerging fields of engineering, finance, and computer sciences. It comprises a collection of articles in the *Axioms* Special Issue of "Mathematical Fuzzy Logic in the Emerging Fields of Engineering, Finance, and Computer Sciences". The publications in this book target both the theoretical and practical aspects of MFL and FST. Several publications present the formal approaches to applying MFL to address real-world problems.

The volume opens with the theoretical contribution of the paper by Dai et al. [1], where authors extensively studied the properties of overlap and grouping functions concerning operations such as meet, join, convex combination, and ⊛-composition. The outcome of this work may be utilized as a norm for selecting the generation approach of overlap and grouping functions.

In another significant contribution, the fuzzy logic extension to the Algebraic Routley–Meyer-style (ARM) semantics for basic substructural logic is introduced by Yang [2]. Overcoming the drawbacks of earlier semantics such as Kripke and Urquhart, ARM semantics signifies operations interpreting ternary relations, which eventually followed similar structures as algebraic semantics.

Jiang and Qiu [3] proposed a novel granular division for the division of type-1 fuzzy numbers. The authors first critically analyzed the relationships among the already available gH-division, g-division, and gr-division. Numerical examples were then added, in order to provide young researchers with a comprehensive overview of this domain.

Thanh and Lan [4] targeted the supplier selection problem pertaining to Vietnam's Food Processing industry. They proposed novel hybrid metrics comprising Triple Bottom Line Metrics, the Fuzzy Analytical Hierarchy Process, and the Combined Compromise Solution approach for sustainable supplier selection.

Another case study of Vietnam focused on petroleum supply chain design was conducted by Wang et al. [5]. The authors proposed a methodology comprised of a heuristic-based location-determination algorithm and a fuzzy multi-objective mixed-integer linear programming optimization model. The uncertainty parameters in this model, such as cost, demand, capacity import/export quota, and cost, are modeled using fuzzy triangular numbers. Maximizing profits and energy security and minimizing transport emissions are the objectives framed under the fuzzy min-max goal programming model.

Moving to another continent, Martin et al. [6] presented an interesting study that analyzes the key factors needed to identify immigrants in Ecuador. This study is administered on the inputs provided by the immigrants themselves, which first process it using a fuzzy hybrid multi-criteria decision-making method, and then a fuzzy clustering approach is used to study the variations in the main determinants.

Another paper targeting a specific geographical area was composed by Simjanović et al. [7]. The authors explored the criteria for the successful design of an e-commerce platform in the Western Balkans. The involved factors were studied during and after the COVID-19 pandemic and modeled using fuzzy triangular numbers under the framework of a fuzzy analytical hierarchy process.

Another computational study focused on the post-COVID-19 effect is presented by Castillo et al. [8]. A financial forecasting problem is addressed using the fuzzy system aggregation of neural networks. Here, the authors utilize the interval type-3 fuzzy theory for the fuzzy system and propose a novel mathematical formulation. The ensemble of COVID-19 and the Dow Jones time series is used for the experimental analysis.

Indelicato et al. [9] studied the attitude of European countries such as Belgium, Germany, Spain, France, the United Kingdom, and Portugal towards various immigrants using the Fuzzy-Hybrid TOPSIS method. The fuzzy triangular numbers are used to model the uncertain parameters, and the data for this study are extracted from the International Social Survey Program.

With the application to brain tumor classification, Nayak et al. [10] suggested an upgraded dense EfficientNet convolutional neural network (CNN) architecture. This CNN model is fully automatic and follows min-max normalization for the multi-classification of brain tumors. The authors advised that fuzzy logic could be used as a pre-processing step for improving brain images. Further, the proposed architecture may be employed as a decision-making tool.

The application of fuzzy logic for assessing students in education is studied by Doz et al. [11]. It integrates the teacher-assigned student's grades with the Italian national assessment of mathematical knowledge score for the final judgment. The teacher grades include grades on oral and written evaluations.

Mishra et al. [12] explored the area of explainable artificial intelligence (XAI) based on the background of the Explainable Fuzzy AI Challenge 2022. The authors proposed a fully autonomous and optimized XAI algorithm that can play the Python arcade game "Asteroid Smasher". A computationally efficient and explainable solution is presented for an XAI agent to work in this fast-paced environment, using fuzzy inference systems (FIS) such as Mamdani FIS and TSK-based FIS.

Castelló-Sirvent and Meneses-Eraso [13] present a systemic review study that focuses on the ideology and agenda in multiple-criteria decision making (MCDM) with the perspective of the business and management domain. The bibliometric section explores the major thematic clusters, international research collaboration networks, and the bibliographic coupling of the MCDM-related publications.

With such a diverse publication, ranging from several theoretical contributions to applications for solving real-world problems, this book will be of great interest to students, as well as young and established researchers.

Conflicts of Interest: The author declares no conflict of interest.

References

1. Dai, S.; Du, L.; Song, H.; Xu, Y. On the Composition of Overlap and Grouping Functions. *Axioms* **2021**, *10*, 272. [CrossRef]
2. Yang, E. Basic Core Fuzzy Logics and Algebraic Routley–Meyer-Style Semantics. *Axioms* **2021**, *10*, 273. [CrossRef]
3. Jiang, Y.; Qiu, D. The Relationships among Three Kinds of Divisions of Type-1 Fuzzy Numbers. *Axioms* **2022**, *11*, 77. [CrossRef]

4. Thanh, N.V.; Lan, N.T.K. A new hybrid triple bottom line metrics and fuzzy MCDM model: Sustainable supplier selection in the food-processing industry. *Axioms* **2022**, *11*, 57. [CrossRef]
5. Wang, C.-N.; Nhieu, N.-L.; Tran, K.-P.; Wang, Y.-H. Sustainable Integrated Fuzzy Optimization for Multimodal Petroleum Supply Chain Design with Pipeline System: The Case Study of Vietnam. *Axioms* **2022**, *11*, 60. [CrossRef]
6. Martin, J.C.; Bustamante-Sánchez, N.S.; Indelicato, A. Analyzing the Main Determinants for Being an Immigrant in Cuenca (Ecuador) Based on a Fuzzy Clustering Approach. *Axioms* **2022**, *11*, 74. [CrossRef]
7. Simjanović, D.J.; Zdravković, N.; Vesić, N.O. On the Factors of Successful e-Commerce Platform Design during and after COVID-19 Pandemic Using Extended Fuzzy AHP Method. *Axioms* **2022**, *11*, 105. [CrossRef]
8. Castillo, O.; Castro, J.R.; Melin, P. Interval Type-3 Fuzzy Aggregation of Neural Networks for Multiple Time Series Prediction: The Case of Financial Forecasting. *Axioms* **2022**, *11*, 251. [CrossRef]
9. Indelicato, A.; Martín, J.C.; Scuderi, R. Comparing Regional Attitudes toward Immigrants in Six European Countries. *Axioms* **2022**, *11*, 345. [CrossRef]
10. Nayak, D.R.; Padhy, N.; Mallick, P.K.; Zymbler, M.; Kumar, S. Brain Tumor Classification Using Dense Efficient-Net. *Axioms* **2022**, *11*, 34. [CrossRef]
11. Doz, D.; Felda, D.; Cotič, M. Combining Students' Grades and Achievements on the National Assessment of Knowledge: A Fuzzy Logic Approach. *Axioms* **2022**, *11*, 359. [CrossRef]
12. Mishra, S.; Shukla, A.K.; Muhuri, P.K. Explainable Fuzzy AI Challenge 2022: Winner's Approach to a Computationally Efficient and Explainable Solution. *Axioms* **2022**, *11*, 489. [CrossRef]
13. Castelló-Sirvent, F.; Meneses-Eraso, C. Research Agenda on Multiple-Criteria Decision-Making: New Academic Debates in Business and Management. *Axioms* **2022**, *11*, 515. [CrossRef]

Article

On the Composition of Overlap and Grouping Functions

Songsong Dai, Lei Du, Haifeng Song and Yingying Xu *

School of Electronics and Information Engineering, Taizhou University, Taizhou 318000, China; ssdai@tzc.edu.cn (S.D.); dulei2109@tzc.edu.cn (L.D.); isshf@126.com (H.S.)
* Correspondence: yyxu@tzc.edu.cn

Abstract: Obtaining overlap/grouping functions from a given pair of overlap/grouping functions is an important method of generating overlap/grouping functions, which can be viewed as a binary operation on the set of overlap/grouping functions. In this paper, firstly, we studied closures of overlap/grouping functions w.r.t. ⊛-composition. In addition, then, we show that these compositions are order preserving. Finally, we investigate the preservation of properties like idempotency, migrativity, homogeneity, k-Lipschitz, and power stable.

Keywords: overlap functions; grouping functions; composition; closures; properties preservation

Citation: Dai, S.; Du, L.; Song, H.; Xu, Y. On the Composition of Overlap and Grouping Functions. *Axioms* **2021**, *10*, 272. https://doi.org/10.3390/axioms10040272

Academic Editor: Amit K. Shukla

Received: 9 September 2021
Accepted: 20 October 2021
Published: 24 October 2021

Publisher's Note: MDPI stays neutral with regard to jurisdictional claims in published maps and institutional affiliations.

Copyright: © 2021 by the authors. Licensee MDPI, Basel, Switzerland. This article is an open access article distributed under the terms and conditions of the Creative Commons Attribution (CC BY) license (https://creativecommons.org/licenses/by/4.0/).

1. Introduction

Overlap function [1] is a special case of aggregation functions [2]. Grouping function [3] is the dual concept of overlap function. In recent years, overlap and grouping functions have attracted wide interest. In the field of application, they are used in image processing [1,4], classification [5,6], and decision-making [7,8]. In the field of theoretical research, the concepts of general, Archimedean, n-dimensional, interval-valued, and complex-valued overlap/grouping functions have been introduced [9–17]. In the literature about overlap/grouping functions, much attention have been recently paid to their properties, this study has enriched overlap/grouping functions. Bedregal [9] studied some properties such as migrativity, idempotency, and homogeneity of overlap/overlap functions. Gomez et al. [12] also considered these properties of N-dimensional overlap functions. Costa and Bedregal [18] introduced quasi-homogeneous overlap functions. Qian and Hu [19] studied the migrativity of uninorms and nullnorms over overlap/grouping functions. They [13,20,21] also studied multiplicative generators and additive generators of overlap/grouping functions and the distributive laws of fuzzy implication functions over overlap functions [9,12,13,18–21]. Moreover, overlap/grouping functions also can be viewed as binary connectives on [0, 1], then they can be used to construct other fuzzy connectives. Residual implication, (G, N)-implications, QL-implications, (IO, O)-fuzzy rough sets, and binary relations induced from overlap/grouping functions have been studied [22–27].

The construction of the following overlap/grouping functions was developed in many literature works [1,4,13,15,16,21,27,28]. Obtaining overlap/grouping functions from given overlap/grouping functions is one of the methods to generate overlap/grouping functions. We consider this work as a composition of two or more overlap/grouping functions. As mentioned above, some properties are important for overlap/grouping functions. Thus, it raises the question of whether the new generated overlap/grouping function still satisfies the properties of overlap/grouping functions. In this paper, we consider properties preservation of four compositions such as meet operation, join operation, convex combination, and ⊛-composition of overlap/grouping functions. These results might serve as a certain criteria for choices of generation methods of overlap/grouping functions from given overlap/grouping functions.

The paper is organized as follows: In Section 2, we recall the concepts of overlap/grouping functions and their properties. In Section 3, we studied the closures of overlap/grouping functions w.r.t. ⊛-composition. In Section 4, we study the order preservation of compositions. In Section 5, we study properties' preservation of compositions. In Section 6, conclusions are briefly summed up.

2. Preliminaries

2.1. Overlap and Grouping Functions

First, we recall the concepts of overlap/grouping functions and their properties; for details, see [1,9,12,13].

Definition 1 ([1]). *A bivariate function $O : [0,1]^2 \to [0,1]$ is an overlap function if it has the following properties:*

(O1) *It is commutative;*
(O2) $O(\eta, \xi) = 0$ *if and only if* $\eta\xi = 0$;
(O3) $O(\eta, \xi) = 1$ *if and only if* $\eta\xi = 1$;
(O4) *It is non-decreasing;*
(O5) *It is continuous.*

Definition 2 ([1]). *A bivariate function $G : [0,1]^2 \to [0,1]$ is a grouping function if it has the following properties:*

(G1) *It is commutative;*
(G2) $G(\eta, \xi) = 0$ *if and only if* $\eta = \xi = 0$;
(G3) $G(\eta, \xi) = 1$ *if and only if* $\eta = 1$ *or* $\xi = 1$.
(G4) *It is non-decreasing;*
(G5) *It is continuous.*

If O is an overlap function, then the function $G(\eta, \xi) = 1 - O(1 - \eta, 1 - \xi)$ is the dual grouping function of G.

2.2. Properties of Overlap and Grouping Functions

For any two overlap (or grouping) functions O and O', if $O(\eta, \xi) \leq O'(\eta, \xi)$ holds for all $(\eta, \xi) \in [0,1]^2$, then we say that O is weaker than O', denoted $O \preceq O'$. For example, consider the following three overlap functions $O_M(\eta, \xi) = \min(\eta, \xi)$, $O_P(\eta, \xi) = \eta\xi$ and $O_{Mid}(\eta, \xi) = \eta\xi\frac{\eta+\xi}{2}$, we get this ordering for these overlap functions:

$$O_{Mid} \preceq O_P \preceq O_M.$$

Some interesting properties for overlap (or grouping) functions are:

(ID) Idempotency:
$$O(\eta, \eta) = \eta$$
for all $\eta \in [0,1]$;

(MI) Migrativity:
$$O(\alpha\eta, \xi) = O(\eta, \alpha\xi)$$
for all $\alpha, \eta, \xi \in [0,1]$;

(HO-k) Homogeneous of order $k \in\,]0, \infty[$:
$$O(\alpha\eta, \alpha\xi) = \alpha^k O(\eta, \xi)$$
for all $\alpha \in [0, \infty[$ and $\eta, \xi \in [0,1]$ such that $\alpha\eta, \alpha\xi \in [0,1]$;

(k-LI) k-Lipschitz:
$$|O(\eta_1,\xi_1) - O(\eta_2,\xi_2)| \le k(|\eta_1 - \eta_2| + |\xi_1 - \xi_2|)$$
for all $\eta_1, \eta_2, \xi_1, \xi_2 \in [0,1]$.

(PS) Power stable [29]:
$$O(\eta^r, \xi^r) = O(\eta, \xi)^r$$
for all $r \in]0, \infty[$ and $\eta, \xi \in [0,1]$.

3. Compositions of Overlap and Grouping Functions and Their Closures

In the following, we list four compositions of overlap/grouping functions including meet, join, convex combination, and ⊛-composition. In addition, we then studied their closures.

3.1. Compositions of Overlap and Grouping Functions

For any two overlap (or grouping) functions O_1 and O_2, meet and join operations of O_1 and O_2 are defined by

$$(O_1 \vee O_2)(\eta,\xi) = \max\left(O_1(\eta,\xi), O_2(\eta,\xi)\right), \tag{1}$$
$$(O_1 \wedge O_2)(\eta,\xi) = \min\left(O_1(\eta,\xi), O_2(\eta,\xi)\right) \tag{2}$$

for all $(\eta,\xi) \in [0,1]^2$.

For any two overlap (or grouping) functions O_1 and O_2, a convex combination of O_1 and O_2 is defined as

$$O_\lambda = \lambda O_1(\eta,\xi) + (1-\lambda) O_2(\eta,\xi) \tag{3}$$

for all $(\eta,\xi) \in [0,1]^2$ and $\lambda \in [0,1]$.

For any two overlap (or grouping) functions O_1 and O_2, the ⊛-composition of O_1 and O_2 is defined as

$$(O_1 \circledast O_2)(\eta,\xi) = O_1(\eta, O_2(\eta,\xi)) \tag{4}$$

for all $(\eta,\xi) \in [0,1]^2$.

3.2. Closures of the Compositions

Closures of the meet operation, join operation, and convex combination have been obtained in [1,3,9]. The ⊛-composition of two overlap functions is closed means ⊛-composition of two bivariate functions on $[0,1]$ preserves (O1), (O2), (O3), (O4) and (O5). Similarly, the ⊛-composition of two grouping functions is closed means ⊛-composition of two bivariate functions on $[0,1]$ preserves (G1), (G2), (G3), (G4) and (G5).

Theorem 1. *If two bivariate functions $O_1, O_2 : [0,1]^2 \to [0,1]$ satisfy (O2)$\big((O3), (G2), (G3),$ (O4), (O5)$\big)$, then $(O_1 \circledast O_2)$ also satisfies (O2)$\big((O3), (G2), (G3), (O4), (O5)\big)$.*

Proof. First, we show that ⊛-composition preserves (O2). If
$$(O_1 \circledast O_2)(\eta,\xi) = O_1(\eta, O_2(\eta,\xi)) = 0,$$
then, since O_1 satisfies (O2), we have $\eta O_2(\eta,\xi)=0$. Case I, if $\eta = 0$ and $O_2(\eta,\xi) \neq 0$, then $\eta\xi = 0\xi = 0$; Case II, if $\eta = 0$ and $O_2(\eta,\xi) = 0$, then $\eta\xi = 0\xi = 0$; Case III, if $\eta \neq 0$ and $O_2(\eta,\xi) = 0$, since O_2 satisfies (O2), then $\eta\xi = 0$.

Next, we show that ⊛-composition preserves (O3). If
$$(O_1 \circledast O_2)(\eta,\xi) = O_1(\eta, O_2(\eta,\xi)) = 1,$$

then, since O_1 satisfies (O3), we have $\eta O_2(\eta,\xi)=1$. Then, $\eta = 1$ and $O_2(\eta,\xi) = 1$, since O_2 satisfies (O3), then $\eta\xi = 1$.

Then, we show that $\circledast$-composition preserves (G2). If

$$(O_1 \circledast O_2)(\eta,\xi) = O_1(\eta, O_2(\eta,\xi)) = 0,$$

then, since O_1 satisfies (G2), we have $\eta = O_2(\eta,\xi)=0$. Since O_2 satisfies (G2), then $\eta = \xi = 0$.

Afterwards, we show that $\circledast$-composition preserves (G3). If

$$(O_1 \circledast O_2)(\eta,\xi) = O_1(\eta, O_2(\eta,\xi)) = 1,$$

then, since O_1 satisfies (G3), we have $\eta = 1$ or $O_2(\eta,\xi)=1$. Since O_2 satisfies (G3), $O_2(\eta,\xi)=1$ means $\eta = 1$ or $\xi = 1$.

The case for (O4) and (O5) are straightforward. □

Unfortunately, $\circledast$-composition of two bivariate functions does not preserve (O1). For example, let $O_1(\eta,\xi) = O_2(\eta,\xi) = \eta\xi$; then, $(O_1 \circledast O_2)(\eta,\xi) = \eta^2\xi$ is not commutative. This means $\circledast$-composition of two overlap/grouping functions is not closed.

However, it is possible to find an example that $\circledast$-composition of two overlap/grouping functions is also an overlap/grouping function. For example, for two given overlap functions $O_1(\eta,\xi) = O_2(\eta,\xi) = \min(\eta,\xi)$, their $\circledast$-composition $(O_1 \circledast O_2)(\eta,\xi) = \min(\eta,\xi)$ is an overlap function.

The summary of the closures of two bivariate functions w.r.t. these compositions is shown in Table 1.

Table 1. Closures of the compositions.

Property	O_1	O_2	$O_1 \vee O_2$	$O_1 \wedge O_2$	O_λ	$O_1 \circledast O_2$
O_1	✓	✓	✓	✓	✓	×
O_2	✓	✓	✓	✓	✓	✓
O_3	✓	✓	✓	✓	✓	✓
G_2	✓	✓	✓	✓	✓	✓
G_3	✓	✓	✓	✓	✓	✓
O_4	✓	✓	✓	✓	✓	✓
O_5	✓	✓	✓	✓	✓	✓

4. Order Preservation

In the following we show that the meet operation, join operation, convex combination, and $\circledast$-composition of overlap/grouping functions are order preserving.

Theorem 2. *Suppose that four overlap functions have $O_1 \preceq O_2$ and $O_3 \preceq O_4$, then $(O_1 \vee O_3) \preceq (O_2 \vee O_4)$, $(O_1 \wedge O_3) \preceq (O_2 \wedge O_4)$ $(O_{1,3,\lambda}) \preceq (O_{2,4,\lambda})$ and $(O_1 \circledast O_3) \preceq (O_2 \circledast O_4)$, where $O_{1,3,\lambda} = \lambda O_1(\eta,\xi) + (1-\lambda)O_3(\eta,\xi)$ and $O_{2,4,\lambda} = \lambda O_2(\eta,\xi) + (1-\lambda)O_4(\eta,\xi)$.*

Proof. The case for meet operation, join operation, and convex combination are straightforward. We show only that $\circledast$-composition preserves order. For any $\eta,\xi \in [0,1]$, from $O_3 \preceq O_4$, we have $O_3(\eta,\xi) \leq O_4(\eta,\xi)$. Since O_1 is non-decreasing and $O_1 \preceq O_2$, we have

$$\begin{aligned}(O_1 \circledast O_3)(\eta,\xi) &= O_1(\eta, O_3(\eta,\xi)) \\ &\leq O_1(\eta, O_4(\eta,\xi)) \\ &\leq O_2(\eta, O_4(\eta,\xi)) \\ &= (O_2 \circledast O_4)(\eta,\xi).\end{aligned}$$

Thus, $(O_1 \circledast O_3) \preceq (O_2 \circledast O_4)$. □

Theorem 3. *Suppose that four grouping functions have $G_1 \preceq G_2$ and $G_3 \preceq G_4$, then $(G_1 \vee G_3) \preceq (G_2 \vee G_4)$, $(G_1 \wedge G_3) \preceq (G_2 \wedge G_4)$ $(G_{1,3,\lambda}) \preceq (G_{2,4,\lambda})$ and $(G_1 \circledast G_3) \preceq (G_2 \circledast G_4)$, where $G_{1,3,\lambda} = \lambda G_1(\eta,\xi) + (1-\lambda)G_3(\eta,\xi)$ and $G_{2,4,\lambda} = \lambda G_2(\eta,\xi) + (1-\lambda)G_4(\eta,\xi)$.*

5. Properties Preservation

In the following, we study properties preserved by meet operation, join operation, convex combination, and $\circledast$-composition of overlap/grouping functions.

5.1. Properties Preserved by Meet and Join Operations of Overlap/Grouping Functions

First, we consider the meet and join operations of overlap/grouping functions.

Theorem 4. *If two overlap functions O_1 and O_2 satisfy* **(ID)**$\big($**(MI)**, **(HO-k)**, **(k-LI)**, **(PS)**$\big)$*, then $(O_1 \vee O_2)$ and $(O_1 \wedge O_2)$ also satisfy* **(ID)**$\big($**(MI)**, **(HO-k)**, **(k-LI)**, **(PS)**$\big)$.

Proof. First, we show that meet operation preserves **(ID)**. Assume that O_1 and O_2 satisfy **(ID)**; then, for any $\lambda, \eta \in [0,1]$,

$$\begin{aligned}(O_1 \vee O_2)(\eta,\eta) &= \max\big(O_1(\eta,\eta), O_2(\eta,\eta)\big) \\ &= \max(\eta,\eta) \\ &= \eta.\end{aligned}$$

Next, we show that meet operation preserves **(MI)**. Assume that O_1 and O_2 satisfy **(MI)**, then, for any $\alpha, \eta, \xi \in [0,1]$,

$$\begin{aligned}(O_1 \vee O_2)(\alpha\eta,\xi) &= \max\big(O_1(\alpha\eta,\xi), O_2(\alpha\eta,\xi)\big) \\ &= \max\big(O_1(\eta,\alpha\xi), O_2(\eta,\alpha\xi)\big) \\ &= (O_1 \vee O_2)(\eta,\alpha\xi).\end{aligned}$$

Then, we show that the meet operation preserves **(HO-k)**. Assuming that O_1 and O_2 satisfy **(HO-k)**, then, for any $\alpha, \eta, \xi \in [0,1]$,

$$\begin{aligned}(O_1 \vee O_2)(\alpha\eta,\alpha\xi) &= \max\big(O_1(\alpha\eta,\alpha\xi), O_2(\alpha\eta,\alpha\xi)\big) \\ &= \max\big(\alpha^k O_1(\eta,\xi), \alpha^k O_2(\eta,\xi)\big) \\ &= \alpha^k \max\big(O_1(\eta,\xi), O_2(\eta,\xi)\big) \\ &= \alpha^k (O_1 \vee O_2)(\eta,\xi).\end{aligned}$$

Afterwards, we show that meet operation preserves **(k-LI)**. Assume that O_1 and O_2 satisfy **(k-LI)**, then, for any $\eta_1, \eta_2, \xi_1, \xi_2 \in [0,1]$,

$$\begin{aligned}&|(O_1 \vee O_2)(\eta_1,\xi_1) - (O_1 \vee O_2)(\eta_2,\xi_2)| \\ &= |\max\big(O_1(\eta_1,\xi_1), O_2(\eta_1,\xi_1)\big) - \max\big(O_1(\eta_2,\xi_2), O_2(\eta_2,\xi_2)\big)| \\ &\leq \max\big(|O_1(\eta_1,\xi_1) - O_1(\eta_2,\xi_2)|, |O_2(\eta_1,\xi_1) - O_2(\eta_2,\xi_2)|\big) \\ &\leq \max\big(k(|\eta_1-\eta_2|+|\xi_1-\xi_2|), k(|\eta_1-\eta_2|+|\xi_1-\xi_2|)\big) \\ &= k(|\eta_1-\eta_2|+|\xi_1-\xi_2|).\end{aligned}$$

Finally we show that meet operation preserves **(PS)**. Assume that O_1 and O_2 satisfy **(PS)**, then, for any $r, \eta, \xi \in [0,1]$,

$$\begin{aligned}(O_1 \vee O_2)(\eta^r,\xi^r) &= \max\big(O_1(\eta^r,\xi^r), O_2(\eta^r,\xi^r)\big) \\ &= \max\big(O_1(\eta,\xi)^r, O_2(\eta,\xi)^r\big) \\ &= \Big(\max\big(O_1(\eta,\xi), O_2(\eta,\xi)\big)\Big)^r \\ &= (O_1 \vee O_2)(\eta,\xi)^r.\end{aligned}$$

Similarly, we can show that the join operation also preserves $(\mathbf{ID})\big((\mathbf{MI}), (\mathbf{HO\text{-}k}), (k\text{-}\mathbf{LI}), (\mathbf{PS})\big)$. □

5.2. Properties Preserved by Convex Combination of Overlap/Grouping Functions

Second, we consider the convex combination of overlap/grouping functions.

Theorem 5. *If two overlap functions O_1 and O_2 satisfy* $(\mathbf{ID})\big((\mathbf{MI}), (\mathbf{HO\text{-}k}), (k\text{-}\mathbf{LI})\big)$, *then, for any $\lambda \in [0,1]$, their convex combination of O_λ also satisfies* $(\mathbf{ID})\big((\mathbf{MI}), (\mathbf{HO\text{-}k}), (k\text{-}\mathbf{LI})\big)$.

Proof. First, we show that convex combination preserves **(ID)**. Assume that O_1 and O_2 satisfy **(ID)**, then, for any $\lambda, \eta \in [0,1]$,

$$\begin{aligned} O_\lambda(\eta, \eta) &= \lambda O_1(\eta, \eta) + (1-\lambda) O_2(\eta, \eta) \\ &= \lambda \eta + (1-\lambda) \eta \\ &= \eta. \end{aligned}$$

Next, we show that convex combination preserves **(MI)**. Assume that O_1 and O_2 satisfy **(MI)**, then, for any $\lambda, \alpha, \eta, \xi \in [0,1]$,

$$\begin{aligned} O_\lambda(\alpha\eta, \xi) &= \lambda O_1(\alpha\eta, \xi) + (1-\lambda) O_2(\alpha\eta, \xi) \\ &= \lambda O_1(\eta, \alpha\xi) + (1-\lambda) O_2(\eta, \alpha\xi) \\ &= O_\lambda(\eta, \alpha\xi). \end{aligned}$$

Then, we show that convex combination preserves **(HO-k)**. Assume that O_1 and O_2 satisfy **(HO-k)**, then, for any $\lambda, \alpha, \eta, \xi \in [0,1]$,

$$\begin{aligned} O_\lambda(\alpha\eta, \alpha\xi) &= \lambda O_1(\alpha\eta, \alpha\xi) + (1-\lambda) O_2(\alpha\eta, \alpha\xi) \\ &= \lambda \alpha^k O_1(\eta, \xi) + (1-\lambda) \alpha^k O_2(\eta, \xi) \\ &= \alpha^k (\lambda O_1(\eta, \xi) + (1-\lambda) O_2(\eta, \xi)) \\ &= \alpha^k O_\lambda(\eta, \xi). \end{aligned}$$

Finally, we show that convex combination preserves **(k-LI)**. Assume that O_1 and O_2 satisfy **(k-LI)**, then, for any $\lambda, \alpha, \eta, \xi \in [0,1]$,

$$\begin{aligned} &|O_\lambda(\eta_1, \xi_1) - O_\lambda(\eta_2, \xi_2)| \\ &= |\lambda O_1(\eta_1, \xi_1) + (1-\lambda) O_2(\eta_1, \xi_1) - \lambda O_1(\eta_2, \xi_2) - (1-\lambda) O_2(\eta_2, \xi_2)| \\ &= |\lambda (O_1(\eta_1, \xi_1) - O_1(\eta_2, \xi_2)) + (1-\lambda)(O_2(\eta_1, \xi_1) - O_2(\eta_2, \xi_2))| \\ &\leq |\lambda k(|\eta_1 - \eta_2| + |\xi_1 - \xi_2|) + (1-\lambda) k(|\eta_1 - \eta_2| + |\xi_1 - \xi_2|)| \\ &= k(|\eta_1 - \eta_2| + |\xi_1 - \xi_2|). \end{aligned}$$

□

Note that convex combination does not preserve **(PS)**, since we have

$$\begin{aligned} O_\lambda(\eta^r, \xi^r) &= \lambda O_1(\eta^r, \xi^r) + (1-\lambda) O_2(\eta^r, \xi^r) \\ &= \lambda O_1(\eta, \xi)^r + (1-\lambda) O_2(\eta, \xi)^r, \end{aligned}$$

and

$$\begin{aligned} O_\lambda(\eta, \xi)^r &= \big(\lambda O_1(\eta, \xi) + (1-\lambda) O_2(\eta, \xi)\big)^r \\ &\neq \lambda O_1(\eta, \xi)^r + (1-\lambda) O_2(\eta, \xi)^r \end{aligned}$$

for some $\lambda, r, \eta, \xi \in [0,1]$.

5.3. Properties Preserved by ⊛-Composition of Overlap/Grouping Functions

Third, we consider the ⊛-composition of overlap/grouping functions.

Theorem 6. *If two overlap functions O_1 and O_2 satisfy* **(ID)**$\big($**(HO-1), (PS)**$\big)$, *then, their* ⊛-*composition $(O_1 \circledast O_2)$ also satisfies* **(ID)**$\big($**(HO-1), (PS)**$\big)$.

Proof. First, we show that ⊛-composition preserves **(ID)**. Assume that O_1 and O_2 satisfy **(ID)**, then, for any $\lambda, \eta \in [0,1]$,

$$\begin{aligned}(O_1 \circledast O_2)(\eta,\eta) &= O_1(\eta, O_2(\eta,\eta)) \\ &= O_1(\eta,\eta) \\ &= \eta.\end{aligned}$$

Next, we show that ⊛-composition preserves **(HO-1)**. Assume that O_1 and O_2 satisfy **(HO-1)**, then, for any $\alpha, \eta, \xi \in [0,1]$,

$$\begin{aligned}(O_1 \circledast O_2)(\alpha\eta, \alpha\xi) &= O_1(\alpha\eta, O_2(\alpha\eta, \alpha\xi)) \\ &= O_1(\alpha\eta, \alpha O_2(\eta,\xi)) \\ &= \alpha O_1(\eta, O_2(\eta,\xi)) \\ &= \alpha(O_1 \circledast O_2)(\eta,\xi).\end{aligned}$$

Then, we show that ⊛-composition preserves **(PS)**. Assume that O_1 and O_2 satisfy **(PS)**, then, for any $r, \eta, \xi \in [0,1]$,

$$\begin{aligned}(O_1 \circledast O_2)(\eta^r, \xi^r) &= O_1(\eta^r, O_2(\eta^r, \xi^r)) \\ &= O_1(\eta^r, O_2(\eta,\xi)^r) \\ &= O_1(\eta, O_2(\eta,\xi))^r \\ &= (O_1 \circledast O_2)(\eta,\xi)^r.\end{aligned}$$

□

Note that we only show that ⊛-composition preserves **(HO-1)**, it does not preserve **(HO-k)** for $k \in]0, \infty[$ and $k \neq 1$. For example, let $O_1(\eta,\xi) = O_2(\eta,\xi) = \eta^2\xi^2$, then $(O_1 \circledast O_2)(\eta,\xi) = \eta^6\xi^4$, we know that O_1 and O_2 satisfy **(HO-2)**, i.e., $O_1(\alpha\eta, \alpha\xi) = \alpha^2 O_1(\eta,\xi)$, but $(O_1 \circledast O_2)(\eta,\xi)$ does not satisfy **(HO-2)** since $(O_1 \circledast O_2)(\alpha\eta, \alpha\xi) = \alpha^{10}\eta^6\xi^4 \neq \alpha^2\eta^6\xi^4 = \alpha^2(O_1 \circledast O_2)(\eta,\xi)$.

The ⊛-composition does not preserve **(MI)**. Assume that O_1 and O_2 satisfy **(MI)**, then

$$\begin{aligned}(O_1 \circledast O_2)(\eta, \alpha\xi) &= O_1(\eta, O_2(\eta, \alpha\xi)) \\ &= O_1(\eta, O_2(\alpha\eta, \xi)) \\ &\neq O_1(\alpha\eta, O_2(\alpha\eta, \xi)) \\ &= (O_1 \circledast O_2)(\alpha\eta, \xi)\end{aligned}$$

for some $\alpha, \eta, \xi \in [0,1]$.

The ⊛-composition does not preserve **(k-LI)**.

Example 1. *Let $O_1(\eta,\xi) = O_2(\eta,\xi) = \eta\xi$, then $(O_1 \circledast O_2)(\eta,\xi) = \eta^2\xi$,*

$$\begin{aligned}|O_1(\eta_1,\xi_1) - O_2(\eta_2,\xi_2)| &= |\eta_1\xi_1 - \eta_2\xi_2| \\ &= |\eta_1\xi_1 - \eta_1\xi_2 + \eta_1\xi_2 - \eta_2\xi_2| \\ &= |\eta_1(\xi_1 - \xi_2) + \xi_2(\eta_1 - \eta_2)| \\ &\leq |\eta_1(\xi_1 - \xi_2)| + |\xi_2(\eta_1 - \eta_2)| \\ &\leq |\xi_1 - \xi_2| + |\eta_1 - \eta_2|.\end{aligned}$$

Thus, O_1 and O_2 satisfy **(1-LI)**. Let $\eta_1 = \xi_1 = 0.8$ and $\eta_2 = \xi_2 = 1$, then $(O_1 \circledast O_2)(0.8, 0.8) - (O_1 \circledast O_2)(1,1) = 0.488 > 0.4 = (|0.8-1| + |0.8-1|)$, so $O_1 \circledast O_2$ does not satisfy **(1-LI)**.

However, we have the following result.

Theorem 7. *If two overlap functions O_1 and O_2 respectively satisfy (k_1-**LI**) and (k_2-**LI**), then their ⊛-composition $(O_1 \circledast O_2)$ satisfies $((k_1 + k_1k_2)$-**LI**).*

Proof. Assume that O_1 and O_2 respectively satisfy (k_1-**LI**) and (k_2-**LI**), then, for any $\eta_1, \eta_2, \xi_1, \xi_2 \in [0,1]$, we have

$$\begin{aligned} |(O_1 \circledast O_2)(\eta_1, \xi_1) - (O_1 \circledast O_2)(\eta_2, \xi_2)| &= |O_1(\eta_1, O_2(\eta_1, \xi_1)) - O_1(\eta_2, O_2(\eta_2, \xi_2))| \\ &\leq k_1(|\eta_1 - \eta_2| + |O_2(\eta_1, \xi_1) - O_2(\eta_2, \xi_2)|) \\ &\leq k_1(|\eta_1 - \eta_2| + k_2|\eta_1 - \eta_2| + k_2|\xi_1 - \xi_2|) \\ &= (k_1 + k_1k_2)|\eta_1 - \eta_2| + k_1k_2|\xi_1 - \xi_2| \\ &\leq (k_1 + k_1k_2)\left(|\eta_1 - \eta_2| + |\xi_1 - \xi_2|\right). \end{aligned}$$

□

5.4. Summary

Thus far, we have studied the basic properties of overlap/grouping functions w.r.t. the meet operation, join operation, convex combination, and ⊛-composition. The summary of the properties of overlap/grouping functions w.r.t. the meet operation, join operation, convex combination, and ⊛-composition is shown in Table 2.

Table 2. Properties preservation of the compositions.

Property	O_1	O_2	$O_1 \vee O_2$	$O_1 \wedge O_2$	O_λ	$O_1 \circledast O_2$
ID	✓	✓	✓	✓	✓	✓
MI	✓	✓	✓	✓	✓	✗
HO-k	✓	✓	✓	✓	✓	✗
k-LI	✓	✓	✓	✓	✓	✗
PS	✓	✓	✓	✓	✗	✓

6. Conclusions

This paper studies the properties preservation of overlap/grouping functions w.r.t. meet operation, join operation, convex combination, and ⊛-composition. The main conclusions are listed as follows.

(1) Closures of two bivariate functions w.r.t. meet operation, join operation, convex combination, and ⊛-composition have been obtained in Table 1. Note that ⊛-composition does not preserve (**O1**), and ⊛-composition of overlap/grouping functions is not closed. In other words, ⊛-composition can not be used to generate new overlap/grouping functions.

(2) We show that meet operation, join operation, convex combination, and ⊛-composition of overlap/grouping functions are order preserving, see Theorems 2 and 3.

(3) We have investigated the preservation of the law of (**ID**), (**MI**), (**HO-k**), (**k-LI**), and (**PS**) w.r.t. meet operation, join operation, convex combination, and ⊛-composition, which can be summarized in Table 2.

These results can be served as a certain criteria for choices of generation methods of overlap/grouping functions from given overlap/grouping functions. For example, convex combination does not preserve (**PS**). Thus, we can not generate a power stable overlap function from two power stable overlap functions by their convex combination.

As we know, overlap/grouping functions have been extended to interval-valued and complex-valued overlap/grouping functions. Could similar results be carried over to the interval-valued and complex-valued settings? Moreover, special overlap/grouping functions such as Archimedean and multiplicatively generated overlap/grouping functions have been studied. In these cases, many restrictions have been added. For further works, it follows that we intend to consider properties preservation of these overlap/grouping functions w.r.t. different composition methods.

Author Contributions: Funding acquisition, S.D. and Y.X.; Writing—original draft, S.D. and Y.X.; Writing—review and editing, L.D. and H.S. All authors have read and agreed to the published version of the manuscript.

Funding: This research was funded by the National Science Foundation of China (Grant Nos. 62006168 and 62101375) and Zhejiang Provincial Natural Science Foundation of China (Grant Nos. LQ21A010001 and LQ21F020001).

Institutional Review Board Statement: Not applicable

Informed Consent Statement: Not applicable

Data Availability Statement: Not applicable.

Conflicts of Interest: The authors declare no conflict of interest.

References

1. Bustince, H.; Fernández, J.; Mesiar, R.; Montero, J.; Orduna, R. Overlap functions. *Nonlinear Anal. Theory Methods Appl.* **2010**, *72*, 1488–1499. [CrossRef]
2. Beliakov, G.; Pradera, A.; Calvo, T. *Aggregation Functions: A Guide for Practitioners*; Springer: Berlin, Germany, 2007.
3. Bustince, H.; Pagola, M.; Mesiar, R.; Hüllermeier, E.; Herrera, F. Grouping, overlaps, and generalized bientropic functions for fuzzy modeling of pairwise comparisons. *IEEE Trans. Fuzzy Syst.* **2012**, *20*, 405–415. [CrossRef]
4. Jurio, A.; Bustince, H.; Pagola, M.; Pradera, A.; Yager, R. Some properties of overlap and grouping functions and their application to image thresholding. *Fuzzy Sets Syst.* **2013**, *229*, 69–90. [CrossRef]
5. Elkano, M.; Galar, M.; Sanz, J.; Bustince, H. Fuzzy Rule-Based Classification Systems for multi-class problems using binary decomposition strategies: On the influence of n-dimensional overlap functions in the Fuzzy Reasoning Method. *Inf. Sci.* **2016**, *332*, 94–114. [CrossRef]
6. Elkano, M.; Galar, M.; Sanz, J.; Fernández, A.; Barrenechea, E.; Herrera, F.; Bustince, H. Enhancing multi-class classification in FARC-HD fuzzy classifier: On the synergy between n-dimensional overlap functions and decomposition strategies. *IEEE Trans. Fuzzy Syst.* **2015**, *23*, 1562–1580. [CrossRef]
7. Elkano, M.; Galar, M.; Sanz, J.A.; Schiavo, P.F.; Pereira, S.; Dimuro, G.P.; Borges, E.N.; Bustince, H. Consensus via penalty functions for decision making in ensembles in fuzzy rule-based classification systems. *Appl. Soft Comput.* **2018**, *67*, 728–740. [CrossRef]
8. Santos, H.; Lima, L.; Bedregal, B.; Dimuro, G.P.; Rocha, M.; Bustince, H. Analyzing subdistributivity and superdistributivity on overlap and grouping functions. In Proceedings of the 8th International Summer School on Aggregation Operators (AGOP 2015), Katowice, Poland, 7–10 July 2015; pp. 211–216.
9. Bedregal, B.; Dimuro, G.P.; Bustince, H.; Barrenechea, E. New results on overlap and grouping functions. *Inf. Sci.* **2013**, *249*, 148–170. [CrossRef]
10. Bedregal, B.; Bustince, H.; Palmeira, E.; Dimuro, G.; Fernandez, J. Generalized interval-valued OWA operators with interval weights derived from interval-valued overlap functions. *Int. J. Approx. Reason.* **2017**, *90*, 1–16. [CrossRef]
11. Dimuro, G.P.; Bedregal, B. Archimedean overlap functions: The ordinal sum and the cancellation, idempotency and limiting properties. *Fuzzy Sets Syst.* **2014**, *252*, 39–54. [CrossRef]
12. Gómez, D.; Rodríguez, J.T.; Montero, J.; Bustince, H.; Barrenechea, E. N-dimensional overlap functions. *Fuzzy Sets Syst.* **2016**, *287*, 57–75. [CrossRef]
13. Qiao, J.; Hu, B.Q. On interval additive generators of interval overlap functions and interval grouping functions. *Fuzzy Sets Syst.* **2017**, *323*, 19–55. [CrossRef]
14. Asmus, T.C.; Dimuro, G.P.; Bedregal, B.; Sanz, J.A.; Pereira, S.; Bustince, H. General interval-valued overlap functions and interval-valued overlap indices. *Inf. Sci.* **2020**, *527*, 27–50. [CrossRef]
15. Chen, Y.; Bi, L.; Hu, B.; Dai, S. General Complex-Valued Overlap Functions. *J. Math.* **2021**, *2021*, 6613730.
16. Chen, Y.; Bi, L.; Hu, B.; Dai, S. General Complex-Valued Grouping Functions. *J. Math.* **2021**, *2021*, 5793151.
17. Santos, H.; Dimuro, G.P.; Asmus, T.C.; Lucca, G.; Bueno, E.; Bedregal, B.; Bustince, H. General grouping functions. In Proceedings of 18th International Conference on Information Processing and Management of Uncertainty in Knowledge-Based Systems, Lisbon, Portugal, 15–19 June 2020; Series Communications in Computer and Information Science; Springer: Cham, Switzerland, 2020.
18. Costa, L.M.; Bedregal, B.R.C. Quasi-homogeneous overlap functions. In *Decision Making and Soft Computing*; World Scientific: Joao Pessoa, Brazil, 2014; pp. 294–299.
19. Qiao, J.; Hu, B.Q. On the migrativity of uninorms and nullnorms over overlap and grouping functions. *Fuzzy Sets Syst.* **2018**, *354*, 1–54. [CrossRef]
20. Qiao, J.; Hu, B.Q. On the distributive laws of fuzzy implication functions over additively generated overlap and grouping functions. *IEEE Trans. Fuzzy Syst.* **2017**. [CrossRef]
21. Qiao, J.; Hu, B.Q. On multiplicative generators of overlap and grouping functions. *Fuzzy Sets Syst.* **2018**, *332*, 1–24. [CrossRef]
22. Dimuro, G.P.; Bedregal, B. On residual implications derived from overlap functions. *Inf. Sci.* **2015**, *312*, 78–88. [CrossRef]

23. Dimuro, G.P.; Bedregal, B. On the laws of contraposition for residual implications derived from overlap functions. In Proceedings of the 2015 IEEE International Conference on Fuzzy Systems (FUZZ-IEEE), Los Alamitos, CA, USA, 2–5 August 2015; pp. 1–7.
24. Dimuro, G.P.; Bedregal, B.; Santiago, R.H.N. On (G, N)-implications derived from grouping functions. *Inf. Sci.* **2014**, *279*, 1–17. [CrossRef]
25. Qiao, J. On binary relations induced from overlap and grouping functions. *Int. J. Approx. Reason.* **2019**, *106*, 155–171. [CrossRef]
26. Qiao, J. On (IO, O)-fuzzy rough sets based on overlap functions. *Int. J. Approx. Reason.* **2021**, *132*, 26–48. [CrossRef]
27. Dimuro, G.P.; Bedregal, B.; Bustince, H.; Asiáin, M.J.; Mesiar, R. On additive generators of overlap functions. *Fuzzy Sets Syst.* **2016**, *287*, 76–96. [CrossRef]
28. Wang, H. Constructions of overlap functions on bounded lattices. *Int. J. Approx. Reason.* **2020**, *125*, 203–217. [CrossRef]
29. Kolesarova, A.; Mesiar, R. 1-Lipschitz power stable aggregation functions. *Inf. Sci.* **2015**, *294*, 57–63. [CrossRef]

Article

Basic Core Fuzzy Logics and Algebraic Routley–Meyer-Style Semantics

Eunsuk Yang

Department of Philosophy & Institute of Critical Thinking and Writing,
Colleges of Humanities & Social Science Blvd., Jeonbuk National University, Rm 417, Jeonju 54896, Korea;
eunsyang@jbnu.ac.kr

Abstract: Recently, algebraic Routley–Meyer-style semantics was introduced for basic substructural logics. This paper extends it to fuzzy logics. First, we recall the basic substructural core fuzzy logic **MIAL** (Mianorm logic) and its axiomatic extensions, together with their algebraic semantics. Next, we introduce two kinds of ternary relational semantics, called here linear *Urquhart-style* and *Fine-style* Routley–Meyer semantics, for them as *algebraic* Routley–Meyer-style semantics.

Keywords: operational semantics; Routley–Meyer-style semantics; algebraic semantics; (core) fuzzy logics; implicational tonoid fuzzy logics

Citation: Yang, E. Basic Core Fuzzy Logics and Algebraic Routley–Meyer-Style Semantics. *Axioms* **2021**, *10*, 273. https://doi.org/10.3390/axioms10040273

Academic Editor: Amit K. Shukla

Received: 21 September 2021
Accepted: 21 October 2021
Published: 25 October 2021

Publisher's Note: MDPI stays neutral with regard to jurisdictional claims in published maps and institutional affiliations.

Copyright: © 2021 by the authors. Licensee MDPI, Basel, Switzerland. This article is an open access article distributed under the terms and conditions of the Creative Commons Attribution (CC BY) license (https://creativecommons.org/licenses/by/4.0/).

1. Introduction

The author [1] recently introduced algebraic Routley–Meyer-style (ARM for simplicity) semantics for basic substructural logics. Here, the term *ARM semantics* means semantics with operations interpreting ternary relations, the frames of which have the same structures as algebraic semantics. This paper extends it to *fuzzy* logics. To this end, we first recall some historical facts associated with Routley–Meyer semantics.

Using binary accessibility relations, Kripke [2–4] first established relational semantics, the so-called *Kripke Semantics*, for modal and intuitionistic logics. Since then, many semantics have been introduced as its generalizations. In particular, Urquhart provided operational semantics, called Urquhart semantics in [1]; for relevant implication see [5–7]. From an operational semantic point of view, this semantics is interesting since instead of binary relations for accessibility it has groupoid operations. More precisely, it provides the valuation of implication using the binary operation $\circ$ such that

$(\to_{\circ_U})$ $a \Vdash A \to B$ if and only if (iff) for any $b \in X$, $b \Vdash A$ implies $a \circ b \Vdash B$,

instead of using the binary relation R such that

$(\to_{R_K})$ $a \Vdash A \to B$ iff for any $b \in X$, aRb and $b \Vdash A$ imply $b \Vdash B$.

Urquhart semantics has the following additional valuations for extensional conjunction and disjunction: For sentences A, B,

($\wedge$) $a \Vdash A \wedge B$ iff $a \Vdash A$ and $a \Vdash B$; and
($\vee$) $a \Vdash A \vee B$ iff $a \Vdash A$ or $a \Vdash B$.

As is well known, these three valuation conditions do not work together for substructural logics in general. As Urquhart himself mentioned in [7,8], while sentences such as (a) $((A \to (B \vee C)) \wedge (B \to C)) \to (A \to C)$ are valid in their semantics, the distributive substructural logic **R** of relevance does not prove such sentences. Because of this negative fact, Routley–Meyer [9–11] instead introduced the so-called Routley–Meyer semantics for implication as a ternary relational semantics (see [12]).

Please note that Urquhart [7] provided the binary operational valuation for implication $(\to_{\circ_U})$, whereas Fine [13] did the following ternary relational valuation for implication.

($\rightarrow_{\circ_F}$) $a \Vdash A \rightarrow B$ iff for all $b, c \in X$, $a \circ b \leq c$ and $b \Vdash A$ imply $c \Vdash B$.

Although these two valuations are not free from the above negative fact, they have been extensively used in substructural logics: Using ($\rightarrow_{\circ_U}$), many logicians such as Došen and Ono have introduced similar semantics for modal and substructural logics [14–16]; with the title "Kripke-style semantics", Montagna–Ono [17], Montagna–Sacchetti [18], and Yang [19,20] introduced similar semantics for substructural fuzzy logics. Using ($\rightarrow_{\circ_F}$), logicians such as Ono–Komori [21], Ishihara [22], and Kamide [23] have introduced analogous semantics for some (modal) substructural logics (For more detailed introduction of these semantics, see [1]).

The starting point for the current work is the observation that, as the author [1] mentioned, using ternary relation $Rabc$, the valuations ($\rightarrow_{\circ_U}$) and ($\rightarrow_{\circ_F}$) can be rephrased as:

($\rightarrow_{R_U}$) $a \Vdash A \rightarrow B$ iff for all $b, c \in X$, if $Rabc$ (:= $a \circ b = c$ (df_U)) and $b \Vdash A$, then $c \Vdash B$, (We take c in place of $a * b$ in $a * b \Vdash B$ because $a \circ b = c$. This was introduced by Dunn in [24]) and

($\rightarrow_{R_F}$) $a \Vdash A \rightarrow B$ iff for all $b, c \in X$, if $Rabc$ (:= $a \circ b \leq c$ (df_F)) and $b \Vdash A$, then $c \Vdash B$, (As Došen [15] and Dunn [25,26] already mentioned, Fine [13] interpreted $Rabc$ as $a \circ b \leq c$. Although Urquhart [7] did not consider to reinterpret ($\rightarrow_{\circ_U}$) using ternary relation, Bimbó and Dunn [27] and Restall [12] introduced such reformulation.), respectively.

In particular, using ($\rightarrow_{R_U}$) and ($\rightarrow_{R_F}$), the author first introduced ARM semantics for basic substructural logics in general. Then, since fuzzy logics are also substructural logics and further prove sentences such as (a), one can ask the following.

$Q:$ Could one establish ARM semantics, i.e., operational and ternary relational semantics equivalent to algebraic semantics, for basic substructural fuzzy logics, using the clauses ($\wedge$), ($\vee$), and either ($\rightarrow_{R_U}$) or ($\rightarrow_{R_F}$) together?

As a positive answer to this question, we introduce such semantics with the conditions ($\wedge$), ($\vee$) and the corresponding implication conditions for basic (core) fuzzy logics. (A logic L is called *fuzzy* if it is complete on linearly ordered models, and *core* fuzzy if it is fuzzy on $[0, 1]$ (see [28,29])). This will verify that the clauses ($\wedge$), ($\vee$), and either ($\rightarrow_{R_U}$) or ($\rightarrow_{R_F}$) work together for basic substructural fuzzy logics.

The more detailed other reasons to study this are as follows: The first and most important reason is that while algebraic Kripke-style (briefly AK) semantics (The term *AK semantics* means semantics with operations in place of binary accessibility relations, the frames of which have the same structures as algebraic semantics.) for substructural fuzzy logics have been introduced extensively (see, e.g., [17–20,30–32]), ARM semantics for such logics have not. Only, the author [33,34] introduced such semantics for **MTL** (Monoidal t-norm logic) and its involutive extension **IMTL**. In particular, the author [1] introduced ARM semantics for substructural logics in general, whereas he did not for substructural fuzzy logics. This is the direct specific reason to consider ARM semantics for *fuzzy logics* in general.

The following are more reasons related to ARM semantics itself, some of which are mentioned in [1]. First, "the definitions (df_U) and (df_F) provide more intuitive ways to understand or interpret the ternary relation R. Please note that using the ternary relation R in $Rxyz$ itself we cannot say how to understand or interpret R, whereas we can say it using $x * y = z$ and $x * y \leq z$". Second, this semantics provides a *direct* way to understand *equivalence relations* between algebraic and relational semantics. "An n-ary operation is an $n+1$-ary relation, but not always conversely. If one shows its converse, one can state an equivalence between the operation and the relation". Associated with this, most well-known method to consider this equivalence is to use 'canonical extensions' investigated with the titles such as 'representation' and 'duality' (see [35–41]). However, the way to use (df$_U$) and (df$_F$) is different from it and more direct in the sense that the way defines ternary relations by virtue of binary operations and (in)equations. The third is the fact that ARM semantics uses forcing relations. It means that this semantics is a study still in the tradition of relational semantic research. The last but not least one is that ARM semantics is a common area between algebraic semantics and ternary relational semantics. Since algebraic semantics and ARM semantics are both based on the same algebraic structures, this last semantics gives a chance to study similarities and differences between algebraic semantics and relational semantics.

We organize the paper as follows. In Section 2, we first recall some basic (core) fuzzy logics, together with their algebraic semantics. In Section 3, we introduce ARM semantics for them. More precisely, we introduce ARM semantics with ($\to_{R_U}$) in Section 3.1 and that with ($\to_{R_F}$) in Sectio 3.2. In Section 4, we consider advantages and limitations of these two semantics as ARM semantics.

We finally note that, as in [1], our ARM semantics in Sections 3.1 and 3.2 provides frames as some reducts of their corresponding algebras and defines ternary relations using binary operations and (in)equations. However, unlike the semantics in [1], this semantics is provided based on linear theories. More precisely, it is an ARM semantics with linearly ordered models. In this sense, this semantics is a *novel* one to connect n-nary operations and $n+1$-nary relations. By ARM^ℓ semantics, we henceforth mean this kind of ARM semantics.

2. Algebraic Semantics for Basic Core Fuzzy Logics

Here we recall the most basic substructural core fuzzy logic **MIAL** and its axiomatic extensions (extensions for short) and their algebraic semantics (See [42] for more detailed introduction of these logics and semantics). The language for these logics is provided over a countable propositional language with Fm (a set of formulas) built from VAR (a set of propositional variables), propositional constants $t, f, \mathbf{F}, \mathbf{T}$, and connectives $\to, \leadsto, \wedge, \vee, \&$. We further define $A \leftrightarrow B$ and A_t as $(A \to B) \wedge (B \to A)$ and $A \wedge t$, respectively.

The variables are denoted by lowercase Latin letters $p, q, r, \ldots$ and the formulas by uppercase ones $A, B, C \ldots$. Theories as sets of formulas are denoted by uppercase Greek letters $\Gamma, \Delta, \ldots$. Please note that variables are also formulas. We provide a consequence relation, denoted by $\vdash$, on axiom systems.

Definition 1 ([43,44]). *MIAL consists of the axioms and rules below:*

$(A \wedge B) \to A, (A \wedge B) \to B$ ($\wedge$-elimination, $\wedge$-E);
$((A \to B) \wedge (A \to C)) \to (A \to (B \wedge C))$ ($\wedge$-introduction, $\wedge$-I);
$A \to (A \vee B), B \to (A \vee B)$ ($\vee$-introduction, $\vee$-I);
$((A \to C) \wedge (B \to C)) \to ((A \vee B) \to C)$ ($\vee$-elimination, $\vee$-E);
$F \to A$ (ex falsum quodlibet, EF);
$(t \to A) \leftrightarrow A$ (push and pop, PP);
$A \to (B \to (B \& A))$ (&-adjunction, &-Adj);
$A \to (B \leadsto (A \& B))$ (&-adjunction, &-Adj$_\leadsto$);
$(A_t \& B_t) \to (A \wedge B)$ (&$\wedge$);
$(B \& (A \& (A \to (B \to C)))) \to C$ (residuation, Res');
$((A \& (A \leadsto (B \to C))) \& B) \to C$ (residuation, Res'$_\leadsto$);
$((A \to (A \& (A \to B))) \& (B \to C)) \to (A \to C)$ (transitivity, T');
$((A \leadsto ((A \leadsto B) \& A)) \& (B \to C)) \to (A \leadsto C)$ (transitivity, T'$_\leadsto$);
$(A \to B)_t \vee ((C \& D) \to (C \& (D \& (B \to A)_t)))$ (prelinearity, $PL_{\alpha_{C,D}}$);
$(A \to B)_t \vee ((C \& D) \to ((C \& (B \to A)_t) \& D))$ (prelinearity, $PL_{\alpha'_{C,D}}$);
$(A \to B)_t \vee ((C \to (D \to ((D \& C) \& (B \to A)_t)))$ (prelinearity, $PL_{\beta_{C,D}}$);
$(A \to B)_t \vee ((C \to (D \leadsto ((C \& D) \& (B \to A)_t)))$ (prelinearity, $PL_{\beta'_{C,D}}$);
$A \to B, A \vdash B$ (modus ponens, mp);
$A \vdash A_t$ (adj$_U$);
$A \vdash (C \& D) \to (C \& (D \& A))$ (α);
$A \vdash (C \& D) \to ((C \& A) \& D)$ (α');

$A \vdash C \to (D \to ((D\&C)\&A))$ (β);
$A \vdash C \to (D \rightsquigarrow ((C\&D)\&A))$ (β').

A logic is called an extension of a logic **L** if it is obtained from **L** by adding further axioms.

Definition 2. *The following are basic structural axioms:*
(exchange, e) $A\&B \to B\&A$;
(expansion, p) $(A\&A) \to A$;
(contraction, c) $A \to (A\&A)$;
(left weakening, i) $A \to (B \to A)$;
(right weakening, o) $f \to A$;
(associativity, a) $A\&(B\&C) \leftrightarrow (A\&B)\&C$.
MIAL$_S$, $S \subseteq \{e, p, c, i, o, a\}$, *is a substructural (core) fuzzy logic extending* **MIAL**.

Example 1. *The following well-known core fuzzy logics are extensions of* **MIAL**.

(1) *Micanorm logic* **MICAL** *is* **MIAL**$_e$.
(2) *Uninorm logic* **UL** *is* **MIAL**$_{ea}$.
(3) *Monoidal t-norm logic* **MTL** *is* **MIAL**$_{eai}$.

By L^ℓs, we denote the set of substructural fuzzy logics introduced in Definition 2, i.e., $L^\ell s = \{\textbf{MIAL}_S : S \subseteq \{e, p, c, i, o, a\}\}$.

A theory of $L^\ell \in L^\ell s$ (L^ℓ-theory for short) is a set Γ of formulas such that $\Gamma \vdash_{L^\ell} A$ entails $A \in \Gamma$. Since $\emptyset \subseteq \Gamma$, the set of theorems of L^ℓ is a subset of all L^ℓ-theories. We define a *proof* in an L^ℓ-theory Γ as a sequence of formulas, the elements of which are either axioms of L^ℓ, members of Γ, or derived from its precedent elements using rules of L^ℓ. For each pair of formulas A, B and a theory Γ, if $\Gamma \vdash A \to B$ or $\Gamma \vdash B \to A$, we call Γ a *linear theory*.

Definition 3. *A bounded, pointed residuated lattice-ordered groupoid with unit (bprlu-groupoid for simplicity) is an algebra* $\mathcal{A} = (A, \bot, \top, 0, 1, \backslash, /, \wedge, \vee, \circ)$ *such that:* $(A, \circ, 1)$ *is a unital groupoid;* $(A, \bot, \top, \wedge, \vee)$ *is a bounded lattice; 0 is an arbitrary element in A; for all* $a, b, c \in A$, $a \circ b \leq c$ *iff* $a \leq c/b$ *iff* $b \leq a\backslash c$ *(residuation)*.

Please note that the notations '$\wedge$' and '$\vee$' are used both as propositional connectives and as algebraic operators.

Definition 4 (L^ℓ-algebras). *Let* a_1 *be a* $\wedge 1$. *A bprlu-groupoid is a* **MIAL**-*algebra if it satisfies the following prelinearity properties: for all* $a, b, c, d \in A$,
$(PL^{\mathcal{A}}_{\alpha_{C,D}})$ $1 \leq (a\backslash b)_1 \vee ((c \circ d)\backslash(c \circ (d \circ (b\backslash a)_1)))$;
$(PL^{\mathcal{A}}_{\alpha'_{C,D}})$ $1 \leq (a\backslash b)_1 \vee ((c \circ d)\backslash((c \circ (b\backslash a)_1) \circ d))$;
$(PL^{\mathcal{A}}_{\beta_{C,D}})$ $1 \leq (a\backslash b)_1 \vee ((c\backslash(d\backslash((d \circ c) \circ (b\backslash a)_1)))$;
$(PL^{\mathcal{A}}_{\beta'_{C,D}})$ $1 \leq (a\backslash b)_1 \vee ((c\backslash(((d \circ c) \circ (b\backslash a)_1)/d))$.

The following are the (in)equations corresponding to the structural axioms above: for all $a, b, c \in A$,
$(e^{\mathcal{A}})$ $a \circ b \leq b \circ a$;
$(p^{\mathcal{A}})$ $a \circ a \leq a$;
$(c^{\mathcal{A}})$ $a \leq a \circ a$;
$(i^{\mathcal{A}})$ $a \leq 1$;
$(o^{\mathcal{A}})$ $0 \leq a$;
$(a^{\mathcal{A}})$ $a \circ (b \circ c) = (a \circ b) \circ c$.

Thus, for any $S \subseteq \{e^{\mathcal{A}}, p^{\mathcal{A}}, c^{\mathcal{A}}, i^{\mathcal{A}}, o^{\mathcal{A}}, a^{\mathcal{A}}\}$, **MIAL**$_S$-*algebras are defined with S. We call all these algebras* L^ℓ-*algebras and linearly ordered* L^ℓ-*algebras* L^ℓ-*chains*.

Given an L^ℓ-algebra $\mathcal{A}$, an $\mathcal{A}$-valuation is defined as a map $v : Fm \to \mathcal{A}$ such that $v(\#(A_1,\ldots,A_n)) = \#^\mathcal{A}(v(A_1),\ldots,v(A_n))$, where $\# \in \{\mathbf{F},\mathbf{T},f,t,\to,\leadsto,\wedge,\vee,\&\}$ and $\#^\mathcal{A} \in \{\bot, \top, 0, 1, \backslash, /, \wedge, \vee, \circ\}$. A formula A is said to be an $\mathcal{A}$-*tautology* if for each $\mathcal{A}$-valuation v, $1 \leq v(A)$. An $\mathcal{A}$-valuation v is said to be an $\mathcal{A}$-*model* of an L^ℓ-theory Γ if $1 \leq v(A)$ for all $A \in \Gamma$. By $Mod(\Gamma, \mathcal{A})$, we denote the class of all $\mathcal{A}$-models of Γ. Over a class $\mathcal{L}^\ell$ of L^ℓ-algebras, a formula A is called a *semantic consequence* of Γ, denoted by $\Gamma \models_{\mathcal{L}^\ell} A$, if $Mod(\Gamma \cup \{A\}, \mathcal{A}) = Mod(\Gamma, \mathcal{A})$ for all $\mathcal{A} \in \mathcal{L}^\ell$. If $\mathcal{A}$ is a semantic consequence of Γ with respect to regarding $\{A\}$ whenever A is provable in Γ on L^ℓ, $\mathcal{A}$ is called an L^ℓ-*algebra*. By $MOD(L^\ell)$ and $MOD^\ell(L^\ell)$, we denote the set of such algebras and the set of linearly ordered ones, respectively, and write $\Gamma \models_{L^\ell} A$ and $\Gamma \models^\ell_{L^\ell} A$ instead of $\Gamma \models_{MOD(L^\ell)} A$ and $\Gamma \models_{MOD^\ell(L^\ell)} A$, respectively.

Theorem 1 (*Completeness*). *For a theory Γ over $L^\ell \in L^\ell s$ and a formula A, $\Gamma \vdash_{L^\ell} A$ iff $\Gamma \models_{L^\ell} A$ iff $\Gamma \models^\ell_{L^\ell} A$.*

Proof. As a corollary of Theorem 3.1.8 in [45], we obtain the claim. □

An L^ℓ-algebra is said to be *standard* if it has the real interval $[0, 1]$ as its carrier set.

Theorem 2 ([42]). *Let ε be a unit element in $[0, 1]$.*

(i) *For $L^\ell \in L^\ell{}_T = \{MIAL_T : T \subseteq \{e, p, c, i, o\}\}$, $\Gamma \vdash_{L^\ell} A$ iff for each standard L^ℓ-algebra and for each valuation v, $\varepsilon \leq v(B)$ for all $B \in \Gamma$ implies $\varepsilon \leq v(A)$.*

(ii) *For $L^\ell \in L^\ell{}_U$ such that $\{i, a\} \subseteq U \subseteq \{e, p, c, i, o, a\}$, $\Gamma \vdash_{L^\ell} A$ iff for each standard L^ℓ-algebra and for each valuation v, $\varepsilon \leq v(B)$ for all $B \in \Gamma$ implies $\varepsilon \leq v(A)$.*

Example 2. *For $L^\ell \in \{MIAL_a, MIAL_{ac}, MIAL_{ap}, MIAL_{ao}, MIAL_{aco}, MIAL_{cpo}, MIAL_{acpo}\}$, L^ℓ is not standard complete since (A) $1 \leq (z\backslash y) \vee ((x\backslash y)\backslash (1/(z\backslash a)))$ or (B) $x \circ y \leq 1$ iff $y \circ x \leq 1$ holds in standard L^ℓ-algebras but not in general in linearly ordered L^ℓ-algebras (see [42,46]).*

3. ARM$^\ell$ Semantics

In this section, we deal with the ARM semantics for fuzzy extensions of the basic substructural logics introduced in [1]. As in [1], we introduce two kinds of ARM$^\ell$ semantics: one is the semantics with the definition (df$_U$) and linearly ordered models, called here *linear Urquhart-style Routley–Meyer semantics* (briefly U-RM$^\ell$ semantics), and the other is the semantics with the definition (df$_F'$) below and linearly ordered models, called here *linear Fine-style Routley–Meyer semantics* (briefly F-RM$^\ell$ semantics). Please note that unlike the semantics in [1], these two semantics are provided using *linear theories* in place of closed theories. However, these semantics still have the same structures as algebraic semantics and so are ARM semantics.

3.1. U-RM$^\ell$ Semantics

Here we consider U-RM$^\ell$ semantics for $L^\ell_{eq} = \{MIAL_{eq} : eq \subseteq \{e, o, a\}\}$. We first define several Routley–Meyer (RM for short) frames.

Definition 5.

(i) *(RM frames [1]) An RM frame is a structure $\mathbf{F} = (F, 1, R)$ such that 1 is a special element in F and $R \subseteq F^3$. We call the elements of F nodes.*

(ii) *(Linear RM frames) A linear RM (briefly, RM$^\ell$) frame is an RM frame $\mathbf{F} = (F, 1, \leq, R)$, where $(F, \leq)$ is a linearly order set.*

(iii) *((Residuated) Urquhart operational RM$^\ell$ frames) An Urquhart operational RM$^\ell$ (briefly, U-RM$^\ell$) frame is an RM$^\ell$ frame $\mathbf{F} = (F, 1, \circ, \leq, R)$, where $\circ$ is a groupoid operation satisfying (df$_U$) $a \circ b = c := Rabc$. A U-RM$^\ell$ frame is called residuated if for any $a, b \in F$, the sets $\{c : a \circ c \leq b\}$ and $\{c : c \circ a \leq b\}$ have suprema.*

(iv) (Bounded, pointed U-RM$^\ell$ frames) A U-RM$^\ell$ frame is said to be pointed if it further has an arbitrary element 0, and bounded if it further has top and bottom elements $\top$ and $\bot$.

(v) (U-RM$^\ell$ MIAL frames) A U-RM$^\ell$ MIAL frame is a bounded pointed residuated U-RM$^\ell$ frame, where $\circ$ is left-continuous and conjunctive and R satisfies the postulates below: for any $a \in F$,

p1. $R1aa$
p2. $Ra1a$.

(vi) (U-RM$^\ell$ L^ℓ_{eq} frames) Consider the definitions and postulates below: for any $a, b, c, d \in F$,

df1. $R^2 a(bc)d := (\exists x)(Raxd \wedge Rbcx)$
df2. $R^2 abcd := (\exists x)(Rabx \wedge Rxcd)$
p_e. $Rabc$ implies $Rbac$.
p_o. $R10a$ iff $R1\bot a$, where $\bot$ is the bottom element in F.
p_a. $R^2 abcd$ iff $R^2 a(bc)d$.

For any $eq \subseteq \{p_e, p_o, p_a\}$, U-RM$^\ell$ MIAL$_{eq}$ frames are defined, along with their corresponding postulates. We call all these frames U-RM$^\ell$ L^ℓ_{eq} frames (briefly U-L^ℓ_{eq} frames).

Remark 1. *Definition 1 has some interesting facts to note.*

(1) ([1]) The definition of an RM frame in (i) is the same as that of a frame structure for R^+ (the positive R), which eliminates all the definitions and postulates for the ternary relation R introduced in [8].

(2) The definitions in (ii) and (iii) are a fuzzy specification of partially ordered RM frames and (residuated) Urquhart operational RM frames introduced in [1]. (Please note that if $\leq$ is a partial ordering in place of a linear ordering in (ii) and (iii), the definitions in (ii) and (iii) form partially ordered RM frames and (residuated) Urquhart operational RM frames introduced in [1].)

(3) ([1]) The postulates p1 and p2 in (v) are for a unit element since we have that $1 \circ a = a = a \circ 1$ using (df$_U$).

(4) ([1]) The indices of the postulates in (vi) denote their corresponding axioms. For example, the postulate p_e is for the exchange axiom e. In particular, (df$_U$) assures that the postulates satisfy the equational forms of their corresponding algebraic properties. For instance, using the postulate p_o and (df$_U$), we have that $0 = 1 \circ 0 = 1 \circ \bot = \bot$, i.e., $0 = \bot$.

A *valuation* on a bounded pointed residuated U-RM$^\ell$ frame is a forcing relation $\Vdash$ between the nodes and the propositional variables, propositional constants, and formulas satisfying the below conditions. For each propositional variable p,

(AHC) $b \leq a$ and $a \Vdash p$ imply $b \Vdash p$;
(min) $\bot \Vdash p$,

for the propositional constants f, t, and $\mathbf{F}$,

(0) $a \Vdash f$ iff $a \leq 0$;
(1) $a \Vdash t$ iff $a \leq 1$;
($\bot$) $a \Vdash \mathbf{F}$ iff $a = \bot$, and

for formulas A, B,

($\rightarrow$) $a \Vdash A \rightarrow B$ iff for all $b, c \in F$, $Rbac$ and $b \Vdash A$ imply $c \Vdash B$;
($\rightsquigarrow$) $a \Vdash A \rightsquigarrow B$ iff for all $b, c \in F$, $Rabc$ and $b \Vdash A$ imply $c \Vdash B$;
($\wedge$) $a \Vdash A \wedge B$ iff $a \Vdash A$ and $a \Vdash B$;

(∨) $a \Vdash A \vee B$ iff $a \Vdash A$ or $a \Vdash B$;
(&) $a \Vdash A \& B$ iff there exist $b, c \in F$ such that $b \Vdash A, c \Vdash B$, and $a \leq b \circ c$.

A valuation on a U-L_{eq}^{ℓ} frame is a valuation further satisfying that (max) for every propositional variable p, $\{a : a \Vdash p\}$ has a maximum.

Definition 6 (U-L_{eq}^{ℓ} model). *An* U-L_{eq}^{ℓ} *model is a pair* $(F, \Vdash)$, *where F is a* U-L_{eq}^{ℓ} *frame and* $\Vdash$ *is a valuation on F. This model is said to be* complete *if F is a complete frame and $\Vdash$ is a valuation on F.*

Definition 7. *For a* U-L_{eq}^{ℓ} *model* $(F, \Vdash)$, *a node a of F and a formula A, a is said to* force *A if $a \Vdash A$. A is said to be* true *in $(F, \Vdash)$ if $1 \Vdash A$, and* valid *in the frame F if A is true in $(F, \Vdash)$ for any valuation $\Vdash$ on F. For a class $\mathcal{UL}^{\ell}$ of U-L_{eq}^{ℓ} frames and for a theory Γ, by $\Gamma \models_{\mathcal{UL}^{\ell}} A$, we mean that A is valid in $F \in \mathcal{UL}^{\ell}$ whenever B is valid in it for all $B \in \Gamma$. This A is called a* semantic consequence *of Γ on $\mathcal{UL}^{\ell}$.*

Now we consider soundness and completeness of L_{eq}^{ℓ}.

Lemma 1 (Hereditary Lemma).

(i) *Let F be a residuated U-RM$^{\ell}$ frame. For any formula A and for any nodes $a, b \in F$, if $a \Vdash A$ and $b \leq a$, then $b \Vdash A$.*

(ii) *Let $\Vdash$ be a forcing relation on a U-L_{eq}^{ℓ} frame and A be a formula. Then the set $\{a \in F : a \Vdash A\}$ has a maximum.*

Proof. It is easy to prove (i). For the proof of (ii), see Proposition 3.3 in [30] and Lemma 2.11 in [18]. □

Lemma 2. $1 \Vdash A \to B$ *iff for any $a \in F$, $a \Vdash A$ implies $a \Vdash B$.*

Proof. ($\Rightarrow$) See Lemma 3 in [1]. ($\Leftarrow$) Suppose $Ra1b$ and $a \Vdash A$ and that $a \Vdash A$ implies $a \Vdash B$. We prove $b \Vdash B$. Using the suppositions and (df$_U$), we obtain that $a \Vdash B$ and $a = a \circ 1 = b$; therefore, $b \Vdash B$. □

Theorem 3 (Soundness). *For a linear theory Γ over $L^{\ell} \in L_{eq}^{\ell}$, a formula A, and a class $\mathcal{UL}^{\ell}$ of all U-L_{eq}^{ℓ} frames, $\Gamma \vdash_{L^{\ell}} A$ only if $\Gamma \models_{\mathcal{UL}^{\ell}} A$.*

Proof. For the system **MIAL**, we consider the axiom (EF) as an example. For (EF), by Lemma 2, we assume that $a \Vdash \mathbf{F}$ and show that $a \Vdash A$. This result directly follows from the supposition and the condition ($\bot$). The other axioms and rules for **MIAL** can be proved similarly.

For the other systems, we need to consider the other structural axioms, i.e., $S \in \{e, o, a\}$.

(e): Suppose that $a \Vdash A \& B$. We have to prove that $a \Vdash B \& A$. By the supposition and the condition (&), there are $b, c \in F$ such that $b \Vdash A$, $a \leq b \circ c$, and $c \Vdash B$. Then, p_e and (df$_U$) ensure that $b \circ c = c \circ b$ and so $a \leq c \circ b$. Hence, we obtain $a \Vdash B \& A$ by (&).

(o): Suppose that $a \Vdash f$. We have to prove $a \Vdash A$. Please note that **MIAL**$_o$ proves $\mathbf{F} \leftrightarrow f$. Then, since p_o and (df$_U$) assure that $0 = \bot$, we can obtain that $a \Vdash A$ using ($\bot$) and (EF).

(a): Suppose $a \Vdash A \& (B \& C)$. We have to prove $a \Vdash (A \& B) \& C$. By the supposition, the condition (&), and (df$_U$), there are $b, c \in F$ so that $b \Vdash A$, $a \leq b \circ c$, and $c \Vdash B \& C$; therefore, for some d, e, we have that $d \Vdash B$, $c \leq d \circ e$, and $e \Vdash C$. Then, $b \circ c \leq b \circ (d \circ e)$ and so $b \circ c \leq (b \circ d) \circ e$ since p_a, df1, df2, and (df$_U$) assure that $b \circ (d \circ e) = (b \circ d) \circ e$. Since $b \circ d \leq b \circ d$ and $a \leq (b \circ d) \circ e$, we may take some x so that $a \leq x \circ e$ and $x \leq b \circ d$. Hence, by the condition (&), we obtain $x \Vdash A \& B$; therefore, $a \Vdash (A \& B) \& C$. The proof for the other direction is analogous. □

The following shows a connection between postulates for U-L^ℓ_{eq} frames and algebraic (in)equations for the structural axioms of $L^\ell \in L^\ell_{eq}$.

Proposition 1. *The postulates for U-L^ℓ_{eq} frames introduced in Definition 1 as p_e, p_o, and p_a are reducible to algebraic (in)equations $e^\mathcal{A}$, $o^\mathcal{A}$, and $a^\mathcal{A}$, respectively.*

Proof. We show that p_{eq}, $eq \in \{e, o, a\}$, is reducible to $eq^\mathcal{A}$.
    (e): Using p_e and (df$_U$), we obtain that for arbitrary $a, b, c \in F$, $c = a \circ b$ implies $c = b \circ a$; therefore, $a \circ b \leq b \circ a$, i.e., $e^\mathcal{A}$, since $a \circ b = b \circ a$.
    (o): Using p_o and (df$_U$), we obtain that $a = 1 \circ 0 = 0$ iff $a = 1 \circ \bot = \bot$ for any $a \in F$ and so $0 \leq a$, i.e., $0^\mathcal{A}$, since $0 = \bot$.
    (a): Using p_a, df1, df2, and (df$_U$), we obtain that for arbitrary $a, b, c, d \in F$, there is x such that $x = a \circ b$ and $d = x \circ c$ and thus $d = (a \circ b) \circ c$ iff $x' = b \circ c$ and $d = a \circ x'$ for some x' and so $d = a \circ (b \circ c)$; therefore, $(a \circ b) \circ c = a \circ (b \circ c)$, i.e., $a^\mathcal{A}$. □

Corollary 1. *Every U-$L^\ell_{eq'}$, $eq \in \{o, e\}$, frame is embeddable into a complete U-L^ℓ_{eq} frame.*

Proof. This corollary directly follows from Theorem 2 and Proposition 1. □

The next proposition connects algebraic semantics and U-RM$^\ell$ semantics for $L^\ell \in L^\ell_{eq}$.

Proposition 2.

(i) The $\{\top, \bot, 1, 0, \leq, \circ\}$ reduct of an L^ℓ-chain $\mathcal{A}$ is a U-L^ℓ_{eq} frame, which is complete iff $\mathcal{A}$ is complete.

(ii) Let $F = (F, \top, \bot, 1, 0, \leq, \circ)$ be a U-L^ℓ_{eq} frame. Then, the structure $\mathcal{A} = (F, \top, \bot, 1, 0, \min, \max, \backslash, /, \circ)$ is an L^ℓ-algebra (where min and max are meant on $\leq$).

(iii) If F is the $\{\top, \bot, 1, 0, \leq, \circ\}$ reduct of an L^ℓ-chain $\mathcal{A}$ and v is a valuation in $\mathcal{A}$, then $(F, \Vdash)$ is a U-L^ℓ_{eq} model and for any formula A and for any $a \in \mathcal{A}$, it holds that $a \Vdash A$ iff $a \leq v(A)$.

(iv) Let $(F, \Vdash)$ be a U-L^ℓ_{eq} model and $\mathcal{A}$ be the L^ℓ-algebra defined as in (ii). Define for every propositional variable p, $v(p) = \max\{a \in F : a \Vdash p\}$. Then, for every formula A, $v(A) = \max\{a \in F : a \Vdash A\}$.

Proof. Here we consider (iii) because the proof for (i) and (ii) is easy and (iv) follows almost directly from (iii) and Lemma 1 (ii). We consider the induction steps, where $A = B \to C$ and $A = B \leadsto C$. For the induction step of $A = B \& C$, see Proposition 3.9 in [33]. The proof for the other cases is easy.
    Suppose $A = B \to C$. By the condition $(\to)$, $a \Vdash B \to C$ iff for any $b, c \in F$, $Rbac$ and $b \Vdash B$ entail $c \Vdash C$, hence by the induction hypothesis, iff for any $b, c \in F$, $b \circ a = c$ and $b \leq v(B)$ entail $c \leq v(C)$ and so iff $v(B) \circ a \leq v(C)$; therefore, iff $a \leq v(B) \to v(C) = v(B \to C)$ by residuation. The proof for the case $A = B \leadsto C$ is analogous. □

Theorem 4 (*Completeness*). *Let Γ be a linear theory on $L^\ell \in L^\ell_{eq}$, A a formula, and $\mathcal{UL}^\ell$ a class of all U-L^ℓ_{eq} frames.*

(i) $\Gamma \vdash_{L^\ell} A$ iff $\Gamma \vDash_{\mathcal{UL}^\ell} A$.

(ii) Let $L^\ell \in L^\ell_{eq'}$, $eq' = \{e, o\}$, and $\mathcal{UL}^\ell_c$ a class of all complete U-$L^\ell_{eq'}$ frames. Then, $\Gamma \vdash_{L^\ell} A$ iff $\Gamma \vDash_{\mathcal{UL}^\ell_c} A$.

Proof. (i) follows from Proposition 2 and Theorems 1 and 3 and (ii) from Proposition 2 and Theorems 2 (i) and 3. □

Example 3. *Among the examples introduced in Example 1, the systems **MICAL** and **UL** have U-RM$^\ell$ semantics but **MTL** does not since the postulates e, a are equationally definable by (df$_U$) but the postulate i is not. Therefore, we can say the following.*

(1) *Micanorm logic **MICAL** has a U-RM$^\ell$ semantics.*
(2) *Uninorm logic **UL** has a U-RM$^\ell$ semantics.*
(3) *Monoidal t-norm logic **MTL** does not have a U-RM$^\ell$ semantics.*

Please note that one is capable of defining the ternary relation R using (df$_U$) and the forcing relation $\Vdash$ using $\leq$. This means that for $L^\ell \in L^\ell_{eq}$, U-RM$^\ell$ semantics can be considered in the context of algebraic semantics and vice versa.

As in [1], using the definition (df$_U$) and the valuation conditions ($\to$) and ($\leadsto$), we can show the following derived conditions of a valuation.

Proposition 3 ([1]).

(i) *For any $b \in F$, $b \Vdash A$ implies $b \circ a \Vdash B$ iff for any $b, c \in F$, $Rbac$ and $b \Vdash A$ imply $c \Vdash B$.*
(ii) *For any $b \in F$, $b \Vdash A$ implies $a \circ b \Vdash B$ iff for any $b, c \in F$, $Rabc$ and $b \Vdash A$ imply $c \Vdash B$.*

Proposition 3 ensures that, as far as we accept (df$_U$), the conditions of a valuation are reducible to those of AK semantics for L^ℓ_{eq}. Thus, U-RM$^\ell$ semantics for L^ℓ_{eq} can be reduced to the AK semantics for L^ℓ_{eq} with the definition (df$_U$). Therefore, this semantics can be called ARM$^\ell$ semantics reducible to AK semantics.

3.2. F-RM$^\ell$ Semantics

Here we consider F-RM$^\ell$ semantics for L^ℓs. We first define some further RM frames.

Definition 8.

(i) *(Operational RM frame [1]) An operational RM frame is a structure $F = (F, 1, \leq, \circ, R)$, where $(F, 1, R)$ is an RM frame, $(F, 1, \circ)$ is a groupoid with unit, and R satisfies the postulates below: for all $a, b, c \in F$,*

p_s. $R1ab$ and $R1ba$ imply $a = b$;
p_t. $R1ab$ and $R1bc$ imply $R1ac$;
$p_\leq$. $a \leq b$ iff $R1ba$.

(ii) *((Residuated) Fine operational RM$^\ell$ frame) Linear RM frames are defined as in Definition 5 (ii). A Fine operational RM$^\ell$ frame (F-RM$^\ell$ frame for short) is an operational RM frame, where $\circ$ satisfies (df$_F'$) $a \circ b \geq c := Rabc$ (Notice that $\leq$ in (df$_F'$) is considered order reversely. Please compare it with $\leq$ in (df$_F$).) and R satisfies the postulate below: for all $a, b \in F$,*

$p0$. $R1ab$ or $R1ba$.

Residuated F-RM$^\ell$ frames are defined as in Definition 5 (iii).

(iii) *(Bounded, pointed F-RM$^\ell$ MIAL frames) Bounded, pointed F-RM$^\ell$ frames are defined as in Definition 5 (iv). An F-RM$^\ell$ MIAL frame is a bounded pointed residuated F-RM$^\ell$ frame, where $\circ$ is conjunctive and left-continuous.*

(iv) *(F-L$^\ell$ frames) Consider the definitions and postulates df1, df2, p_e, p_o, p_a and the below additional postulates: for all $a, b, c, d \in F$,*

p_p. $Raab$ implies $R1ab$.
p_c. $Raaa$
p_i. $Rabc$ implies $R1bc$.

For any $S \subseteq \{p_e, p_p, p_c, p_i, p_o, p_a\}$, F-RM$^\ell$ MIAL$_S$ frames are defined, along with their corresponding postulates. We call all these frames F-L$^\ell$ frames.

Remark 2.

(1) One is capable of showing that $(F, \leq)$ is a linearly ordered set, using (df$_F'$), identity $a \leq a$, p_s, p_t, and p0 in F-RM$^\ell$ frames and so these frames are linearly ordered.

(2) ([1]) The indices of the postulates in (iv) denote their corresponding axioms. For example, the postulate p_p is for the expansion axiom p. Moreover, (df$_F'$) assures that those postulates satisfy their corresponding algebraic properties.

The conditions for a valuation on an F-L$^\ell$ frame are the same as in Section 3.1 except for the following:

(&$_R$) $a \Vdash A\&B$ iff there exist $b, c \in F$ so that $Rbca$, $b \Vdash A$ and $c \Vdash B$.

We can prove Proposition 3 and the condition (&) using (df$_F'$). Moreover, we can further show the following additional derived condition.

Proposition 4. $a \leq v(A) \circ v(B)$ iff there exist $b, c \in F$ such that $Rcba$, $b \leq v(A)$ and $c \leq v(B)$.

Proof. ($\Rightarrow$) Assume that $a \leq v(A) \circ v(B)$. We take b, c satisfying that $b = v(A)$ and $c = v(B)$. Then, using (df$_F'$), we can obtain that $Rcba$, $b \leq v(A)$, and $c \leq v(B)$. ($\Leftarrow$) Suppose that $Rcba$, $b \leq v(A)$ and $c \leq v(B)$. Then, using (df$_F'$), we obtain $a \leq b \circ c$, $b \leq v(A)$, and $c \leq v(B)$; therefore, $a \leq v(A) \circ v(B)$. □

Notice that Lemmas 1 and 2 also hold for F-L$^\ell$ frames and models.

Theorem 5 (Soundness). *For a linear theory Γ over $L^\ell \in L^\ell s$, a formula A, and a class $\mathcal{FL}^\ell$ of all F-L$^\ell$ frames, $\Gamma \vdash_{L^\ell} A$ only if $\Gamma \models_{\mathcal{FL}^\ell} A$.*

Proof. We need to consider the structural axioms c, p, i. For c, we assume that $a \Vdash A$ and show that $a \Vdash A\&A$. By the supposition, p_c, and (&), we obtain that $a \Vdash A\&A$. The proof for the other ones p, i is analogous. □

Now, we recall a connection between postulates for F-L$^\ell$ frames and algebraic (in)equations for the structural axioms of $L^\ell \in L^\ell s$.

Proposition 5 ([1]). *The postulates for F-L$^\ell$ frames introduced in Definition 1 are reducible to algebraic (in)equations for the structural axioms of L^ℓ introduced in Definition 4.*

The next proposition connects F-RM$^\ell$ semantics and algebraic semantics for L^ℓs.

Proposition 6.

(i) The $\{\top, \bot, 1, 0, \leq, \circ\}$ reduct of an L^ℓ-chain $\mathcal{A}$ is an F-L$^\ell$ frame, which is complete iff $\mathcal{A}$ is complete.

(ii) Let $F = (F, \top, \bot, 1, 0, \leq, \circ)$ be an F-L$^\ell$ frame. Then, the structure $\mathcal{A} = (F, \top, \bot, 1, 0, max, min, \circ, \backslash, /)$ is an L^ℓ-algebra.

(iii) If F is the $\{\top, \bot, 1, 0, \leq, \circ\}$ reduct of an L^ℓ-chain $\mathcal{A}$ and v is a valuation in $\mathcal{A}$, then $(F, \Vdash)$ is an F-L$^\ell$ model and for all formulas A and for all $a \in \mathcal{A}$, we obtain that $a \Vdash A$ iff $a \leq v(A)$.

(iv) Let $(F, \Vdash)$ be an F-L$^\ell$ model and $\mathcal{A}$ be the L^ℓ-algebra defined as in (ii). Define for every propositional variable p, $v(p) = max\{a \in F : a \Vdash p\}$. Then, for every formula A, $v(A) = max\{a \in F : a \Vdash A\}$.

Proof. As above, we prove (iii). We consider the induction steps, where $A = B\&C$, $A = B \to C$ and $A = B \leadsto C$, since the other cases can be easily proved.

Suppose $A = B\&C$. The condition $(\&_R)$ assures that $a \Vdash B\&C$ iff there are $b, c \in F$ so that $b \Vdash B$, $c \Vdash C$, and $Rbca$, hence by the induction hypothesis and (df_F'), iff there are $b, c \in F$ such that $b \leq v(B)$, $c \leq v(C)$, and $a \leq b \circ c$. It then holds true that $a \leq b \circ c \leq v(B) \circ v(C) = v(B\&C)$. Conversely, suppose $a \leq v(B) \circ v(C) = v(B\&C)$ and take $b = v(B)$ and $c = v(C)$. Then we can obtain $b \Vdash B$, $c \Vdash C$ and $a \leq b \circ c$; hence, $a \Vdash B\&C$ by $(\&_R)$ and (df_F').

Suppose $A = B \to C$. The condition $(\to)$ assures that $a \Vdash B \to C$ iff for all $b, c \in F$, $Rbac$ and $b \Vdash B$ entail $c \Vdash C$, hence by the induction hypothesis and (df_F'), iff for all $b, c \in F$, $c \leq b \circ a$ and $b \leq v(B)$ entail $c \leq v(C)$. Then, we obtain $a \leq v(B)\backslash v(C) = v(B \to C)$ since $c \leq b \circ a \leq v(B) \circ a \leq v(C)$. Suppose conversely that $a \leq v(B)\backslash v(C) = v(B \to C)$. Then we have that $v(B) \circ a \leq v(C)$ and so $c \leq v(C)$ for $c \leq b \circ a$ and $b \leq v(B)$. This ensures that $Rbac$ and $b \Vdash B$ entail $c \Vdash C$; hence, $a \Vdash B \to C$ by $(\to)$.

The proof of the case $A = B \leadsto C$ is analogous to the case $A = B \to C$. □

Theorem 6 (Completeness). *Let Γ be a linear theory over $L^\ell \in L^\ell s$, A a formula, and $\mathcal{FL}^\ell$ a class of all F-L^ℓ frames.*

(i) $\Gamma \vdash_{L^\ell} A$ iff $\Gamma \models_{\mathcal{FL}^\ell} A$.

(ii) Let L^ℓ be a member of $L^\ell_{S'} = \{\mathbf{MIAL}_{S'} : S' \subseteq \{e, p, c, i, o\}\}$ or $L^\ell_{S''}$ such that $\{i, a\} \subseteq S'' \subseteq \{e, p, c, i, o, a\}$, and $\mathcal{FL}^\ell_c$ a class of all complete F-L^ℓ frames. Then, $\Gamma \vdash_{L^\ell} A$ iff $\Gamma \models_{\mathcal{FL}^\ell_c} A$.

Proof. (i) follows from Proposition 6 and Theorems 1 and 5 and (ii) from Proposition 6 and Theorems 2 and 5. □

Example 4. *All the systems introduced in Example 1 have F-RM$^\ell$ semantics since the postulates e, a, i are inequationally definable by (df_F'). However, the non-fuzzy system $\mathbf{R}^+$ (the positive $\mathbf{R}$) does not have such semantics since, while F-RM$^\ell$ semantics validates sentences such as (a) in Section 1, $\mathbf{R}^+$ does not proves such sentences. Therefore, we can say the following.*

(1) *Micanorm logic $\mathbf{MICAL}$ has an F-RM$^\ell$ semantics.*

(2) *Uninorm logic $\mathbf{UL}$ has an F-RM$^\ell$ semantics.*

(3) *Monoidal t-norm logic $\mathbf{MTL}$ has an F-RM$^\ell$ semantics.*

(4) *The positive relevance logic $\mathbf{R}^+$ does not have an F-RM$^\ell$ semantics.*

As above, one is capable of defining the ternary relation R using (df_F') and the forcing relation $\Vdash$ using $\leq$. This means that for $L^\ell \in L^\ell s$, F-RM$^\ell$ semantics can be considered in the context of algebraic semantics and vice versa.

4. Advantages and Limitations of ARM$^\ell$ Semantics

4.1. Advantages and Limitations: General

Here we consider the advantages and limitations of U-RM$^\ell$ and F-RM$^\ell$ semantics as ARM$^\ell$ semantics in general. The most important advantage of these semantics is that the clauses $(\wedge)$, $(\vee)$, and either $(\to_{R_U})$ or $(\to_{R_F})$ can be used together. Please note that these clauses are not working together on distributive substructural logic systems in general, whereas they are still working on linearly ordered related substructural systems (see Examples 3 and 4). This means that these semantics use the standard clauses $(\wedge)$, $(\vee)$, and so are more powerful than such semantics introduced in [1] in a *pragmatic* sense. Because most people working for semantics of a formal system would be familiar with these standard clauses and thus U-RM$^\ell$ and F-RM$^\ell$ semantics would be easier to understand to them. (Please note that in fuzzy logic prime theories are interchangeable with linear theories (see, e.g., [29]) and so the clause $(\vee)$ can be used in ARM$^\ell$ semantics. Note also that the ARM semantics in [1] uses closed theories in place of linear theories.)

ARM$^\ell$ semantics is also very powerful in a *philosophical* sense that one may understand concretely the connections between nodes to force a formula. For instance, the inequation (e^A) shows that any pair of nodes a, b must be *exchangeable* in order to force the formula $(A\&B) \to (B\&A)$ in the logic **MIAL**$_e$ (= **MICAL**). Hence, one can say that the basic feature of the postulate p_e is the commutativity property. Please note that it is not easy for us to understand that the postulate p_e has the commutativity feature if we do not interpret it using the definition (df$_U$) (or (df$_F'$)). The definition (df$_U$) says that the ternary relation R for accessibility is replaced by the operator $\circ$ and equality $=$ and similarly for the definition (df$_F'$). Using these definitions, one can achieve an intuitive understanding of the meaning of p_e.

As is well known, Routley–Meyer semantics for relevance logics need not require structures equivalent to algebraic semantics for those logics. For example, the Routley–Meyer semantics for **R** introduced by Dunn [8] has the ternary relation R indefinable by (df$_U$) and (df$_F'$) and the postulates for this semantics cannot be interpreted by those definitions (see [1,8]). Thus, related to accessibility, we may introduce two different approaches to Routley–Meyer-style semantics: One is Routley–Meyer-style semantics based on accessibility relations themselves and the other is that instead based on accessibility operations. The Routley–Meyer semantics for **R** above is a representative example of the former sort and the ARM$^\ell$ semantics for the substructural fuzzy logics here is a representative example of the latter sort. Therefore, ARM$^\ell$ semantics as a representative of the latter sort is *very useful* to deal with substructural fuzzy logics.

However, on the other side of the same coin, ARM$^\ell$ semantics has clear limitations. First, it does not have its own semantics distinguished from algebraic semantics in that frames for the ARM$^\ell$ semantics have the same structures as algebraic semantics. In this sense, ARM$^\ell$ semantics is not very interesting in terms of the novelty of semantics. Second, it is not applicable to Routley–Meyer frames not having such algebraic structures. Thirdly, is not applicable to non-fuzzy substructural logics in general. These three are the limitations of U-RM$^\ell$ and F-RM$^\ell$ semantics as ARM$^\ell$ semantics in general.

4.2. Advantages and Limitations: Specific

Here we deal with comparative advantages and limitations between U-RM$^\ell$ and F-RM$^\ell$ semantics. We first introduce advantages of each semantics. First, consider U-RM$^\ell$ semantics. As mentioned in Section 3.1, Position 3 implies that this semantics can be regarded as ARM$^\ell$ semantics reducible to AK semantics. This shows that U-RM$^\ell$ semantics is related to both Kripke-style semantics and algebraic semantics. More precisely, U-RM$^\ell$ semantics belongs to a common area of algebraic, Kripke-style, and Routley–Meyer-style semantics. This is the most important *logical* advantage of U-RM$^\ell$ semantics in that it provides a chance to investigate similarities and differences between the three sorts of semantics. U-RM$^\ell$ frames have the postulates $p1, p2$, whereas F-RM$^\ell$ frames do not. This means that U-RM$^\ell$ frames have relational conditions for a unit element but F-RM$^\ell$ frames do not. This is another advantage of U-RM$^\ell$ semantics in a *technical* point of view for relational semantics when it is compared to F-RM$^\ell$ semantics.

Next, consider F-RM$^\ell$ semantics. Proposition 6 assures that if one accepts (df$_F'$), one is capable of providing ARM$^\ell$ semantics being equivalent to algebraic semantics for $\tilde{L}^\ell$s. This implies that F-RM$^\ell$ semantics can cover all the systems introduced in Definition 2. This is the most important *logical* advantage of F-RM$^\ell$ semantics in that this semantics as one sort of ARM$^\ell$ semantics is as powerful as algebraic semantics. Please note that, as is shown in Section 3.2, substructural (core) fuzzy logics being algebraically complete are also complete regarding this sort of semantics and vice versa. F-RM$^\ell$ frames have the postulates $p_s, p_t, p_\leq, p0$, whereas U-RM$^\ell$ frames do not. This means that F-RM$^\ell$ frames have relational conditions for the *linear ordering* of $\leq$ but U-RM$^\ell$ frames do not. Moreover, it has the relational clause ($\&_R$) defined using the ternary relation R for a valuation of the intensional conjunction &. These provide a *technical* advantage of F-RM$^\ell$ semantics for relational semantics when it is compared to U-RM$^\ell$ semantics.

We next introduce limitations of each semantics. Like the face and back of a coin, the advantages of U-RM$^\ell$ provide limits of F-RM$^\ell$ semantics, and the advantages of F-RM$^\ell$ give limitations of U-RM$^\ell$ semantics. We state this. For the limitations of U-RM$^\ell$ semantics, first consider the following example.

Example 5. *As in [1], (df_U) does not work for the postulates $p_p, p_c,$ and p_i introduced in Section 3.2. To verify this, apply (df_U) to $p_c, p_p,$ and p_i. Then, we obtain the following:*

p'_c. $a \circ a = a$.
p'_p. $b = a \circ a$ implies $b = 1 \circ a$.
p'_i. $c = a \circ b$ implies $c = 1 \circ b$.

Since p'_c implies p'_p and vice versa, the postulates p_c and p_p are the same; therefore, the MIAL$_c$-RM (MIAL$_p$-RM resp) frame validates the axiom p (c resp), which is not provable in MIAL$_c$ (MIAL$_p$ resp). Similarly, the postulate p_i implies that $b = a * b$ and thus the MIAL$_i$-RM frame validates formulas such as $\varphi \to (\psi \& \varphi)$, which is not provable in MIAL$_i$.

This example shows that as semantics for basic (core) fuzzy logics U-RM$^\ell$ semantics is *less powerful* than F-RM$^\ell$ semantics in a *logical* point of view. Moreover, using the ternary relation R, one cannot provide the postulates for the above linear ordering and the clause ($\&_R$). These two are the limitations of U-RM$^\ell$ semantics compared to F-RM$^\ell$ semantics.

For the limitations of F-RM$^\ell$ semantics, first consider the following example, which can be easily verified.

Example 6. *Using the definition (df_F') and the valuation conditions ($\to$) and ($\rightsquigarrow$), one can prove the following.*

(i) *For any $b \in F$, $b \Vdash A$ implies $b \circ a \Vdash B$ only if for any $b, c \in F$, $Rbac$ and $b \Vdash A$ imply $c \Vdash B$.*

(ii) *For any $b \in F$, $b \Vdash A$ implies $a \circ b \Vdash B$ only if for any $b, c \in F$, $Rabc$ and $b \Vdash A$ imply $c \Vdash B$.*

However, one cannot prove the reverse direction of each (i) and (ii) and so cannot do Proposition 3.

This example shows that F-RM$^\ell$ semantics is not reducible to AK semantics. Therefore, such semantics can be called ARM$^\ell$ semantics irreducible to AK semantics for L^ℓs. It implies that F-RM$^\ell$ semantics is not helpful to study a common area between Kripke-style semantics and Routley–Meyer-style semantics. Hence, F-RM$^\ell$ semantics is *less powerful* than U-RM$^\ell$ semantics in a logical research of common areas between different sorts of semantics. Moreover, using the ternary relation R, one cannot provide the postulates for the unit element. These two are the limitations of F-RM$^\ell$ semantics compared to U-RM$^\ell$ semantics.

As a summary we note the following facts. First, U-RM$^\ell$ semantics covers all the (core) fuzzy systems with equationally definable substructural axioms, whereas F-RM$^\ell$ semantics those systems with inequationally definable substructural axioms. Second, in these two sorts of ARM$^\ell$ semantics, (df_U) and (df_F') provide ways to interpret the ternary relation R using binary operation $\circ$ and (in)equation. Third, these two semantics are not applicable to Routley–Meyer-style semantics irreducible to algebraic one. For instance, while the RM semantics for **R** introduced in [8] requires the postulate $Raaa$ for the rule (mp), U-RM$^\ell$ and F-RM$^\ell$ semantics cannot have $a = a \circ a$ (by (df_U)) and $a \leq a \circ a$ (by (df_F')), respectively, as semantic postulates for **MIAL**.

5. Discussion and Conclusions

We investigated ARM semantics for substructural (core) fuzzy logics based on mianorms. More precisely, we provided U-RM$^\ell$ and F-RM$^\ell$ semantics as two sorts of ARM semantics for them. We in particular deal with advantages and limitations of these semantics.

We note that U-RM$^\ell$ and F-RM$^\ell$ semantics provide frames as some reducts of their corresponding algebras and so are ARM$^\ell$ semantics for fuzzy extensions of substructural logics. Especially, those semantics define ternary relations using binary operations and (in)equations like the semantics for substructural logics in [1]. However, unlike these semantics, they are provided based on linear theories and conditions for linear ordering, and so work for linearly ordered models. As mentioned in Section 1, ARM$^\ell$ semantics as a relational semantics for substructural fuzzy logics in general is a *novel* one to connect n-nary operations and $n+1$-nary relations.

The author [47] introduced implicational tonoid *fuzzy* logics as fuzzy extensions of implicational tonoid logics, the class of logics satisfying transitivity, reflexivity, tonicity, and modus ponens introduced by the author and Dunn [48]. Please note that all the logic systems introduced in Definition 2 can be regarded as such fuzzy logics because they also satisfy the conditions for an implicational tonoid logic and are complete over linearly ordered models. Hence, this investigation can be thought of as an introduction of ARM semantics for *concrete* implicational tonoid fuzzy logics.

However, any more exact connection between semantics for implicational tonoid fuzzy logics and those for substructural (core) fuzzy logics is not studied here. For instance, while the former logics do not introduce any concrete connectives, the substructural (core) fuzzy logics do. For these logics, the connectives ∨ and ∧ need to be interpreted by *join* and *meet* as lattice operators and need their corresponding relational consideration. Thus, in the context of implicational tonoid fuzzy logics, these things have to be dealt with. Furthermore, while non-operational RM semantics can be established for substructural logics, e.g., the system **R** (see [8]), such semantics for the fuzzy logics is not considered either. The author has a plan to study these two in the future, i.e., leave these for another day. By these two works, we can fill gaps between abstract logic (implicational tonoid fuzzy logics) and concrete logic (substructural (core) fuzzy logics) and between algebraic and non-algebraic Routley–Meyer-style semantics.

It is well known that lattices can be defined as ordered sets and as algebraic structures. To show the equivalence between the first relational definition of a lattice and its second algebraic definition, one has to have some definitions such as (b) $x \leq y$ iff $join(x,y) = y$ iff $meet(x,y) = x$. Similarly, we can consider the algebraic and ARM semantics and the definitions (df$_U$) and (df$_F'$) regarding substructural (core) fuzzy logics. Associated with this, the author [49] studied basic logico-algebraic properties of micanorms characterizing the logic **MICAL** such as (left-)continuity, residuated implications, conjunctive and disjunctive micanorms, idempotent, nilpotent, and divisor micanorms, and so on. This implies that such theoretic applications of micanorms can be considered in the context of U-RM$^\ell$ and F-RM$^\ell$ frames. Namely, one can treat such properties as applications of U-RM$^\ell$ and F-RM$^\ell$ frames. More exact treatment of such applications is an another problem to solve in the future.

Funding: This work was supported by the Ministry of Education of the Republic of Korea and the National Research Foundation of Korea (NRF-2019S1A5A2A01034874).

Data Availability Statement: The author does not have any data supporting.

Conflicts of Interest: The author declares no conflict of interest.

References

1. Yang, E. Algebraic relational semantics for basic substructural logics. *Log. Anal.* **2020**, *252*, 415–441.
2. Kripke, S. Semantic analysis of modal logic I: Normal modal propositional calculi. *Z. Math. Logik Grund. Math.* **1963**, *9*, 67–96. [CrossRef]
3. Kripke, S. Semantic analysis of intuitionistic logic I. In *Formal Systems and Recursive Functions*; Crossley, J., Dummett, M. Eds.; North-Holland Publ. Co.: Amsterdam, The Nederland, 1965; pp. 92–129.

4. Kripke, S. Semantic analysis of modal logic II. In *The Theory of Models*; Addison. J., Henkin, L., Tarski, A. Eds.; North-Holland Publ. Co.: Amsterdam, The Nederland, 1965; pp. 206–220.
5. Urquhart, A. The completeness of weak implication. *Theoria* **1972**, *37*, 274–282. [CrossRef]
6. Urquhart, A. A general theory of implication. *J. Symb. Log.* **1972**, *37*, 443.
7. Urquhart, A. Semantics for relevant logics. *J. Symb. Log.* **1972**, *37*, 159–169. [CrossRef]
8. Dunn, J.M. Relevance logic and entailment. In *Handbook of Philosophical Logic*; Gabbay, D., Guenthner, F. Eds.; Reidel Publ. Co.: Dordrecht, The Nederland, 1986; Volume III, pp. 117–224.
9. Routley, R.; Meyer, R.K. The semantics of entailment (II). *J. Phil. Log.* **1972**, *1*, 53–73. [CrossRef]
10. Routley, R.; Meyer, R.K. The semantics of entailment (III). *J. Phil. Log.* **1972**, *1*, 192–208. [CrossRef]
11. Routley, R.; Meyer, R.K. The semantics of entailment (I). In *Truth, Syntax, and Modality*; Lebranc, H. Ed.; North-Holland: Amsterdam, The Nederland, 1973; pp. 199–243.
12. Restall, G. *An Introduction to Substructural Logics*; Routledge: London, UK, 2000.
13. Fine, K. Models for entailment. *J. Phil. Log.* **1974**, *3*, 347–372. [CrossRef]
14. Došen, K. Sequent systems and groupoid models I. *Stud. Log.* **1988**, *47*, 353–385.
15. Došen, K. Sequent systems and groupoid models II. *Stud. Log.* **1989**, *48*, 41–65.
16. Ono, H. Completions of algebras and completeness of modal and substructural logics. In *Advances in Modal Logic*; Balbiani, P., Ed.; College Publications: London, UK, 2003; Volume 4, pp. 335–353.
17. Montagna, F.; Ono, H. Kripke Semantics, undecidability and standard completeness for Esteva and Godo's Logic MTL∀. *Stud. Log.* **2002**, *71*, 227–245. [CrossRef]
18. Montagna F.; Sacchetti, L. Kripke-style semantics for many-valued logics. *Math. Log. Quart.* **2003**, *49*, 629–641. [CrossRef]
19. Yang, E. Kripke-style semantics for UL. *Korean J. Log.* **2012**, *15*, 1–15.
20. Yang, E. Algebraic Kripke-style semantics for substructural fuzzy logics. *Korean J. Log.* **2016**, *19*, 295–322.
21. Ono, H.; Komori, Y. Logics without the contraction rule. *J. Symb. Log.* **1985**, *50*, 169–201. [CrossRef]
22. Ishihara, H. A canonical construction for substructural logics. *J. UCS.* **2000**, *6*, 155–168.
23. Kamide, N. Kripke Semantics for modal substructural logics. *J. Logic Lang. Inform.* **2002**, *11*, 453–470. [CrossRef]
24. Dunn, J.M. *Logics as Tools, or Humans as Rational Tool Making Animals*; Jeonbuk National University: Jeonju, Korea, 2018.
25. Dunn, J.M. Ternary relational semantics and beyond: Programs as data and programs as instructions. *Log. Stud.* **2001**, *7*, 1–20.
26. Dunn, J.M. The relevance of relevance to relevance logic. In *ICLA 2015: Logic and Its Applications*; Banerjee. M., Krishna, S.N. Eds.; Springer: Berlin, Germany, 2015; pp. 11–29.
27. Bimbó, K.; Dunn, J.M. The emergence of set-theoretic semantics for relevance logics around 1970. *J. Appl. Log.* **2017**, *4*, 557–589.
28. Běhounek, L.; Cintula, P. Fuzzy logics as the logics of chains. *Fuzzy Sets Syst.* **2006**, *157*, 604–610.
29. Cintula, P. Weakly Implicative (Fuzzy) Logics I: Basic properties. *Arch. Math. Log.* **2006**, *45*, 673–704. [CrossRef]
30. Diaconescu, D. Kripke-style semantics for non-commutative monoidal t-norm logic. *J. Mult.-Valued Log. Soft Comput.* **2010**, *16*, 247–263.
31. Diaconescu, D.; Georgescu, G. On the forcing semantics for monoidal t-norm-based logic. *J. UCS* **2007**, *13*, 1550–1572.
32. Yang, E. Algebraic Kripke-style semantics for an extension of HpsUL, CnHpsUL*. *Korean J. Log.* **2016**, *19*, 107–126.
33. Yang, E. Algebraic Routley–Meyer-style semantics for the fuzzy logic MTL. *Korean J. Log.* **2018**, *21*, 353–371.
34. Yang, E. Algebraic Routley–Meyer-style semantics for the involutive monoidal t-norm logic IMTL. *Korean J. Log.* **2020**, *23*, 177–195.
35. Allwein, G.; Dunn, J.M. Kripke models for linear logics. *J. Symb. Log.* **1993**, *58*, 514–545. [CrossRef]
36. Bimbó K.; Dunn, J.M. *Generalized Galois Logics*; CSLI: Stanford, CA, USA, 2008.
37. Chernilovskaya, A.; Gehrke, M.; van Rooijen, L. Generalized Kripke Semantics for Lambek-Grishin calculus. *Log. J. IGPL* **2012**, *20*, 1110–1132. [CrossRef]
38. Dunn, J.M. Partial gaggles applied to logics with restricted structural rules. In *Substructural Logics*; Schroeder-Heister, P., Došen, K. Eds.; Clarendon: Oxford, UK, 1993; pp. 63–108.
39. Dunn, J.M.; Gehrke, M.; Palmigiano, A. Canonical extensions and relational completeness of some structural logics. *J. Symb. Log.* **2005**, *70*, 713–740. [CrossRef]
40. Gehrke, M. Generalized Kripke Semantics. *Stud. Log.* **2006**, *84*, 241–275. [CrossRef]
41. Hartonas C.; Dunn, J.M. Stone Duality for Lattices. *Alg. Univ.* **1997**, *37*, 391–401. [CrossRef]
42. Yang, E. Basic substructural core fuzzy logics and their extensions: Mianorm-based logics. *Fuzzy Sets Syst.* **2016**, *301*, 1–18. [CrossRef]
43. Cintula, P.; Horčík, R.; Noguera, C. Non-associative substructural logics and their semilinear extensions: axiomatization and completeness properties. *Rev. Symb. Log.* **2013**, *6*, 394–423. [CrossRef]
44. Cintula, P.; Horčík, R.; Noguera, C. The quest for the basic fuzzy logic. In *Petr Hájek on Mathematical Fuzzy Logic*; Montagna, F., Ed.; Springer: Dordrecht, The Nederland, 2015; pp. 245–290.
45. Cintula, P.; Noguera, C. A general framework for mathematical fuzzy logic. In *Handbook of Mathematical Fuzzy Logic*; Cintula, P., Hájek, P., Noguera, C. Eds.; College Publications; London, UK 2011; Volume 1, pp. 103–207.
46. Horčík, R. Algebraic semantics: semilinear FL-algebras. In *Handbook of Mathematical Fuzzy Logic*; Cintula, P., Hájek, P., Noguera, C., Eds.; College Publications: London, UK, 2011; Volume 1, pp. 283–353.

47. Yang, E. Implicational Tonoid Fuzzy Logics. In *Frontiers in Artificial Intelligence and Applications: Fuzzy Systems and Data Mining IV*; Tallón-Ballesteros, A.J., Li, K. Eds.; IOS Press: Amsterdam, The Nederland, 2018; Volume 309, pp. 223–230.
48. Yang, E.; Dunn, J.M. Implicational tonoid logics: Algebraic and relational semantics. *Log. Universalis* **2021**. s11787-021-00288-z. [CrossRef]
49. Yang, E. Micanorm aggregation operators: Basic logico-algebraic properties. *Soft Comput.* **2021**, *25*, 13167–13180. [CrossRef]

Article

The Relationships among Three Kinds of Divisions of Type-1 Fuzzy Numbers

Yadan Jiang and Dong Qiu *

College of Sciences, Chongqing University of Posts and Telecommunications, Chongqing 400065, China; s200601001@stu.cqupt.edu.cn
* Correspondence: qiudong@cqupt.edu.cn or dongqiumath@163.com

Abstract: The division operation for type-1 fuzzy numbers in its original form is not invertible for the multiplication operation. This is an essential drawback in some applications. To eliminate this drawback several approaches are proposed: the generalized Hukuhara division, generalized division and granular division. In this paper, the expression of granular division is introduced, and the relationships among generalized Hukuhara division, generalized division and granular division are clarified.

Keywords: generalized Hukuhara division; generalized division; granular division

1. Introduction

The search for some invertible operations has been an issue for a long time. In 1965, Ref. [1] proposed a difference based on the extension principle, which is an extension of the interval subtraction operation according to the addition and multiplication operations of type-1 fuzzy numbers (T1FNs). This method provides a difference between T1FNs. However, this difference is not the invertible operation of addition for T1FNs. The pioneer work of finding an invertible operation for the addition can be traced to 1967 [2] when Hukuhara proposed the Hukuhara difference (H-difference), which is well known and largely used. However, the existence of H-difference has very restrictive limitations [3]. To overcome this weakness, Stefanini, Bede and Mazandarani introduced a generalized Hukuhara difference (gH-difference) [3], a generalized difference (g-difference) [4,5] and a granular difference (gr-difference) [6].

The division operation of T1FNs has also received much attention. Similarly to the gH-difference, which is defined by Stefanin in [3], the idea is to introduce the generalized division of real intervals and T1FNs by Stefanini [7] (we called the generalized division gH-division in this paper, while Stefanini called it g-division), which gives an inverse operation for the multiplication operation of T1FNs. However, Stefanini also illustrated that the result of the gH-division between two T1FNs is not always a T1FN. Then, Stefanini proposed another division in [7] (we called it g-division, while Stefanini considered it as a generalization of the division of T1FNs). The introduction of this kind of division opens up more fields of applications to interval and fuzzy arithmetic and analysis, such as the concepts of differentiability [3,4,8], the solution of equations [9,10], interval and fuzzy regression analysis [11–13], interval and fuzzy integral and differential equations [14–17], etc.

The horizontal membership function was introduced by Piegat [15], which transforms T1FNs as an algebraic form with a variable that called a relative distance measure (RDM) variable (Please refer to [18] for more details about RDM variable). Through this expression, we could transform the four arithmetic operations of T1FNs into four arithmetic operations of an algebraic expression in order to calculate them easily, which includes the gr-difference and granular division (gr-division). Details on the horizontal membership function and the gr-division are discussed in later sections.

Citation: Jiang, Y.; Qiu, D. The Relationships among Three Kinds of Divisions of Type-1 Fuzzy Numbers. *Axioms* **2022**, *11*, 77. https://doi.org/10.3390/axioms11020077

Academic Editor: Amit K. Shukla

Received: 19 December 2021
Accepted: 11 February 2022
Published: 15 February 2022

Publisher's Note: MDPI stays neutral with regard to jurisdictional claims in published maps and institutional affiliations.

Copyright: © 2022 by the authors. Licensee MDPI, Basel, Switzerland. This article is an open access article distributed under the terms and conditions of the Creative Commons Attribution (CC BY) license (https://creativecommons.org/licenses/by/4.0/).

To know which of these three divisions is more practical, we have to consider the relationships among these divisions. Costa et al. in [19] discussed the inclusion isotonic relationship of the gH-division and found that the gH-division was not inclusion isotonic. However, we analyze the relationships among gH-division, g-division and gr-division more clearly in this paper. Furthermore, the following problems are well worth considering in order to help people reasonably select the corresponding division operation in practice. The basic questions posed below are then discussed and conclusions are drawn.

(1) It has been proved that if the g-division or the gr-division exists between any two T1FNs, then the following question arises: do they get the same results?
(2) It is also obvious that the g-division is more general than the gH-division and they have the same result if the gH-division exists. Therefore, another question is: does the gH-division have the same relationship with the gr-division or not?

This paper is organized as follows. We first briefly described some related concepts in Section 2. After the statement of these basic problems above, we give an expression of the gr-division between two T1FNs and the complete relationships characterization among gH-division, g-division and gr-division are studied, then we analyze the properties of these approaches, and some examples are illustrated in Section 3. Finally, conclusions and future work are summarized in Section 4.

2. Basic Concepts

We provide some basic terminologies and related definitions which are necessary for the understanding of subsequent results in this section.

Throughout this paper, the set of all real numbers, bounded closed intervals of real numbers and T1FNs on real numbers is denoted by $\mathbb{R}$, K_c and $\mathcal{F}_1$, respectively. $cl(A)$ denotes the closure of set A.

Definition 1. *Let $u \in \mathcal{F}_1$. For $\alpha \in (0,1]$, the α-level set of u is defined by $[u]_\alpha = \{x|x \in \mathbb{R}, u(x) \geq \alpha\}$ and for $\alpha = 0$ by the closure of the support $[u]_0 = cl\{x|x \in \mathbb{R}, u(x) > \alpha\}$ whose lower and upper endpoints are represented as u_α^- and u_α^+ with $\alpha \in [0,1]$.*

A division of fuzzy numbers and real intervals can be introduced, which is similar to the gH-difference. Let $A = [a^-, a^+] \in K_c$ and $B = [b^-, b^+] \in K_c$ with $b^+ < 0$ or $b^- > 0$, which means that $0 \notin B$. The multiplication $C = AB = [c^-, c^+]$ and the multiplicative "inverse" of A is given by

$$c^- = \min\{a^-b^-, a^-b^+, a^+b^-, a^+b^+\}, \quad c^+ = \max\{a^-b^-, a^-b^+, a^+b^-, a^+b^+\}, \quad (1)$$

and

$$A^{-1} = \left[\frac{1}{a^+}, \frac{1}{a^-}\right]. \quad (2)$$

Definition 2 ([7]). *Let $A, B \in K_c$ with $A = [a^-, a^+]$ and $B = [b^-, b^+]$, then the gH-division $\div_{gH}$ is defined as*

$$A \div_{gH} B = C \iff \begin{cases} (i) A = BC, \\ \text{or} \\ (ii) B = AC^{-1}. \end{cases} \quad (3)$$

We called it gH_i-division or gH_{ii}-division if (i) or (ii) in (3) holds, respectively.

Remark 1. *We can get the following results for the gH-division from the definition (see [7] for more details).*

(1) If $0 < a^- \le a^+, b^- \le b^+ < 0$ and $a^-b^- \ge a^+b^+$, then
$$c^- = \frac{a^+}{b^-}, c^+ = \frac{a^-}{b^+}, \quad (4)$$

(2) If $0 < a^- \le a^+, 0 < b^- \le b^+$ and $a^-b^+ \le a^+b^-$, then
$$c^- = \frac{a^-}{b^-}, c^+ = \frac{a^+}{b^+}, \quad (5)$$

(3) If $a^- \le a^+ < 0, b^- \le b^+ < 0$ and $a^+b^- \le a^-b^+$, then
$$c^- = \frac{a^+}{b^+}, c^+ = \frac{a^-}{b^-}, \quad (6)$$

(4) If $a^- \le a^+ < 0, 0 < b^- \le b^+$ and $a^-b^- \le a^+b^+$, then
$$c^- = \frac{a^-}{b^+}, c^+ = \frac{a^+}{b^-}, \quad (7)$$

(5) If $a^- \le 0, a^+ \ge 0, b^- \le b^+ < 0$ and
$$c^- = \frac{a^+}{b^-}, c^+ = \frac{a^-}{b^-}, \quad (8)$$

(6) If $a^- \le 0, a^+ \ge 0, 0 < b^- \le b^+$ and
$$c^- = \frac{a^-}{b^+}, c^+ = \frac{a^+}{b^+}, \quad (9)$$

and (i) in (3) is satisfied which means that (1)–(6) are gH_i-divisions.

(7) If $0 < a^- \le a^+, b^- \le b^+ < 0$ and $a^-b^- \le a^+b^+$, then
$$c^- = \frac{a^-}{b^+}, c^+ = \frac{a^+}{b^-}, \quad (10)$$

(8) If $0 < a^- \le a^+, 0 < b^- \le b^+$ and $a^-b^+ \ge a^+b^-$, then
$$c^- = \frac{a^+}{b^+}, c^+ = \frac{a^-}{b^-}, \quad (11)$$

(9) If $a^- \le a^+ < 0, b^- \le b^+ < 0$ and $a^+b^- \ge a^-b^+$, then
$$c^- = \frac{a^-}{b^-}, c^+ = \frac{a^+}{b^+}, \quad (12)$$

(10) If $a^- \le a^+ < 0, 0 < b^- \le b^+$ and $a^-b^- \ge a^+b^+$, then
$$c^- = \frac{a^+}{b^-}, c^+ = \frac{a^-}{b^+}, \quad (13)$$

and (ii) in (3) is satisfied which means that (7)–(10) are gH_{ii}-divisions.
In conclusion, we have that
$$\div_{gH}[b^-, b^+] := [\min \frac{a^\pm}{b^\pm}, \max \frac{b^\pm}{b^\pm}]. \quad (14)$$

Definition 3 ([7]). *Let $a, b \in \mathcal{F}_1$ have α-level sets $[a]_\alpha = [a_\alpha^-, a_\alpha^+]$ and $[b]_\alpha = [b_\alpha^-, b_\alpha^+]$ with $0 \notin [b]_\alpha$, for each $\alpha \in [0, 1]$. The gH-division $\div_{gH}$ calculates the T1FN $c = a \div_{gH} b \in \mathcal{F}_1$ is defined by*

$$[a]_\alpha \div_{gH} [b]_\alpha = [c]_\alpha \iff \begin{cases} (i) [a]_\alpha = [b]_\alpha [c]_\alpha, \\ \text{or} \\ (ii) [b]_\alpha = [a]_\alpha [c]_\alpha^{-1}, \end{cases} \quad (15)$$

where the α-level sets and the multiplicative "inverse" are written as $[c]_\alpha = [c_\alpha^-, c_\alpha^+]$ and $[c]_\alpha^{-1} = [1/c_\alpha^+, 1/c_\alpha^-]$.

However, there exist two T1FNs whose gH-division is not a T1FN, for more details, please refer to [7]. If the gH-division $[a]_\alpha \div_{gH} [b]_\alpha$ do not define a proper T1FN, Stefanini [7] proposed a new division named g-division ($\div_g$) with α-level sets that can obtain an approximated division for T1FNs. Similarly to what is done in [5], the convexification is necessary for the new division to always be a T1FN.

Definition 4 ([7]). *For any $a, b \in \mathcal{F}_1$, the g-division with α-level sets is defined as*

$$[a \div_g b]_\alpha = cl\left(conv \bigcup_{\mu \geq \alpha} ([a]_\mu \div_{gH} [b]_\mu)\right). \quad (16)$$

Here, $conv(A)$ denotes the convex hull of set A. It can be considered that $z = a \div_g b$ is a generalization of the division of T1FNs because the g-division exists for any a, b with $0 \notin [b]_\mu$ for all $\mu \in [0, 1]$.

Piegat et al. examined a new definition of membership function based on constraint interval arithmetic (CIA) about T1FNs, multidimensional relative distance measure interval arithmetic (RDM-IA) and multidimensional fuzzy arithmetic based on RDM (MD-RDM-F arithmetic), which have been studied as a powerful and effective tool in interval arithmetic and fuzzy mathematics (see [15,20–24]), which overcomes the difficulties found in traditional membership function.

Definition 5 ([6,15]). *Let $a : [p, q] \to [0, 1]$ be a T1FN. The horizontal membership function $a^{gr} : [0, 1] \times [0, 1] \to [p, q]$ is written as $a^{gr}(\mu, \alpha_a) = a_\mu^- + (a_\mu^+ - a_\mu^-)\alpha_a$ where "gr" represents the granule of information in $x \in [p, q], \mu \in [0, 1]$ is the membership degree of x in $a(x)$ and $\alpha_a \in [0, 1]$ is called an RDM variable.*

Remark 2 ([6,25]). *$\mathcal{H}(a) \triangleq a^{gr}(\mu, \alpha_a)$ can be denoted as the horizontal membership function of $a(x) \in \mathcal{F}_1$ and using*

$$\mathcal{H}^{-1}(a^{gr}(\mu, \alpha_a)) = [a]_\mu = \left[\inf_{\beta \geq \mu} \min_{\alpha_a} a^{gr}(\beta, \alpha_a), \sup_{\beta \geq \mu} \max_{\alpha_a} a^{gr}(\beta, \alpha_a)\right] \quad (17)$$

we can obtain the μ-level sets of span of the information granule named vertical membership function of $a(x)$.

Definition 6 ([6]). *We say that two T1FNs a and b are equal if and only if for all $\alpha_a = \alpha_b \in [0, 1]$, $\mathcal{H}(a) = \mathcal{H}(b)$ holds.*

Next, we give the definition of four arithmetic operations between T1FNs based on horizontal membership functions.

Definition 7 ([6,25]). *Let a and b be two T1FNs and $a^{gr}(\mu, \alpha_a)$ and $a^{gr}(\mu, \alpha_a)$ be their horizontal membership functions. Then, the granular division (gr-division) $a \div_{gr} b$ is a T1FN, with w such that $\mathcal{H}(w) \triangleq a^{gr}(\mu, \alpha_a) \div b^{gr}(\mu, \alpha_b)$ with $0 \notin b^{gr}(\mu, \alpha_b)$.*

Remark 3 ([6]). *Let $w = a \div_{gr} b$. Then, $[w]_\mu = \mathcal{H}^{-1}\left(\frac{a^{gr}(\mu, \alpha_a)}{b^{gr}(\mu, \alpha_b)}\right)$ always presents μ-level sets of w.*

3. Main Results

In this section, we give a complete characterization of the relationships among gH-division, g-division and gr-division. Recently, the search for the division operation between T1FNs has received much attention, in order to find the inverse operation of multiplication, such as the study in [26–31].

We give the expression of gr-division first. For any $m, n \in \mathcal{F}_1$, $[m]_\beta = [m_\beta^-, m_\beta^+]$ and $[n]_\beta = [n_\beta^-, n_\beta^+]$ are their α-level sets, $\mathcal{H}(\cdot)$ denotes the horizontal membership function of "·". According to Definition 5 we have

$$\mathcal{H}(v) = \frac{\mathcal{H}(m)}{\mathcal{H}(n)} = \frac{m_\alpha^- + (m_\alpha^+ - m_\alpha^-)\alpha_m}{n_\alpha^- + (n_\alpha^+ - n_\alpha^-)\alpha_n}. \quad (18)$$

Because of the monotonicity of numerator and denominator with respect to α_m, α_n we can get the following extreme values:

$$\begin{aligned}
\alpha_m &= 0, \min\{m_\alpha^- + (m_\alpha^+ - m_\alpha^-)\alpha_m\} = m_\alpha^-, \\
\alpha_m &= 1, \max\{m_\alpha^- + (m_\alpha^+ - m_\alpha^-)\alpha_m\} = m_\alpha^+, \\
\alpha_n &= 0, \min\{n_\alpha^- + (n_\alpha^+ - n_\alpha^-)\alpha_n\} = n_\alpha^-, \\
\alpha_n &= 1, \max\{n_\alpha^- + (n_\alpha^+ - n_\alpha^-)\alpha_n\} = n_\alpha^+.
\end{aligned} \quad (19)$$

Moreover, with (17), we can get the expression of the gr-division in the following theorem.

Theorem 1. *For any $m, n \in \mathcal{F}_1$, $m \div_{gr} n$ is a T1FN u such that $\mathcal{H}(u) = \mathcal{H}(m)/\mathcal{H}(n)$ and*

$$[u]_\alpha = [m \div_{gr} n]_\alpha = [\inf_{\beta \geq \alpha} \min \frac{m_\beta^\pm}{n_\beta^\pm}, \sup_{\beta \geq \alpha} \max \frac{m_\beta^\pm}{n_\beta^\pm}]. \quad (20)$$

Proof of Theorem 1. The horizontal membership functions of m and n are written as

$$\begin{aligned}
\mathcal{H}(m) &= m_\alpha^- + (m_\alpha^+ - m_\alpha^-)\alpha_m, \\
\mathcal{H}(n) &= n_\alpha^- + (n_\alpha^+ - n_\alpha^-)\alpha_n,
\end{aligned} \quad (21)$$

respectively. Then, by (18) we can get the horizontal membership function of $m \div_g n$ (which is represented as the T1FN u) as follows:

$$\mathcal{H}(u) = \frac{\mathcal{H}(m)}{\mathcal{H}(n)} = \frac{m_\alpha^- + (m_\alpha^+ - m_\alpha^-)\alpha_m}{n_\alpha^- + (n_\alpha^+ - n_\alpha^-)\alpha_n}. \quad (22)$$

From (19) and (17), we have

$$\mathcal{H}^{-1}(u^{gr}(\mu, \alpha_u)) = [u]_\mu = [\inf_{\beta \geq \alpha} \min \frac{m_\beta^\pm}{n_\beta^\pm}, \sup_{\beta \geq \alpha} \max \frac{m_\beta^\pm}{n_\beta^\pm}]. \quad (23)$$

□

Next we clarify the relationships among the three divisions. For any $m, n \in \mathcal{F}_1$, let $[m \div_{gH} n]_\alpha = [u^{gH}]_\alpha$, $[m \div_g n]_\alpha = [u^g]_\alpha$ and $[m \div_{gr} n]_\alpha = [u^{gr}]_\alpha$ denote the gH-division, g-division and gr-division, respectively. The following theorems hold.

Theorem 2. *If there exists $u = m \div_{gH} n \in \mathcal{F}_1$, then $[u^{gH}]_\alpha \subseteq [u^{gr}]_\alpha$ holds. Moreover, if $m = n$ then we have $[u^{gH}]_\alpha = [u^{gr}]_\alpha$.*

Proof of Theorem 2. Based on (14) and (20) we have

$$[u^{gH}]_\alpha = [\min \frac{m_\alpha^\pm}{n_\alpha^\pm}, \max \frac{m_\alpha^\pm}{n_\alpha^\pm}] \subseteq [\inf_{\beta \geq \alpha} \min \frac{m_\beta^\pm}{n_\beta^\pm}, \sup_{\beta \geq \alpha} \max \frac{m_\beta^\pm}{n_\beta^\pm}] = [u^{gr}]_\alpha, \quad (24)$$

which implies that $[m \div_{gH} n]_\alpha \subseteq [m \div_{gr} n]_\alpha$ holds.

If $m = n$, according to Definition 6 and (17), $\mathcal{H}(u^{gr}) = \mathcal{H}(m)/\mathcal{H}(n) = 1$, $[u^{gr}]_\alpha = [1,1]$. Since $[u^{gH}]_\alpha \subseteq [u^{gr}]_\alpha$ we have $[u^{gH}]_\alpha = [u^{gr}]_\alpha = [1,1]$. □

Theorem 3. $[u^g]_\alpha \subseteq [u^{gr}]_\alpha$ *holds for all $m, n \in \mathcal{F}_1$. Moreover, if $m = n$ then we have $[u^g]_\alpha = [u^{gr}]_\alpha$.*

Proof of Theorem 3. The relation (20) is equivalent to

$$[u^{gr}]_\alpha = [\inf_{\beta \geq \alpha} \min \frac{m_\beta^\pm}{n_\beta^\pm}, \sup_{\beta \geq \alpha} \max \frac{m_\beta^\pm}{n_\beta^\pm}] = cl\left(conv \bigcup_{\beta \geq \alpha} ([m]_\beta \div_{gr} [n]_\beta)\right). \quad (25)$$

According to (16) we have

$$[u^g]_\alpha = [m \div_g n]_\alpha = cl\left(conv \bigcup_{\beta \geq \alpha} ([m]_\beta \div_{gH} [n]_\beta)\right). \quad (26)$$

Because of $[m]_\beta \div_{gH} [n]_\beta \subseteq [m]_\beta \div_{gr} [n]_\beta$, we have $[u^g]_\alpha \subseteq [u^{gr}]_\alpha$.
If $m = n$ then $[u^{gr}]_\alpha = [1,1]$. Since $[u^g]_\alpha \subseteq [u^{gr}]_\alpha$ we have $[u^g]_\alpha = [u^{gr}]_\alpha = [1,1]$. □

We illustrate Theorems 2 and 3 with some examples in which the T1FNs are defined in terms of their α-level sets.

Example 1. $[1+2\alpha, 7-4\alpha] \div_{gH} [-3+\alpha, -1-\alpha] = [(7-4\alpha)/(-3+\alpha), (1+2\alpha)/(-1-\alpha)]$ [7]. *Based on (20) we can get the gr-division:*

$$\beta = [\inf_{\alpha \geq \beta} \frac{5-3.5\alpha}{-1-\alpha}, \sup_{\alpha \geq \beta} \frac{1+0.5\alpha}{-4+2\alpha}]$$

$$= [\frac{5-3.5\beta}{-1-\beta}, \frac{1+0.5\beta}{-4+2\beta}] \quad (27)$$

$$\supset [\frac{7-4\beta}{-3+\beta}, \frac{1+2\beta}{-1-\beta}] = [u^{gH}]_\beta;$$

$$\beta = cl\left(conv \bigcup_{\alpha \geq \beta} ([m]_\alpha \div_{gH} [n]_\alpha)\right)$$

$$= cl\left(conv \bigcup_{\alpha \geq \beta} [\frac{7-4\alpha}{-3+\alpha}, \frac{1+2\alpha}{-1-\alpha}]\right) \quad (28)$$

$$= [\frac{7-4\beta}{-3+\beta}, \frac{1+2\beta}{-1-\beta}] = [u^{gH}]_\beta.$$

Example 2. $[1+0.5\alpha, 5-3.5\alpha] \div_{gH} [-4+2\alpha, -1-\alpha] = [(5-3.5\alpha)/(-4+2\alpha), (1+0.5\alpha)/(-1-\alpha)]$ exists but the resulting intervals are not the α-level sets of a T1FN. Using (16) and (20) we can get the g-division and the gr-division:

$$[m \div_g n]_\alpha = cl\left(conv \bigcup_{\beta \geq \alpha}([m]_\beta \div_{gH} [n]_\beta)\right)$$

$$= cl\left(conv \bigcup_{\beta \geq \alpha}\left[\frac{5-3.5\beta}{-4+2\beta}, \frac{1+0.5\beta}{-1-\beta}\right]\right) \qquad (29)$$

$$= \left[\frac{5-3.5\alpha}{-4+2\alpha}, -0.75\right];$$

$$[m \div_{gr} n]_\alpha = cl\left(conv \bigcup_{\beta \geq \alpha}([m]_\beta \div_{gr} [n]_\beta)\right)$$

$$= cl\left(conv \bigcup_{\beta \geq \alpha}\left[\frac{5-3.5\beta}{-1-\beta}, \frac{1+0.5\beta}{-4+2\beta}\right]\right) \qquad (30)$$

$$= \left[\frac{5-3.5\alpha}{-1-\alpha}, \frac{1+0.5\alpha}{-4+2\alpha}\right]$$

$$\supset \left[\frac{5-3.5\alpha}{-4+2\alpha}, -0.75\right] = [u^g]_\alpha.$$

In terms of generalization, the gr-division and the g-division are the most generalized but they have different results, and the gH-division has the minimum application range among these three division we talked about.

The relationships among gH-division, g-division and gr-division have been shown in Table 1.

Table 1. The relationships between m^{gH}, m^g and m^{gr}.

	gH-Division	g-Division	gr-division
gH-division exists	\	g-division exists and $m^g = m^{gH}$ (see [7])	gr-division exists and $[m^{gH}]_\alpha \subseteq [m^{gr}]_\alpha$ (Theorem 2)
g-division exists	gH-division does not necessarily exist (see [7])	\	gr-division exists and $[m^g]_\alpha \subseteq [m^{gr}]_\alpha$ (Theorem 3)
gr-division exists	gH-division does not necessarily exist (Example 2)	g-division exists and $[m^g]_\alpha \subseteq [m^{gr}]_\alpha$ (Theorem 3)	\

As the table shows, resulting from Theorem 2, if there exists $u \in \mathcal{F}_1$ such that $m \div_{gH} n = u$, then we have $[u^{gH}]_\alpha = [u^g]_\alpha \subseteq [u^{gr}]_\alpha$ such as Example 1. Due to Theorem 3, if the gH-division between m and n does not exist, then we can calculate the g-division and the gr-division, and we have $[u^g]_\alpha \subseteq [u^{gr}]_\alpha$ as in the case of Example 2. We can also see their relationships in Figure 1.

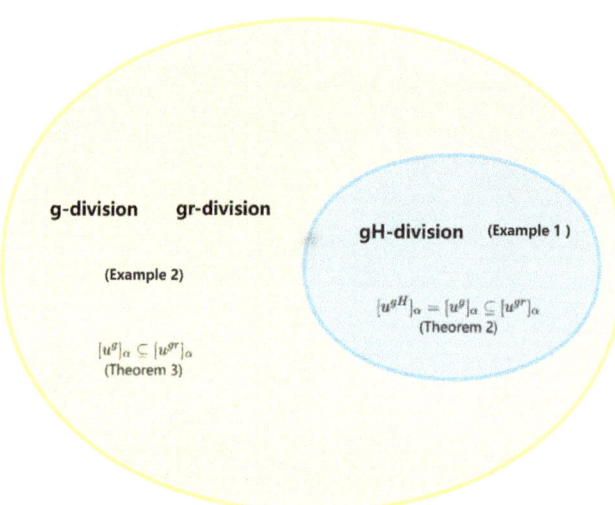

Figure 1. The relationships between gH-division, g-division and gr-division.

4. Conclusions

As is known to all, the division operation for type-1 fuzzy number in its original form is not invertible for multiplication operation. This is an essential drawback in some applications. Furthermore, there are several approaches proposed: gH-division, g-division and gr-division to eliminate this drawback. However, one should figure out how they relate to each other in order to analyze practical problems, which was the point of this paper.

From the above discussion, the conclusion can be reached that the gr-division exists between any two T1FNs, as well as g-division, but the result of the g-division is contained in that of the gr-division (see Table 1). Costa et al. [19] also discussed the inclusion isotonic relationship of the gH-division and found that the gH-division was not inclusion isotonic. We have pointed out the relations among the gH-division, the g-division and the gr-division in this paper more clearly. In terms of generalization, the gr-division and the g-division are the most generalized, and the gH-division has the minimum application range among these three division types (see Figure 1).

Since different practical problems exist, we can choose a reasonable division according to the above conclusions to deal with specific issues. The division operation of T1FNs present some cues from the theory of fuzzy sets application to fuzzy differential equations and fuzzy regression analysis.

In the future, we will devote ourselves to the four arithmetic operations between fuzzy numbers and use our conclusion to analyze the differentiability and differential equations about fuzzy numbers, which are based on the four arithmetic operations.

Author Contributions: Y.J. is responsible for writing and theoretical derivation; D.Q. is responsible for conceptual and theoretical construction. All authors have read and agreed to the published version of the manuscript.

Funding: This work was supported by the National Natural Science Foundations of China (grant nos. 12171065 and 11671001 and 61901074) and the Science and Technology Research Program of Chongqing Municipal Education Commission (grant no. KJQN201900636).

Institutional Review Board Statement: This study did not require ethical approval; all data are available in the public domain.

Informed Consent Statement: This paper is a pure theoretical study, not involving human and animal experiments.

Data Availability Statement: No additional data is covered in this article.

Acknowledgments: The authors would like to thank the referee for his valuable comments.

Conflicts of Interest: All authors declare no conflict of interest in this paper.

References

1. Zadeh, L.A. Fuzzy sets. *Inf. Control* **1965**, *8*, 338–353. [CrossRef]
2. Hukuhara, M. Integration des applications measurables dont la valeur est un compact convexe. *Funkcialaj Ekvacioj* **1967**, *10*, 205–223.
3. Stefanin, L. A generalization of Hukuhara difference. In *Soft Methods for Handling Variability and Imprecision*; Springer: Berlin/Heidelberg, Germany, 2008; Volume 48, pp. 203–210.
4. Bede, B.; Stefanini, L. Generalized differentiability of fuzzy-valued functions. *Funkc. Ekvacioj* **2013**, *230*, 119–141. [CrossRef]
5. Gomes, L.T.; Barros, L.C. A note on the generalized difference and the generalized differentiability. *Fuzzy Sets Syst.* **2015**, *280*, 142–145. [CrossRef]
6. Mazandarani, M.; Pariz, N.; Kamyad, A.V. Granular differentiability of fuzzy-number-valued functions. *IEEE Trans. Fuzzy Syst.* **2018**, *26*, 310–323. [CrossRef]
7. Stefanini, L. A Generalization of Hukuhara difference and division for interval and fuzzy arithmetic. *Fuzzy Sets Syst.* **2010**, *161*, 1564–1584. [CrossRef]
8. Bede, B.; Gal, S.G. Generalizations of the differentiability of fuzzy-number-valued functions with applications to fuzzy differential equations. *Fuzzy Sets Syst.* **2005**, *151*, 581–599. [CrossRef]
9. Liu, R.; Wang, J.; O'Regan, D. On the solutions of first-order linear impulsive fuzzy differential equations. *Fuzzy Sets Syst.* **2020**, *400*, 1–33. [CrossRef]
10. Samadpour Khalifeh Mahaleh, V.; Ezzati, R. Existence and uniqueness of solution for fuzzy integral equations of product type. *Soft Comput.* **2020**, *25*, 13287–13295. [CrossRef]
11. Chukhrova, N.; Johannssen, A. Fuzzy regression analysis: Systematic review and bibliography. *Appl. Soft Comput.* **2019**, *84*, 105708. [CrossRef]
12. Sener, Z.; Karsak, E.E. A Fuzzy regression and optimization approach forsetting target levels in software quality function deployment. *Softw. Qual. J.* **2010**, *18*, 323–339. [CrossRef]
13. Toyoura, Y.; Kambara, M.; Uemura, M.; Miyake, T.; Kawasaki, K.; Watada, J. Evaluation of Fuzzy Regression Analysis and Its Application to Oral Age Model. *Int. J. Biomed. Soft Comput. Hum. Sci.* **2017**, *6*, 41–49.
14. Muzzioli, S.; Reynaerts, H. Solving linear fuzzy systems of the form $A_1 x + b_1 = A_2 x + b_2$. *Fuzzy Sets Syst.* **2006**, *157*, 939–951. [CrossRef]
15. Piegat, A.; Landowski, M. Horizontal membership function and examples of its applications. *Int. J. Fuzzy Syst.* **2015**, *17*, 22–30. [CrossRef]
16. Sevastjanov, P.; Dymova, L. A new method for solving interval and fuzzy equations: Linear case. *Inf. Sci.* **2009**, *179*, 925–937. [CrossRef]
17. Wasowski, J. On solutions to fuzzy equations. *Control Cybern. (Warsaw)* **1997**, *26*, 653–658.
18. Piegat, A.; Landowski, M. On Fuzzy RDM-Arithmetic. In *International Multi-Conference on Advanced Computer Systems*; Springer: Cham, Switzerland, 2016.
19. Costa, T.M.; Lodwick, W.A.; De Baets, B. The Hukuhara difference, gH-difference and gH-division are not inclusion isotonic. *Fuzzy Sets Syst.* **2021**. [CrossRef]
20. Piegat, A.; Landowski, M. Is the conventional interval-arithmetic correct? *J. Theor. Appl. Comp. Sci.* **2012**, *6*, 27–44.
21. Piegat, A.; Tomaszewska, K. Decision-making under uncertainty using info-gap theory and a new multidimensional RDM interval arithmetic. *Electrotech. Rev.* **2013**, *89*, 71–76.
22. Piegat, A.; Landowski, M. Two interpretations of multidimensional RDM interval arithmetic-multiplication and division. *Int. J. Fuzzy Syst.* **2013**, *15*, 488–496.
23. Piegat, A.; Landowski, M. Correctness-checking of uncertain equation solutions on example of the interval-modal method. In *Modern Approaches in Fuzzy Sets, Intuitionistic Fuzzy Sets, Generalized Nets and Related Topics*; System Research Institute, Polish Academy of Sciences: Warsaw, Poland, 2014; Volume I, pp. 159–170.
24. Tomaszewska, K.; Piegat, A. Application of the horizontal membership function to the uncertain displacement calculation of a composite mass less rod under a tensile load. *Soft Comput. Comput. Inf. Sci.* **2015**, *342*, 63–72.
25. Najariyan, M.; Pariz, N.; Vu, H. Fuzzy Linear Singular Differential Equations Under Granular Differentiability Concept. *Fuzzy Sets Syst.* **2022**, *429*, 169–187. [CrossRef]
26. Benvenuti, P.; Mesiar, R. Pseudo arithmetical operations as a basis for the general measure and integration theory. *Inf. Sci.* **2004**, *160*, 1–11. [CrossRef]
27. Boukezzoula, R.; Galichet, S.; Foulloy, L. Inverse arithmetic operators for fuzzy intervals. In Proceedings of the 5th EUSFLAT Conference, Ostrava, Czech Republic, 11–14 September 2007.
28. Klir, G.J. Fuzzy arithmetic with requisite constraints. *Fuzzy Sets Syst.* **1997**, *91*, 165–175. [CrossRef]
29. Ma, M.; Friedman, M.; Kandel, A. A new fuzzy arithmetic. *Fuzzy Sets Syst.* **1999**, *108*, 83–90. [CrossRef]

30. Mares, M. Weak arithmetic of fuzzy numbers. *Fuzzy Sets Syst.* **1997** *91*, 143–153. [CrossRef]
31. Stefanini, L.; Guerra, M.L. On fuzzy arithmetic operations: Some properties and distributive approximations. *Int. J. Appl. Math.* **2006**, *19*, 171–199.

Article

A New Hybrid Triple Bottom Line Metrics and Fuzzy MCDM Model: Sustainable Supplier Selection in the Food-Processing Industry

Nguyen Van Thanh [1] and Nguyen Thi Kim Lan [2,*]

[1] Faculty of Commerce, Van Lang University, Ho Chi Minh City 70000, Vietnam; thanh.nguyenvan@vlu.edu.vn
[2] International Education Institute, Van Lang University, Ho Chi Minh City 70000, Vietnam
* Correspondence: lan.ntk@vlu.edu.vn

Abstract: Vietnam's food processing and production industries in the past have managed to receive many achievements, contributing heavily to the growth of the country's economic growth, especially the production index. Even with an increase of 7% per year over the past five years, the industry currently also faces problems and struggles that require business managers to rewrite legal documents and redevelop the business environment as well as the production conditions in order to compete better and use the available resources. Xanthan gum (a food additive and a thickener) is one of the most used ingredients in the food-processing industry. Xanthan gum is utilized in a number of variety of products such as canned products, ice cream, meats, breads, candies, drinks, milk products, and many others. Therefore, in order to improve competitiveness, the stage of selecting raw-material suppliers is a complicated task. The purpose of this study was to develop a new composite model using Triple Bottom Line Metrics, the Fuzzy Analytical Hierarchy Process (FAHP) method, and the Combined Compromise Solution (CoCoSo) algorithm for the selection of suppliers. The application process was accomplished for the Xanthan-gum (β-glucopyranose $(C_{35}H_{49}O_{29})n$) supplier selection in a food processing industry. In this study, the model building, solution, and application processes of the proposed integrated model for the supplier selection in the food-processing industry are presented.

Keywords: fuzzy theory; FAHP; CoCoSo; MCDM; chemistry; supplier selection model; food-processing industry

1. Introduction

In recent years, Vietnam's food-processing industry has been on a strong growth trend, gradually supplying more competitive products, dominating the domestic market, and increasing exports. Statistics from the Vietnam Ministry of Industry and Trade show that Vietnam's annual food consumption value is estimated at about 15% of GDP. In the last 5 years, consumption of processed foods and beverages has increased by an average annual rate of 9.68% and 6.66%, respectively [1]. Seizing this opportunity, many businesses have expanded their investment and increased production in the food-processing sector.

The food-processing industry is one of the industry groups selected by the Vietnamese Government to prioritize sustainable development. To develop a sustainable food-processing industry, there needs to be a methodical investment in production, ensuring the source of good quality raw materials, meeting the requirements of food hygiene and safety and other environmental factors [2].

In order to pursue sustainability management, companies utilize stable decision-making tools in order to support their change process, including the development of sustainable materials, products, and procedures [3]. For choosing the best suppliers in a supplier selection process, the integration of social, ethical, and environmental evaluation is key for sourcing decisions. Constructing the strong bond with suppliers is the final goal that all businesses want to achieve. Changing and evaluating performance on environmental, social, and ethical issues is vital to developing such relationships [4].

A Multicriteria Decision-Making (MCDM) model is based on the theory that fuzzy sets are a strong tool for calculating complex supplier selection problems including multiple standards (qualitative and quantitative) with multiple options [5]. Qualitative standards often have unclear characteristics, making it hard to distinguish accuracy and resulting in the difficulty to achieve the suitability of the evaluation according to the standards and the delivery decision. The MCDM method will quantify these criteria and calculate the total score of these alternatives. There have been many studies on the application of MCDM in the sustainable-supplier-selection processes. A number of methods are commonly used today and include The Technique for Order of Preference by Similarity to Ideal Solution (TOPSIS), AHP, the analytic network process (ANP), CoCoSo, etc. [6].

In this study, the authors developed a new composite model using Triple Bottom Line Metrics, the Fuzzy Analytical Hierarchy Process (FAHP) method, and the Combined Compromise Solution (CoCoSo) Algorithm for the selection of suppliers in the food-processing industry. The supplier selection criteria were identified by the Triple Bottom Line (TPL) model (environmental, economic, and social factors) and literature reviews. In addition, the FAHP method was utilized to identify the weight of all criteria in the second stage. The CoCoSo is an MCDM method, which is utilized for ranking the suppliers list in the result stage.

One of the tools that can assist businesses in evaluating and selecting sustainable suppliers is the Triple Bottom Line (TBL). The TPL is an accounting framework that incorporates three dimensions of performance: social, environmental, and financial (Figure 1) [7]. TBL reporting can be an important tool to support sustainability goals.

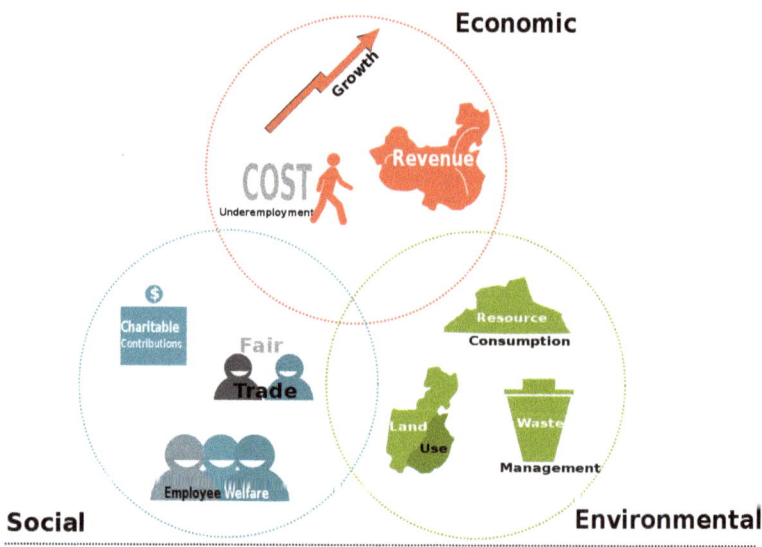

Figure 1. Graphic describing the three types of bottom lines.

In recent decades, due to the rapid consumption of natural resources and the need for environmental protection, sustainability in supply chain management has emerged as an increasingly important issue. Therefore, in this study, supplier selection was performed in order to achieve sustainability, taking into account all aspects: economic, social, and environmental criteria. For this purpose, a combined TPL–FAHP–CoCoSo approach was used for selecting the optimal Xanthan-gum (β-glucopyranose ($C_{35}H_{49}O_{29}$)n) supplier. The research goal of this study can be described as following:

- Developing a new composite model for supplier selection for a sustainable food-processing supply chain.
- Achieving sustainable goals, the author used the Triple Bottom Line (TPL) for defining criteria that affect the decision-making process. Then, a Fuzzy Analytical Hierarchy Process (FAHP) method and the Combined Compromise Solution (CoCoSo) model was used to select an optimal supplier (Xanthan gum (β-glucopyranose ($C_{35}H_{49}O_{29}$)n) supplier).
- Evaluating the fuzzy multi-criteria decision model for a case study.

2. Literature Review

The supplier evaluation and the selection processes is a typical multicriteria decision problem, and a more complex variation of it is the sustainable supplier selection that should consider many qualitative and quantitative factors. There are many approaches that have been applied to address this decision process, some of which are based on MCDM/multi-criteria decision analysis (MCDA) methods, applied individually, or combined with other MCDM/MCDA methods, and/or other different techniques [8].

Mirko Stojčić et al. [9] showed that sustainability is one of the main challenges of the recent decades. In this study, the authors reviewed many MCDM models that are applied in the sustainability engineering sector. Bojan Matić et al. [10] presented a new hybrid MCDM model for evaluating and selecting sustainable suppliers in the supply chain for a construction company. In this study, the authors applied four MCDM models including rough simple additive weighting (SAW), rough weighted aggregated sum product assessment (WASPAS), rough additive ratio assessment (ARAS), and rough multi-attributive border approximation area comparison (MABAC). SemihÖnüt et al. [11] developed a new MCDM model for supplier evaluation in telecommunication company. This MCDM model was developed based on the analytic network process (ANP) and the technique for order performance by similarity to ideal solution (TOPSIS) methods.

S. Nallusamy et al. [12] proposed a MCDM model based on the Analytical Hierarchy Process (AHP), Fuzzy Logic (FL), and Artificial Neural Networks (ANN) for selection of suppliers in manufacturing industries. Morteza Yazdani [13] found the right supplier based on a fuzzy Multi-Criteria Decision Making (MCDM) process. In this study, the author applied the AHP and the TOPSIS model for ranking potential suppliers. Joseph Sarkis and Dileep G. Dhavale [14] proposed a triple-bottom-line approach using a Bayesian framework for supplier selection for sustainable operations. The author considered a TBL model approach and considered business operations as well as environmental impacts and social responsibilities of the suppliers while they evaluated and selected optimal suppliers in their search.

Kannan Govindan et al. [15] presented an effective model for supplier-selection operations in supply chains by triple-bottom-line metrics, the fuzzy theory, and the multicriteria approach. Ioannis E. Nikolaou et al. [16] proposed a new framework of performance indicators for measuring reverse logistics social responsibility performance based on the TPL approach. Maedeh Rezaeisaray et al. [17] merged three decision-making techniques including decision-making trial and evaluation (DEMATEL), the fuzzy analytic network process (FANP), and the data envelopment analysis (DEA) model into a hybrid MCDM model for outsourcing supplier selection in pipe and fittings manufacturing. Alireza Fallahpour et al. [18] presented a fuzzy decision-making model for the sustainable resilient supplier-selection problem. In this research, they used fuzzy DEMATEL, the fuzzy Best Worst Method, the fuzzy ANP, and the fuzzy inference system. For showing the applicability of this hybrid decision-making model, an industrial case of palm oil in Malaysia was presented. He-Yau Kang et al. [19] used a fuzzy analytic network process model to evaluate various aspects of suppliers in IC packaging company selection. Hengameh Hadian et al. [20] integrated VIKOR-AHP-BOCR (Benefits, Opportunities, Costs, and Risks) to select the best providers of galvanized steel sheets for Iran Khodro (IKCO), which is the largest Iranian automaker. Wang et al. [21] introduced a MCDM model for N-hexane solvent (C_6H_{14}) supplier evaluation and selection for vegetable-oil production. In this study, the authors used fuzzy ANP and the TOPSIS model for the supplier-selection process. Wang et al. [22] applied FAHP and Green DEA for sustainable supplier selection in the SMEs food-processing industry.

Vladimir R. Milovanović et al. [23] discusses the selection of the most optimal supplier using the example of an unmanned aircraft when the decision-maker has data of a qualitative nature. In this study, the authors used intuitive fuzzy numbers (IF ELECTRE) to rank some potential suppliers. Hamed Fazlollahtabar and Navid Kazemitash [24] represented the relation between Information Systems (IS) and Green Supplier Selection (GSS) as two vital components of firms in a novel way, which has not been done before.

Zeeshan Ali et al. [25] proposed a novel complex interval-valued Pythagorean fuzzy setting with application in green supplier chain management. Marko Radovanovic [26] proposed a MCDM model based on the fuzzy AHP method and the VIKOR method in selection of the most efficient procedure for rectification of the optical sight of the long-range rifle. Tapas Biswas et al. [27] presented an integrated criteria importance through inter-criteria correlation (CRITIC)—Combined Compromise Solution (CoCoSo) method for selection of commercially available alternative passenger vehicles in the automotive environment. Aleksandra Bączkiewicz et al. [28] provided a reliable recommendation to the consumer in the form of a compromise ranking constructed from the five MCDM methods: the hybrid model TOPSIS-COMET, COCOSO, EDAS, MAIRCA, and MABAC. Each of the methods used contributes significantly to the final compromise ranking built with the Copeland strategy. Wojciech Sałabun et al. [29] have benchmarked Multi-Criteria Decision Analysis (MCDA) methods. To achieve that, a set of feasible MCDA methods was identified. Based on reference literature guidelines, a simulation experiment was planned. Wang and Hongjun [30] studied interval-valued fuzzy and Muirhead Mean algorithms. We deduced new algorithms named as the Hesitant Interval-Valued Fuzzy Muirhead Mean (HIVFMM) and the Hesitant Interval-Valued Fuzzy Muirhead Mean (HIVFWMM) with Muirhead Mean algorithms based on the Hesitant Interval-Valued Fuzzy Set (HIVFS). Then, we combined them both and gave the proof process of properties and theorems, a mathematic model applying to MADM.

Pamučar Dragan S. and Savin Lazar M. [31] proposed the Best Worst Method (BWM) and the Compressed Proportional Assessment (COPRAS) models for the selection of the optimal off-road vehicle for the needs of the Serbian Armed Forces (SAF). Elmina Durmić et al. [32] combined FUCOM—Rough SAW for sustainable supplier selection. Fatih Ecera and Dragan Pamucarb [33] proposed a new FMCDM model for sustainability supplier selection (SSS). In this research, a real-world example of a home-appliance manufacturer in Serbia is discussed. Madjid Tavana et al. [34] proposed a fuzzy group BWM and CoCoSo for supplier selection in reverse supply chains. Morteza Yazdani et al. [35] presented a two-phase sustainable multitier supplier selection model for food supply chains based on an integrated decision analysis under multi-criteria perspectives considering sustainability criteria, suppliers, and sub-suppliers. Seyed Amirali Hoseini et al. [36] proposed a hybrid fuzzy best worst method, and a fuzzy inference system model was developed for sustainable supplier selection. Morteza Yazdani et al. [37] proposed a combined compromise solution (CoCoSo) method for multi-criteria decision-making problems. The purpose of this study was to discuss the advantage of a combinatory methodology; the study also suggested that the comparison with the results of previously developed methods is in high agreement.

As a literature review, MCDM is a branch of operational research dealing with finding optimal results in complex scenarios including various indicators and conflicting objectives and criteria. This popular tool in the sustainable-supplier-selection field is receiving attention due to the flexibility it provides for decision-makers in finalizing decisions while considering all the criteria, but there are very few studies using the MCDM based on fuzzy sets to develop a decision-making tool in the food-processing industry. Thus, the author proposed a fuzzy MCDM model for sustainable supplier selection in this research.

3. Methodology

Supplier selection is a multi-criteria problem that includes both tangible and intangible factors. In this research, the authors developed a new composite model using Triple Bottom Line Metrics, the Fuzzy Analytical Hierarchy Process (FAHP) method, and the Combined Compromise Solution (CoCoSo) Algorithm for the selection of suppliers in the food-processing industry. There are three step in the decision-making process (Figure 2) as follows:

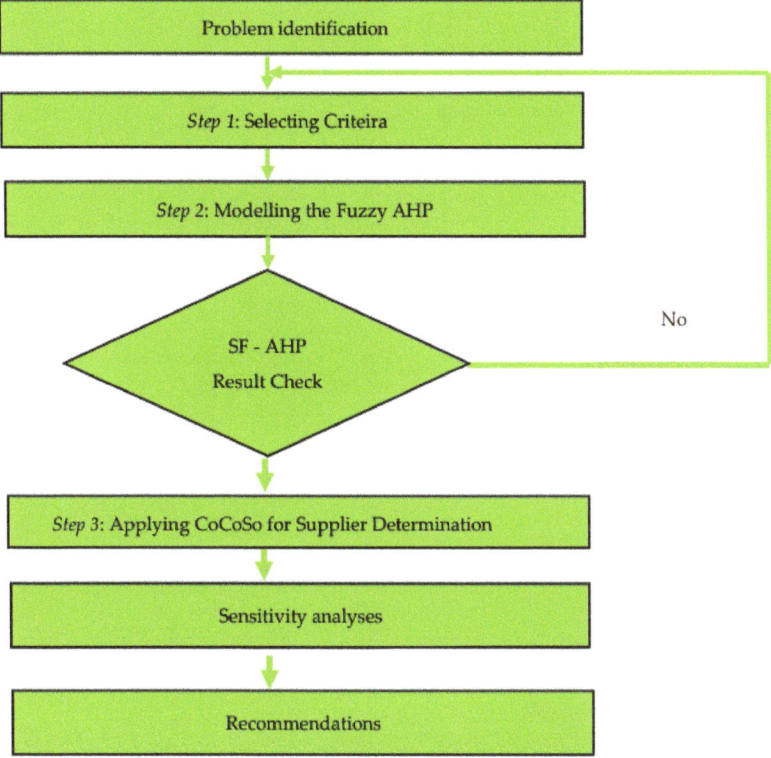

Figure 2. Research process.

Step 1: All important criteria affecting the decision process are defined based on Triple Bottom Line and the literature review.

Step 2: The Fuzzy Analytical Hierarchy Process (FAHP) is employed to determine the important weights of criteria under fuzzy environment conditions.

Step 3: The CoCoSo model is an MCDM technique that applies an integrated simple additive methodology with an exponentially weighted product model. The CoCoSo approach is used to evaluate and rank the potential sustainable suppliers.

3.1. Fuzzy Analytical Hierarchy Process (FAHP) Method
3.1.1. Theoretical Fuzziness

The triangular fuzzy number (TFN) is defined (k, h, g), where k, h, and g $(k \leq h \leq g)$ are parameters that determine the least likely value, the most promising value, and the greatest conceivable value in TFN. TFN are seen in Figure 3 and may be characterized as follows:

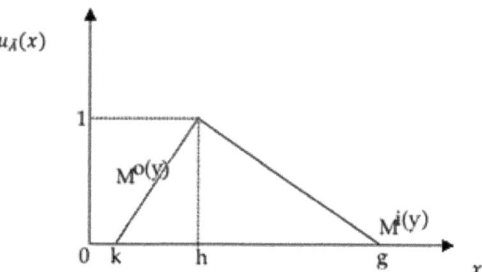

Figure 3. Triangular fuzzy number.

The following is an example of a fuzzy number:

$$\tilde{M} = (M^{o(y)}, M^{i(y)}) = [k + (h-k)y, \ g + (h-g)y], y \in [0,1] \quad (1)$$

The left and right sides of a fuzzy number are represented by $o(y)$ and $i(y)$, respectively. The fundamental computations shown below utilize two positive TFN, (k_1, h_1, g_1) and (k_2, h_2, g_2).

$$\begin{aligned}
(k_1, h_1, g_1) + (k_2, h_2, g_2) &= (k_1 + k_2, h_1 + h_2, g_1 + g_2) \\
(k_1, h_1, g_1) - (k_2, h_2, g_2) &= (k_1 - k_2, h_1 - h_2, g_1 - g_2) \\
(k_1, h_1, g_1) \times (k_2, h_2, g_2) &= (k_1 \times k_2, h_1 \times h_2, g_1 \times g_2) \\
\frac{(k_1, h_1, g_1)}{(k_2, h_2, g_2)} &= (k_1/k_2, h_1/h_2, g_1/g_2)
\end{aligned} \quad (2)$$

3.1.2. Fuzzy Analytical Hierarchy Process (FAHP)

The Fuzzy Analytical Hierarchy Process (FAHP) is the fuzzy extension of the AHP methodology that would assist its limitation in opinionated with unclear decision-making environments. Let $X = \{x_1, x_2, \ldots x_n\}$ be the set of objects and $K = \{k_1, k_2, \ldots k_n\}$ be the final ranking set. According to Chang [38,39], in the extent analysis method, each alternative is counted for, and an extended analysis of its goals are analyzed. Therefore, the l extended analysis values for each alternative can be determined. These values are defined as:

$$L_{k_i}^1, L_{k_i}^2, \ldots, L_{k_i}^m, \quad i = 1, 2, \ldots, n \quad (3)$$

where $L_k^j (j = 1, 2, \ldots, m)$ are the TFNs

The fuzzified extent number of the ith object is calculated as:

$$S_i = \sum_{j=1}^{m} L_{k_i}^j \otimes \left[\sum_{i=1}^{n} \sum_{j=1}^{m} L_{k_i}^j \right]^{-1} \quad (4)$$

The possibility that $L_1 \geq L_2$ is calculated as;

$$V(L_1 \geq L_2) = sup_{y \geq x}[min(\mu_{L_1}(x),), (\mu_{L_2}(y))] \quad (5)$$

where the pair (x, y) are shown with $x \geq y$ and $\mu_{L_1}(x) = \mu_{L_2}(y)$, then we finally have $V(L_1 \geq L_2) = 1$.

Since L_1 and L_2 are convex fuzzy numbers, we have:

$$V(L_1 \geq L_2) = 1, \ if \ l_1 \geq l_2 \quad (6)$$

and

$$V(L_2 \geq L_1) = hgt(L_1 \frown L_2) = \mu_{L_1}(d) \quad (7)$$

where d is the ordinate of the highest crossing point D of μ_{L_1} and μ_{L_2}.

With $L_1 = (o_1, p_1, q_1)$ and $L_2 = (o_2, p_2, q_2)$, the ordinate of point D is calculated by (7):

$$V(L_2 \geq L_1) = hgt(L_1 \cap L_2) = \frac{l_1 - q_2}{(p_2 - q_2) - (p_1 - o_1)} \tag{8}$$

In order to compare L_1 and L_2, we need to calculate the values of $V(L_1 \geq L_2)$ and $V(L_2 \geq L_1)$.

The possibility for a convex fuzzy number to be higher than the k convex fuzzy numbers $L_i (i = 1, 2, \ldots k)$ is calculated as:

$$\begin{aligned} V(L \geq L_1, L_2, \ldots, L_k) &= V[(L \geq L_1) \text{ and } (L \geq L_2)] \\ \text{and, } (L \geq L_k) &= \min V (L \geq L_i), \ i = 1, 2, \ldots, k \end{aligned} \tag{9}$$

Assume that:

$$d'(B_i) = minV(S_i \geq S_k), \tag{10}$$

For $k = 1, 2, \ldots n$ and $k \neq i$, the weight vector is calculated as:

$$W' = (d'(B_1), d'(B_2), \ldots d'(B_n))^T, \tag{11}$$

where B_i are n elements.

The normalized weight vectors are defined as

$$W = (d(B_1), d(B_2), \ldots, d(B_n))^T \tag{12}$$

where W is a defuzzified number.

3.2. Combined Compromise Solution (CoCoSo)

CoCoSo is an MCDM technique that applies an integrated simple additive methodology with an exponentially weighted product model [37]:

Stage 1: Creating the first decision-making matrix:

$$x_{ij} = \begin{bmatrix} x_{11} & x_{12} & \cdots & x_{1n} \\ x_{21} & x_{22} & \cdots & x_{2n} \\ \cdots & \cdots & \cdots & \cdots \\ x_{m1} & x_{m2} & & x_{mn} \end{bmatrix} \tag{13}$$

with $i = 1, 2, \ldots, m; \ j = 1, 2, \ldots, n$, where m represents the number of alternatives, and n represents the number of criteria.

Stage 2: Normalizing the values of the criteria

In terms of the benefit criteria:

$$r_{ij} = \frac{x_{ij} - \min_i x_{ij}}{\max_i x_{ij} - \min_i x_{ij}} \tag{14}$$

In terms of the cost criteria:

$$r_{ij} = \frac{\max_i x_{ij} - x_{ij}}{\max_i x_{ij} - \min_i x_{ij}} \tag{15}$$

Stage 3: Total the weighted comparability sequence (S_i) and the sum of the weighted comparability sequences (P_i) for each alternative, as well as the total power weight of comparability sequences for each alternative:

$$S_i = \sum_{j=1}^{n} (w_j r_{ij}) \tag{16}$$

The grey relational generation technique is used to compute this S_i value:

$$P_i = \sum_{j=1}^{n}(r_{ij}^{w_j}) \quad (17)$$

Stage 4: Determining the relative weights of each alternative.
Calculate the overall mean for the summation of the WSM and WPM values:

$$k_{ia} = \frac{P_i + S_i}{\sum_{i=1}^{m}(P_i + S_i)}, \quad (18)$$

Calculate the total of the relative WSM and WPM scores in comparison to the best alternative:

$$k_{ib} = \frac{S_i}{\min_i S_i} + \frac{P_i}{\min_i P_i} \quad (19)$$

Determine the weighted average of the WSM and WPM values:

$$k_{ic} = \frac{\lambda(S_i) + (1-\lambda)P_i}{\lambda \max_i S_i + (1-\lambda)\max_i P_i} \quad (20)$$

where λ is a coefficient (usually $\lambda = 0.5$) that is chosen by the decision-makers.
Stage 5: Defining the ultimate alternative rating k_i

$$k_i = (k_{ia}k_{ib}k_{ic})^{\frac{1}{3}} + \frac{1}{3}(k_{ia} + k_{ib} + k_{ic}) \quad (21)$$

4. Case Study

With Vietnam's expected turnover for agriculture, forestry, and fishery products to be 200% of the current turnover by 2030, the food-production sector has great attraction for investments [40]. However, there are still many difficulties for the food-processing industry when there are clear shortcomings in the supply chain of raw materials and a shortage in the goods flow resulting in the accumulation in warehouses [41].

As an initiative to minimize food manufacturing's environmental impact in the future, businesses are trying to innovate different methods in order to embrace the potential challenges [42].

In order to reveal the potentiality of the proposed model, a sustainable-supplier-selection case study for Xanthan-gum (β-glucopyranose ($C_{35}H_{49}O_{29}$)n) supplier selection in the food-processing industry was considered. Xanthan gum is actually a very familiar additive in food technology, with international code E415, and is used in the following applications: as a binding agent for sauces, including salad dressings; to create gel for beverage products; bakery technology; ice cream; and gluten-free flour-based foods (vermicelli, pho, rice flour cakes, etc.).

In this study, a Multicriteria Decision-Making (MCDM) model using Triple Bottom Line Metrics, a Fuzzy Hierarchy Network Process (FAHP) method, and the Combined Compromise Solution (CoCoSo) Algorithm was used for the selection of Xanthan-gum suppliers. In the decision process, the authors identified all criteria based on the Triple Bottom Line (TBL) model (economic, environmental, and social aspects) and the literature reviews.

All criteria were used for assessment of sustainable suppliers as defined by 15 experts; the literature review and the initial decision-making matrix were defined by experts. Some information about the criteria is shown in Figure 4.

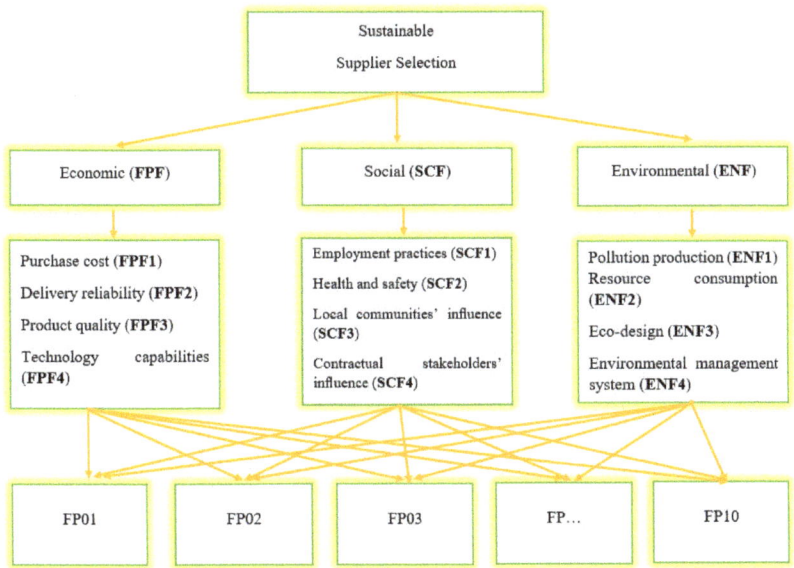

Figure 4. Structure of FAHP model.

In the first stage, the Fuzzy Analytic Hierarchy Process (FAHP) method was applied for identifying the weight of 12 criteria. AHP allows a certain degree of inconsistency that may occur during the pairwise comparisons of criteria and other decision elements. This approach, however, cannot capture the uncertainty of the preference ratings for scoring the criteria. Combining fuzzy logic with AHP overcomes this problem of AHP by allowing the decision-makers to give their assessments in terms of a range of values in the fuzzy scale instead of the AHP scale. The weight of all criteria is shown in Table 1.

Table 1. The weight of criteria.

Criteria	Fuzzy Geometric Mean of Each Row			Fuzzy Weights			BNP	Normalization
FPF1	0.7826	1.0928	1.5255	0.0471	0.0895	0.1704	0.102	0.0905
FPF2	0.7423	1.0208	1.3842	0.0447	0.0836	0.1546	0.094	0.0834
FPF3	1.0156	1.4132	1.8999	0.0612	0.1157	0.2122	0.130	0.1147
FPF4	0.7778	1.0613	1.4265	0.0469	0.0869	0.1593	0.098	0.0864
SCF1	0.9556	1.3108	1.7732	0.0576	0.1073	0.1981	0.121	0.1069
SCF2	0.6177	0.8340	1.1373	0.0372	0.0683	0.1270	0.078	0.0685
SCF3	0.5958	0.8236	1.1620	0.0359	0.0674	0.1298	0.078	0.0687
SCF4	0.7313	0.9981	1.3208	0.0440	0.0817	0.1475	0.091	0.0805
ENF1	0.7376	0.9978	1.3213	0.0444	0.0817	0.1476	0.091	0.0807
ENF2	0.6489	0.8768	1.2198	0.0391	0.0718	0.1363	0.082	0.0728
ENF3	0.5461	0.7051	0.9682	0.0329	0.0577	0.1081	0.066	0.0586
ENF4	0.8013	1.0781	1.4638	0.0483	0.0883	0.1635	0.100	0.0884

CoCoSo is an MCDM technique that applies an integrated simple additive methodology with an exponentially weighted product model. In this stage, the CoCoSo model was used for ranking 10 potential suppliers.

From the weighted comparability sequence and S_i (Table 2) and the exponentially weighted comparability sequence and P_i (Table 3), the final results are shown in Table 4.

Table 2. Weighted comparability sequence and S_i.

	A1	A2	A3	A4	A5	A6	A7	A8	A9	A10
FPF1	0.04523	0.04523	0.00000	0.04523	0.00000	0.09047	0.09047	0.04523	0.00000	0.00000
FPF2	0.08336	0.04168	0.00000	0.04168	0.00000	0.08336	0.00000	0.04168	0.08336	0.04168
FPF3	0.00000	0.05733	0.00000	0.05733	0.05733	0.00000	0.05733	0.00000	0.11465	0.05733
FPF4	0.08636	0.00000	0.04318	0.04318	0.00000	0.08636	0.00000	0.08636	0.04318	0.00000
SCF1	0.10695	0.05347	0.00000	0.05347	0.00000	0.00000	0.05347	0.10695	0.05347	0.00000
SCF2	0.06852	0.03426	0.03426	0.06852	0.03426	0.03426	0.03426	0.00000	0.03426	0.06852
SCF3	0.06869	0.00000	0.06869	0.00000	0.06869	0.00000	0.06869	0.00000	0.00000	0.00000
SCF4	0.08054	0.04027	0.08054	0.00000	0.04027	0.04027	0.08054	0.04027	0.04027	0.08054
ENF1	0.04033	0.04033	0.00000	0.08065	0.04033	0.04033	0.08065	0.08065	0.04033	0.08065
ENF2	0.07282	0.05462	0.07282	0.05462	0.05462	0.01821	0.05462	0.00000	0.07282	0.05462
ENF3	0.05857	0.04393	0.04393	0.02929	0.01464	0.02929	0.01464	0.02929	0.00000	0.04393
ENF4	0.08842	0.05894	0.02947	0.05894	0.02947	0.05894	0.05894	0.00000	0.02947	0.05894

Table 3. Exponentially weighted comparability sequence and P_i.

	A1	A2	A3	A4	A5	A6	A7	A8	A9	A10
FPF1	0.93922	0.93922	0.00000	0.93922	0.00000	1.00000	1.00000	0.93922	0.00000	0.00000
FPF2	1.00000	0.94386	0.00000	0.94386	0.00000	1.00000	0.00000	0.94386	1.00000	0.94386
FPF3	0.00000	0.92360	0.00000	0.92360	0.92360	0.00000	0.92360	0.00000	1.00000	0.92360
FPF4	1.00000	0.00000	0.94189	0.94189	0.00000	1.00000	0.00000	1.00000	0.94189	0.00000
SCF1	1.00000	0.92855	0.00000	0.92855	0.00000	0.00000	0.92855	1.00000	0.92855	0.00000
SCF2	1.00000	0.95362	0.95362	1.00000	0.95362	0.95362	0.95362	0.00000	0.95362	1.00000
SCF3	1.00000	0.00000	1.00000	0.00000	1.00000	0.00000	1.00000	0.00000	0.00000	0.00000
SCF4	1.00000	0.94571	1.00000	0.00000	0.94571	0.94571	1.00000	0.94571	0.94571	1.00000
ENF1	0.94563	0.94563	0.00000	1.00000	0.94563	0.94563	1.00000	1.00000	0.94563	1.00000
ENF2	1.00000	0.97927	1.00000	0.97927	0.97927	0.90398	0.97927	0.00000	1.00000	0.97927
ENF3	1.00000	0.98329	0.98329	0.96021	0.92201	0.96021	0.92201	0.96021	0.00000	0.98329
ENF4	1.00000	0.96479	0.90743	0.96479	0.90743	0.96479	0.96479	0.00000	0.90743	0.96479

Table 4. Final aggregation and ranking.

Alternatives	Ka	Ranking	Kb	Ranking	Kc	Ranking	K
A1	0.1285	1	3.9590	1	1.0000	1	2.4942
A2	0.1098	4	2.7852	4	0.8539	4	1.8887
A3	0.0788	10	2.0980	10	0.6127	10	1.3959
A4	0.1113	3	2.9811	3	0.8656	3	1.9790
A5	0.0871	8	2.1166	9	0.6775	8	1.4602
A6	0.1007	5	2.6960	6	0.7835	5	1.7904
A7	0.1129	2	3.1732	2	0.8785	2	2.0685
A8	0.0794	9	2.2679	8	0.6179	9	1.4694
A9	0.1005	6	2.7778	5	0.7818	6	1.8220
A10	0.0911	7	2.5803	7	0.7087	7	1.6769

Supplier evaluation and selection is the process of appraising and evaluating potential existing and potential suppliers by quantifying, helping to choose the right supplier to ensure the business's production, business without interruption, and a move towards driving continuous improvement. Supplier selection is very important for every business, especially those with long supply chains that depend on many suppliers. The authors developed a new composite model using Triple Bottom Line Metrics, the Fuzzy Analytical Hierarchy Process (FAHP) method, and the Combined Compromise Solution (CoCoSo) Algorithm for the selection of suppliers in the food-processing industry. As a result from Table 4, A01 is the optimal supplier. This approach was demonstrated with a real-world case study involving six main evaluation criteria that the company determined to choose the most-appropriate supplier.

5. Sensitivity Analysis

It is shown that besides Equation (21) being the general method for the results of the coefficient λ, a fixed value in the range of 0.1, 0.2, 0.3, ... , 1.0 can be used. Therefore, in the first part of the sensitivity analysis, a modification in the coefficient λ was conducted. The ranking performance of CoCoSo for varying λ values is exhibited in Table 5.

Table 5. Rankings of robots for varying λ values.

	$\lambda = 0.1$	$\lambda = 0.2$	$\lambda = 0.3$	$\lambda = 0.4$	$\lambda = 0.5$	$\lambda = 0.6$	$\lambda = 0.7$	$\lambda = 0.8$	$\lambda = 0.9$	$\lambda = 1$
A1	2.4952	2.3842	2.4002	2.5042	2.3972	2.4350	2.5142	2.4768	2.4979	2.4904
A2	1.8987	1.8971	1.8950	1.8923	1.8887	1.8836	1.8757	1.8621	1.8329	1.7251
A3	1.4014	1.4005	1.3994	1.3979	1.3959	1.3930	1.3887	1.3811	1.3651	1.3065
A4	1.9866	1.9854	1.9838	1.9818	1.9790	1.9751	1.9692	1.9590	1.9371	1.8575
A5	1.4697	1.4682	1.4662	1.4637	1.4602	1.4554	1.4479	1.4351	1.4074	1.3038
A6	1.7973	1.7961	1.7947	1.7929	1.7904	1.7868	1.7814	1.7721	1.7522	1.6797
A7	2.0737	2.0728	2.0718	2.0704	2.0685	2.0658	2.0617	2.0547	2.0397	1.9858
A8	1.4724	1.4719	1.4713	1.4705	1.4694	1.4678	1.4654	1.4613	1.4525	1.4212
A9	1.8274	1.8266	1.8254	1.8240	1.8220	1.8193	1.8150	1.8077	1.7921	1.7359
A10	1.6808	1.6802	1.6794	1.6783	1.6769	1.6750	1.6719	1.6667	1.6557	1.6159

Table 5 show the relative calculated values of the options according to the value of the coefficient λ. Note that the values of the coefficient λ do not affect the change in the rank of the alternative. The research successfully created a hybrid MCDM model, using FAHP and CoCoSo, to determine the supplier evaluation and selection procedure in the food-processing industry.

6. Conclusions

In the domestic market, Vietnam, with a population of nearly 94 million people and with more than half of them of working age, is also a great opportunity for processed-food consumption. Currently, food and beverages account for the highest proportion in the monthly consumption structure of the Vietnamese with about 35%. Vietnam's annual food-consumption value also accounts for about 15% of GDP and will increase as income levels improve in the future.

Therefore, in order to survive and develop, businesses constantly improve their production processes towards the goal of sustainable development, especially in the selection of raw material suppliers. Supplier selection is a multi-criteria decision, and the decision-maker must evaluate many qualitative and quantitative criteria, which may conflict with each other, with the aim of selecting the optimal supplier. In this research, the authors developed a new composite model for supplier selection for a sustainable food-processing supply chain. The authors also evaluated the proposed fuzzy multi-criteria decision model for a case study. Given the results from Table 4, the ranking list of the robot alternatives was achieved as A1–A7–A4–A2–A6–A9–A10–A5–A8–A3 for a λ value of 0.5; thus, supplier 1 (A1) is the optimal supplier.

The contribution of this study includes modeling the sustainable supplier selection decision problem in the food-processing industry under fuzzy environment. The most significant contributions and successes in this study can be described as follows:

➢ The proposed FMCDM model is the first Xanthan-gum (β-glucopyranose $(C_{35}H_{49}O_{29})n$) supplier evaluation and selection model in Vietnam by interviewing experts and reviewing the literature.

➢ Second, this is the first study to provide a case study on evaluating suppliers for the food-processing industry utilizing the model proposed by the combination of FAHP and CoCoSo models.

➢ The proposed model can also address different complex problems in supplier selection in other industries.

There are also some limitations in this study. Because Saaty's AHP produces rank reversal, a new procedure was proposed based on a simple algebraic system of equations, called "Alpha-Discounting Method for Multi-Criteria Decision Making" [43], which will be considered for multi-criteria decision-making in a future study.

Author Contributions: Conceptualization, N.V.T. and N.T.K.L.; Data curation, N.V.T. and N.T.K.L.; Formal analysis, N.V.T.; Funding acquisition, N.V.T.; Investigation, N.T.K.L.; Methodology, N.V.T. and N.T.K.L.; Project administration, N.V.T.; Resources, N.T.K.L.; Supervision, N.V.T.; Validation, N.T.K.L.; Writing—original draft, N.V.T. and N.T.K.L.; Writing—review and editing, N.T.K.L. All authors have read and agreed to the published version of the manuscript.

Funding: This research was funded by Van Lang University and The APC was funded by Van Lang University.

Acknowledgments: The authors wish to express their gratitude to Van Lang University, Vietnam for financial support for this research.

Conflicts of Interest: The authors declare no conflict of interest.

References

1. Sức Hút Của Ngành Công Nghiệp Chế Biến Thực Phẩm Việt Nam. Available online: https://thanguy.com/tin-thi-truong-4/ (accessed on 18 October 2021).
2. Làm gì để Phát Triển Bền Vững Công Nghiệp Chế Biến Thực Phẩm? Available online: https://dantocmiennui.vn/lam-gi-de-phat-trien-ben-vung-cong-nghiep-che-bien-thuc-pham/180544.html (accessed on 18 October 2021).
3. Beske-Janssen, P.; Johnson, M.P.; Schaltegger, S. 20 years of performance measurement in sustainable supply chain management—What has been achieved? *Supply Chain. Manag. Int. J.* **2015**, *20*, 664–680. [CrossRef]
4. What Is Sustainable Sourcing? Available online: https://ecovadis.com/glossary/sustainable-sourcing/#:~{}:text=Sustainable%20sourcing%20is%20the%20integration,the%20process%20of%20selecting%20suppliers.&text=The%20ultimate%20goal%20of%20sustainable,long%2Dterm%20relationships%20with%20suppliers (accessed on 18 October 2021).
5. Zadeh, L.A. Fuzzy sets. *Inf. Control* **1965**, *8*, 338–353. [CrossRef]
6. Đạt, L.Q.; Phượng, B.H.; Thu, N.T.P.; Anh, T.T.L. Xây dựng mô hình ra quyết định đa tiêu chuẩn tích hợp để lựa chọn và phân nhóm nhà cung cấp xanh. *Tạp Chí Khoa Học Đhqghn Kinh Tế Và Kinh Doanh Tập* **2017**, *33*, 43–54.
7. Slaper, T.F.; Hall, T.J. The triple bottom line: What is it and how does it work. *Indiana Bus. Rev.* **2011**, *86*, 4–8.
8. Schramm, V.B.; Cabral, L.P.B.; Schramm, F. Approaches for supporting sustainable supplier selection—A literature review. *J. Clean. Prod.* **2020**, *273*, 123089. [CrossRef]
9. Stojčić, M.; Zavadskas, E.K.; Pamučar, D.; Stević, Ž.; Mardani, A. Application of MCDM methods in sustainability engineering: A literature review 2008–2018. *Symmetry* **2019**, *11*, 350. [CrossRef]
10. Matić, B.; Jovanović, S.; Das, D.K.; Zavadskas, E.K.; Stević, Ž.; Sremac, S.; Marinković, M. A new hybrid MCDM model: Sustainable supplier selection in a construction company. *Symmetry* **2019**, *11*, 353. [CrossRef]
11. Önüt, S.; Kara, S.S.; Işik, E. Long term supplier selection using a combined fuzzy MCDM approach: A case study for a telecommunication company. *Expert Syst. Appl.* **2009**, *36*, 3887–3895. [CrossRef]
12. Nallusamy, S.; Sri Lakshmana Kumar, D.; Balakannan, K.; Chakraborty, P.S. MCDM tools application for selection of suppliers in manufacturing industries using AHP, Fuzzy Logic and ANN. *Int. J. Eng. Res. Afr.* **2016**, *19*, 130–137. [CrossRef]
13. Yazdani, M. An integrated MCDM approach to green supplier selection. *Int. J. Ind. Eng. Comput.* **2014**, *5*, 443–458. [CrossRef]
14. Sarkis, J.; Dhavale, D.G. Supplier selection for sustainable operations: A triple-bottom-line approach using a Bayesian framework. *Int. J. Prod. Econ.* **2015**, *166*, 177–191. [CrossRef]
15. Govindan, K.; Khodaverdi, R.; Jafarian, A. A fuzzy multi criteria approach for measuring sustainability performance of a supplier based on triple bottom line approach. *J. Clean. Prod.* **2013**, *47*, 345–354. [CrossRef]
16. Nikolaou, I.E.; Evangelinos, K.I.; Allan, S. A reverse logistics social responsibility evaluation framework based on the triple bottom line approach. *J. Clean. Prod.* **2013**, *56*, 173–184. [CrossRef]
17. Rezaeisaray, M.; Ebrahimnejad, S.; Khalili-Damghani, K. A novel hybrid MCDM approach for outsourcing supplier selection: A case study in pipe and fittings manufacturing. *J. Model. Manag.* **2016**, *11*, 536–559. [CrossRef]
18. Fallahpour, A.; Nayeri, S.; Sheikhalishahi, M.; Wong, K.Y.; Tian, G.; Fathollahi-Fard, A.M. A hyper-hybrid fuzzy decision-making framework for the sustainable-resilient supplier selection problem: A case study of Malaysian Palm oil industry. *Environ. Sci. Pollut. Res.* **2021**, 1–21. [CrossRef] [PubMed]
19. Kang, H.Y.; Lee, A.H.; Yang, C.Y. A fuzzy ANP model for supplier selection as applied to IC packaging. *J. Intell. Manuf.* **2012**, *23*, 1477–1488. [CrossRef]
20. Hadian, H.; Chahardoli, S.; Golmohammadi, A.M.; Mostafaeipour, A. A practical framework for supplier selection decisions with an application to the automotive sector. *Int. J. Prod. Res.* **2020**, *58*, 2997–3014. [CrossRef]

21. Wang, C.N.; Tsai, H.T.; Nguyen, V.T.; Nguyen, V.T.; Huang, Y.F. A hybrid fuzzy analytic hierarchy process and the technique for order of preference by similarity to ideal solution supplier evaluation and selection in the food processing industry. *Symmetry* **2020**, *12*, 211. [CrossRef]
22. Wang, C.-N.; Nguyen, V.T.; Thai, H.T.N.; Tran, N.N.; Tran, T.L.A. Sustainable Supplier Selection Process in Edible Oil Production by a Hybrid Fuzzy Analytical Hierarchy Process and Green Data Envelopment Analysis for the SMEs Food Processing Industry. *Mathematics* **2018**, *6*, 302. [CrossRef]
23. Milovanović, V.R.; Aleksić, A.V.; Sokolović, V.S.; Milenkov, M.A. Uncertainty modeling using intuitionistic fuzzy numbers. *Vojnotehnički Glasnik/Mil. Tech. Cour.* **2021**, *69*, 905–929. [CrossRef]
24. Fazlollahtabar, H.; Kazemitash, N. Green supplier selection based on the information system performance evaluation using the integrated best-worst method. *Facta Univ. Ser. Mech. Eng.* **2021**, *19*, 345–360. [CrossRef]
25. Ali, Z.; Mahmood, T.; Ullah, K.; Khan, Q. Einstein Geometric Aggregation Operators using a Novel Complex Interval-valued Pythagorean Fuzzy Setting with Application in Green Supplier Chain Management. *Rep. Mech. Eng.* **2021**, *2*, 105–134. [CrossRef]
26. Radovanovic, M.; Ranđelović, A.; Jokić, Ž. Application of hybrid model fuzzy AHP-VIKOR in selection of the most efficient procedure for rectification of the optical sight of the long-range rifle. *Decis. Mak. Appl. Manag. Eng.* **2020**, *3*, 131–148. [CrossRef]
27. Biswas, T.; Chatterjee, P.; Choudhuri, B. Selection of commercially available alternative passenger vehicle in automotive environment. *Oper. Res. Eng. Sci. Theory Appl.* **2020**, *3*, 16–27. [CrossRef]
28. Bączkiewicz, A.; Kizielewicz, B.; Shekhovtsov, A.; Wątróbski, J.; Sałabun, W. Methodical Aspects of MCDM Based E-Commerce Recommender System. *J. Theor. Appl. Electron. Commer. Res.* **2021**, *16*, 2192–2229. [CrossRef]
29. Sałabun, W.; Wątróbski, J.; Shekhovtsov, A. Are mcda methods benchmarkable? A comparative study of topsis, vikor, copras, and promethee ii methods. *Symmetry* **2020**, *12*, 1549. [CrossRef]
30. Wang, H. Models for MADM with hesitant interval-valued fuzzy information under uncertain environment. *Int. J. Knowl.-Based Intell. Eng. Syst.* **2021**, *25*, 315–322. [CrossRef]
31. Pamučar, D.S.; Savin, L.M. Multiple-criteria model for optimal off-road vehicle selection for passenger transportation: BWM-COPRAS model. *Vojnoteh. Glas.* **2020**, *68*, 28–64. [CrossRef]
32. Durmić, E.; Stević, Ž.; Chatterjee, P.; Vasiljević, M.; Tomašević, M. Sustainable supplier selection using combined FUCOM–Rough SAW model. *Rep. Mech. Eng.* **2020**, *1*, 34–43. [CrossRef]
33. Ecer, F.; Pamucar, D. Sustainable supplier selection: A novel integrated fuzzy best worst method (F-BWM) and fuzzy CoCoSo with Bonferroni (CoCoSo'B) multi-criteria model. *J. Clean. Prod.* **2020**, *266*, 121981. [CrossRef]
34. Tavana, M.; Shaabani, A.; Di Caprio, D.; Bonyani, A. An integrated group fuzzy best-worst method and combined compromise solution with Bonferroni functions for supplier selection in reverse supply chains. *Clean. Logist. Supply Chain.* **2021**, *2*, 100009. [CrossRef]
35. Yazdani, M.; Pamucar, D.; Chatterjee, P.; Torkayesh, A.E. A multi-tier sustainable food supplier selection model under uncertainty. *Oper. Manag. Res.* **2021**, 1–30. [CrossRef]
36. Hoseini, S.A.; Fallahpour, A.; Wong, K.Y.; Mahdiyar, A.; Saberi, M.; Durdyev, S. Sustainable Supplier Selection in Construction Industry through Hybrid Fuzzy-Based Approaches. *Sustainability* **2021**, *13*, 1413. [CrossRef]
37. Gogus, O.; Boucher, T.O. Strong transitivity, rationality and weak monotonicity in fuzzy pairwise comparisons. *Fuzzy Sets Syst.* **1998**, *94*, 133–144. [CrossRef]
38. Chang, D.-Y. Applications of the extent analysis method on fuzzy AHP. *Eur. J. Oper. Res.* **1996**, *95*, 649–655. [CrossRef]
39. Yazdani, M.; Zarate, P.; Zavadskas, E.K.; Turskis, Z. A combined compromise solution (CoCoSo) method for multi-criteria decision-making problems. *Manag. Decis.* **2019**, *57*, 2501–2519. [CrossRef]
40. Công nghiệp thực phẩm Việt Nam có tiềm năng lớn trong thu hút đầu tư. Available online: https://tapchitaichinh.vn/nghien-cuu-trao-doi/cong-nghiep-thuc-pham-viet-nam-co-tiem-nang-lon-trong-thu-hut-dau-tu-315296.html (accessed on 18 October 2021).
41. Thách Thức và cơ hội cho ngành chế biến thực phẩm ở Việt Nam năm. 2021. Available online: https://fbsp.ftu.edu.vn/thach-thuc-va-co-hoi-cho-nganh-che-bien-thuc-pham-o-viet-nam-nam-2021/ (accessed on 18 October 2021).
42. 4 Ways to Make Food Processing More Sustainable. Available online: https://certification.bureauveritas.com/magazine/4-ways-make-food-processing-more-sustainable (accessed on 18 October 2021).
43. Smarandache, F. α-Discounting Method for Multi-Criteria Decision Making. 2016. Available online: https://digitalrepository.unm.edu/math_fsp/243/ (accessed on 18 October 2021).

Article

Sustainable Integrated Fuzzy Optimization for Multimodal Petroleum Supply Chain Design with Pipeline System: The Case Study of Vietnam

Chia-Nan Wang [1,*], Nhat-Luong Nhieu [1,*], Kim-Phong Tran [1,*] and Yen-Hui Wang [2,*]

1. Department of Industrial Engineering and Management, National Kaohsiung University of Science and Technology, Kaohsiung 807778, Taiwan
2. Department of Information Management, Chihlee University of Technology, New Taipei City 220305, Taiwan
* Correspondence: cn.wang@nkust.edu.tw (C.-N.W.); nnluong.iem@gmail.com (N.-L.N.); tkphongspkt@gmail.com (K.-P.T.); ttxyhw@mail.chihlee.edu.tw (Y.-H.W.)

Abstract: Over the years, oil-related energy sources have played an irreplaceable role in both developed and developing countries. Therefore, the efficiency of petroleum supply chains is a key factor that significantly affects the economy. This research aimed to optimize the configuration of the uncertainty multimodal petroleum supply chain in terms of economy, energy and environment (3E assessment). This study proposes a novel integration methodology between a heuristic algorithm and exact solution optimization. In the first stage, this study determines the facilities' potential geographical coordinates using heuristic algorithm. Then, the fuzzy min-max goal programming model (FMMGPM) was developed to find the multi-objective solutions. In particular, this model allows analysis of supply chain uncertainty through simultaneous factors such as demand, resource, cost and price. These uncertainty factors are expressed as triangular fuzzy parameters that can be analyzed in terms of both probability and magnitude. Moreover, the model is applied to the entire petroleum supply chain in Vietnam, including downstream and upstream activities. In addition, another novelty is that for the first time, pipeline systems in logistics activities are considered in Vietnam's petroleum supply chain optimization study. The results also show the short-term and long-term benefits of developing a pipeline system for oil transportation in Vietnam's petroleum supply chain. To evaluate the effects of uncertainty on design decisions, this study also performed a sensitivity analysis with scenarios constructed based on different magnitudes and probabilities of uncertainty.

Keywords: fuzzy sets; multiple criteria decision making; operation research; mixed integer linear programming; supply chain management

1. Introduction

Renewable energy sources have been shown to be efficient in most modern industries. However, fossil resources still play a major role in providing the energy that powers most of the world's economies [1]. Of these fossil energy sources, the most common are oil and its related products. Therefore, in addition to political issues, the optimization of petroleum supply chains is a topic of interest to governments, businesses, supply chain managers and researchers [2,3]. In addition, sustainable development requires not only economic efficiency optimization, but also environmental impacts and energy security. These objectives are commonly known as the 3E evaluation, which entails the economy, environment and energy [4]. Furthermore, the impact of uncertainties such as consumption demand, capacity, costs and prices can cause changes in supply chain configurations [5–9]. Therefore, mid- and long-term decisions in petroleum supply chain design should include an uncertainty factor analysis.

Known as one of the fastest growing economies in the region, Vietnam has a high potential petroleum supply chain, which includes upstream, middle stream and downstream activities. Statistics show that Vietnam has played an important crude oil export role in Southeast Asia over the past two decades [10]. On the other hand, Vietnam's petroleum demand is increasing year-over-year. However, this demand is heavily dependent on imports because of the domestic limited oil refining capacity. Possessing large crude oil reserves but still having to import petroleum for the domestic market is a special situation in Vietnam's petroleum supply chain [10]. The government's revised energy plan also clearly states the major role of petroleum in the structure of energy sources from now to 2030, with approximately 22.8% [11]. Therefore, effectively implementing both import and export tasks is an essential problem for petroleum supply chain managers in Vietnam. Therefore, medium- and long-term design decisions, such as the location and size of facilities or the appropriate mode of transport for transit routes, can partially address this pressing issue. In addition, petroleum transportation in Vietnam is currently mainly carried out by roadways, waterways and railways. Meanwhile, recent studies have shown the efficiency of pipeline systems in the petroleum supply chain [12]. In other words, decisions related to pipeline system development are also included in the petroleum supply chain design problem.

The oil and gas supply chain considered in this study includes upstream, midstream and downstream facilities, as shown in Figure 1. In the first tier of the supply chain, oil rigs are responsible for extracting and transporting crude oil. This amount of crude oil is either exported at ports or filtered into other products at the refineries. At the same time, these seaports are also responsible for importing refined oil products. The third tier of the supply chain is a system of distribution centers in different forms of regional centralized warehouses. The primary role of these distribution centers is to maintain inventory and perform crossdocking processes before shipping gasoline and diesel oil to retail stores in the fourth tier. The transport system between the tiers of the supply chain consists of four common modes for domestic oil and gas transport: roads, waterways, railways and pipelines.

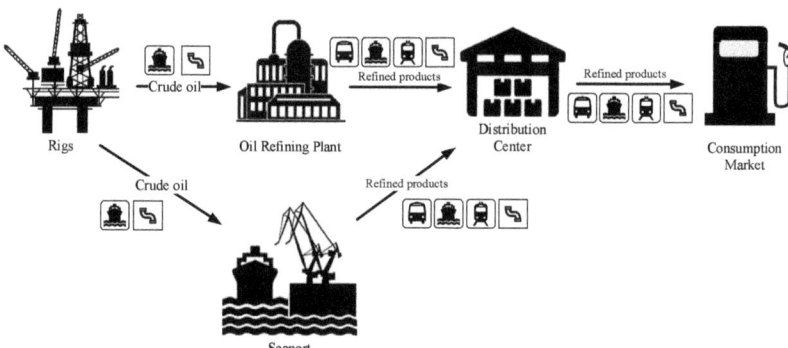

Figure 1. Petroleum supply chain network.

The contributions of this study are intended to provide recommendations for design decisions in the above identified problem. Firstly, this study develops an integrated methodology composed of a heuristic algorithm and a fuzzy multi-objective mixed integer linear programming (FMOMILP) optimization model. In this, the heuristic algorithm allows users to determine the potential coordinates of the markets based on the population density of each region. Then, the FMOMILP model, which includes the properties of multi-objective, multimodal, multi-product, multi-scale and uncertainty simultaneously, is used to suggest the optimal design for the petroleum supply chain. Through the decision variables, this model supports decisions related to the development of distribution centers, transportation, imports and exports and development of the pipeline system. Moreover, uncertainty is considered in the model as fuzzy parameters that relate to consumption demand, cost, price, capacity and import/export quota. The variety of uncertain sources allows the model to comprehensively analyze possible variations in the long-term configuration of the supply chain. These uncertainty factors are expressed as triangular fuzzy parameters that can be analyzed in terms of both probability and magnitude. In addition, this model balances the three objectives of maximizing profits, maximizing energy security and minimizing transport emissions by applying the min-max variant of the goal programming approach. This variation helps the model avoid goal-oriented extremism in finding solutions according to goal programming approaches. Secondly, the above integrated methodology is applied in practice for the petroleum supply chain in Vietnam. In this managerial contribution, a detailed petroleum supply chain configuration is proposed for managers in Vietnam based on the results of the optimization model. This includes a proposal for the process of developing a pipeline system for both crude oil exports and gasoline imports. As a third contribution, this study analyzes scenarios that are developed based on two factors, including amplitude and probability of fuzzy parameters, to evaluate the impact of uncertainty on supply chain configuration.

The organization of the following sections of this paper is as follows: Section 2 is a literature review related to petroleum supply chain design; the integrated methodology is presented in Section 3; in Section 4, the study describes the application of the methodology to the case of Vietnam's petroleum industry and uncertainty sensitivity analyses; and finally, conclusions, limitations and suggestions for future research are discussed in Section 5.

2. Literature Review

Over the past decades, the efficiency of different upstream to downstream segments of petroleum supply chains has been improved by researchers using various approaches. Approaches to this topic can be classified into two main groups: heuristic algorithms/simulation/strategic analysis and mathematical optimization models [2]. As one of the approaches without an optimization mathematical model, the combined framework, which was introduced by Ghasemzadeh et al. in 2017, shows that identifying key metrics for prioritizing supply chain segment strategies can determine the optimal strategy in the total supply chain and the players within it. The study also confirms that the most important strategic decisions of each segment and the total supply chain are not necessarily the same [13]. Using a different approach, Eslami et al. proposed a genetic algorithm to search for the multi-objective problem's set of solutions. This approach supports the selection of safety measures that minimize the cost and risk of hazards for petroleum facilities [14]. Grudz et al.'s study, published in 2020, analyzed the difference between forecast and actual performance indicators of the underground gas pumping plunger operation modes [15]. In 2017, Guliman presented several logistics performance evaluation methods for the petroleum industry. This study aims to clarify the purpose of both original, improved and modern methods to achieve the necessary suitability when applying these methods [3]. In a review paper, Sahebi et al. classified the optimization mathematical models for this topic in the last three decades in terms of supply chain structure, decision levels, uncertain factors and environmental impact. The results of this study show that the application of mathematical models in the petroleum supply chain design problem has emerged, and there are still many avenues for future research [16].

For decades, multiple criteria decision-making (MCDM) methods and optimization mathematical models have been widely applied to decision-making problems [17–22]. In 2019, Ahmed M. Attia introduced the mixed integer linear programming (MILP) model to address the problem of hydrocarbon supply chain (HCSC) optimization in terms of perspectives and goals in the oil and gas industry. Furthermore, this study investigates the balance between the different goals of the HCSC. Therefore, the results showed that gas production depends on many aspects [23]. In 2020, Sheel's study provides ideas for application to the model, which was developed by Gligor et al. (2016), on India's petroleum supply chain transportation. At the same time, the study elaborates on the difficult points affecting the development of the oil and gas transportation industry in this country [24]. Pipeline systems, which require large investments, have a significant impact on the performance of petroleum supply chains. Therefore, this infrastructure factor is also more commonly considered in strategic studies on petroleum supply chain management [25–35]. In 2017, an optimization model and a decomposition algorithm were applied in combination in Roger Rocha's study to optimize the cost of activities in the petroleum supply chain [36]. Meanwhile, Wang used the MILP model to optimize downstream oil supply chain design addresses and consider transportation planning and pipeline evaluation oil. The results of this study show that it is necessary to build a new pipeline system [12]. In the article, published in 2017, H. Devold presented the installation of advanced systems, along with the application of modern technologies and MILP methods [37].

Besides cost optimization models, other studies are more interested in other impacts of petroleum supply chains in developing countries, such as emissions, energy and society [38–43]. The multi-objective sustainable competitive petroleum supply chain (SCPSC) model, which was developed by N. Moradinasab, was used to solve existing problems deposited in refineries, distribution centers and consumption markets. As a result, a certain distribution center can be applied across many supply chains, leading to better distribution center usage and better practice [44]. In 2019, Meng Yuan proposed a pipeline network reform method and highlighted the importance of influence on other aspects, such as China's 3E and downstream oil supply chain. The results of this study are extremely efficient as a year-over-year improvement of overall energy efficiency, as well as a reduction in electricity consumption [4]. In 2020, another study by Ayman Alghanmi applied mathematical modeling in combination with fuzzy rule-based and Bayesian networks theory to stimulate, explain and analyze operational risks. The performance of the model achieved the desired results, and this is also one of the first studies to address the problem of uncertain data from the point of view of the petroleum transportation system [45]. FoomaniDana's study provides a comprehensive assessment to analyze the competition between road and pipeline systems in different regions. Then, the functional demand and profit for both competing systems were analyzed and compared in detail [46]. Zhou's contribution used the MILP model to solve the problem of supply chain management in both the economy and CO_2 emissions dimensions. According to the above model implementation, the research has optimized the design to reduce not only carbon emissions, but also cost in the pipeline oil system [47].

As a reinforcement, this study aims to fill in the remaining gaps in terms of both the problem properties and methods of the optimization mathematical models in this field, as described in Tables 1 and 2 below.

Table 1. Related research problem characteristic.

No.	Author	Year	Upstream	Downstream	Facility Scale	Pipeline System Development	Intermodal Transportation	Economic	Environment	Energy Security
1	H.-J. Zimmerman [17]	1978	X			X				
2	T. N. Sear [18]	1993	X			X				
3	Don A. Eichmann [39]	2000	X			X		X	X	X
4	A. Konak et al. [19]	2006	X						X	
5	Y. Kim et al. [26]	2008	X			X	X			

Table 1. Cont.

No.	Author	Year	Oil and Gas Supply Chain		Problem Characteristic			Objective Function		
			Upstream	Downstream	Facility Scale	Pipeline System Development	Intermodal Transportation	Economic	Environment	Energy Security
6	T.-H. Kuo and C.-T. Chang [27]	2008	X	X	X	X	X			
7	A. Elkamel et al. [48]	2008	X			X				X
8	W. B.E. Al-Othman et al. [29]	2008	X	X		X	X			X
9	K. Al-Qahtani and A. Elkamel [28]	2008	X		X	X				
10	Pierre Guyonnet et al. [49]	2009	X		X	X				
11	F. M. Song [32]	2009		X		X	X			X
12	Maryam Hamedi et al. [30]	2009		X		X	X			X
13	Jie Chen et al. [31]	2010	X			X	X			
14	Jian-ling Jiao et al. [20]	2010	X				X			X
15	A. Khosrojerdi et al. [41]	2012	X			X	X	X		
16	David T. Allen et al. [40]	2013		X					X	X
17	Luiz Aizemberg et al. [33]	2014	X	X		X	X			
18	Y. Kazemi et al. [34]	2015	X			X	X	X		
19	L. J. Fernandes et al. [21]	2015	X	X			X			
20	V. R. Ghezavati et al. [35]	2015	X	X		X	X			
21	B. Anifowose and M. Odubela [38]	2015	X		X	X	X	X		X
22	Y. Guo et al. [25]	2016		X		X	X	X		
23	N. M. Nasab and M. R. Amin-Naseri [42]	2016		X	X	X		X		X
24	F. Ghasemzadeh et al. [13]	2017		X				X	X	X
25	B. Guliman et al. [3]	2017	X	X		X	X	X	X	X
26	R.Rocha et al. [36]	2017	X			X	X			X
27	A. M. Ghaithan et al. [43]	2017	X	X	X	X	X			X
28	B. Wang et al. [12]	2019		X	X	X		X		
29	N. Moradinasab et al. [44]	2018	X	X	X	X			X	X
30	M. Yuan et al. [4]	2019		X		X		X	X	
31	A. E. Baladeh et al. [14]	2019		X	X					
32	X. Zhou et al. [47]	2020	X	X		X		X	X	
33	Ahmed M. Attia et al. [23]	2019	X	X	X		X			X
34	A. C. FoomaniDana and M. Tamannaei [46]	2020	X		X	X	X	X	X	X
35	A. Alghanmi et al. [45]	2020	X		X			X	X	
36	Ashutosh Sheel et al. [24]	2020	X		X					
37	V. Grudz et al. [15]	2020		X		X	X			
38	C. Lima et al. [50]	2021		X		X		X		X
39	P. Pudasaini [51]	2021		X		X	X	X		
40	E. Santibanez-Borda et al. [52]	2021	X			X		X	X	
41	This study	2021	X	X	X	X	X	X	X	X

Table 2. Related research methodology.

No.	Author	Year	Uncertainty Approach		Uncertainty Factor			Methodology	
			Stochastic	Fuzzy	Demand	Resource	Cost	Linear/Mixed Integer Programming	Heuristic Algorithm/Others
1	H.-J. Zimmermann [17]	1978		X	X		X	X	
2	T. N. Sear [18]	1993			X		X	X	
3	Don A. Eichmann [39]	2000			X	X	X	X	
4	A. Konak et al. [19]	2006	X				X	X	
5	Y. Kim et al. [26]	2008					X	X	
6	T.-H. Kuo and C.-T. Chang [27]	2008			X	X	X	X	
7	A. Elkamel et al. [48]	2008			X		X	X	
8	W.B.E. Al-Othman et al. [29]	2008	X		X	X	X	X	
9	K. Al-Qahtani and A. Elkamel [28]	2008		X	X	X	X	X	
10	Pierre Guyonnet et al. [49]	2009	X		X		X		X
11	F.M. Song [32]	2009					X	X	
13	Maryam Hamedi et al. [30]	2009	X		X		X	X	
14	Jie Chen et al. [31]	2010			X		X	X	
15	Jian-ling Jiao et al. [20]	2010	X		X		X	X	
16	A. Khosrojerdi et al. [41]	2012					X	X	
17	David T. Allen et al. [40]	2013						X	
18	Luiz Aizemberg et al. [33]	2014	X		X	X	X	X	
19	Y. Kazemi et al. [34]	2015			X	X	X	X	
20	L. J. Fernandes et al. [21]	2015	X		X	X	X	X	
21	V.R. Ghezavati et al. [35]	2015	X		X		X	X	
22	B. Anifowose and M. Odubela [38]	2015						X	
23	Y. Guo et al. [25]	2016		X				X	
24	N. M. Nasab and M. R. Amin-Naseri [42]	2016	X		X		X	X	
25	F. Ghasemzadeh et al. [13]	2017	X	X	X	X	X		X
26	B. Guliman et al. [3]	2017		X	X	X	X		X
27	R. Rocha et al. [36]	2017					X	X	
28	A. M. Ghaithan et al. [43]	2017			X	X	X	X	
29	N. Moradinasab et al. [44]	2018			X	X	X	X	
30	M. Yuan et al. [4]	2019						X	
31	A. E. Baladeh et al. [14]	2019						X	
32	B. Wang et al. [12]	2019						X	
33	X. Zhou et al. [47]	2020						X	
34	Ahmed M. Attia et al. [23]	2019	X		X	X	X	X	

Table 2. Cont.

			Uncertainty Approach		Uncertainty Factor			Methodology	
No.	Author	Year	Stochastic	Fuzzy	Demand	Resource	Cost	Linear/Mixed Integer Programming	Heuristic Algorithm/Others
35	A. C. FoomaniDana and M. Tamannaei [46]	2020			X		X	X	
36	A. Alghanmi et al. [45]	2020		X				X	
37	Ashutosh Sheel et al. [24]	2020			X	X	X	X	
38	V. Grudz et al. [15]	2020					X		X
39	C. Lima et al. [50]	2021		X		X	X	X	
40	P. Pudasaini [51]	2021	X		X	X		X	
41	E. Santibanez-Borda et al. [52]	2021	X			X		X	
42	This study	2021		X	X	X	X	X	X

3. Methodology

This section first describes the structure of the oil and gas supply chain network considered in this study. Next, a two-phase methodology including a heuristic algorithm and fuzzy multi-objective mixed-integer linear programming optimization model is proposed to design a multimodal oil and gas supply network. The integrated methodology is described in Figure 2.

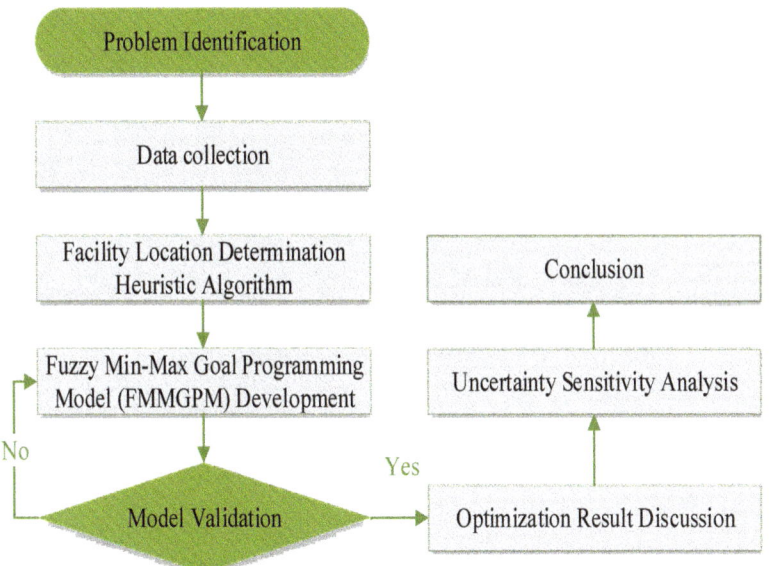

Figure 2. Proposed methodology.

3.1. Location Determination Algorithm

The first phase of this research is to propose a four-step heuristic algorithm for determining the potential locations of distribution centers. In addition, because of the very large number of petroleum retailers at the end of the supply chain, this algorithm is also used to determine the central point of consumption zones. In the first step, the algorithm determines the initial trial location (x^*, y^*) based on the longitude a_q, latitude b_q and weight w_q of the related locations $(q = 1 \ldots Q)$ in the area under consideration, as in Equations (1) and (2). In the second step, in Equation (3), the ratio between the weight of each relevant position and its distance to the trial location is used to determine the relative weight f_q. Next, the algorithm modifies the coordinates of the potential position, as in Equations (4) and (5). This modification was repeated until there was no difference in the coordinates of the trial position in two consecutive iterations.

Step 1: Determine initial potential location:

$$x^* = \frac{\sum_{q=1}^{Q} w_q \times a_q}{\sum_{q=1}^{Q} w_q} \tag{1}$$

$$y^* = \frac{\sum_{q=1}^{Q} w_q \times b_q}{\sum_{q=1}^{Q} w_q} \tag{2}$$

Step 2: Consider a trial location (x, y), for the first iteration $(x, y) = (x^*, y^*)$. For each location (a_q, b_q) compute:

$$f_q = \frac{w_q}{\sqrt{(x - a_q)^2 + (y - b_q)^2}} \tag{3}$$

Step 3: Modify the x and y values as follows:

$$x = \frac{\sum_{q=1}^{Q} f_q \times a_q}{\sum_{q=1}^{Q} f_q} \tag{4}$$

$$y = \frac{\sum_{q=1}^{Q} f_q \times b_q}{\sum_{q=1}^{Q} f_q} \tag{5}$$

Step 4: If one or both of (x, y) change, repeat the process with modified (x, y). Go to step 2 with modified (x, y). If none of (x, y) changes, then stop.

3.2. Fuzzy Mixed-Integer Programming Model
3.2.1. Sets and Parameters

This fuzzy optimization model is developed on sets that relate the type of product $(p = 1 \ldots P)$ in the supply chain along with the modes of transport $(m = 1 \ldots M)$. In addition, the assemblies represent facilities at all levels of the supply chain, such as rigs $(i = 1 \ldots I)$, refinery plants $(j = 1 \ldots J)$, ports $(l = 1 \ldots L)$, distribution centers $(k = 1 \ldots K)$ and market central points $(n = 1 \ldots N)$. In addition, the distribution centers are also considered by the model with many different construction scales $(s = 1 \ldots S)$.

In addition to the deterministic parameters, the operating efficiency of the oil and gas supply chains is influenced by the uncertainties that are represented by the fuzzy parameters in this model. These parameters are related to product price $\left(\widetilde{PI}_p^{oil}, \widetilde{PI}_p^{refined}\right)$, unit costs $\left(\widetilde{TC}_m, \widetilde{FC}_s, \widetilde{SC}, \widetilde{PC}, \widetilde{RC}_p, \widetilde{PUC}_p\right)$, environmental impact coefficients $\left(\widetilde{EF}_m\right)$, consumption demand $(\widetilde{D}_{np})$, refinery ratio $\left(\widetilde{RR}_p\right)$, export-import quotas $\left(\widetilde{EQ}, \widetilde{IQ}\right)$ and facility capacity $\left(\widetilde{CA}_i^{rig}, \widetilde{CA}_j^{plant}\right)$.

To handle the uncertainty, the triangular fuzzy numbers (TFN) are defined as (l, m, u) representing the most pessimistic, most likely and most optimistic value as Equation (6):

$$\mu_{\tilde{A}}(x) = \begin{cases} \frac{(x-l)}{(m-l)}, & \forall l < x \leq m \\ \frac{(u-x)}{(u-m)}, & \forall m < x \leq u \\ 0, & otherwise \end{cases} \quad (6)$$

In this study, the above fuzzy parameters are defined as TFN (A^{lower}, A^{mean}, A^{upper}) as shown in Figure 3. As Equations (7) and (8), from the known mean of the parameters (A^{mean}), the lower and upper boundary values (A^{lower}, A^{upper}) of the fuzzy parameter are determined based on the coefficient of variation. These two boundary coefficients are valid in the interval [0, 1] and are denoted as ε^- and ε^+, respectively.

$$A^{lower} = (1 - \varepsilon^-) \times A^{mean} \quad (7)$$

$$A^{upper} = (1 + \varepsilon^+) \times A^{mean} \quad (8)$$

Next, the defuzzification values of the fuzzy parameters are determined by the model based on the probabilities of the boundary values, as shown in Equation (9):

$$\tilde{A} = \theta^{lower} \times A^{lower} + \theta^{mean} \times A^{mean} + \theta^{upper} \times A^{upper} \quad (9)$$

The fuzzy and non-fuzzy parameters mentioned above are listed in Table 3 below.

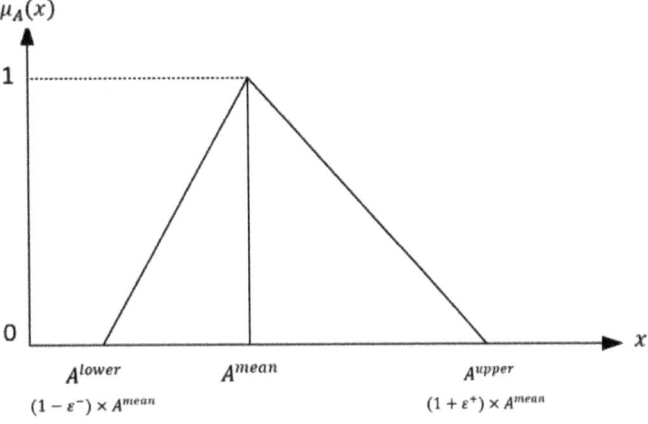

Figure 3. Fuzzy parameter membership function.

3.2.2. Decision Variables

For product flow decisions, integer variables $X1_{ijm}$ and $X2_{ilm}$ represent the amount of crude oil transported from the oil rigs ($i = 1 \ldots I$) to the refineries ($j = 1 \ldots J$) and export ports ($l = 1 \ldots L$) by transportation modes ($m = 1 \ldots M$), respectively. Meanwhile, the integer variables $Y1_{jkpm}$ and $Y2_{lkpm}$ represent the quantity of refined products ($p = 1 \ldots P$) that are transported from refineries and import ports to distribution centers ($k = 1 \ldots K$). Next, the amount of refined product transported from the distribution centers to the consumer markets ($n = 1 \ldots N$) is described by this model through the integer variable Z_{knpm}.

Table 3. Fuzzy and non-fuzzy parameters.

Notation	Unit	Description
Fuzzy Parameters		
$\widetilde{PI}^{oil}$	USD/barrel	Unit price of exported crude oil
$\widetilde{PI}_p^{refined}$	USD/barrel	Unit price of post-refining products p for domestic consumption
$\widetilde{TC}_m$	USD/km	The unit transport cost of mode m
$\widetilde{FC}_s$	USD	Fixed costs of setting up distribution centers with scale s
$\widetilde{SC}$	USD/km	Fixed cost of pipeline system setup
$\widetilde{PC}$	USD/barrel	Unit exploitation cost of crude oil
$\widetilde{RC}_p$	USD/barrel	Unit refining cost of post-refining product p
$\widetilde{PUC}_p$	USD/barrel	Unit importing cost of post-refining product p
$\widetilde{EF}_m$	gram CO_2/km	Transportation environment factor of mode m
$\widetilde{D}_{np}$	Barrel	Domestic demand for product p in region n
$\widetilde{RR}_p$	%	Expected refining ratio of post-refining product p
$\widetilde{EQ}$	Barrel	Export quota for crude oil
$\widetilde{IQ}_p$	Barrel	Import quota for post-refining product p
$\widetilde{CA}_i^{rig}$	Barrel	Maximum capacity of drilling rig i
$\widetilde{CA}_j^{plant}$	Barrel	Maximum capacity of refining plant j
Non-fuzzy parameters		
CA_s^{DC}	Barrel	Maximum capacity of distribution center with scale s
$RD_{ijm}^{Rig2Plant}$	Km	Transportation distance from drilling rig i to refining plant j by mode m
$RD_{ilm}^{Rig2Port}$	Km	Transportation distance from drilling rig i to seaport l by mode m
$RD_{jkm}^{Plant2DC}$	Km	Transportation distance from refining plant j to distribution center k by mode m
$RD_{lkm}^{Port2DC}$	Km	Transportation distance from seaport l to distribution center k by mode m
$RD_{knm}^{DC2Market}$	Km	Transportation distance from distribution center k to market region n by mode m
M		Big M value

In addition to supporting initial investment decisions, the proposed model uses the binary variables $OP_{ij}^{Rig2Plant}$, $OP_{il}^{Rig2Port}$, $OP_{jk}^{Plant2DC}$, $OP_{lk}^{Port2DC}$ and $OP_{kn}^{DC2Market}$ to represent the decision to develop oil pipelines and the binary variable V_{ks} to describe the decision to build different scale distribution centers. Finally, the float variable ESL_{np} is used as an intermediary to determine the supply chain's demand response rate in consumer markets. The decision variables which mentioned above are presented Figure 4.

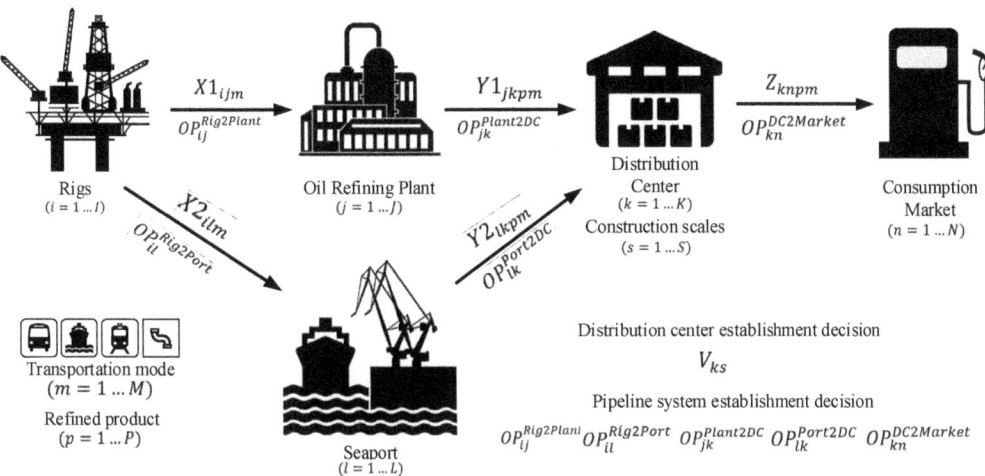

Figure 4. Fuzzy parameter membership function.

3.2.3. Objective Functions

Towards sustainable development, the objective functions of this model revolve around the three pillars of sustainability: economic, social and environmental. First, this study formulates the factors that influence supply chain profitability and optimizes them. As described in Equation (10), supply chain profit is determined by the difference between revenue and costs.

Maximize Profit

$$
\begin{aligned}
&= Revenue - Transportation\ Cost - Facility\ Cost \\
&\quad - \frac{Pipeline\ Setup\ Cost}{Project\ Length} - Exploitation\ Cost - Refining\ Cost \\
&\quad - Purchasing\ Cost
\end{aligned}
\tag{10}
$$

$$
Revenue = \sum_{i\in I}\sum_{l\in L}\sum_{m\in M} X2_{ilm} \times \widetilde{PI}^{oil} + \sum_{k\in K}\sum_{n\in N}\sum_{p\in P}\sum_{m\in M} Z_{knpm} \times \widetilde{PI}^{refined}_p \tag{11}
$$

Transportation Cost

$$
\begin{aligned}
&= \sum_{i\in I}\sum_{j\in J}\sum_{m\in M} X1_{ijm} \times RD^{Rig2Plant}_{ijm} \times \widetilde{TC}_m \\
&+ \sum_{i\in I}\sum_{l\in L}\sum_{m\in M} X2_{ilm} \times RD^{Rig2Port}_{ilm} \times \widetilde{TC}_m \\
&+ \sum_{j\in J}\sum_{k\in K}\sum_{p\in P}\sum_{m\in M} Y1_{jkpm} \times RD^{Plant2DC}_{jkm} \times \widetilde{TC}_m \\
&+ \sum_{l\in L}\sum_{k\in K}\sum_{p\in P}\sum_{m\in M} Y2_{lkpm} \times RD^{Port2DC}_{lkm} \times \widetilde{TC}_m \\
&+ \sum_{k\in K}\sum_{n\in N}\sum_{p\in P}\sum_{m\in M} Z_{knpm} \times RD^{DC2Market}_{knm} \times \widetilde{TC}_m
\end{aligned}
\tag{12}
$$

$$
Facility\ Cost = \sum_{k\in K}\sum_{s\in S} V_{ks} \times \widetilde{FC}_s \tag{13}
$$

Pipeline Setup Cost
$$= \sum_{i\in I}\sum_{j\in J} OP_{ij}^{Rig2Plant} \times RD_{ijm}^{Rig2Plant} \times \widetilde{SC}$$
$$+ \sum_{i\in I}\sum_{l\in L} OP_{il}^{Rig2Port} \times RD_{ilm}^{Rig2Port} \times \widetilde{SC}$$
$$+ \sum_{j\in J}\sum_{k\in K}\sum_{p\in P} OP_{jk}^{Plant2DC} \times RD_{jkm}^{Plant2DC} \times \widetilde{SC} \qquad (14)$$
$$+ \sum_{l\in L}\sum_{k\in K}\sum_{p\in P} OP_{lk}^{Port2DC} \times RD_{lkm}^{Port2DC} \times \widetilde{SC}$$
$$+ \sum_{k\in K}\sum_{n\in N}\sum_{p\in P} OP_{kn}^{DC2Market} \times RD_{knm}^{DC2Market} \times \widetilde{SC}, \quad m=4$$

$$Exploitation\ Cost = \sum_{i\in I}\sum_{j\in J}\sum_{m\in M} X1_{ijm} \times \widetilde{PC} + \sum_{i\in I}\sum_{l\in L}\sum_{m\in M} X2_{ilm} \times \widetilde{PC} \qquad (15)$$

$$Refining\ Cost = \sum_{j\in J}\sum_{k\in K}\sum_{p\in P}\sum_{m\in M} Y1_{jkpm} \times \widetilde{RC}_p \qquad (16)$$

$$Purchasing\ Cost = \sum_{l\in L}\sum_{k\in K}\sum_{p\in P}\sum_{m\in M} Y2_{lkpm} \times \widetilde{PUC}_p \qquad (17)$$

In Equation (11), the revenue is obtained from the value of exported crude oil plus the value of refined oil products in the consuming markets. In Equations (12)–(17), this is the transportation cost of crude oil or refining products in the supply chain, the distribution center construction cost, the oil pipeline system development cost, the oil exploitation cost at rigs, the refining cost at plants and the refined oil products import cost.

The second objective function of this model is to maximize the ratio between the quantity supplied and demanded as Equation (18). This ratio represents the level of energy security guaranteed by the supply chain.

$$\textbf{\textit{Maximize}}\ Energy\ Security = \sum_{n\in N}\sum_{p\in P} (ESL_{np})/(N \times P) \qquad (18)$$

In the final objective function, the model aims to minimize the number of emissions generated during the transportation of crude oil and finished products in Equation (19).

Minimize Transportation Emission
$$= \sum_{i\in I}\sum_{j\in J}\sum_{m\in M} X1_{ijm} \times RD_{ijm}^{Rig2Plant} \times \widetilde{EF}_m$$
$$+ \sum_{i\in I}\sum_{l\in L}\sum_{m\in M} X2_{ilm} \times RD_{ilm}^{Rig2Port} \times \widetilde{EF}_m$$
$$+ \sum_{j\in J}\sum_{k\in K}\sum_{p\in P}\sum_{m\in M} Y1_{jkpm} \times RD_{jkm}^{Plant2DC} \times \widetilde{EF}_m \qquad (19)$$
$$+ \sum_{l\in L}\sum_{k\in K}\sum_{p\in P}\sum_{m\in M} Y2_{lkpm} \times RD_{lkm}^{Port2DC} \times \widetilde{EF}_m$$
$$+ \sum_{k\in K}\sum_{n\in N}\sum_{p\in P}\sum_{m\in M} Z_{knpm} \times RD_{knm}^{DC2Market} \times \widetilde{EF}_m$$

3.2.4. Constraints

Constraints (20) and (21) ensure that the total volume of finished products does not exceed their demand's crisp value in markets. At the same time, the quantity of this product cannot be less than the lower boundary of demand. In Equation (22), the total amount of finished product that is produced by refineries and imported at ports is shipped to DCs is greater than that shipped from DCs to markets. Constraint (23) ensures that the amount of product shipped out of the refineries is equal to the amount refined based on the refinery ratio coefficient. Constraints (24) and (25) ensure that the amount of crude oil shipped to ports for export purposes is greater than the crisp value of the export quota and less than the upper boundary of the export quota. Similarly, the amount of a finished product imported and shipped from ports to DCs does not exceed the import quota, as described in

Equation (26). Constraint (27) shows that the total amount of crude oil transported from a particular rig to refineries and ports for export does not exceed the rig's capacity. However, as shown in Equations (28) and (29), the total amount of crude oil delivered to a particular refinery is neither above its design capacity nor below its utilization factor. For DCs, the total amount of finished product that is shipped to markets is limited by the capacity of the DCs depending on the design scale, as described in Equation (30). In addition, constraint (31) ensures that the DCs are designed with only one size at a location.

$$\sum_{k \in K} \sum_{m \in M} Z_{knpm} \leq \widetilde{D}_{np} \quad \forall n \in N, p \in P \tag{20}$$

$$\sum_{k \in K} \sum_{m \in M} Z_{knpm} \geq D_{np}^{lower} \quad \forall n \in N, p \in P \tag{21}$$

$$\sum_{j \in J} \sum_{m \in M} Y1_{jkpm} + \sum_{l \in L} \sum_{m \in M} Y2_{lkpm} \geq \sum_{n \in N} \sum_{m \in M} Z_{knpm} \quad \forall k \in K, p \in P \tag{22}$$

$$\sum_{i \in I} \sum_{m \in M} X1_{ijm} \times \widetilde{RR}_p = \sum_{k \in K} \sum_{m \in M} Y1_{jkpm} \quad \forall j \in J, p \in P \tag{23}$$

$$\sum_{i \in I} \sum_{l \in L} \sum_{m \in M} X2_{ilm} \geq \widetilde{EQ} \tag{24}$$

$$\sum_{i \in I} \sum_{l \in L} \sum_{m \in M} X2_{ilm} \leq EQ^{upper} \tag{25}$$

$$\sum_{l \in L} \sum_{k \in K} \sum_{m \in M} Y2_{lkpm} \leq \widetilde{IQ}_p \quad \forall p \in P \tag{26}$$

$$\sum_{j \in J} \sum_{m \in M} X1_{ijm} + \sum_{l \in L} \sum_{m \in M} X2_{ilm} \leq \widetilde{CA}_i^{rig} \quad \forall i \in I \tag{27}$$

$$\sum_{i \in I} \sum_{m \in M} X1_{ijm} \leq \widetilde{CA}_j^{plant}, \quad \forall j \in J \tag{28}$$

$$\sum_{i \in I} \sum_{m \in M} X1_{ijm} \geq \delta \times \widetilde{CA}_j^{plant}, \quad \forall j \in J \tag{29}$$

$$\sum_{n \in N} \sum_{p \in P} \sum_{m \in M} Z_{knpm} \leq \sum_{s \in S} CA_s^{DC} \times v_{ks}, \quad \forall k \in K \tag{30}$$

$$\sum_{s \in S} v_{ks} \leq 1, \quad \forall k \in K \tag{31}$$

$$X1_{ijm} \leq M \times RF_{ijm}^{Rig2Plant} \quad \forall i \in I, j \in J, m \neq m_{pipeline} \tag{32}$$

$$X2_{ilm} \leq M \times RF_{ilm}^{Rig2Port} \quad \forall i \in I, l \in L, m \neq m_{pipeline} \tag{33}$$

$$Y1_{jkpm} \leq M \times RF_{jkm}^{Plant2DC} \quad \forall j \in J, k \in K, p \in P, m \neq m_{pipeline} \tag{34}$$

$$Y2_{lkpm} \leq M \times RF_{lkm}^{Port2DC} \quad \forall l \in L, k \in K, p \in P, m \neq m_{pipeline} \tag{35}$$

$$Z_{knpm} \leq M \times RF_{knm}^{DC2Market} \quad \forall k \in K, n \in N, p \in P, m \neq m_{pipeline} \tag{36}$$

For modes of transport other than pipelines, Big-M constraints (32)–(36) ensure that crude oil and finished goods are transported only if and only if the route is feasible for a certain mode of transportation. For the pipeline mode of transport, the Big-M constraints (37)–(41) assist in determining the routes needed to develop the pipeline system through variables such as $OP_{ij}^{Rig2Plant}$, $OP_{il}^{Rig2Port}$, $OP_{jk}^{Plant2DC}$, $OP_{lk}^{Port2DC}$ and $OP_{kn}^{DC2Market}$.

$$X1_{ijm} \leq M \times OP_{ij}^{Rig2Plant} \quad \forall i \in I, j \in J, m = m_{pipeline} \tag{37}$$

$$X2_{ilm} \leq M \times OP_{il}^{Rig2Port} \quad i \in I, l \in L, m = m_{pipeline} \tag{38}$$

$$Y1_{jkpm} \leq M \times OP_{jk}^{Plant2DC} \quad \forall j \in J, k \in K, p \in P, m = m_{pipeline} \tag{39}$$

$$Y2_{lkpm} \leq M \times OP_{lk}^{Port2DC} \quad \forall l \in L, k \in K, p \in P, m = m_{pipeline} \tag{40}$$

$$Z_{knpm} \leq M \times OP_{kn}^{DC2Market} \quad \forall k \in K, n \in N, p \in P, m = m_{pipeline} \tag{41}$$

To determine the level of energy security from the designed supply chain, constraint (42) estimates the ratio (ESL_{np}) of product supply to demand in markets.

$$ESL_{np} = \left(\sum_{k \in K} \sum_{m \in M} Z_{knpm} \right) / \tilde{D}_{np} \quad \forall n \in N, p \in P \tag{42}$$

3.3. Fuzzy Min-Max Goal Programming Model (FMMGPM)

To search for solutions with weighted compromise between objective functions, this study applies a goal-programming approach with a min-max variant. This approach is followed by the following four-step procedure:

First, the single-objective optimal solutions are determined. The objective function values from these single-objective solutions are aggregated and used as the goals (G_1, G_2, G_3) of each related objective. In step two, constraints (43)–(45) are established to estimate the under-attainment (U_1, U_2, U_3) and over-attainment (O_1, O_2, O_3) deviation variables between the objective function values and the goal value.

$$Profit + U_1 - O_1 = G_1 \tag{43}$$

$$Energy\ Security + U_2 - O_2 = G_2 \tag{44}$$

$$Transportation\ Emission + U_3 - O_3 = G_3 \tag{45}$$

In step three, as described in Equations (47)–(50), the product of the objectives' weight and the ratio of the undesirable variables to the goal value are controlled by the same variable, α. In other words, this variable represents the maximum weighted difference ratio. Finally, the optimal solutions with a weighted compromise between the objective functions are determined by minimizing the variable α.

$$\left(\frac{U_1}{G_1} \right) \times W_1 \leq \alpha \tag{46}$$

$$\left(\frac{U_2}{G_2} \right) \times W_2 \leq \alpha \tag{47}$$

$$\left(\frac{O_3}{G_3} \right) \times W_3 \leq \alpha \tag{48}$$

$$\text{Minimize } \alpha \tag{49}$$

4. Numerical Results

4.1. Case Study Description

In Southeast Asia, Vietnam is known as one of the most potential developing economies due to its advantages of location, low human cost and political stability. In just two years, this potential economy has consumed more than a thousand terawatt-hours of energy each year. Energy sources from oil and oil products accounted for 25.92% to 35.68% in the decade in Vietnam [53]. On the other hand, the petroleum supply chain in Vietnam includes not only upstream roles such as oil exploration, refining and crude oil exports, but also downstream roles such as importing oil products and retailing. However, with the middle stream, the accompanying logistics system is mainly water and road, while pipeline systems that are believed to be more efficient do not yet exist. Therefore, the model proposed in this study is applied to find optimal design solutions for both the petroleum supply chain in general and the pipeline system, particularly in Vietnam.

As described in Table 4, the upstream petroleum facilities consist of six oil rigs, two refinery plants owned by the Vietnam National Petroleum Group (Petrolimex), three import/export seaports in Haiphong City, Quinhon City and Hochiminh City. The downstream supply chain includes distribution centers in direct-controlled municipalities such as Hanoi, Danang, Hochiminh and Cantho, along with the retail system in the northern, central and southern regions of Vietnam. The design decisions of distribution centers will be chosen at three different scales with different fixed costs. In addition to crude oil, the supply chain also distributes two main product groups, gasoline and diesel, through four modes of transport: waterways, railways, roads and pipelines. In particular, the model aims to propose the development of a pipeline system on necessary transport sections, while the feasibility of other modes of transport is based on the current state of infrastructure. Railways are almost not feasible in the southern region because of the terrain with an interlaced river network, leading to challenges in railway development.

Table 4. Set descriptions.

Set Description	Indices	Notation
Rigs	$i = 1 \ldots 6$	{PV Drilling, I; PV Drilling II; PV Drilling III; TAD—PV Drilling V; PV Drilling VI; PV Drilling 11}
Refinery plants	$j = 1 \ldots 2$	{Dungquat; Nghison}
Ports	$l = 1 \ldots 3$	{Haiphong; Quinhon; Hochiminh city}
Distribution centers	$k = 1 \ldots 4$	{Hanoi; Danang; Hochiminh city; Cantho}
Market central points	$n = 1 \ldots 3$	{Northern; Central; Southern}
Product types	$p = 1 \ldots 2$	{Gasoline; Diesel Oil}
Transportation modes	$m = 1 \ldots 4$	{Waterway; Railway; Roadway; Pipeline}
Construction scales	$s = 1 \ldots 3$	{Small; Medium; Large}

As mentioned above, the input parameters include fuzzy and non-fuzzy groups that are collected from open databases [10,54–57], government statistics [11,58,59] and other publications [4,7,12,14,23,47,60–63]. For the fuzzy triangular parameters, the lower and upper boundary values are estimated using Equations (7) and (8), with boundary coefficients $\varepsilon^- = \varepsilon^+ = 0.3$ in the first optimization. In addition, as in Equation (9), the defuzzification values of those fuzzy parameters are determined to transform the model from a fuzzy form to a crisp form with probabilities that are chosen as $\theta^{lower} = 1/6$, $\theta^{mean} = 4/6$ and $\theta^{upper} = 1/6$. The data of these input parameters are presented in the Appendix A. In addition, based on the coordinates of the provinces and cities in the northern, central and southern regions of Vietnam, this study first determines the center point coordinates of each of the above-mentioned consuming regions through the heuristic algorithm discussed in Section 3.1 above. The results of this algorithm are listed in Table 5.

Table 5. Market region center point determination.

Market Region	Center Point Coordinates		No. of Related Provinces and Cities	No. of Solving Iteration
	Latitude	Longitude		
Northern	21.0245	105.8412	26	8
Central	15.9357	108.1827	18	90
Southern	10.8166	106.6333	19	

4.2. Multiple Objective Optimization Results

Next, to determine the solution for FMMGPM, the model is resolved with the addition of new constraints and objective functions, such as Equations (43)–(49). The weights of the objective functions related to profit, energy security and emissions are chosen equally to imply the balance of 3E for sustainable development. The values of the objective functions provided by the compromise solution are listed in Table 6. As shown in Figure 5, the results show that FMMGPM's solution almost reaches the goal value at the objective functions that maximize profit and energy security while sacrificing little in minimizing emissions.

Table 6. FMMGPM objective value.

Objective Function	Objective Goal	FMMGPM Objective Value
Profit (Mil. USD)	53,196.95	52,161.85
Energy Security (%)	100%	82.70%
Transportation Emission (Ton CO_2/Barrel-km)	527,783.91	696,005.89

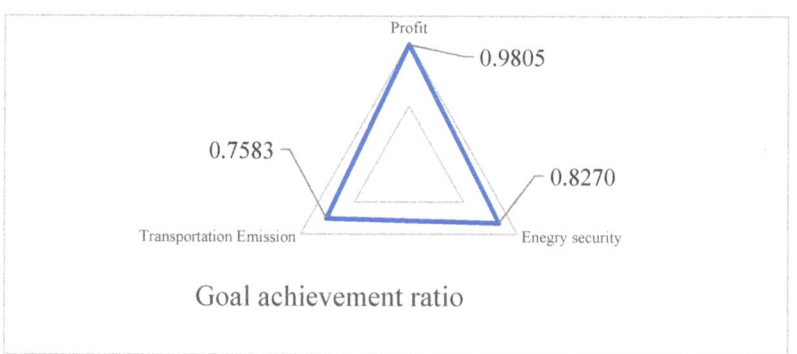

Figure 5. FMMGPM goal achievement ratio.

Based on the value of the decision variables in the solution of FMMGPM, the configuration of the petroleum supply chain, as well as the product flow for both crude oil, gasoline and diesel oil, is depicted in Figure 6. This configuration includes all components of the upstream, middle-stream and downstream petroleum supply chains across Vietnam.

In the northern market, the supply chain establishes a large-scale distribution center that plays the role of storing and distributing gasoline and diesel. The amount of gasoline and diesel oil in this distribution center comes entirely from imported sources from abroad through the Haiphong seaport by pipeline.

In the south, the seaport in Hochiminh City is identified as the pharynx of the country's crude oil exports, with a total annual output of approximately four billion barrels. This amount of crude oil is exploited at PV Drilling II, PV Drilling III, TAD—PV Drilling V and a part from PV Drilling I. In addition to its export role, this port is also in charge of importing all gasoline and diesel oil that is consumed in southern Vietnam. After being imported to the seaport of Hochiminh City, this product is transported by an inland waterway to the distribution center in the largest city in the Mekong Delta, Cantho. They are then distributed from the Can Tho distribution center to retailers in the southern market through the trucking system.

In general, the income of a petroleum supply chain depends mainly on crude oil exports. Meanwhile, approximately 69.7% of gasoline products and 73.9% of domestic diesel products are imported products. Owing to capacity limitations, post-refined products obtained from oil refineries are only sufficient to supply the central market. Therefore, other refinery projects that have been invested and developed by the government are expected to change to reduce the import rate. An overview of the transport infrastructure and supply chain configuration proposed by this optimization model using a combination of all modes of transport is considered, based on the advantages of each mode for each area's infrastructure. According to the above configuration, the shared structure of transport modes used in the supply chain logistics system is shown in Figure 7. The chart presents the share of modes of transport for crude oil, gasoline and diesel. Because of the large transportation volume, the transportation of crude oil is primarily operated by pipelines (97.10%), and a negligible proportion by waterways (2.90%). For gasoline and diesel, the share of pipelines and waterways, which includes both inland waterways and coastal waterways, is approximately 34% to 36%. In addition, the trucking mode plays a key role in distributing gasoline and diesel from distribution centers to consumer markets that cover a large area, such as the north and south of Vietnam. Thus, trucking constitutes approximately one-fifth of the overall logistics system. Finally, with the lowest proportion (6.75–7.77%), the railway system shows its advantage in the long vertical and narrow horizontal areas, such as central Vietnam. In summary, the results of FMMGPM imply that the pipeline mode of transport, without infrastructure development in Vietnam, has the potential to have a positive impact, as well as a key role in the 3E sustainable development of Vietnam.

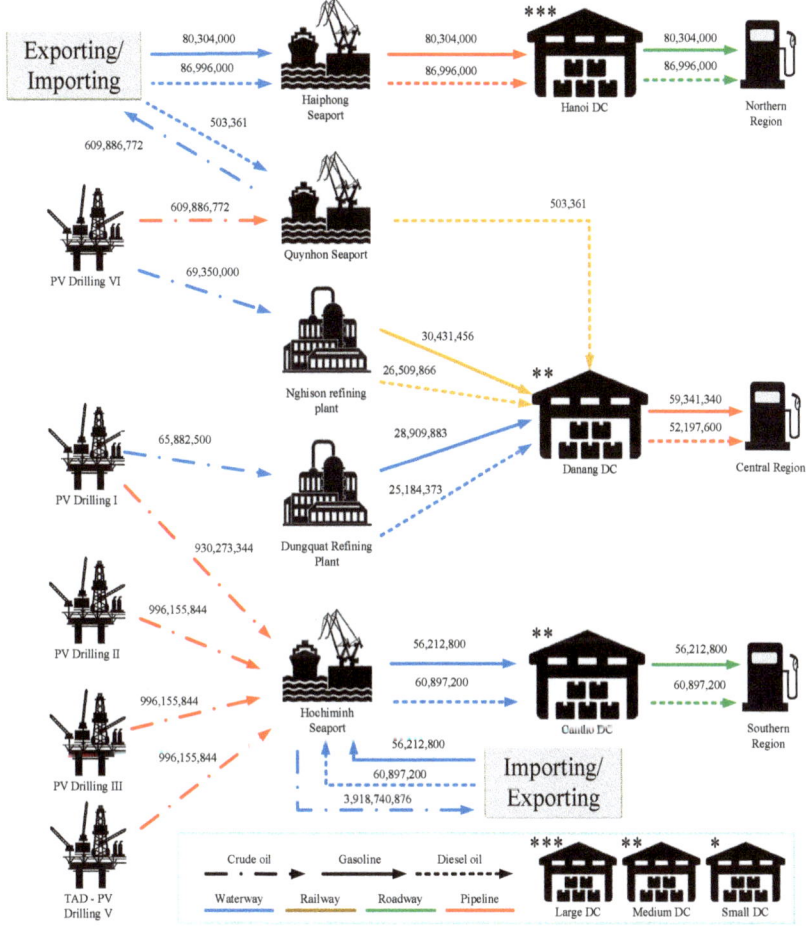

Figure 6. FMMGPM Vietnam Petroleum Supply Chain Configuration and Transportation Flow (in barrel).

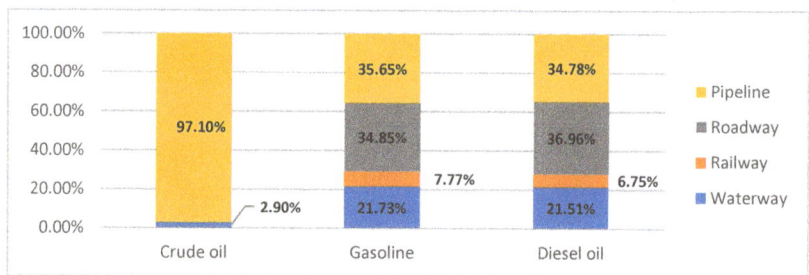

Figure 7. Transportation mode sharing.

In addition, fixed costs such as distribution center development and pipeline systems account for a negligible proportion of variable costs, as shown in Figure 8. Accordingly, because of the large export volume of crude oil, the cost of exploiting this amount of oil also accounts for more than 80% of the variable cost structure. However, this study focuses on logistics systems with concerns about the necessity of developing pipeline systems, which directly affect transportation costs, as well as transportation emissions. According to the optimization results of the model, transportation costs account for approximately a quarter of the total variable costs. At the same time, it ranks second in terms of the impact of crude oil exploitation costs. In short, a five-year-project fixed-cost pipeline system that is insignificant compared to the large transportation needs, but designed at a few key segments in the supply network, is a factor that positively affects the efficiency of the supply chain.

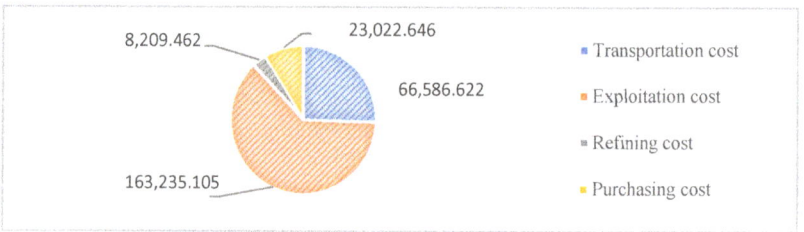

Figure 8. Variable cost structure.

4.3. Uncertainty Sensitivity Analysis

Because fuzzy parameters are defined as triangular fuzzy numbers, as discussed in Section 3, the mean and boundary values of these fuzzy parameters, as well as their probabilities, can affect the model's crisp form. Therefore, these variations also change the configuration of the petroleum supply chain, which is proposed through a multi-objective optimization solution. Therefore, in this section, we analyze the sensitivity of the models under the influence of uncertainty of fuzzy parameters through scenarios developed based on the following two factors, as shown in Figure 9. The first factor is the slope to the sides of the fuzzy triangular number, which is determined by the two variables ε^- and ε^+, as described in Equations (7) and (8). This factor implies the magnitude of volatility in both the positive and negative directions. Accordingly, this analysis develops four situations for this factor, as shown in Table 7.

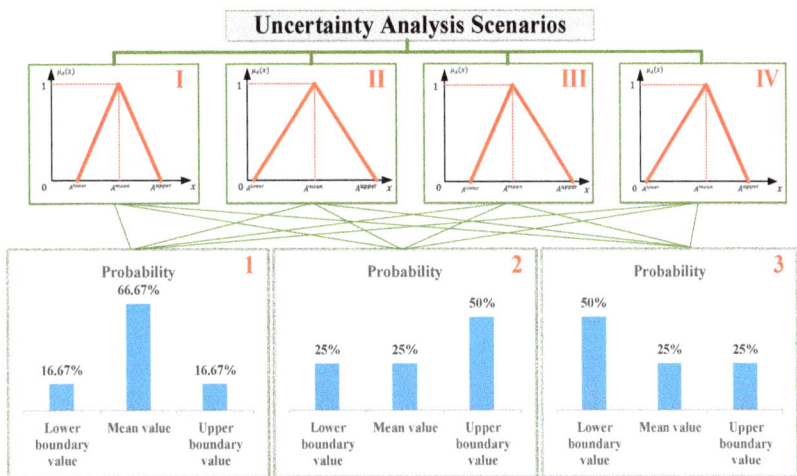

Figure 9. Two-dimension Uncertainty Sensitivity Analysis.

Table 7. Variation magnitude analyze situations.

Case Notation	ε^- Value	ε^+ Value
I	0.3	0.3
II	0.5	0.5
III	0.3	0.5
IV	0.5	0.3

The second factor is the probability distribution of the variation expressed in terms of the probability of occurrence of the mean and boundary values. Accordingly, there are three situations analyzed in this study: the probability of concentration on the mean value; the probability of bias on the upper boundary value; and the probability of bias on the lower boundary value. In the case of probability centered on the mean, this factor implies that the uncertainties have a high stability at the mean. The other two situations imply that volatility tends to go in either pessimistic or optimistic directions. By combining the above two factors, this study develops 12 scenarios whose notations and goal values of single-objective optimization are presented in Table 8. Scenario I-1's solution is detailed above.

Table 8. Scenario goal.

Scenarios	Objective Goal		
	Profit	Energy Security	Transportation Emission
I-1	53,196.947	100%	527,783.910
I-2	56,389.000	100%	600,616.000
I-3	51,644.389	100%	447,239.035
II-1	62,158.088	100%	498,839.088
II-2	71,782.463	100%	643,816.850
II-3	53,975.732	100%	377,372.806
III-1	61,869.010	100%	560,090.422
III-2	71,781.496	100%	707,191.723
III-3	58,291.575	100%	501,678.521
IV-1	54,577.516	100%	468,320.016
IV-2	56,347.103	100%	520,171.822
IV-3	46,485.418	100%	322,997.157

The optimization results of the scenarios show that the nature and intensity of the uncertainty factor can be the cause of the improvisation chain profits ranging from $20 billion to $30 billion. In particular, managers should pay attention to scenarios I-3 and IV-3, in which the uncertainty parameters tend to move in the negative direction. For energy security, the average value of the scenarios of 83.48% is an acceptable value in uncertain situations, as the market may also involve other private supply chains. Even so, the Group II and Group IV scenarios with large negative margins should be of interest to managers, due to the energy market supply levels of these two groups being lower than the rest. Finally, the comparison between scenarios suggests that scenarios with a wider margin, such as III-1, III-2 and III-3, have larger transportation emissions. In addition, in each group with the same volatility, the situation tends to develop positively. In other words, the expanded scale of operations also increases the impact of the supply chain on the environment.

In addition, the sensitivity analysis of the uncertainty parameters also shows that the proportion of the pipeline transport mode changes under different uncertainty situations. As shown in Figure 10, except for scenario III-3, fluctuations in the share of pipeline transport for crude oil were not significantly different between the scenarios. This implies that the pipeline system is a necessary investment for the transportation of crude oil, a product group with high traffic volumes, despite changing uncertainty conditions. In addition, this analysis also shows that the logistics system can utilize pipelines for gasoline and diesel by approximately 30% to 40%. In several scenarios where the probability of uncertainty parameters tends to increase in the negative direction, such as II-3 and III-3, other modes of transport can be achieved more economically. In short, according to the multi-objective optimization results in this study, the investment and development of pipeline transport systems at several locations in Vietnam brings long-term value in both economic and environmental terms.

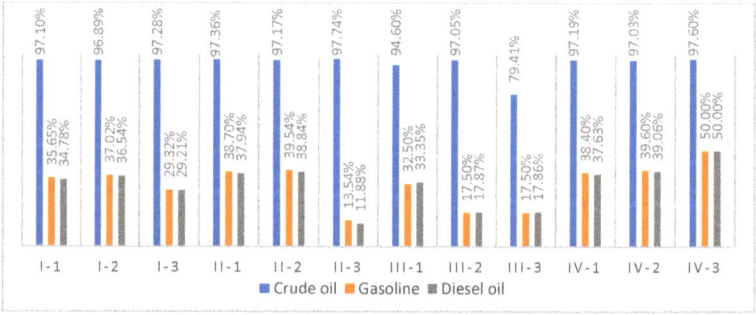

Figure 10. Pipeline transportation proportion.

In summary, in this section, the authors have applied the optimization model to the Vietnam petroleum industry case, one of the countries with great potential for the oil and gas industry. This result suggests suitable configurations for the multimodal petroleum supply chain that are interested in sustainable development based on 3E. In addition, sensitivity analyses were performed to predict changes in design when uncertainty conditions fluctuated. According to the results of the optimization and uncertainty sensitivity analysis, the role of pipeline transport system development, which has not been fully developed in the infrastructural mode, is also confirmed. The FMMGPM is then applied to the case of Vietnam's petroleum supply chain, which has both upstream and downstream activities.

5. Conclusions

An integrated methodology was presented to support tactical and strategic decisions in petroleum supply chain development. In the first step, the facilities' potential coordinates were determined using a heuristic algorithm. Subsequently, a fuzzy multi-objective mixed integer programming optimization model was developed to provide solutions that harmoniously improve the economics, energy and environment of the multimodal petroleum supply chain. Min-max goal programming and fuzzy sets are approaches to augmenting the mixed-integer programming model to deal with this multiple objective and uncertain problem. The FMMGPM is then applied to the case of Vietnam's petroleum supply chain, which has both upstream and downstream activities. The optimization results suggested the supply chain configuration for the Vietnamese situation, which simultaneously satisfied the 3E assessment. This solution includes decisions on transportation volume, transportation mode, facilities development, export/import volume and recommendations on pipeline system development. Then, uncertainty scenarios are developed and analyzed to assess the impact of these factors on the strategic decisions of Vietnam's petroleum supply chain. The results of the analysis show that in some situations where uncertainty factors change in the downward direction, it affects the utilization of facilities such as the pipeline system. However, these impacts are not as significant as the long-term benefits that this infrastructure system has developed at the locations proposed by the model.

The main limitations of this study are the lack of expert opinion survey on the weights of the objective functions, as well as the intensity and probability predictive analyzes of uncertainty. In addition, for sustainable development, the offshore petroleum pipeline system development in this study has not considered marine-protected areas in Vietnam.

In future studies, the uncertainty that affects the supply chain configuration can be approached with more complex random distributions. In addition, other real-world properties may be of interest in models such as logistics services, transportation modes and other post-refinery products.

Author Contributions: Conceptualization, C.-N.W. and N.-L.N.; methodology, C.-N.W. and N.-L.N.; formal analysis, N.-L.N.; investigation, N.-L.N. and Y.-H.W.; data curation, N.-L.N. and K.-P.T.; writing—original draft preparation, N.-L.N. and K.-P.T.; writing—review and editing, C.-N.W. and N.-L.N.; project administration, C.-N.W.; and funding acquisition, C.-N.W. and Y.-H.W. All authors have read and agreed to the published version of the manuscript.

Funding: This research received no external funding.

Acknowledgments: The authors appreciate the support from the National Kaohsiung University of Science and Technology and the Ministry of Sciences and Technology in Taiwan. The authors would like to thank the anonymous reviewers of Axioms for their comments and recommendations, which helped to improve this article's quality significantly.

Conflicts of Interest: The authors declare no conflict of interest.

Appendix A

Table A1. Annual domestic demand (barrel).

Region	Gasoline	Diesel Oil
Northern	80,304,000	86,996,000
Central	68,832,000	74,568,000
Southern	80,304,000	86,996,000

Table A2. Transportation-related parameter value.

Parameter	Waterway	Railway	Roadway	Pipeline
Transportation Cost (USD/Barrel-Km)	0.081	0.147	0.334	0.074
Transportation Emission Factor (g/Barrel-km)	2.17	1.58	4.09	0.68

Table A3. Product-related parameter value.

Parameter	Crude Oil	Gasoline	Diesel Oil
Annual export quota (Barrel)	3,483,559,729	-	-
Annual import quota (Barrel)	-	3,710,546,452	2,473,697,635
Expected refining ratio (%)	-	46	40
Sell price (USD/Barrel)	60	121.88	90.31
Refining cost (USD/Barrel)	-	85.94	60.16
Purchasing cost (USD/Barrel)	-	92.32	70.22
Exploitation cost (USD/Barrel)	35	-	-

Table A4. Facility-related parameter value.

Parameter	Scale		
	Small	Medium	Large
Distribution center capacity (Barrel/year)	100,000,000	150,000,000	200,000,000
Distribution center fixed cost (USD)	1,000,000	1,500,000	2,000,000
Pipeline construction cost (USD/Km)		2,880,000	

Table A5. Production-related parameter value.

Parameter	Refining Plant	
	Dungquat	Nghison
Refining capacity (Barrel/year)	69,350,000	73,000,000
Rig Exploitation capacity (Barrel/year-rig)	996,155,844	

Table A6. Acronym list.

Abbreviation	Definition
3E assessment	Economy, Energy and Environment
FMMGPM	Fuzzy Min-Max Goal Programming Model
FMOMILP	Fuzzy Multi-Objective Mixed Integer Linear Programming
MILP	Mixed Integer Linear Programming
MCDM	Multiple Criteria Decision Making
HCSC	Hydrocarbon Supply Chain
SCPSC	Sustainable Competitive Petroleum Supply Chain
TFN	Triangular Fuzzy Numbers
DC	Distribution Center

References

1. Brutschin, E.; Fleig, A. Innovation in the energy sector—The role of fossil fuels and developing economies. *Energy Policy* **2016**, *97*, 27–38. [CrossRef]
2. Emenike, S.N.; Falcone, G. A review on energy supply chain resilience through optimization. *Renew. Sustain. Energy Rev.* **2020**, *134*, 110088. [CrossRef]
3. Guliman, B.; Ionescu, S.; Niculescu, A. Modern Logistics Methods. *FAIMA Bus. Manag. J.* **2017**, *5*, 64–74.
4. Yuan, M.; Zhang, H.; Wang, B.; Shen, R.; Long, Y.; Liang, Y. Future scenario of China's downstream oil supply chain: An energy, economy and environment analysis for impacts of pipeline network reform. *J. Clean. Prod.* **2019**, *232*, 1513–1528. [CrossRef]
5. Hosseini, S.; Ivanov, D. Bayesian networks for supply chain risk, resilience and ripple effect analysis: A literature review. *Expert Syst. Appl.* **2020**, *161*, 113649. [CrossRef]
6. Chen, Z.; Ming, X.; Zhou, T.; Chang, Y. Sustainable supplier selection for smart supply chain considering internal and external uncertainty: An integrated rough-fuzzy approach. *Appl. Soft Comput.* **2020**, *87*, 106004. [CrossRef]
7. Wang, C.-N.; Nhieu, N.-L.; Chung, Y.-C.; Pham, H.-T. Multi-Objective Optimization Models for Sustainable Perishable Intermodal Multi-Product Networks with Delivery Time Window. *Mathematics* **2021**, *9*, 379. [CrossRef]
8. Wang, C.-N.; Nhieu, N.-L.; Tran, T.T.T. Stochastic Chebyshev Goal Programming Mixed Integer Linear Model for Sustainable Global Production Planning. *Mathematics* **2021**, *9*, 483. [CrossRef]
9. Sahin, B.; Soylu, A. Multi-Layer, Multi-Segment Iterative Optimization for Maritime Supply Chain Operations in a Dynamic Fuzzy Environment. *IEEE Access* **2020**, *8*, 144993–145005. [CrossRef]
10. U.S. Energy Information Administration. *Vietnam Petroleum and Other Liquids*; U.S. Energy Information Administration: Washington, DC, USA, 2021.
11. *Decision on the Approval of the Revised National Power Development Master Plan for the 2011–2020 Period with the Vision to 2030*; Prime Minister; Vietnam Department of Prime Minister: Hanoi, Vietnam, 2016.
12. Wang, B.; Liang, Y.; Zheng, T.; Yuan, M.; Zhang, H. Optimisation of a downstream oil supply chain with new pipeline route planning. *Chem. Eng. Res. Des.* **2019**, *145*, 300–313. [CrossRef]
13. Ghasemzadeh, F.; Pishdar, M.; Antuchevičienė, J. Prioritization of Petroleum Supply Chains' Disruption Management Strategies Using Combined Framework of Bsc Approach, Fuzzy Ahp and Fuzzy Choquet Integral Operator. *J. Bus. Econ. Manag.* **2017**, *18*, 897–919. [CrossRef]
14. Eslami Baladeh, A.; Cheraghi, M.; Khakzad, N. A multi-objective model to optimal selection of safety measures in oil and gas facilities. *Process Saf. Environ. Prot.* **2019**, *125*, 71–82. [CrossRef]
15. Grudz, V.; Grudz, Y.; Zapukhliak, V.; Chudyk, I.; Poberezhny, L.; Slobodyan, N.; Bodnar, V. Optimal Gas Transport Management Taking into Account Reliability Factor. *Manag. Syst. Prod. Eng.* **2020**, *28*, 202–208. [CrossRef]
16. Sahebi, H.; Nickel, S.; Ashayeri, J. Strategic and tactical mathematical programming models within the crude oil supply chain context—A review. *Comput. Chem. Eng.* **2014**, *68*, 56–77. [CrossRef]
17. Zimmermann, H.-J. Fuzzy Programming and Linear Programming with Several Objective Functions. *Fuzzy Sets Syst.* **1978**, *1*, 45–55. [CrossRef]
18. Sear, T.N. Logistics Planning in the Downstream Oil Industry. *J. Opl. Res. Soc.* **1993**, *44*, 9–17. [CrossRef]
19. Konak, A.; Coit, D.W.; Smith, A.E. Multi-objective optimization using genetic algorithms: A tutorial. *Reliab. Eng. Syst. Saf.* **2006**, *91*, 992–1007. [CrossRef]
20. Jiao, J.-L.; Zhang, J.-L.; Tang, Y.-S. A Model for the Optimization of the Petroleum Supply Chain in China and its Empirical Analysis. In Proceedings of the 2010 International Conference on E-Business and E-Government, Guangzhou, China, 7–9 May 2010; pp. 3327–3330.
21. Fernandes, L.J.; Relvas, S.; Barbosa-Póvoa, A.P. Downstream Petroleum Supply Chain Planning under Uncertainty. In *Computer Aided Chemical Engineering*; Elsevier: Amsterdam, The Netherlands, 2015; Volume 37, pp. 1889–1894.
22. Wang, C.N.; Nhieu, N.L.; Nguyen, H.P.; Wang, J.W. Simulation-based Optimization Integrated Multiple Criteria Decision-Making Framework for Wave Energy Site Selection: A Case Study of Australia. *IEEE Access* **2021**, *9*, 167458–167476. [CrossRef]
23. Attia, A.M.; Ghaithan, A.M.; Duffuaa, S.O. A multi-objective optimization model for tactical planning of upstream oil & gas supply chains. *Comput. Chem. Eng.* **2019**, *128*, 216–227.
24. Sheel, A.; Singh, Y.P.; Nath, V. Managing agility in the downstream petroleum supply chain. *Int. J. Bus. Excell.* **2020**, *20*, 269–294. [CrossRef]
25. Guo, Y.; Meng, X.; Wang, D.; Meng, T.; Liu, S.; He, R. Comprehensive risk evaluation of long-distance oil and gas transportation pipelines using a fuzzy Petri net model. *J. Nat. Gas Sci. Eng.* **2016**, *33*, 18–29. [CrossRef]
26. Kim, Y.; Yun, C.; Park, S.B.; Park, S.; Fan, L.T. An integrated model of supply network and production planning for multiple fuel products of multi-site refineries. *Comput. Chem. Eng.* **2008**, *32*, 2529–2535. [CrossRef]
27. Kuo, T.-H.; Chang, C.-T. Application of a Mathematic Programming Model for Integrated Planning and Scheduling of Petroleum Supply Networks. *Ind. Eng. Chem. Res.* **2008**, *47*, 1935–1954. [CrossRef]
28. Al-Qahtani, K.; Elkamel, A. Multisite facility network integration design and coordination: An application to the refining industry. *Comput. Chem. Eng.* **2008**, *32*, 2189–2202. [CrossRef]
29. Al-Othman, W.B.E.; Lababidi, H.M.S.; Alatiqi, I.M.; Al-Shayji, K. Supply chain optimization of petroleum organization under uncertainty in market demands and prices. *Eur. J. Oper. Res.* **2008**, *189*, 822–840. [CrossRef]

30. Hamedi, M.; Zanjirani Farahani, R.; Husseini, M.M.; Esmaeilian, G.R. A distribution planning model for natural gas supply chain: A case study. *Energy Policy* **2009**, *37*, 799–812. [CrossRef]
31. Jie, C.; Jing, L.; Shilong, Q. Transportation network optimization of import crude oil in China based on minimum logistics cost. In Proceedings of the 2010 IEEE International Conference on Emergency Management and Management Sciences, Beijing, China, 8–10 August 2010; IEEE: Piscataway, NJ, USA, 2010.
32. Song, F.M. A comprehensive model for predicting CO_2 corrosion rate in oil and gas production and transportation systems. *Electrochim. Acta* **2010**, *55*, 689–700. [CrossRef]
33. Aizemberg, L.; Kramer, H.H.; Pessoa, A.A.; Uchoa, E. Formulations for a problem of petroleum transportation. *Eur. J. Oper. Res.* **2014**, *237*, 82–90. [CrossRef]
34. Kazemi, Y.; Szmerekovsky, J. Modeling downstream petroleum supply chain: The importance of multi-mode transportation to strategic planning. *Transp. Res. Part E Logist. Transp. Rev.* **2015**, *83*, 111–125. [CrossRef]
35. Ghezavati, V.R.; Ghaffarpour, M.H.; Salimian, M. A hierarchical approach for designing the downstream segment for a supply chain of petroleum production systems. *J. Ind. Syst. Eng.* **2015**, *8*, 1–17.
36. Rocha, R.; Grossmann, I.E.; de Aragão, M.V.S.P. Petroleum supply planning: Reformulations and a novel decomposition algorithm. *Optim. Eng.* **2017**, *18*, 215–240. [CrossRef]
37. Devold, H.; Graven, T.; Halvorsrød, S.O. Digitalization of Oil and Gas Facilities Reduce Cost and Improve Maintenance Operations. In Proceedings of the Offshore Technology Conference 2017, Houston, TX, USA, 1–4 May 2017.
38. Anifowose, B.; Odubela, M. Methane emissions from oil and gas transport facilities—Exploring innovative ways to mitigate environmental consequences. *J. Clean. Prod.* **2015**, *92*, 121–133. [CrossRef]
39. Creating a High-Performance Downstream Petroleum Supply Chain. 2000. Available online: http://kambing.ui.ac.id/onnopurbo/library/library-ref-eng/ref-eng-1/application/e-commerce/eichmann.pdf (accessed on 22 February 2021).
40. Allen, D.T.; Torres, V.M.; Thomas, J.; Sullivan, D.W.; Harrison, M.; Hendler, A.; Herndon, S.C.; Kolb, C.E.; Fraser, M.P.; Hill, A.D.; et al. Measurements of methane emissions at natural gas production sites in the United States. *Proc. Natl. Acad. Sci. USA* **2013**, *110*, 17768–17773. [CrossRef] [PubMed]
41. Hadizadeh, A.K.A.; Allen, J.K. Designing a Dynamic Bi-Objective Network Model for a Petroleum Supply Chain. In Proceedings of the 2012 Industrial and Systems Engineering Research Conference; Institute of Industrial and Systems Engineers (IISE): Peachtree Corners, GA, USA, 2012.
42. Moradi Nasab, N.; Amin-Naseri, M.R. Designing an integrated model for a multi-period, multi-echelon and multi-product petroleum supply chain. *Energy* **2016**, *114*, 708–733. [CrossRef]
43. Ghaithan, A.M.; Attia, A.; Duffuaa, S.O. Multi-objective optimization model for a downstream oil and gas supply chain. *Appl. Math. Model.* **2017**, *52*, 689–708. [CrossRef]
44. Moradinasab, N.; Amin-Naseri, M.R.; Behbahani, T.J.; Jafarzadeh, H. Competition and cooperation between supply chains in multi-objective petroleum green supply chain: A game theoretic approach. *J. Clean. Prod.* **2018**, *170*, 818–841. [CrossRef]
45. Alghanmi, A.; Yang, Z.; Blanco-Davis, E. Risk analysis of petroleum transportation using fuzzy rule-based Bayesian reasoning. *Int. J. Shipp. Transp. Logist.* **2020**, *12*, 39–64. [CrossRef]
46. Chamani FoomaniDana, A.; Tamannaei, M. A Game-Theoretic Approach for Transportation of Oil Products in a Duopolistic Supply Chain. *AUT J. Civ. Eng.* **2020**, *5*, 7.
47. Zhou, X.; Zhang, H.; Xin, S.; Yan, Y.; Long, Y.; Yuan, M.; Liang, Y. Future scenario of China's downstream oil supply chain: Low carbon-oriented optimization for the design of planned multi-product pipelines. *J. Clean. Prod.* **2020**, *244*, 118866. [CrossRef]
48. Elkamel, A.; Ba-Shammakh, M.; Douglas, P.; Croiset, E. An Optimization Approach for Integrating Planning and CO_2 Emission Reduction in the Petroleum Refining Industry. *Ind. Eng. Chem. Res.* **2008**, *47*, 760–776. [CrossRef]
49. Guyonnet, P.; Grant, F.H.; Bagajewicz, M.J. Integrated Model for Refinery Planning, Oil Procuring and Product Distribution. *Ind. Eng. Chem. Res.* **2009**, *48*, 463–482. [CrossRef]
50. Lima, C.; Relvas, S.; Barbosa-Póvoa, A. Corrigendum to Designing and planning the downstream oil supply chain under uncertainty using a fuzzy programming approach. *Comput. Chem. Eng.* **2021**, *153*, 107400. [CrossRef]
51. Pudasaini, P. Integrated planning of downstream petroleum supply chain: A multi-objective stochastic approach. *Oper. Res. Perspect.* **2021**, *8*, 100189. [CrossRef]
52. Santibanez-Borda, E.; Korre, A.; Nie, Z.; Durucan, S. A multi-objective optimisation model to reduce greenhouse gas emissions and costs in offshore natural gas upstream chains. *J. Clean. Prod.* **2021**, *297*, 126625. [CrossRef]
53. Panos, E.; Densing, M.; Volkart, K. Access to electricity in the World Energy Council's global energy scenarios: An outlook for developing regions until 2030. *Energy Strategy Rev.* **2016**, *9*, 28–49. [CrossRef]
54. Vietnam Gasoline Prices. 2021. Available online: https://www.globalpetrolprices.com/Vietnam/gasoline_prices/ (accessed on 21 March 2021).
55. Annual Statistical Bulletin. 2020. Available online: https://asb.opec.org/ (accessed on 20 January 2021).
56. Vietnam Oil Consumption. 2021. Available online: https://www.ceicdata.com/en/indicator/vietnam/oil-consumption (accessed on 20 February 2021).
57. Vietnam Cities Database. 2020. Available online: https://simplemaps.com/data/vn-cities (accessed on 15 December 2020).
58. Vietnam Energy Sector. 2019. Available online: https://www.ukabc.org.uk/wp-content/uploads/2019/07/Energy-Sector-Update-April-2019.pdf (accessed on 10 February 2021).

59. The Vietnam Household Living Standards Survey 2018. May 2020. Available online: https://www.gso.gov.vn/en/data-and-statistics/2020/05/result-of-the-vietnam-household-living-standards-survey-2018 (accessed on 27 July 2021).
60. Vietnam's Crude Oil Export Price. 2021. Available online: https://tuoitre.vn/viet-nam-xuat-khau-dau-tho-gia-thap-20210322075805618.htm (accessed on 10 March 2021).
61. Blancas, L.C.; El-Hifnawi, M.B. *Facilitating Trade through Competitive, Low-Carbon Transport: The Case for Vietnam's Inland and Coastal Waterways*; The World Bank: Washington, DC, USA, 2014.
62. Tencati, A.; Russo, A.; Quaglia, V. Sustainability along the global supply chain: The case of Vietnam. *Soc. Responsib. J.* **2010**, *6*, 91–107. [CrossRef]
63. Oil and Gas Pipeline Construction Costs. 2021. Available online: https://www.gem.wiki/Oil_and_Gas_Pipeline_Construction_Costs#:~{}:text=For%20proposed%20onshore%20US%20gas,(%244.10%20million%2Fkm) (accessed on 30 December 2020).

Article

Analyzing the Main Determinants for Being an Immigrant in Cuenca (Ecuador) Based on a Fuzzy Clustering Approach

Juan Carlos Martín [1,*], Natalia Soledad Bustamante-Sánchez [2] and Alessandro Indelicato [1]

[1] Institute of Tourism and Sustainable Economic Development, University of Las Palmas de Gran Canaria, 35017 Las Palmas de Gran Canaria, Spain; alessandro.indelicato101@alu.ulpgc.es
[2] Departamento de Ciencias Empresariales, Universidad Técnica Particular de Loja, Loja 110107, Ecuador; nsbustamante@utpl.edu.ec
* Correspondence: jcarlos.martin@ulpgc.es

Abstract: The study aims to analyze the determinants for being an immigrant in Cuenca (Ecuador). Our analysis is based on the answers given to a scale formed by 30 items included in a questionnaire administered to a representative sample of 369 immigrants. A fuzzy hybrid multi-criteria decision-making method, TOPSIS (Technique for Order Preference by Similarity to an Ideal Solution), is used to analyze whether immigrants are more or less exigent regarding the items included in the scale to reside in Cuenca. Then, a fuzzy clustering method is applied to analyze the differences observed in the main determinants observed over a number of traits according to their similarities to three obtained profiles: (1) extreme exigent immigrants; (2) extreme unneedful immigrants; and (3) intermediate exigent immigrants. Results show that items such as access to internet and benefits for retirees were highly valued by some immigrants. In addition, the authors found that information channels, reasons for immigrating, house location, main transport mode, income and main income source are the main determinants that differentiate whether the immigrants in Cuenca (Ecuador) are more or less demanding with respect to the exigency scale developed in the study. The main contributions to the body of knowledge, the policy implications and lines for future research are finally discussed.

Keywords: immigrants; fuzzy logic; triangular fuzzy numbers; TOPSIS; fuzzy-hybrid cluster

1. Introduction

The negative representations that immigrants have especially in Europe [1] are the result of the labels created by a polarization process that has distorted attitude formation over immigrants and refugees. The labels have important implications regarding the legitimacy of a newcomer's desire to settle in a country. Some of the negative attitudes towards immigrants are rooted in the perceived economic and cultural cost of having this group settling in Europe [2]. This negative perception of economic costs is particularly linked to developed welfare systems that provide houses, clothes, education and health care to immigrants. For this reason, a number of recent studies have found that attitudes towards immigrants in Western European countries are becoming more negative than in the past [1,3–7].

The situation in the European countries contrasts highly with other less developed or developing countries, such as Ecuador, which are implementing programs that favor the entrance of immigrants, especially those who want to be retired in the country [8]. This well-known phenomenon is also studied as second-home tourism or retirement migration [9]. There are a number of reasons that can influence the migrants in deciding whether to settle in another country; these depend on different traits, such as income, cultural background and lifestyle [10,11]. Martín and Bustamante-Sánchez [8] categorized the main reasons to be retired immigrants as: (1) improving the quality of life; (2) retiring and living in countries that they knew on their vacation; (3) looking for a lower cost of life and warmer climates; (4) moving out to escape from their home countries or to be away from relatives; (5) knowing different people, cultures and places; (6) relaxing in quieter cities and towns where they can live away from noise and globalization; and (7) adjusting the preferences according to the place attachment.

It is out of the scope of the current introduction to review the main theories that have been developed to explain the many controversies that exist in migrant studies. Interested readers are referred to [12], in which the authors discussed, in Chapter 2, the appreciation of who the immigrants are. Immigrant groups differed greatly by race, ethnic, age, income or religion. All these characteristics might put immigrants at risks of being seen as permanent and disadvantaged minorities separated from the majority. The authors compare the immigrants' integration to the US from Canada or the UK with the situation experienced by those who come from Latin America. Apart from integration, other topics of interests are related to national identity, political economy, distinctions between settler societies with a long immigration tradition vs. new immigrant societies and competing theories that explain the main reasons to emigrate to other countries.

As seen, the literature is abundant in the analysis of the attitudes towards immigrants from the perspective of the residents [1,7]. Nevertheless, the number of migrant studies analyzing the phenomenon from the perspective of immigrants is still scarce. It would be interesting to analyze why immigrants migrate to other countries. What are the main pull factors that a particular city needs to have or develop in order to attract the settlement of newcomers? In addition, the analysis of immigrants is equally uneven in favor of immigrants coming to the rich countries of the world for improving their well-being, but much less is known about the immigration processes from high-income countries to low-income countries. In this case, the well-being gain can be sustained by the existing tradeoff between the initial willingness to accept less quality in public services, such as the health system, libraries, and public administration, in exchange for the possibility of enjoying a better climate, nicer houses and relatively higher income than in their countries of origin. For example, Hayes [13] analyzed the notions of 'active' and 'successful' aging by exploring the narratives of aging for a group of retired immigrants from Canada and the US in Cuenca, Ecuador.

The present study attempts to correct, in part, the commented scarcity presenting empirical evidence of the most important determinants that Cuenca (Ecuador) has to be considered the place of settlement for a group of immigrants. The current study is based on a quantitative method grounded in fuzzy logic theory, a multi-criteria decision-making model and a fuzzy clustering method with the aim to provide interesting insights on: (1) obtaining the degree of exigency of immigrants (DEI) according the calculus of a synthetic index based on 30 items; (2) analyzing the level of exigency in every item with the help of the ideal solutions in order to determine if some items present more or less variability; (3) analyzing DEIs and sensitivity of results using some traits; (4) segmenting the immigrants without assuming that each immigrant belongs to only one segment; and (5) analyzing whether there are differences on the segments obtained according to some socioeconomic traits. Thus, the current study provides an empirical contribution to a body of knowledge that has been scarcely explored; the interest is justified because migration mainly from high-income countries to low-income countries is changing in less developed countries, such as Ecuador, and there is a need to understand the main pull factors that affect immigrants' decisions.

2. Materials and Methods

2.1. Questionnaire and Data

Unfortunately, we could not find any DEI scale that was previously developed by other researchers, so we decided to develop an instrument that contained the preferences of the immigrants related to what items are important or not when they decide to emigrate to a different country. At the end, the instrument consists of 30 items rated on a 5-point semantic response scale as follows: (1) not important at all; (2) slightly important; (3) somewhat important; (4) important; and (5) very important. The total scale score can be calculated as the sum of all individual item scores and can range from 30 to 150. Higher scores indicate higher levels of degree of exigency related to the preferences of immigrants.

The development of the scale was obtained by identifying the diverse factors that were mentioned by other scholars in the analysis of the main determinants that lead individual to emigrate. There exists an ample consensus in the existing literature about the main causes for both flows immigrants and refugees [14]. Thus, the list of thirty items correspond to the categories of factors that include economic variables, globalization, political variables, social variables, cultural variables and access variables [15–30]. Other items were obtained from the items included in the studies of secondary houses as these are also related to the objective of the study [31–35].

A focus group with administrative officials of the city of Cuenca, as well as with a group of professors at the Universities of Loja and Cuenca in Ecuador and the University of Las Palmas de Gran Canaria in Spain was finally consulted in order to obtain the final list of the relevant items. Table 1 shows the final list of the 30 items included in the questionnaire to measure *DEI*.

Table 1. Items included in the degree of exigency of immigrants who live in Cuenca, Ecuador.

Item	Description
1	Climate
2	Cost of Living
3	Safety
4	Language
5	Local Culture
6	General Image and Landscape
7	Social Atmosphere [1]
8	Local Gastronomy
9	Tourist Attractions
10	Leisure and Entertainment
11	Ease of integration
12	Lifestyle
13	Banks. Monetary Exchange
14	Shops; Commercial Activity
15	Accessibility of Roads
16	Means of Transport
17	Variety of Types of Houses
18	House Rental Costs
19	Quality of Water
20	Quality of Air
21	Quality of Grounds and Cleanliness
22	General Vegetation/Green Space
23	Medical Assistance
24	Quality of Urban Services
25	Access to Internet
26	Tourist Services
27	Education
28	Programs for Foreigners
29	Benefits for Retirees
30	Sport facilities

[1] Social Atmosphere is related to social capital.

The questionnaire was divided into three different sections: (1) the first part included sociodemographic and economic information, such as nationality, gender, age, marital status, income and visa; (2) the second part included 26 items that measure the degree of importance given by respondents to buy a house in the city of Cuenca; and (3) the last part contained the items that measure *DEI* (Table 1).

The questionnaire was administered in Cuenca during the months of January and February in the year 2018. The socioeconomic characteristics of the immigrants are relevant in the study in order to analyze the extent *DEI* could be determined by income, age, visa permit or occupation. The sample size was determined by considering the data of the last census conducted by the National Institute of Census and Statistics, and knowing that the population of immigrants was approximately 9000 in the municipality, by applying the formula of finite population with a confidence level of 95 percent and an error margin of 5.0 percent, a representative sample of 369 immigrants who answered the questionnaires was obtained. To our surprise, we did not find any particular resistance of immigrants to participate in the survey, as we expected that some illegal immigrants could be more reluctant to be part of the survey process. In fact, it was well known that of the total 9000 immigrants, only 2422 were legal immigrants. The administration of the questionnaire was carried out face-to-face with the help of well-trained students, taking about 13 min to complete. A number of hot spots (19) were selected in the city to administer the questionnaires; these places were frequently used by the immigrants for entertainment, or for having coffee or a drink.

Table 2 shows the sociodemographic profile of the total sample of immigrants who responded to the questionnaire. Analyzing the most important categories for the sample of immigrants of some variables, namely nationality, gender, age, marital status and whether the immigrant was retired or not, it can be seen that: (1) nationalities of the US, Colombia, Canada, Argentina and Peru were those most represented; (2) there were slightly more males than females; (3) those between 25 and 34 years old, and between 35 and 44 years old were the two age groups more represented; (4) single and married were the most popular marital status; and (5) immigrants who were not retired were more abundant than retired immigrants, with a proportion of 4:1.

Table 2. Immigrants' Sociodemographic profiles.

Variable	Categories	N	Perc.
Nationality *	United States	76	20.60
	Colombia	38	10.30
	Other South American countries	32	8.67
	Canada	30	8.13
	Argentina	28	7.59
	Other nationality	25	6.78
	Peru	22	5.96
	France	21	5.69
	Venezuela	19	5.15
	Other European countries	16	4.34
	Netherlands	15	4.07
	Germany	13	3.52
	Cuba	10	2.71
	Italy	9	2.44
	Mexico	8	2.17
	Iberian countries	7	1.90
Gender	Male	206	55.83
	Female	163	44.17
Age	$\leq$24 years old	45	12.20
	25–34 years old	116	31.44
	35–44 years old	83	22.49
	45–54 years old	37	10.03
	55–64 years old	47	12.74
	$\geq$65 years old	41	11.11

Table 2. *Cont.*

Variable	Categories	N	Perc.
Marital status	Single	164	44.44
	Married	125	33.88
	Widowed	16	4.34
	Divorced	40	10.84
	Unmarried couple	24	6.50
Retired	Y	66	17.89
	N	303	82.11

* There were 41 different nationalities, so for those with less than 10 respondents, it was decided to group them in territorial categories for ease of exposition.

2.2. Methods

2.2.1. Fuzzy Set Theory Preliminaries

The information provided by the instrument to measure *DEI* is of a subjective and inaccurate nature because, as in many real world applications, preference knowledge is fuzzy rather than precise. Various methods have been developed by researchers to analyze this type of information. In this study, a fuzzy hybrid multi-criteria decision-making approach that integrates fuzzy logic and the technique of similarity to ideal solutions, TOPSIS (Technique for order preference by similarity to an ideal solution), was employed. This method has been successfully used in different fields [36–39].

The vagueness associated to the subjective evaluation is a sort of problem when researchers are finding a way to synthesize the information to apply econometric or mathematical models. Nevertheless, fuzzy logic models are adequate tools to deal in part with the vagueness associated with linguistic terms [40–42]. These models deal with the vague information deconstructing the idea of objective information in a sort of a measurement that that has different degrees of intensity. The degree of intensity is conceptualized by a probability (membership) function breaking into different pieces the objective "crisp information" that is conceptualized, following the fuzzy logic, as the zero-one membership function. This membership function is also known as the characteristic function, discrimination function or indicator function [43] (p.25).

We now introduce the basic terminology of fuzzy set theory as well as some of the algebraic operations based on [44–46]. A fuzzy set A in X is a function A: $X \to [0,1]$ denoted by μ_A, and X is known as the universe or discourse. The value $\mu_A(x)$ at x represents the membership function of x in A, and if the value is closer to one, then x belongs to A with more intensity. The support of A is denoted by S(A) and can be found as all the elements x in the discourse X for which $\mu_A(x) > 0$. A is a normal fuzzy set in X if there exists an element x for which $\mu_A(x) = 1$. We finally introduce the α-cut sets as they are important in the study of the fuzzy arithmetic. We define the α-cut set A_α of the fuzzy set A as those elements x in X for which $\mu_A(x) \geq \alpha$, where $\alpha \in (0,1]$.

Fuzzy numbers were first defined as "numbers that are close to a given real number" [46]. A fuzzy set A in $\mathbb{R}$ is called a fuzzy number if it satisfies the following conditions: (1) A is a normal fuzzy set, (2) A_α is a closed interval for every α in (0,1]; and (3) the support of A is bounded.

The most common fuzzy numbers used by researchers are triangular fuzzy numbers (TFNs), defined by a triplet (a_1, a_2, a_3) of real numbers for which the membership function is given in Equation (1).

$$\mu_A(x) = \begin{cases} \frac{x-a_1}{a_2-a_1}, & a_1 \leq x \leq a_2 \\ \frac{x-a_3}{a_2-a_3}, & a_2 \leq x \leq a_3 \\ 0, & \text{otherwise.} \end{cases} \quad (1)$$

The α-cut set of the TFN (a_1, a_2, a_3) is the closed interval $[a_1 + \alpha(a_2 - a_1), a_3 - \alpha(a_3 - a_2)]$. Now, let $A = (a_1, a_2, a_3)$ and $B = (b_1, b_2, b_3)$ be two TFNs, then with the help of the α-cut sets, the following algebraic operations can be defined:

$$\begin{aligned} A(+)B &= (a_1 + b_1, a_2 + b_2, a_3 + b_3) \\ (-)A &= (-a_1, -a_2, -a_3) \\ kA &= (ka_1, ka_2, ka_3), \ k > 0 \\ A(-)B &= (a_1 - b_1, a_2 - b_2, a_3 - b_3) \end{aligned} \quad (2)$$

In the study, each point of the semantic scale was assigned to a TFN [47,48]. Researchers have used different sets to represent the universe or discourse based on ranges (0, 1) or (0, 100) without loss of generality. The triplet for each point was selected according to previous experience or knowledge of researchers. Table 3 shows the TFNs used in the study. It is interesting to highlight that the central value of the semantic scale (somewhat important) presents the widest range (40 units) of all the TFNs used in the conversion. TFN membership function is characterized because the degree of the truth intensity is the highest in the intermediate point of the triplet used to represent it. Another interesting remark of the table is that the vagueness of the information is properly handled with fuzzy logic because all the consecutive TFNs overlap. A further discussion of the conversion can be consulted in [8].

Table 3. Five-point semantic scale conversion to TFNs.

Semantic Scale	TFN [1]
Not important at all	(0, 0, 30)
Slightly important	(20, 30, 40)
Somewhat important	(30, 50, 70)
Important	(60, 70, 80)
Very important	(70, 100, 100)

[1] (0, 1) interval for the universe is also common.

2.2.2. A Hybrid Fuzzy TOPSIS Model

The hybrid fuzzy TOPSIS model is an extension of the TOPSIS introduced by Hwang and Yoon [49]. This technique is based on the issue that the ideal solution should have the best level for all attributes considered in the analysis, whereas on the opposite, the negative ideal solution should be characterized by having all the worst attribute values. The hybrid fuzzy TOPSIS model is different from the original TOPSIS because the attribute values are represented by fuzzy numbers.

The fuzzy TOPSIS approach has been applied successfully in some previous studies in different fields, such as: (1) the hiring of a system analysis engineering by a software company [50]; (2) the selection of a location for a plant [51]; and (3) the selection of a location for a distribution center [52]. All the previous studies share in common the integration of various linguistic assessments in the form of fuzzy set numbers.

The respondents' information can be aggregated according to the objectives of the study by different population groups. This can be accomplished by calculating the average of the TFNs, and one of the good properties of the fuzzy hybrid model is that this operation is closed in the algebra of TFN [46]. Thus, the aggregated information of each group is also a TFN, and, for this reason, it can be inferred that it inherits the vagueness of the individual information [53]. Mathematically, the average TFN of a group of n individuals is calculated as:

$$\tilde{A} = (a_1, a_2, a_3) = \left(\frac{1}{n}\right) \bullet \left(\tilde{A}_1 \oplus \tilde{A}_2 \oplus \cdots \tilde{A}_n\right) = \left(\frac{\sum_{i=1}^{n} a_1^{(i)}, \sum_{i=1}^{n} a_2^{(i)}, \sum_{i=1}^{n} a_3^{(i)}}{n}\right) \quad (3)$$

Once researchers have selected the number of groups they want to analyze, it is possible to calculate the fuzzy information matrix in which the rows are represented by each item included in the scale of the study and the columns are represented by the different groups under analysis. It is now where the hybrid nature of the method can be explained before applying the TOPSIS method to the TFN matrix. Two possible approaches can be utilized at this stage: TOPSIS can be applied to the TFN matrix that can be seen as a tensor matrix, or a defuzzification method can be applied to the TFN aggregated matrix before applying TOPSIS. In this sense, for example, Li [54] introduced a compromise ratio methodology for the fuzzy hybrid method when TOPSIS is directly applied to a fuzzy set of numbers to resolve a multi-attribute group decision-making problem.

The defuzzification method, also known as the clarification method, converts the fuzzy information matrix into a "crisp" information matrix. Thus, the crisp information value for the TFN needs to adequately synthesize the uncertainty associated to the TFN. There are many defuzzification methods that are based on different assumptions that can be made by the researchers, "mean of maximum", "center-of-area" and "alpha-cut" methods are among the most popular methods.

The defuzzification method used in the study is based on a "center of area" method and it is known as the best-non-fuzzy weighted average that can be calculated as $((a_1 + 2 a_2 + a_3)/4)$. This method is very popular and has been proposed in many previous studies [8,55–57]. The method presents several advantages over other methods because it is simple and does not require any personal researcher value judgment. Thus, the TFN information matrix is converted to a conventional crisp information matrix.

TOPSIS is then applied to the information matrix method [49,58]. The ideal solutions are obtained according to items used to measure DEI and the groups used in the analysis. The items need to be separated according to whether higher or lower values mean more or less value for the synthetic indicator that is constructed. Mathematically, the positive and negative ideal solutions are, in our case, calculated as:

$$A^+ = \{(\max V_{ig}|i \in I), (\min V_{ig}|i \in I'), g = 1, 2, \ldots, G \equiv groups\}, \quad (4)$$

$$A^- = \{(\min V_{ig}|i \in I), (\max V_{ig}|i \in I'), g = 1, 2, \ldots, G \equiv groups\}, \quad (5)$$

where I and I' divide the different items included in the DEI scale according to benefit (higher values are good) or cost (higher values are bad) characteristics regarding the indicator under analysis. In the current study, the whole set of 30 items included in the DEI scale can be considered as a benefit, and the number of groups G depends on are the categories of 17 covariates, such as nationality, gender, age, marital status, occupation, years of residence, residence visa, pension visa, main information channels, reasons to come, house location, house tenancy, house type, main transport mode used, income, main income source and expenditure in the city. A total number of 84 groups were considered in the study.

Once the ideal solutions are calculated, the relative DEI index for each group can be calculated comparing the existing distance from each group to these ideal solutions calculated in Equation (6). Thus, the synthetic DEI indicator for the groups can be obtained as:

$$\begin{aligned} S_g^+ &= dist(V_g, A^+) = \sqrt{\sum_{i=1}^{30} (V_{ig} - A_i^+)^2} \quad g = 1, 2, \ldots, G \\ S_g^- &= dist(V_g, A^-) = \sqrt{\sum_{i=1}^{30} (V_{ig} - A_i^-)^2} \quad g = 1, 2, \ldots, G \\ DEI_g &= \frac{S_g^-}{S_g^+ + S_g^-} \quad g = 1, 2, \ldots, G \end{aligned} \quad (6)$$

where DEI is always in the range (0, 1). Thus, each of the groups included in the analysis can be ranked according to whether the group is more or less exigent according to the increasing order of the synthetic index. TOPSIS is based on the concept that the best alternatives should be more or less similar to the positive or negative ideal solutions.

The synthetic exigency DEI index depends on 30 different items and, sometimes, the knowledge of what items are more or less critical to different groups can be the object of interest for some stakeholders, such as policy makers in charge of the immigrant governance rules. Thus, the elasticity value measuring the sensitivity of DEI with respect to each item will be obtained. Mathematically, the elasticity of the DEI for each group s and each item i can be calculated as:

$$\eta_{ig} = \frac{\Delta\% DEI_g}{\Delta\% V_{ig}} = \frac{dDEI_g}{dV_{ig}} \frac{V_{ig}}{DEI_g}, \qquad (7)$$

2.2.3. Fuzzy Clustering Method

D'Urso [59] discussed different fuzzy clustering models for fuzzy data according to: (1) the informational paradigms and their relationship with the fuzzy clustering methods; (2) fuzzy data features regarding the algebraic and geometric formalization, mathematical transformations and metrics; (3) conceptual aspects, such as elicitation and specification of the membership functions; (4) a systematic overview with a comparative assessment of different fuzzy clustering methods; and (5) an analysis of fuzzy clustering model extensions for complex fuzzy data structures, such as fuzzy data time arrays. The reference is a good starting point to find the main pioneering fuzzy clustering studies in which a great deal of attention was paid to the fuzzy clustering analysis for fuzzy data.

The rest of the section briefly describes the three fuzzy cluster solutions adopted in the study. On occasions, it is preferable to obtain a three-cluster solution rather than a solution with more than three clusters, even though a statistical indicator might suggest that it is more reasonable to obtain more than three clusters [60]. Thus, three representative immigrant profiles were obtained and named as: (1) extreme exigent immigrant; (2) extreme unneedful immigrant; and (3) intermediate exigent immigrant. The fuzzy clustering method provides the membership function assigned to each immigrant that determines the probability that each immigrant has to belong to each of the three clusters. The profiles of the representative immigrant for each of the clusters were based on the individual DEI indicator according to the maximum, minimum and median values. This assumption is very different from other proposed methods in which the prototypes are obtained directly within the method.

Cluster analysis summarizes multivariate data in order to find useful information that facilitates the decision making. Cluster analysis finds meaningful groups for which the similarities within the clusters and the dissimilarity between the groups are maximized [61]. The fuzzy cluster algorithm is presented in Equation (8). The method is an extension of the bagged cluster algorithm introduced by Leisch [62]. The fuzzy C means the algorithm for fuzzy data (FCM-FD) can be expressed as follows:

$$\begin{cases} \min: \sum_{i=1}^{n}\sum_{c=1}^{C} u_{ic}^{m} d_{F}^{2}(\tilde{x}_{i}, \tilde{p}_{c}) = \sum_{i=1}^{n}\sum_{c=1}^{C} u_{ic}^{m} [w_{2}^{2} \|a_{2}^{i} - p_{2}^{c}\|^{2} + \\ \qquad + w_{1}^{2}(\|a_{1}^{i} - p_{1}^{c}\|^{2} + \|a_{3}^{i} - p_{3}^{c}\|^{2})] \\ \text{s.t.} \quad m > 1,\ u_{ic} \geq 0,\ \sum_{c=1}^{C} u_{ic} = 1, \\ \qquad w_{1} \geq w_{2} \geq 0,\ w_{1} + w_{2} = 1 \end{cases} \qquad (8)$$

where, $d_{F}^{2}(\tilde{x}_{i}, \tilde{p}_{c})$ represents the squared fuzzy distance between the ith immigrant and the profile of the cth cluster; the $\tilde{x}_{i} \equiv \{\tilde{x}_{ik} = (a_{1ik}, a_{2ik}, a_{3ik}) : k = 1 \ldots K\}$ denotes the TFN triplet for the ith immigrant obtained from the observation of the 30 items; $\tilde{p}_{c} \equiv \{\tilde{p}_{ck} = (p_{1ck}, p_{2ck}, p_{3ck}) : k = 1 \ldots K\}$ represents the fuzzy profile of the cth cluster; $\|a_{2}^{i} - p_{2}^{c}\|^{2}$ is the squared Euclidean distance between the centers of the TFN vectors of the ith immigrant and the representative immigrant of the cth cluster; $\|a_{1}^{i} - p_{1}^{c}\|^{2}$ and

$\|a_3^i - p_3^c\|^2$ are the squared Euclidian distances between the left and right extreme components of the TFN vectors of the ith immigrant and the representative immigrant of the cth cluster, respectively; $w_1 \geq w_2 \geq 0$ are suitable weights for the center and extreme components for the fuzzy distances considered; $m > 1$ is a weighted exponent that controls the fuzziness of the obtained partition; u_{ic} gives the membership degree of the ith immigrant in the cth cluster.

There are a number of methodological issues associated with the fuzzy cluster analysis proposed in the study, such as the selection of the centroids or medoids, the distance measures, the selection of the parameters m, w_1 and w_2, and the optimal solutions of the method. The medoids strategy is preferred as the profiles of the representing cluster prototypes are real observations. As mentioned, our study is based on selecting three real observations for the prototypes of each cluster. Different distance measures can be adapted to the fuzzy environment, such as a sort of exponential-type distance measure, Hausdorff metrics or dissimilarity parametric approaches. The study uses a parametric dissimilarity approach composed of two distances, the center and spread distances, that are related to the values of the w coefficients. The coefficient m is known as the "fuzziness coefficient". The fuzziness directly increases with m, and when m is closer to one, the fuzziness is lower. In this study, m is equal to 1.5 as in [60]. The weights w_1 and w_2 measure the relative importance given to each of the components of the triplet that represent the respective TFN. In this study, as in other empirical applications, the neutral approach was selected and, accordingly, the weights are equal to 0.5 [56,60].

We end this section with the optimal solutions provided by the Lagrangian multiplier method used to solve the constrained minimization problem. D'Urso and Giordani [63] discussed that the Lagrangian method does not guarantee that the global optimum is obtained, so in order to check the stability of the solution, they suggested to initialize the iterative algorithm by considering several different starting points. The authors used an iterative algorithm in which the weights are directly obtained within the model (internal weighting estimation). As stated, our study uses the neutral approach in which we have not tuned the influence of the two components of the TFNs in the clustering process, and the local optima problem might be less important than in the case in which the prototypes and the weights are determined in the own method. Interested readers in cluster validation and cluster profiles are referred to [59,60,63–65].

3. Results

3.1. Fuzzy Hybrid Model

Table 4 shows the TFNs and the defuzzified (crisp) values that correspond to the total sample of immigrants. A simple analysis of the TFN triplets shows that the information has a clear meaning for fuzzy logic experts, but it is less evident for those who are not so familiar with this tool. It can be seen that the majority of the TFNs overlap. However, this is not the case for the most and least valued items which are quality of water and sport facilities, respectively. The overlapping finding is not a surprise as this is an essential characteristic of the fuzzy logic approach to deal with vague information. The defuzzification method provides the crisp column and facilitates the interpretation of the information. Thus, it can be inferred that the items for which the degree of exigency is higher than 75 are quality of urban services, programs for foreigners, house rental costs, climate, lifestyle, ease of integration, safety, cost of living, medical assistance and quality of water. Meanwhile, there are only two items, sport facilities and education, for which the crisp values are lower than 50, so immigrants are clearly less exigent in these two items.

Table 4. TFN and crisp values of the total sample of immigrants by item and ideal solutions [1].

Item	TFN	Crisp	A^+	A^-
Climate	(58.78, 79.92, 86.59)	76.30	89.69	59.44
Cost of Living	(61.65, 86.04, 90.60)	81.08	92.50	64.03
Safety	(61.76, 83.55, 88.27)	79.28	92.50	53.91
Language	(44.42, 61.11, 74.23)	60.22	70.00	51.41
Local Culture	(45.07, 60.79, 74.55)	60.30	72.31	50.00
General Image and Landscape	(46.83, 62.44, 75.37)	61.77	70.58	50.00
Social Atmosphere	(50.33, 65.45, 77.15)	64.59	75.19	54.31
Local Gastronomy	(42.93, 58.48, 72.66)	58.14	70.68	48.21
Tourist Attractions	(50.95, 65.45, 76.53)	64.59	78.86	40.56
Leisure and Entertainment	(54.25, 72.22, 81.41)	70.03	92.50	59.06
Ease of integration	(59.81, 81.65, 87.40)	77.63	92.50	55.00
Lifestyle	(59.81, 80.70, 87.05)	77.07	92.50	63.75
Banks. Monetary Exchange	(56.59, 78.43, 84.91)	74.59	92.50	36.72
Shops. Commercial Activity	(44.77, 61.65, 74.63)	60.68	78.64	38.33
Accessibility of Roads	(35.72, 51.57, 66.78)	51.41	65.45	42.92
Means of Transport	(36.72, 51.60, 66.23)	51.54	64.22	44.50
Variety of Types of Houses	(51.65, 67.15, 78.02)	66.00	77.50	53.75
House Rental Costs	(59.05, 79.30, 86.12)	75.94	92.50	62.63
Quality of Water	(66.29, 92.41, 94.88)	86.50	92.50	73.28
Quality of Air	(60.46, 76.67, 84.42)	74.55	81.25	59.86
Quality of Grounds and Cleanliness	(47.07, 64.12, 77.51)	63.20	77.41	50.00
General Vegetation/Green Space	(49.59, 66.26, 78.21)	65.08	74.13	50.00
Medical Assistance	(65.15, 91.65, 94.50)	85.74	92.50	60.78
Quality of Urban Services	(58.92, 78.10, 85.34)	75.12	92.50	57.97
Access to Internet	(54.80, 71.25, 80.70)	69.50	92.50	48.00
Tourist Services	(48.75, 63.33, 76.12)	62.89	73.13	49.58
Education	(34.85, 49.89, 64.93)	49.89	87.68	37.17
Programs for Foreigners	(56.69, 79.59, 85.58)	75.37	92.50	52.81
Benefits for Retirees	(44.23, 61.54, 73.50)	60.20	92.50	37.68
Sport facilities	(34.85, 49.30, 64.07)	49.38	81.56	33.28

[1] A^+ and A^- are the positive and negative ideal solutions respectively (Equations (4) and (5)).

The ideal solutions were calculated according to Equations (4) and (5). Through analysis of the ideal solutions (Table 4), it is a surprise that the positive ideal solutions are represented by the highest mark in some items as, for example, cost of living, safety, access to internet, programs for foreigners or benefits for retirees. These results are very different from those obtained in the negative ideal solution in which all the groups of immigrants do not value some item at its minimum value (not important at all). There are 11 items for which the figures are lower than 50. The percentage variation between the values of the positive and negative ideal solutions can be used to conclude that four items are seen more homogeneously by the immigrants, namely quality of water and air, language and social atmosphere. The item which is seen as more heterogeneous is banks and monetary exchange.

Table 5 shows the *DEI* synthetic index obtained according to Equation (6) for the group of groups that were already commented on in Table 1. The results show that by nationality the most exigent immigrants are from Peru, Mexico, Venezuela and Cuba. It is interesting to remark that all the countries are located in South America. Female immigrants are more exigent than male immigrants. The senior group (>= 65 years old) are the most exigent immigrants if the analysis is performed by age. The analysis by marital status shows that widowed and unmarried couple immigrants are the most exigent groups. And finally, retired immigrants are more exigent than non-retired immigrants.

Table 5. *DEI* synthetic index.

Variable	Categories	DEI
Nationality	Germany	0.523
	Argentina	0.525
	Other nationality	0.454
	Other European countries	0.455
	Other South American countries	0.510
	Canada	0.484
	Colombia	0.562
	Cuba	0.600
	Iberian countries	0.518
	United States	0.427
	France	0.491
	Netherlands	0.526
	Italy	0.347
	Mexico	0.623
	Peru	0.625
	Venezuela	0.623
Gender	Male	0.474
	Female	0.547
Age	≤24 years old	0.480
	25–34 years old	0.501
	35–44 years old	0.514
	45–54 years old	0.529
	55–64 years old	0.482
	≥65 years old	0.542
Marital status	Single	0.490
	Married	0.515
	Widowed	0.583
	Divorced	0.498
	Unmarried couple	0.531
Retired	Yes	0.518
	No	0.504

Table 6 shows the elasticities of the total sample of immigrants and the marital status groups with respect to each of the items. The figures of the table can be used to conclude that *DEI* is quite inelastic with respect to all the items and for the total sample of immigrants and for all of the marital status groups under analysis. The table can be analyzed bi-dimensionally by item and group. Focusing first in the whole sample, it can be concluded that the items for which the total sample is more elastic are: (1) banks and monetary exchange; (2) benefits for retirees; and (3) access to internet. On the other hand, *DEI* for the whole sample of immigrants is more inelastic with respect to these three items: (1) language; (2) accessibility of roads; and (3) means of transport.

Table 6. Elasticity values of the total sample and age groups.

Item	Total	Single	Married	Widowed	Divorced	Unmarried Couple
Climate	0.1254	0.1284	0.1194	0.0793	0.1274	0.1100
Cost of Living	0.1252	0.1329	0.1192	0.0896	0.1251	0.1067
Safety	0.1654	0.1729	0.1615	0.1147	0.1592	0.1382
Language	0.0611	0.0620	0.0602	0.0478	0.0600	0.0530
Local Culture	0.0735	0.0749	0.0707	0.0555	0.0783	0.0637
General Image and Landscape	0.0690	0.0712	0.0664	0.0443	0.0719	0.0584
Social Atmosphere	0.0736	0.0766	0.0707	0.0556	0.0770	0.0626
Local Gastronomy	0.0715	0.0727	0.0704	0.0562	0.0681	0.0623
Tourist Attractions	0.1340	0.1437	0.1289	0.0985	0.1269	0.1144

Table 6. Cont.

Item	Total	Single	Married	Widowed	Divorced	Unmarried Couple
Leisure and Entertainment	0.1289	0.1357	0.1235	0.1122	0.1248	0.1121
Ease of integration	0.1578	0.1723	0.1470	0.1181	0.1596	0.1342
Lifestyle	0.1211	0.1232	0.1183	0.0922	0.1176	0.1062
Banks. Monetary Exchange	0.2246	0.2263	0.2200	0.1588	0.2297	0.2036
Shops. Commercial Activity	0.1330	0.1389	0.1297	0.1003	0.1201	0.1259
Accessibility of Roads	0.0636	0.0668	0.0609	0.0494	0.0609	0.0541
Means of Transport	0.0559	0.0562	0.0540	0.0370	0.0538	0.0500
Variety of Types of Houses	0.0854	0.0877	0.0820	0.0560	0.0818	0.0753
House Rental Costs	0.1241	0.1301	0.1194	0.1013	0.1150	0.1114
Quality of Water	0.0897	0.0938	0.0861	0.0574	0.0897	0.0741
Quality of Air	0.0860	0.0896	0.0832	0.0508	0.0858	0.0715
Quality of Grounds and Cleanliness	0.0946	0.0967	0.0913	0.0674	0.0948	0.0818
General Vegetation/Green Space	0.0850	0.0913	0.0798	0.0532	0.0871	0.0709
Medical Assistance	0.1459	0.1548	0.1392	0.0881	0.1474	0.1204
Quality of Urban Services	0.1415	0.1449	0.1397	0.1133	0.1388	0.1216
Access to Internet	0.1688	0.1762	0.1626	0.1349	0.1712	0.1419
Tourist Services	0.0804	0.0858	0.0768	0.0579	0.0757	0.0694
Education	0.1393	0.1484	0.1326	0.1214	0.1216	0.1312
Programs for Foreigners	0.1625	0.1681	0.1585	0.1236	0.1623	0.1397
Benefits for Retirees	0.1809	0.1645	0.1885	0.1561	0.2001	0.1453
Sport facilities	0.1312	0.1399	0.1239	0.1062	0.1334	0.1118

A similar analysis can be carried out now for each of the marital status groups included in the table, but for ease of exposition and in order to synthesize and be concise, the analysis will be based on the overall results for the five groups, namely single, married, widowed, divorced and unmarried couple. Thus, the analysis will be based on the 10 highest figures (more elastic pair group item) and the 10 lowest figures (more inelastic pair group item). Thus, we conclude that regarding the items, ease of integration is added to the list of the elastic items obtained for the whole sample, and that the more elastic groups are those whose marital status is single or divorced.

Analyzing the 10 more inelastic pair group items in the table, it can be seen that quality of air and green space are the two items that are now included in the list of the items for the whole sample mentioned above. The analysis by group concludes that widowed immigrants now have six of the most inelastic pairs, so it seems that this group is more inelastic than the rest of marital status groups.

3.2. The Fuzzy Clusters

Table 7 shows the three representative profiles of each cluster, and for clarity, it was decided to present the semantic scale answers instead of the respective converted TFN. For this reason, the table shows a vector of 30 values in the range 1 to 5 for each of the representative immigrants selected for each of the clusters, namely extreme exigent immigrant, extreme unneedful immigrant and intermediate exigent immigrant. The first cluster is characterized by those immigrants for which DEI synthetic indicator is closer to 1. The second cluster, on the other hand, is characterized by those immigrants who are the least exigent. And finally, the third cluster is an intermediate cluster that represents quite well the greyness area between the other two extreme clusters.

Table 7. Representatives for the clusters.

Item	Extreme Exigent	Extreme Unneedful	Intermediate
Climate	5	3	4
Cost of Living	5	1	5
Safety	5	1	5
Language	5	1	4
Local Culture	5	1	4
General Image and Landscape	5	1	4
Social Atmosphere	5	1	4
Local Gastronomy	5	1	4
Tourist Attractions	5	1	5
Leisure and Entertainment	5	1	3
Ease of integration	5	1	4
Lifestyle	5	1	5
Banks. Monetary Exchange	5	1	5
Shops. Commercial Activity	5	1	4
Accessibility of Roads	5	1	2
Means of Transport	5	1	2
Variety of Types of Houses	5	1	4
House Rental Costs	5	1	4
Quality of Water	5	1	5
Quality of Air	5	1	4
Quality of Grounds and Cleanliness	5	1	3
General Vegetation/Green Space	5	1	4
Medical Assistance	5	1	5
Quality of Urban Services	5	1	5
Access to Internet	5	1	5
Tourist Services	5	1	4
Education	5	1	1
Programs for Foreigners	5	1	5
Benefits for Retirees	5	1	4
Sport facilities	5	1	3

By analysis of Table 7, it can be seen that the representative for the extreme exigent immigrant is characterized by an immigrant who perceives all the items of the scale at the maximum value. The profile of the immigrant was an American retired and widowed woman in the senior age group scale who obtained the visa by investments and lived in a rented house. It is interesting to remark that the score of the scale for the immigrant is the maximum of 150. In empirical applications, when the scale has a relatively large number of items, this result is not common [38,65]. On the contrary, analysis of the extreme unneedful immigrant is very different as it can be seen that the representative is an immigrant who answered all the items with the minimum value with the exception of the climate that is valued as somewhat important. In this case, the score of the scale was 32 and not the minimum 30. The profile for this immigrant was a Bolivian woman of middle age between 35 and 44 years old who lived with an unmarried couple, worked and her house was borrowed. The representative immigrant for the intermediate cluster is characterized by: (1) three low valued items with a value of 1 (education) and a value of 2 (accessibility of roads and means of transport); (2) three intermediate valued items with a value of 3 (leisure and entertainment, quality of grounds and cleaning, and sport facilities); and (3) 24 high valued items with 14 and 10 items showing values of 4 and 5, respectively. Interestingly, it can be seen that the score of the scale for the intermediate exigent immigrant is 120, so the preferences are closer to the extreme exigent immigrant than to the extreme unneedful immigrant. The profile of the representative is characterized for being a married Dutch woman of middle age (35–44 years old) who worked and lived in a rented house.

Figure 1 shows the ternary plot of the whole sample of immigrants. The ternary plots represent graphically how the immigrants are distributed in the triangle according to the probability vector (weights) that characterizes the membership function that each immigrant has to belong to in each of the three clusters. The graph provides a very intuitive understanding about how the immigrants are distributed with respect to the resemblance of being more similar to extreme exigent, extreme unneedful or intermediate. At a simple glance, it seems that the majority of the immigrants are located near the base line that joins extreme exigent and intermediate immigrants. The immigrants near the upper vertex that characterizes the extreme unneedful immigrants are less in number. A summary of the graph can be obtained by the average probabilities for each of the clusters, which is as follows: (1) 26.4% for the extreme exigent cluster; (2) 4.1% for the extreme unneedful cluster; and (3) 69.4% for the intermediate cluster. The summary matches well with the distribution of the immigrants in the triangle. Thus, it can be concluded that the immigrants in Cuenca are a mixture of extreme or intermediate exigent people, and only a very small group of immigrants can be considered unneedful ones.

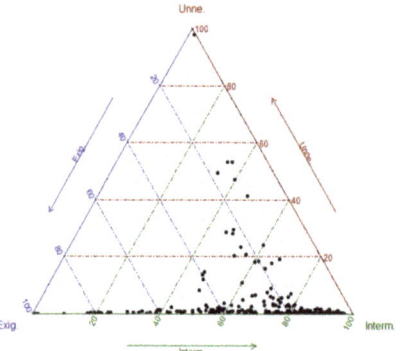

Figure 1. Immigrants' fuzzy clustering ternary graph.

This section ends with a final ANOVA analysis in which the socioeconomic variables that can affect the membership function of the fuzzy clustering method are studied. The analysis will be based on ANOVA and Tukey–Kramer coefficients, and 17 different socioeconomic and demographic variables have been used as factors to analyze differences in the distribution of immigrants according to the fuzzy clusters: (1) nationality; (2) gender; (3) age; (4) marital status; (5) occupation; (6) years of residence; (7) visa of residence; (8) visa by pension; (9) main information channels; (10) reason to come; (11) house location; (12) house tenancy; (13) house type; (14) main transport mode; (15) income; (16) main income source; and (17) expenditure in the city. Interestingly, the main sociodemographic variables, such as nationality, gender, age and marital status do not have any effect on the distribution of the fuzzy clusters. The variables that have a significant effect on the distribution are characterized by being from the economic sphere or inherent to immigrants' lifestyle. Table 8 presents the ANOVA results and the discussion of the differences observed for the factors that have a significant effect, namely on information channels, reasons to come, house location, main transport mode, income and main income source. The expenditure in the city was also a significant factor but has been omitted because the discussion is similar to that of income. The factors that do not have a significant effect are omitted from the table.

Table 8. ANOVA results.

Variable	Categories	Exigent [1]	Unneeded [1]	Interm. [1]	E.p [2]	U.p [2]	I.p [2]
Information channel	Internet	26.4%	3.2%	70.4%	0.0190	0.0000	0.0000
	Social Media	24.0%	2.4%	73.6%			
	Specialized Media	23.6%	3.7%	72.7%			
	TV ads	27.5%	3.3%	69.2%			
	Other channels	35.0%	11.1%	53.9%			
Reasons to come	Tourism	24.4%	2.9%	72.7%	0.0306	0.0002	0.0000
	Work	28.0%	5.1%	66.9%			
	Refugees	19.4%	1.0%	79.7%			
	Studies	39.4%	8.0%	52.6%			
	Retirement	30.2%	4.8%	64.9%			
	Other reasons to come	31.2%	15.8%	53.1%			
House location	Historical center	23.3%	5.2%	71.5%	0.0015	0.4797	0.0029
	Urban area	25.3%	3.2%	71.4%			
	New urban area	34.8%	4.3%	60.9%			
	Rural area	34.9%	5.4%	59.8%			
Main transport mode	Walking	26.9%	3.4%	69.7%	0.0433	0.0004	0.0001
	Bike	32.4%	11.2%	56.4%			
	Public transport	24.1%	2.7%	73.1%			
	Private car	30.1%	2.8%	67.1%			
	Motorcycle	32.4%	12.4%	55.2%			
	Taxi	19.8%	3.3%	76.9%			
	Other transport mode	14.7%	0.4%	84.9%			
Income	ECS 300 or less	28.4%	8.5%	63.2%	0.0002	0.0055	0.0000
	ECS 301–600	21.4%	3.3%	75.3%			
	ECS 601–900	22.9%	2.7%	74.4%			
	ECS 901–1200	36.0%	2.4%	61.6%			
	ECS 1201–1500	31.4%	1.6%	67.1%			
	More than ECS 1500	31.5%	7.2%	61.3%			
Main income source	Salary	24.0%	3.2%	72.8%	0.0476	0.0304	0.0031
	Self-employed salary	29.2%	3.0%	67.7%			
	Other income source	29.3%	6.4%	64.3%			

[1] The figures represent the average probabilities. [2] The figures represent the probability value of the Tukey–Kramer coefficient that can be used to determine the confidence level for which the differences in the probability values are observed for the exigent, unneeded and intermediate immigrants.

The ANOVA results show that exigent immigrants are more numerous when: (1) they receive the information from other channels; (2) they come for studies; (3) they live in the new urban area or in the rural area; (4) they use bikes or motorcycles as the main mode of transport; (5) they are more affluent; and (6) their main source of income comes from self-employment or rent. On the other hand, there are more numerous unneeded immigrants when: (1) they receive the information from other channels; (2) they have other reasons to come; (3) they use bikes or motorcycles as the main mode of transport; (4) they present a duality with respect to the income (lowest and highest income group are more represented in the cluster); and (5) the main source of income comes from rent.

4. Discussion

4.1. Fuzzy Hybrid Model

It was seen that for the average immigrant, the highest valued items were quality of urban services, programs for foreigners, house rental costs, climate, lifestyle, ease of integration, safety, cost of living, medical assistance and quality of water. Meanwhile, there were only two items for which the immigrants in Cuenca were not very exigent, namely sport facilities and education. The comparison of the results with previous studies cannot be directly extracted as several previous studies have analyzed the influence of the determinants for explaining the dependent variable to emigrate or not, and not the influence of each determinant on a synthetic exigency scale as in our case. Nevertheless, the comparison will provide interesting insights into the results obtained in the study.

Migration can be explained by multiple factors, and among them, the most important drivers are the advantageous exchange rate of the currencies between the destination and the origin of the pension, low costs of living and adequate medical services [66]. A warmer climate and lower cost of living are also important drivers to emigrate to other countries for pensioner migrations in Japan, Italy, Great Britain and the United States [67].

It seems that when societies become more prosperous, seniors tend to move to milder climate areas in which their cost of living is lower. This evidence is in line with the findings of [21,32,34], in which the main determinants for immigrants are not exclusively formed by the mild climate and proximity to the sea, but also for the beautiful landscape, culture, gastronomy and a good presence of commercial areas. For example, the pensioner migration from Great Britain to Tuscany has a long tradition, and the destination is selected because of its mild climate conditions, the seaside proximity, its beautiful landscape, high culture, and its great lifestyle immortalized with the concept of the Italian "dolce vita" [34].

Regarding the programs for pensioners, the results are in the same line of [27,34,68], in which individuals choose their emigration destinations due to policies that support pensioners and foreigners from host countries, but above all, they require to be able to take advantage of medical assistance. In this context, retirees spend a high monthly average fee on taxes, entertainment, medical services, and so on in their destinations. This means that emigrating to a less developed country allows them to live a comfortable life for less. Two types of immigrants can be distinguished: those who aim to improve the quality of their life by spending less than in their countries of origin and those who, on the other hand, emigrate to find a warm climate and fun at all costs [34].

From our analysis, it emerged that there were some factors that immigrants do not consider very much when choosing a destination to emigrate. Although, young people from the southern hemisphere dream successfully of sport that generates migratory flows to the countries of the northern hemisphere [69], this finding has not been empirically supported by our results. Similarly, to findings in [70], education could be a stimulus to emigrate but this is not necessarily supported by all the immigrants.

Regarding, the house location, our results concurred with [35], in which migrants move to rural areas to ensure a peaceful lifestyle, seeking a peaceful environment from their destinations to be able to spend a peaceful life. In fact, according to the analysis of [71], emigrants consider green space, access to good water, and air quality to be important. For example, the authors found that urban residents had better access to clean water because China's government gave a higher priority to the quality of drinking water in urban areas than in rural areas.

The analysis of the positive ideal solutions concluded that some additional items are highly valued by some population groups, such as access to internet and benefits for retirees. In addition, the percentage variation between the values of the positive and negative ideal solutions was used to conclude that four items were seen more homogeneously by the immigrants, namely quality of water and air, language and social atmospheric. Meanwhile, only one item, banks and monetary exchange, was seen very heterogeneously.

Digital nomads are defined as individuals who can work remotely from any location, taking advantage of portable computing technologies and widespread internet access [72]. For this group of immigrants characterized by lifestyles based on mobility, minimalism (unneedful orientation), uncertainty and being risk-takers instead of having a sedentary life, materialism, stability and comfort, internet access is absolutely crucial. These new immigrants could select any city of the world which could develop vibrant communities that facilitate the participation in professional and social networks, with good weather, fast internet access and a minimum cost of living.

Regarding pensioners, it was found that due to their growing financial independence and improved health, retirees are nowadays more pushed to emigrate not for work reasons, but rather to improve their health, standards of living as well as and environmental conditions [69].

The synthetic index was used to analyze immigration in Cuenca for a number of population groups based on nationality, gender, age, marital status and whether the immigrants are retired or not. The results showed that Peruvians, Mexicans, Venezuelans and Cubans were the most exigent immigrants of the whole set of nationalities. Females were more exigent than males. The senior age immigrants were more exigent than other age groups. The widowed and unmarried couple immigrants were more exigent than other marital status groups. And finally, retired immigrants were more exigent than non-retired immigrants.

Freirer and Holloway [14] used mixed methods to find that "a Cuban interviewee explained, how she chose Ecuador for many reasons, first because it is a country that is very open to tourists, immigrants, the world. It is a country more open to the world, and apart from that because of the Spanish language, there is a great amount of mixture of Latinos, here in Ecuador, the same Colombians, Peruvians". Thus, it can be inferred that cultural values that are shared by Hispanic heritage can play a determinant role explaining the exigency index.

Age is an important determinant for the number of immigrants at aggregated country levels because a young age structure in the destination was found to be positively associated with a lower number of immigrants, while a young age structure in the origin was associated with a higher number of immigrants [20].

Palloni et al. [22] contended that gender captured unmeasured factors that influenced the propensity to migrate. In particular, many cultural factors, such as household heads, siblings' education, and patriarchal vs. matriarchal roles are highly affected by gender. For example, in many countries the female role is mainly seen as a follower instead of a leader in issues related to reasons to emigrate.

4.2. Elasticities, Fuzzy Clustering and ANOVA

The analysis of elasticities showed that the average immigrant in Cuenca is more elastic with respect to: (1) banks and monetary exchange; (2) benefits for retirees; and (3) access to internet; and more inelastic with respect to: (1) language; (2) accessibility of roads; and (3) means of transport. The three profiles for the fuzzy clusters' representatives were found to be a very extreme exigent American immigrant who answered that every item of the scale was very important, a very extreme unneedful Bolivian immigrant who answered that all the items of the scale were not important at all with the exception of the climate (somewhat important), and finally a Dutch immigrant who was the representative for the intermediate exigent cluster obtained a score of 120 on the scale, which is closer to the extreme exigent representative than to the extreme unneedful representative. The results showed that the immigrants in Cuenca are more similar to the intermediate and the extreme exigent representatives than to the exigent unneedful representative. The probability of the latter cluster was only 4.1 percent, so unneedful immigrants are not common in Cuenca.

The ANOVA results showed that a number of variables had a significant effect on the probability of belonging to the three fuzzy clusters, namely information channels, reasons to come, house location, main transport mode, income, expenditure in the city and main income source. Specifically, the exigent immigrants were found to be more numerous when: (1) they received the information from other channels; (2) they came for studies; (3) they lived in the new urban area or in the rural area; (4) they used bikes or motorcycles as the main mode of transport; (5) they were more affluent; and (6) their main source of income came from self-employment or rent. On the other hand, more numerous unneeded immigrants were found when: (1) they received the information from other channels; (2) they had other reasons to come; (3) they used bikes or motorcycles as the main mode of transport; (4) they presented a duality with respect to the income (lowest and highest income group were more represented in the cluster); and (5) the main source of income came from rent.

Other information channels usually refer to friends or relatives who have previously emigrated to Cuenca, and this result is concordant with [70,73], as migration is highly influenced by the size of the network of previous migrants at destination. It seems evident that those who plan to emigrate to Cuenca, whenever possible, will connect with past migrants to establish the main advantages and disadvantages about Cuenca, thereby significantly reducing the transaction costs of gathering information. It seems also reasonable to highlight that the number of migrants in Cuenca could also be used as an important source of social capital that enhances the lifestyle and well-being of immigrants. There are also specialized media channels that have created a ranking of the best cities to live, and internet access is popularizing this type of information. Real estate dealers have also developed websites with detailed information about many aspects of seniors' life. There are also other social media channels, such as Facebook and twitter accounts, that provide sharing experiences of other immigrants in different destinations.

Regarding the main income source and transport modes, it was not easy to find any comparable evidence. Marjavaara [35] analyzed a cohort of Swedish residents aged 55–70 years to study the retirement transition migration because they argued that this cohort could be compared to that of retirement-age persons. They contended that the migrant drivers are quite similar to those of the cohort of having an empty nest, which is preparing its lifestyle for a transition to the age of retirement. Meanwhile, the issue of the main transport mode used by immigrants in the less developed countries has been clearly unexplored. In Canada, young people appeared to be using public transit more than the previous generations, reversing twentieth century trends, but the importance of such findings depends on whether high transit and other more environmental transport modes use could be affected by residents' lifestyles [74].

5. Conclusions

The migratory phenomenon has been extensively studied as a phenomenon of income of new migrants into European and North American countries. On the other hand, however, there are very distinct realities, such as the case of Ecuador, an upper-middle-income country according to the World Bank, which can be considered both a relatively safe and economically attractive southern destination that can be used as a migratory intermediate stop toward North America [14] that has not been analyzed very much. Paradoxically, Rafael Correa, a former president of Ecuador, promoted a number of legislations that favor the entrance of migrants to the country through guaranteeing universal citizenship and free human mobility in a period in which there was also a massive Ecuadorian emigration. Freier and Holloway [14] recommended migration scholars to better reconceptualize immigrants' drivers beyond simplistic assumptions based on economic motivation and well-being improvements. They also contended that restrictive migrant policies of high-income countries will divert some of the immigrants to the South. Our study contributes to both of the commented issues with a more profound analysis beyond economic and well-being motivations, and with an analysis of a city located in Ecuador. Thus, the study analyses the exigencies of immigrants residing in Cuenca, Ecuador based on a fuzzy hybrid method and a fuzzy clustering method providing some insights on the little knowledge that exists in this region of the world.

As stated, the analysis is based on two related methods: a fuzzy hybrid TOPSIS method and a fuzzy clustering method that have been previously applied in other contexts [8,39,60,64,65]. Results provide interesting insights that were already discussed. First, the importance given to the different items included in the scale is very heterogeneous across different population groups. Second, the fuzzy clustering approach used in the study provides a more flexible characterization of immigrants than other classical clustering methods, and the partitioning around the three selected real immigrants instead of centroids used in other studies are more suitable for results interpretation. The membership coefficients obtained in the fuzzy clustering were analyzed through ANOVA, and results showed that there are some covariates, which have a significant effect on the probability of giving more or less importance to the scale items, such as information channels, reasons to come, house location, main transport mode, income, expenditure in the city and main income source. It was also interesting to note that the same covariate could have a significant effect for being positively associated to extreme exigent and unneedful immigrants. These results should be taken into account for those policy makers in charge of developing immigration policies in Ecuador.

This study is not exempt from a number of limitations that could be studied in a future agenda. For example, the scale to study the importance given to some attributes in order to emigrate to a different country is still under researched, and a more suitable and robust scale needs to be developed. Other interesting issues that can be analyzed in the future are more related to the fuzzy clustering method regarding to the effects of the fuzziness coefficient m, the values of the w coefficients that can be internally calculated within the model or the selection of other medoids in order to analyze the stability of the results.

Author Contributions: Conceptualization, J.C.M. and N.S.B.-S.; methodology, J.C.M.; software, J.C.M. and A.I.; validation, J.C.M., N.S.B.-S. and A.I.; investigation, N.S.B.-S.; resources, N.S.B.-S.; data curation, N.S.B.-S.; writing—original draft preparation, J.C.M., N.S.B.-S. and A.I.; writing—review and editing, J.C.M. All authors have read and agreed to the published version of the manuscript.

Funding: This research received no external funding.

Institutional Review Board Statement: Not applicable.

Informed Consent Statement: Informed consent was obtained from all subjects involved in the study.

Data Availability Statement: The datasets generated during the current study are not publicly available due to participants' confidentiality but are available from the corresponding author on reasonable request.

Acknowledgments: We acknowledge the support given by some colleagues at the Universidad de Cuenca as well as at the Universidad Técnica Particular de Loja during the focus group when the questionnaire was designed. The help received by the master's students for the questionnaire administration is also highly appreciated. We also acknowledge the constructive comments raised by the editor and three anonymous reviewers.

Conflicts of Interest: The authors declare no conflict of interest.

References

1. De Coninck, D. Migrant categorizations and European public opinion: Diverging attitudes towards immigrants and refugees. *J. Ethn. Migr. Stud.* **2020**, *46*, 1667–1686. [CrossRef]
2. Goodman, S.; Burke, S.; Liebling, H.; Zasada, D. 'I Can't Go Back Because If I Go Back I Would Die': How Asylum Seekers Manage Talk about Returning Home by Highlighting the Importance of Safety. *J. Community Appl. Soc. Psychol.* **2015**, *25*, 327–339. [CrossRef]
3. Heath, A.; Davidov, E.; Ford, R.; Green, E.G.T.; Ramos, A.; Schmidt, P. Contested terrain: Explaining divergent patterns of public opinion towards immigration within Europe. *J. Ethn. Migr. Stud.* **2020**, *46*, 475–488. [CrossRef]
4. Hatton, T.J. Public opinion on immigration in Europe: Preference and salience. *Eur. J. Polit. Econ.* **2020**, *66*, 101969. [CrossRef]
5. Meuleman, B.; Abts, K.; Schmidt, P.; Pettigrew, T.F.; Davidov, E. Economic conditions, group relative deprivation and ethnic threat perceptions: A cross-national perspective. *J. Ethn. Migr. Stud.* **2020**, *46*, 593–611. [CrossRef]
6. Davidov, E.; Seddig, D.; Gorodzeisky, A.; Raijman, R.; Schmidt, P.; Semyonov, M. Direct and indirect predictors of opposition to immigration in Europe: Individual values, cultural values, and symbolic threat. *J. Ethn. Migr. Stud.* **2020**, *46*, 553–573. [CrossRef]
7. Martín, J.C.; Indelicato, A. A DEA MCDM Approach Applied to ESS8 Dataset for Measuring Immigration and Refugees Citizens' Openness. *J. Int. Migr. Integr.* **2021**, 1–21. [CrossRef]
8. Martín, J.C.; Bustamante-Sánchez, N.S. A cultural analysis of the secondary housing tourism in Vilcabamba, Ecuador. *Int. J. Hous. Mark. Anal.* **2019**, *12*, 604–625. [CrossRef]
9. Jaakson, R. Second-home domestic tourism. *Ann. Tour. Res.* **1986**, *13*, 367–391. [CrossRef]
10. Gustafson, P. Retirement migration and transnational lifestyles. *Ageing Soc.* **2001**, *21*, 371–394. [CrossRef]
11. Hall, K.; Hardill, I. Retirement migration, the "other" story: Caring for frail elderly British citizens in Spain. *Ageing Soc.* **2016**, *36*, 562–585. [CrossRef] [PubMed]
12. Alba, R.; Foner, N. *Strangers No More: Immigration and the Challenges of Integration in North America and Western Europe*; Princeton University Press: Princeton, NJ, USA, 2015; ISBN 9781400865901.

13. Hayes, M. "Sometimes you gotta get out of your comfort zone": Retirement migration and active ageing in Cuenca, Ecuador. *Ageing Soc.* **2021**, *41*, 1221–1239. [CrossRef]
14. Freier, L.F.; Holloway, K. The Impact of Tourist Visas on Intercontinental South-South Migration: Ecuador's Policy of "Open Doors" as a Quasi-Experiment. *Int. Migr. Rev.* **2019**, *53*, 1171–1208. [CrossRef]
15. Hanson, G.H.; Robertson, R.; Spilimbergo, A. Does Border Enforcement Protect U.S. Workers from Illegal Immigration? *Rev. Econ. Stat.* **2002**, *84*, 73–92. [CrossRef]
16. Stringer, A. Crossing the Border: Latino Attitudes toward Immigration Policy. *J. Int. Migr. Integr.* **2018**, *19*, 701–715. [CrossRef]
17. Miyagiwa, K.; Sato, Y. Illegal immigration, unemployment, and multiple destinations. *J. Reg. Sci.* **2019**, *59*, 118–144. [CrossRef]
18. De Haas, H. A theory of migration: The aspirations-capabilities framework. *Comp. Migr. Stud.* **2021**, *9*, 8. [CrossRef]
19. Pagogna, R.; Sakdapolrak, P. Disciplining migration aspirations through migration-information campaigns: A systematic review of the literature. *Geogr. Compass* **2021**, *15*, e12585. [CrossRef]
20. Kim, K.; Cohen, J.E. Determinants of International Migration Flows to and from Industrialized Countries: A Panel Data Approach beyond Gravity. *Int. Migr. Rev.* **2010**, *44*, 899–932. [CrossRef]
21. Aziz, N.; Chowdhury, M.; Cooray, A. Why do people from wealthy countries migrate? *Eur. J. Polit. Econ.* **2021**, 102156. [CrossRef]
22. Palloni, A.; Massey, D.S.; Ceballos, M.; Espinosa, K.; Spittel, M. Social Capital and International Migration: A Test Using Information on Family Networks. *Am. J. Sociol.* **2001**, *106*, 1262–1298. [CrossRef]
23. Williams, N.E.; Hughes, C.; Bhandari, P.; Thornton, A.; Young-DeMarco, L.; Sun, C.; Swindle, J. When Does Social Capital Matter for Migration? A Study of Networks, Brokers, and Migrants in Nepal. *Int. Migr. Rev.* **2020**, *54*, 964–991. [CrossRef] [PubMed]
24. Thielemann, E.R. How Effective are National and EU Policies in the Area of Forced Migration? *Refug. Surv. Q.* **2012**, *31*, 21–37. [CrossRef]
25. Jo, H.M. Constitutionalizing trans-border nationhood: From Latin American perspectives. *Asian J. Law Soc.* **2020**, *7*, 61–84. [CrossRef]
26. Doña Reveco, C.; Finn, V. Conflicting Priorities in South American Migration Governance. *Bull. Lat. Am. Res.* **2021**, 1–16. [CrossRef]
27. Palop-García, P.; Pedroza, L. Do Diaspora Engagement Policies Endure? An Update of the Emigrant Policies Index (EMIX) to 2017. *Glob. Policy* **2021**, *12*, 361–371. [CrossRef]
28. Hammoud-Gallego, O. A Liberal Region in a World of Closed Borders? The Liberalization of Asylum Policies in Latin America, 1990–2020. *Int. Mig. Rev.* **2022**, *56*, 63–96. [CrossRef]
29. Solano, G.; Wali, A.; Yar, A. *Gaps in Migration Research. Review of Migration Theories and the Quality and Compatibility of Migration Data on the National and International Level. Migration Policies at the Local Level: The Case of Belgian Municipalities View Project*; HIVA-Research Institute for Work and Society: Leuven, Belgium, 2020.
30. Pedroza, L.; Palop-García, P. Diaspora policies in comparison: An application of the Emigrant Policies Index (EMIX) for the Latin American and Caribbean region. *Polit. Geogr.* **2017**, *60*, 165–178. [CrossRef]
31. Müller, D.K. 20 years of Nordic second-home tourism research: A review and future research agenda. *Scand. J. Hosp. Tour.* **2021**, *21*, 91–101. [CrossRef]
32. Stylidis, D.; Cherifi, B.; Melewar, T.C. Exploring Czechs' and Greeks' mental associations of London: A tourist destination or a place to live in? *J. Destin. Mark. Manag.* **2021**, *19*, 100530. [CrossRef]
33. Müller, D.K.; Hoogendoorn, G. Second Homes: Curse or Blessing? A Review 36 Years Later. *Scand. J. Hosp. Tour.* **2013**, *13*, 353–369. [CrossRef]
34. Pytel, S.; Rahmonov, O.; Ruman, M. Internal and external migrations of pensioners in Poland: A directional typology. *Popul. Space Place* **2020**, *26*, e2330. [CrossRef]
35. Marjavaara, R.; Lundholm, E. Does Second-Home Ownership Trigger Migration in Later Life? *Popul. Space Place* **2016**, *22*, 228–240. [CrossRef]
36. Behdioğlu, S.; Acar, E.; Burhan, H.A. Evaluating service quality by fuzzy SERVQUAL: A case study in a physiotherapy and rehabilitation hospital. *Total Qual. Manag. Bus. Excell.* **2019**, *30*, 301–319. [CrossRef]
37. Martínez, M.P.; Cremasco, C.P.; Gabriel Filho, L.R.A.; Braga Junior, S.S.; Bednaski, A.V.; Quevedo-Silva, F.; Correa, C.M.; da Silva, D.; Moura-Leite Padgett, R.C. Fuzzy inference system to study the behavior of the green consumer facing the perception of greenwashing. *J. Clean. Prod.* **2020**, *242*, 116064. [CrossRef]
38. Leon, S.; Martín, J.C. A fuzzy segmentation analysis of airline passengers in the U.S. based on service satisfaction. *Res. Transp. Bus. Manag.* **2020**, *37*, 100550. [CrossRef]
39. Martin, J.C.; Román, C.; Moreira, P.; Moreno, R.; Oyarce, F. Does the access transport mode affect visitors' satisfaction in a World Heritage City? The case of Valparaiso, Chile. *J. Transp. Geogr.* **2021**, *91*, 102969. [CrossRef]
40. Herrera, F.; Herrera-Viedma, E. Linguistic decision analysis: Steps for solving decision problems under linguistic information. *Fuzzy Sets Syst.* **2000**, *115*, 67–82. [CrossRef]
41. Zadeh, L.A. Fuzzy Sets. *Inf. Control* **1965**, *8*, 338–353. [CrossRef]
42. Zimmermann, H.J. *Fuzzy Set Theory and Its Applications*, 2nd ed.; Springer Science: Berlin/Heidelberg, Germany, 2013.
43. Mendel, J.M. *Uncertain Rule-Based Fuzzy Logic Systems: Introduction and New Directions*, 2nd ed.; Springer: Cham, Switzerland, 2017.
44. Kaufmann, A.; Gupta, M.M. *Introduction to Fuzzy Arithmetic Theory and Application*; Van Nortrand Reinhold: New York, NY, USA, 1985.

45. Zimmermann, H.J. *Fuzzy Set Theory and Its Applications*, 4th ed.; Kluwer Academic Publishers: Nowell, MA, USA, 2001; ISBN 9789401038706.
46. Bector, C.R.; Chandra, S. *Fuzzy Mathematical Programming and Fuzzy Matrix Games*; Springer: Berlin/Heidelberg, Germany, 2005; ISBN 3-540-23729-1.
47. Mamdani, E.H.; Assilian, S. An Experiment in Linguistic Synthesis with a Fuzzy Logic Controller. *Int. J. Man-Mach. Stud.* **1975**, *7*, 1–13. [CrossRef]
48. Zadeh, L.A. The Concept of a Linguistic Variable and its Application to Approximate Reasoning-I. *Inf. Sci.* **1975**, *8*, 199–249. [CrossRef]
49. Hwang, C.; Yoon, K. *Multiple Attribute Decision Making: Methods and Application*; Springer: New York, NY, USA, 1981.
50. Chen, C. Extensions of the TOPSIS for group decision-making under fuzzy environment. *Fuzzy Sets Syst.* **2000**, *114*, 1–9. [CrossRef]
51. Chu, T.C. Selecting plant location via a fuzzy TOPSIS approach. *Int. J. Adv. Manuf. Technol.* **2002**, *20*, 859–864. [CrossRef]
52. Chen, C.T. A fuzzy approach to select the location of the distribution center. *Fuzzy Sets Syst.* **2001**, *118*, 65–73. [CrossRef]
53. Buckley, J.J. Ranking alternatives using fuzzy numbers. *Fuzzy Sets Syst.* **1985**, *15*, 21–31. [CrossRef]
54. Li, D.F. Compromise ratio method for fuzzy multi-attribute group decision making. *Appl. Soft Comput. J.* **2007**, *7*, 807–817. [CrossRef]
55. Zhao, R.; Govind, R. Algebraic characteristics of extended fuzzy numbers. *Inf. Sci.* **1991**, *54*, 103–130. [CrossRef]
56. Kaufman, A.; Gupta, M. *Fuzzy Mathematical Models in Engineering and Management Science*; Elsevier: New York, NY, USA, 1988.
57. Chen, S.-M. Evaluating weapon systems using fuzzy arithmetic operations. *Fuzzy Sets Syst.* **1996**, *77*, 265–276. [CrossRef]
58. Zeleny, M. *Multiple Criteria Decision Making*; McGraw-Hill: New York, NY, USA, 1982.
59. D'Urso, P.D. Clustering of fuzzy data. In *Advances in Fuzzy Clustering and Its Applications*; Valente de Oliveira, J., Pedrycz, W., Eds.; J. Wiley and Sons: Chichester, UK, 2007; pp. 155–192.
60. D'Urso, P.D.; Disegna, M.; Massari, R.; Osti, L. Fuzzy segmentation of postmodern tourists. *Tour. Manag.* **2016**, *55*, 297–308. [CrossRef]
61. Caruso, G.; Gattone, S.A.; Balzanella, A.; Di Battista, T. Cluster Analysis: An Application to a Real Mixed-Type Data Set. In *Models and Theories in Social Systems*; Flaut, C., Hošková-Mayerová, Š., Flaut, D., Eds.; Springer International Publishing: Cham, Switzerland, 2019; pp. 525–533. ISBN 978-3-030-00084-4.
62. Dolnicar, S.; Leisch, F. Segmenting Markets by Bagged Clustering. *Australas. Mark. J.* **2004**, *12*, 51–65. [CrossRef]
63. D'Urso, P.; Giordani, P. A weighted fuzzy c-means clustering model for fuzzy data. *Comput. Stat. Data Anal.* **2006**, *50*, 1496–1523. [CrossRef]
64. D'Urso, P.; Disegna, M.; Massari, R.; Prayag, G. Knowledge-Based Systems Bagged fuzzy clustering for fuzzy data: An application to a tourism market. *Knowl.-Based Syst.* **2015**, *73*, 335–346. [CrossRef]
65. Martín, J.C.; Moreira, P.; Román, C. A hybrid-fuzzy segmentation analysis of residents' perception towards tourism in Gran Canaria. *Tour. Econ.* **2020**, *26*, 1282–1304. [CrossRef]
66. Aguila, E.; Zissimopoulos, J. Retirement and health benefits for Mexican migrant workers returning from the United States. *Int. Soc. Secur. Rev.* **2013**, *66*, 101–125. [CrossRef]
67. Longino, C.F.; Bradley, D.E. Geographical distribution and migration. In *Aging and the Social Sciences*; Binstock, R.H., Georg, L.K., Eds.; Oxford Univeristy Press: Oxford, UK, 2001; pp. 103–213.
68. Kureková, L. Welfare Systems as Emigration Factor: Evidence from the New Accession States. *JCMS J. Common Mark. Stud.* **2013**, *51*, 721–739. [CrossRef]
69. Cowper, D.C.; Longino, C.F.; Kubal, J.D.; Manheim, L.M.; Dienstfrey, S.J.; Palmer, J.M. The Retirement Migration of U.S. Veterans, 1960, 1970, 1980, and 1990. *J. Appl. Gerontol.* **2000**, *19*, 123–137. [CrossRef]
70. Van Dalen, H.P.; Groenewold, G.; Schoorl, J.J. Out of Africa: What drives the pressure to emigrate? *J. Popul. Econ.* **2005**, *18*, 741–778. [CrossRef]
71. Chen, H.; Liu, Y.; Zhu, Z.; Li, Z. Does where you live matter to your health? Investigating factors that influence the self-rated health of urban and rural Chinese residents: Evidence drawn from Chinese General Social Survey data. *Health Qual. Life Outcomes* **2017**, *15*, 78. [CrossRef]
72. Mancinelli, F. Digital nomads: Freedom, responsibility and the neoliberal order. *Inf. Technol. Tour.* **2020**, *22*, 417–437. [CrossRef]
73. Docquier, F.; Peri, G.; Ruyssen, I. The Cross-country Determinants of Potential and Actual Migration. *Int. Migr. Rev.* **2014**, *48*, 37–99. [CrossRef]
74. Grimsrud, M.; El-Geneidy, A. Transit to eternal youth: Lifecycle and generational trends in Greater Montreal public transport mode share. *Transportation* **2014**, *41*, 1–19. [CrossRef]

Article

On the Factors of Successful e-Commerce Platform Design during and after COVID-19 Pandemic Using Extended Fuzzy AHP Method

Dušan J. Simjanović [1,*], Nemanja Zdravković [1] and Nenad O. Vesić [2]

1 Faculty of Information Technology, Belgrade Metropolitan University, 11000 Belgrade, Serbia; nemanja.zdravkovic@metropolitan.ac.rs
2 Mathematical Institute, Serbian Academy of Sciences and Arts, 11000 Belgrade, Serbia; n.o.vesic@outlook.com
* Correspondence: dusan.simjanovic@metropolitan.ac.rs

Abstract: The ongoing COVID-19 pandemic has caused a paradigm shift in all aspects of contemporary human life. Everyday activities such as shopping have shifted from traditional methods to the ever-more growing online variants, allowing for an increase in electronic commerce (e-commerce) industry. As more services become available online, consumers often rely on trusted services, which are often reflected on the web and mobile platforms they are presented on. In this paper, we study the factors for successful e-commerce platform design in the Western Balkans region using Fuzzy Analytical Hierarchy Process (FAHP) with triangular fuzzy numbers. After an extensive literature overview, interviews with representatives of top-ranking e-commerce companies in the region, and the analysis of experts' opinions, we select a number of factors and sub-factors for prioritization, taking into account pre-pandemic factors, as well as the ones of the pandemic itself. We extend the FAHP model, which now consists of five (instead of three) points of view. Finally, we present and discuss the results in the form of tables and graphs, as well as an overall recommendation of what should be taken into account when designing an e-commerce platform. Our results rank service quality and security factors first and criteria such as multilingual support last.

Keywords: B2C e-commerce; Fuzzy AHP; MCDM; pandemic

Citation: Simjanović, D.J.; Zdravković, N.; Vesić, N.O. On the Factors of Successful e-Commerce Platform Design during and after COVID-19 Pandemic Using Extended Fuzzy AHP Method. *Axioms* **2022**, *11*, 105. https://doi.org/10.3390/axioms11030105

Academic Editor: Darjan Karabašević

Received: 12 January 2022
Accepted: 25 February 2022
Published: 26 February 2022

Publisher's Note: MDPI stays neutral with regard to jurisdictional claims in published maps and institutional affiliations.

Copyright: © 2022 by the authors. Licensee MDPI, Basel, Switzerland. This article is an open access article distributed under the terms and conditions of the Creative Commons Attribution (CC BY) license (https://creativecommons.org/licenses/by/4.0/).

1. Introduction

In the last 20 years, in the era of new technologies and modernization, Internet use has increased significantly, especially for the purposes of communication, marketing, and electronic commerce (e-commerce) [1,2]. Business of marketing has always been fluid, continuously adapting to ever-evolving consumer preferences. The migration from traditional to electronic commerce was going on long before the events caused by the COVID-19 pandemic, which has only hastened this transition. Indeed, the need for commerce digitization rapidly graduated for many businesses into means for survival once the pandemic hit. Within a matter of weeks to months, brands without online options were hastily implementing new e-commerce platforms, and those already using digital infrastructures were bracing their servers' capacities for the impact of increased online traffic. E-commerce is defined as a type of Internet use mainly to carry out business transactions in which parties communicate electronically instead of in person. These transactions significantly reduce costs, save time, increase profits, and simplify business activities, involving manufacturers, consumers, and service providers that use the Internet [3,4]. There is a clear expectation from consumers that companies should do their part to help them in their daily lives and to keep them informed. Brands must be able to meet consumers where they are and offer personalized services for their specific needs. According to Shaw [5], considering the nature of transactions, there are five major categories of e-commerce: Business to Business (B2B), where e-commerce is done exclusively between companies; Business to Customer (B2C), in which company offers services to consumers; Business to Government (B2G), where companies offer government agencies products and services through online marketing and bidding for projects; Consumer to Business (C2B), where companies tender for projects posted by consumers; and Consumer to Consumer (C2C), where consumers sell their products to consumers online.

Knowing that B2C websites, where consumers directly buy products, present the lifeblood of B2C e-commerce, companies strive to design a successful B2C website and to ultimately make business considerably practical and effective. Amazon and Alibaba, followed by eBay, Walmart, Priceline, and Rakuten, are the most dominant and significant B2C e-commerce companies [6]. The popularity and expeditious advancement of B2C e-commerce make these sorts of transactions the leading retailing channel for ordinary customers [7], and therefore Internet-based commerce in general raises the question of awareness and vulnerability of consumers' privacy and security on B2C platforms [8–10]. Security and privacy of information provided by customers are very important, especially in risky and unpredictable ambiance [11]. Factors such as transaction confidentiality, integrity, and authentication imply trust at the technology level. For the continual performance of B2C online commerce, customer relationship management plays an important role [12] and trust becomes an inevitable factor [13,14].

In recent years, multi-criteria decision-making (MCDM) has been applied in various fields of scientific research in cases where it is desirable to restructure a multi-criteria problem. At the end of this process, the most optimal choice, or an alternative one, is selected. A formal framework for modeling multidimensional decision-making problems is therefore provided by applying MCDM, especially for problems that require systems analysis, the analysis of decision complexity, the relevance of consequences, and the need for the accountability of decisions made [15]. Utilizing Fuzzy MCDM (F-MCDM), an efficient approach for evaluating multiple criteria, can be achieved to support managers, experts, and other decision makers with the goal of balancing and measuring different factors, simplifying and clarifying decisions [16].

In this paper, we study the factors for successful e-commerce platform design using Fuzzy Analytical Hierarchy Process (FAHP) based on triangular fuzzy numbers [17]. In many real-world situations, when applying decision-making approaches, human judgment alone is often insufficient and not reliable. Therefore, the use of triangular fuzzy numbers presents a viable alternative for expert judgment regarding the qualitative factors and their importance. Similarly, trapezoidal, Pythagorean, z-numbers, and the recently introduced Spherical fuzzy numbers [18] may also be considered when applying the FAHP method. Although our research is based solely on triangular fuzzy numbers, we present an extension to the current model of optimism indexes. Firstly, we conduct a literature overview, and afterwards we select a number of factors and sub-factors for prioritization, taking into account factors during the COVID-19 pandemic. As a starting point, we include FAHP with three points of view and further extend to a novel, five-points-of-view ranking of sub-criteria.

The advances in this paper are summarized in the following:

- New sub-criteria influencing e-commerce websites are introduced
- The FAHP method is extended by introducing two new points of view for the decision-maker, namely, semi-pessimistic and semi-optimistic views, with corresponding optimism indexes $\lambda = 0.25$ and $\lambda = 0.75$, respectively.
- The estimation and analysis of ranking similarities in the extended model is conducted and discussed.

As of writing this paper, the authors have not found any article or study regarding e-commerce platform design using FAHP in the region of the Western Balkans. Therefore, our main goal is to provide insights to the decision-making process and further extend one of the well-known MCDM methods. According to this goal, we formulated four research questions (RQs).

RQ1: Can the results presented in our paper help e-commerce companies of the Western Balkans region?

RQ2: Does a highly influencing sub-factor during the COVID-19 pandemic exist?

RQ3: Are there significant changes in the sub-factors ranking when the three values of an optimism index in the FAHP method are expanded to the finite or countable set of values?

RQ4: Do we have complete insight into the interrelations of sub-criteria using Extended FAHP?

The rest of the paper is organized as follows. Section 2 presents the criteria for evaluation of B2C websites, divided into factors and sub-factors. Section 3 deals with methodology used, namely, Fuzzy AHP. Finally, Section 4 gives the results, while the concluding remarks are given in Section 5.

2. Criteria for Evaluation of B2C Websites

In this Section, we firstly give a literature overview on the application of MCDM. Afterwards, we identify the main factors for the design of B2C e-commerce websites.

2.1. Literature Overview

In the past two decades, the application of MCDM and some other approaches in the process of evaluation of B2C e-commerce-website-related tasks has led to a number of published works. These approaches include but are not limited to Analytical Hierarchy Process (AHP) [14,19–21], Analytical Network Process (ANP) and Grey Relational Analysis (GRA) [22], fuzzy Technique for Order Preference by Similarity to Ideal Solution (TOPSIS) [23], VIsekriterijumska optimizacija i KOmpromisno Resenje (VIKOR) [15], fuzzy VIKOR [24], Preference Ranking Organization METHod for Enrichment Evaluation (PROMETHEE) [25], and PROMETHEE for Sustainability Assessment (PROSA) [26]. In addition, the Decision-making Trial and Evaluation Laboratory (DEMATEL) [27,28] is also a very convenient method for assessing the B2C websites criteria. Service quality has been the main aim of the majority of online platforms [29], with emphasis on the difference between levels of perceived and expected service [30]. Customer orientation, marketing, and security have been the most important factors in evaluation of five-star hotel websites in Mashhad, according to the research conducted by Ostovare and Shahraki [25], while price saving, awareness, and security took precedence in the assessment of the website quality of the Turkish e-business market [31]. In [32–34], content quality, service quality, and system availability, followed by security, ease usage, privacy, efficiency, and appearance, have been influence factors in the prioritization of B2C e-commerce websites. Similar investigations of the influence and relevance of each website quality factor have been discussed by Del Vasto-Terrientes et al. [35], Dey et al. [36], and Chou and Cheng [37]. However, there have been other relevant papers with a different viewpoint . For example, Ashraf et al. [7] have dealt with the connection between e-commerce business and their customers; Kang et al. [38] have introduced new E-S-QUAL based TOPSIS approach for evaluation of e-commerce websites; and Ong and Teh [39] have focused on consumer expectations, complaints, and compensations.

Recent studies have dealt with applying MCDM methods for better decision making. For instance, in [16], the authors deal with delivery time, order fulfillment, convenience of payment, and real-time tracking, and their influence on Last Mile Delivery companies utilizing FAHP with triangular fuzzy numbers. They conclude that utilizing MCDM techniques can be valuable for both researchers and decision-makers themselves. In [40], the authors combine data envelopment analysis and Grey model, with the goal of predicting and assessing future efficiency in e-commerce marketplaces. Finally, in [41], the authors apply triangular fuzzy numbers for FAHP, coupled with TOPSIS-Grey techniques to, respectively, determine factors and access alternatives for B2C e-commerce websites.

2.2. Main Factors for B2C e-Commerce Websites

In this paper, we have identified five major factors with corresponding sub-factors for the design of B2C e-commerce websites. The initial factors and sub-factors were obtained from the extensive literature overview given in Section 2.1. Furthermore, we have selected the top-ranking companies from the Western Balkans Region and interviewed their representatives from sales, management, and IT support sectors [42]. These companies' activities mainly deal with consumer products, with a couple of them having an e-Bay like business model. A total of 23 persons representing both companies' points of view, and customers' experience, responded to our interviews. Finally, four experts in the fields of mathematics, artificial intelligence, digital marketing, and management have acknowledged all given answers, and have, in consensus with the authors, obtained the final list of factors and their respective sub-factors.

The opinions we have collected from the representatives of e-commerce companies, professionals, and ourselves as the authors, as well as the selection and ranking of criteria and sub-criteria, will be useful to the managerial part of companies in meeting various challenges posed by the ongoing COVID-19 pandemic, as well as the challenges that will come after.

The summary of each of the main factors with corresponding sub-factors is given in Figure 1, while the detailed descriptions of each are presented below.

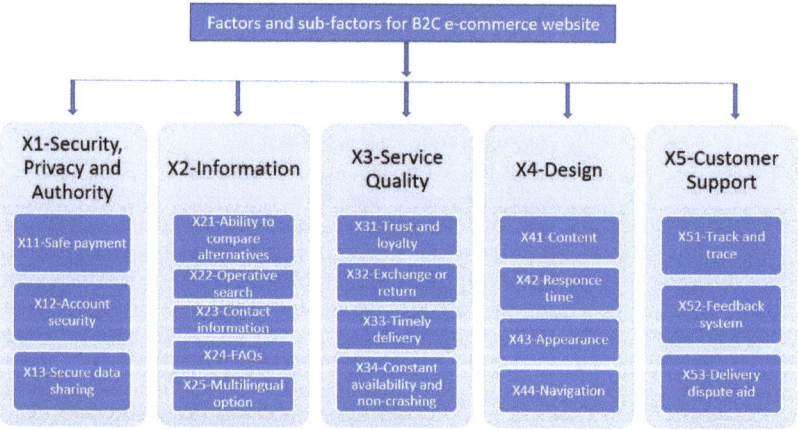

Figure 1. Factors and sub-factors for B2C website.

2.2.1. X1: Security, Privacy and Authority

Security is a dominant concern for all types of e-business web sites [43]. The presence of the somewhat insecure networks and/or servers can lead to the corruption and exploitation of customers' personal data. A company's reputation heavily relies on this type of vulnerability,, and potential attackers should not be able to have access to customers' information by accessing their databases or websites. When customers have to worry about the process of collection and maltreatment of personal information, trust towards online shops decreases [44]; Conversely, if the impression of being secure while browsing a B2C website persists, confidence and trust towards the website increases. When dealing with online payment, companies should accept well-known payment methods as well as globally recognized credit cards, in order to preserve customers' credit card information to an online account and ultimately ensure safety [10]. As soon as the pandemic shopping trends started [42], website security became paramount.

2.2.2. X2: Information

Every customer on the e-commerce website should be able to contact the company for any necessary information and/or regarding disputes [45]. The existence of company contact details also helps in solving problems and contributes to the level of confidence [46]. It is important to have correct and updated information of item availability, a search by keyword options, and the option to compare multiple items' characteristics [34,47]. Having a version of the website in other languages is mandatory nowadays, especially for those websites trading on a global scale. A section for Frequently Asked Questions or similar step-by-step guides can also be useful, especially for new shopper influx due to the pandemic.

2.2.3. X3: Service Quality

Every e-commerce website should be trustworthy. Since e-trust has a positive affect on e-loyalty, and a pleased customer often refers new potential buyers to shops, trust is essential for continual success in long-term online business [48,49]. The constant availability of websites, especially well-known ones, is recommended, with no down-time. In addition, a B2C website's significance and influence are also determined by the purchased items' delivery time, and multiple delivery options should exist [50], with a no-contact delivery option as well. There should be no delays in the process of delivery, nor should delivery schedules change often, as they have a negative influence on e-satisfaction [51]. The opportunity for item replacement or return enhances the number of customers and helps to solve any potential conflicts between the buyer and the company [39].

2.2.4. X4: Design

Online shops' long-term profitability will be strengthened by their content [52]. If the customer is bored by the content of the site, its non-creativeness; or the lack of applications, images, and/or data, or they have difficulties in finding necessary information, the sales potential will be significantly reduced [25,34]. Therefore, according to Ivory [53], good navigation is fundamental, and it should consist of clear and helpful links. Additionally, the appearance on the B2C e-commerce website must be attractive and well-organized, always keeping the customer's attention and encouraging them to come back [32]. Page load and response times should be as short as possible, because if it takes long to load or download the page (e.g., due to many graphic elements), the site's performance will suffer [54]. Customers' satisfaction will increase if the company's staff is responsible, enthusiastic, and happy to give quick responses to queries and provide help [55].

2.2.5. X5: Customer Support

It would be desirable for the B2C e-commerce website to include a customer support service as people need to know the status of the purchased item, whether their order is still in the warehouse, or whether it is being delivered [33,50]. The option of product reviews should be available to customers, and they should include realistic feedback about the negative and/or positive aspects of the service [32,56]. Reimbursement is often a subject of discussion or dispute, so B2C e-commerce should provide a help service for these types of situations [57]. One of the essential factors for a successful business is its communication method with online consumers, meaning that quick and adequate information should be provided by the company in order to increase the return visits by customers [58].

3. Methodology

The fuzzy set theory has been known for over half a century, ever since its proposal by Zadeh in 1965. Even then, it has been employed as guidance for fuzzy decision-making problems. Their original inception was intended for linguistics, and it has enabled uncertainty and imprecision to be represented, and, more importantly, constructed in a deterministic manner [59,60]. Sets defined in such a manner could therefore be identified as a generalization of the well-known set theory, enabling a decision-maker to include incomplete or partially unknown information in the decision model [61].

Whereas in the classic set theory, an element can either belong to a set or not belong at all, in fuzzy sets, the membership of an element can be described by a number from the interval $[0,1]$. Each element of this set can hence be mapped on this interval with a membership function (MF), denoted by μ. In addition, a fuzzy set can have an infinite number of different MFs.

Let all fuzzy sets defined on the set of real numbers $\mathbb{R}$ be represented as $F(\mathbb{R})$. The number $A \in F(\mathbb{R})$ is a fuzzy number if there exists $x_0 \in \mathbb{R}$ so condition $\mu_A(x_0) = 1$ holds, and $A_\lambda = [x, \mu_{A_\lambda}(x) \geq \lambda]$ is a closed interval for every $\lambda \in [0,1]$ (see [17,62]). The membership function, a component of a triangular fuzzy number (TFN) A, is a function $\mu_A : \mathbb{R} \to [0,1]$, defined as

$$\mu_F(x) = \begin{cases} \frac{x-l}{m-l}, & l \leq x \leq m, \\ \frac{u-x}{u-m}, & m \leq x \leq u, \\ 0, & \text{otherwise,} \end{cases} \quad (1)$$

where inequality $l \leq m \leq u$ holds. Variables l, m, and u are the lower, middle, and upper value, respectively, and when $l = m = u$, TFN becomes a crisp number. In the sequel, the triangular fuzzy number will be denoted by $\tilde{A} = (l, m, u)$.

Assume two TFNs, $\tilde{A}_1 = (l_1, m_1, u_1)$, $\tilde{A}_2 = (l_2, m_2, u_2)$, and scalar $k > 0$, $k \in \mathbb{R}$. The arithmetic operation properties are defined as [63–65]:

Addition:

$$\tilde{A}_1 \oplus \tilde{A}_2 = (l_1, m_1, u_1) \oplus (l_2, m_2, u_2) = (l_1 + l_2, m_1 + m_2, u_1 + u_2), \quad (2)$$

Subtraction:

$$\tilde{A}_1 \ominus \tilde{A}_2 = (l_1, m_1, u_1) \ominus (l_2, m_2, u_2) = (l_1 - u_2, m_1 - m_2, u_1 - l_2), \quad (3)$$

Multiplication:

$$\tilde{A}_1 \otimes \tilde{A}_2 = (l_1, m_1, u_1) \otimes (l_2, m_2, u_2) = (l_1 \cdot l_2, m_1 \cdot m_2, u_1 \cdot u_2), \quad (4)$$

Reciprocal:

$$\tilde{A}_1^{-1} = (l_1, m_1, u_1)^{-1} = \left(\frac{1}{u_1}, \frac{1}{m_1}, \frac{1}{l_1}\right), \quad (5)$$

Scalar multiplication:

$$k \cdot \tilde{A}_1 = k \cdot (l_1, m_1, u_1) = (k \cdot l_1, k \cdot m_1, k \cdot u_1). \quad (6)$$

Left and right side of the membership function of triangular number $\tilde{A} = (l, m, u)$, as shown in Figure 2, are denoted by $\mu_{\tilde{A}}^l = \frac{x-l}{m-l}$ and $\mu_{\tilde{A}}^r = \frac{u-x}{u-m}$, and their matching inverse functions are

$$\left(\mu_{\tilde{A}}^l\right)^{-1} = l + (m-l)y, \quad \left(\mu_{\tilde{A}}^r\right)^{-1} = u + (m-u)y, \quad y \in [0,1] \quad (7)$$

Left and right integral values of the triangular fuzzy number $\tilde{A}$, according to [66], are defined as

$$I_L(\tilde{A}) = \int_0^1 \left(\mu_{\tilde{A}}^l\right)^{-1} dy = \int_0^1 (l + (m-l)y) dy = \frac{1}{2}(m+l), \quad (8)$$

and

$$I_R(\tilde{A}) = \int_0^1 \left(\mu_{\tilde{A}}^r\right)^{-1} dy = \int_0^1 (u + (m-u)y) dy = \frac{1}{2}(m+u), \quad (9)$$

and the total integral value, according to [66] as a combination of left and right integral values, is

$$I_T^\lambda(\tilde{A}) = \lambda I_R(\tilde{A}) + (1-\lambda)I_L(\tilde{A}) = \frac{1}{2}\lambda(m+u) + \frac{1}{2}(1-\lambda)(m+l) = \frac{1}{2}(\lambda u + m + (1-\lambda)l), \qquad (10)$$

where λ represents an optimism index. The pessimistic, semi-pessimistic, balanced, semi-optimistic, and optimistic points of view of the decision-maker are, respectively, expressed by the values 0, 0.25, 0.5, 0.75, and 1.

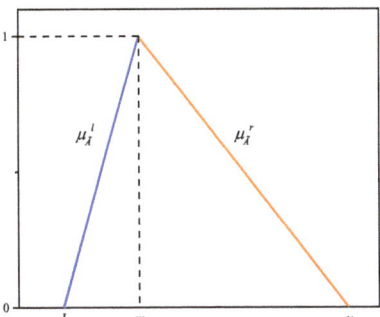

Figure 2. The representation of a triangular membership function.

Fuzzy AHP

Since its creation [67], the AHP had a respectable application in MCDM, enabling the decision makers to solve complex problems by decomposing them into a hierarchical structure, creating the comparison matrix and determining the importance of one indicator above others. The specified level of uncertainty of a team of experts (or even one expert) [68] due to the inability to express the significance of some criteria has led to the introduction of FAHP [69,70] enabling conversion of linguistic statements into mathematical expressions.

The summarized steps in FAHP are as follows [17,71]:

Step 1. Establishing the main goal and hierarchical appearance of criteria. In general, the hierarchical structure has been organized vertically: the main goal is, as the most important component, at the top; the criteria that contribute to the goal are at the intermediate levels; and the sub-criteria are at the lowest level.

Step 2. Determining the pairwise comparison matrix $\tilde{D}$ in terms of TFNs. In this step, a positive fuzzy reciprocal comparison matrix $\tilde{D} = (\tilde{d}_{ij})_{n \times n}$ with a total of $\binom{n}{2}$ comparisons of elements from a higher level with elements from a lower level is developed. The fuzzy value $\tilde{d}_{ij}$ represents the degree of relative importance between criteria; $i = j$, $\tilde{d}_{ij} = (1,1,1)$, and $\tilde{d}_{ij} = 1/\tilde{d}_{ji}$, otherwise. Table 1 shows the fuzzy scale for constructing pairwise comparisons.

Table 1. Marks, linguistic terms, and denotation of TFNs.

Mark	Linguistic Term	Denotation of TFNs	TFNs
E	Equal importance	$\tilde{1}$	(1,1,3)
AW	Absolutely weak dominance	$\tilde{2}$	(1,2,3)
EW	Extremely weak dominance	$\tilde{3}$	(1,3,5)
VW	Very weak dominance	$\tilde{4}$	(3,4,5)
FW	Fairly weak dominance	$\tilde{5}$	(3,5,7)
FS	Fairly strong dominance	$\tilde{6}$	(5,6,7)
VS	Very strong dominance	$\tilde{7}$	(5,7,9)
ES	Extremely strong dominance	$\tilde{8}$	(7,8,9)
AS	Absolutely strong dominance	$\tilde{9}$	(7,9,9)

As it was recommended in [72], a fuzzy distance of 2 and odd values as boundaries for all non-intermediate values are applied in order to achieve better consistency. There are also different scales of triangular fuzzy numbers applicable in the previous case [73–75].

The graphic representation of the used FAHP scale with all three values (lower, median, and upper) is presented in Figure 3.

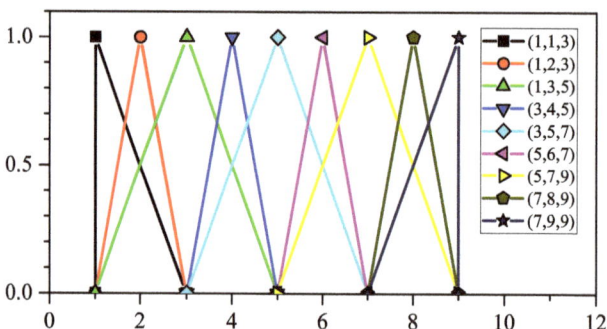

Figure 3. Graphic representation of TFNs.

Step 3. Matrix consistency review.

For a matrix $D = (d_{ij})_{n \times n}$, the consistency index CI and consistency ratio CR are calculated using eqs. from [76]:

$$CI = \frac{\lambda_{\max} - n}{n - 1}, \quad CR = \frac{CI}{RI}, \quad (11)$$

where $\lambda_{\max}$ corresponds to a maximal eigenvalue of matrices D and RI is a random index, as shown in Table 2.

Table 2. The table of Random Index numbers.

Matrix Dimension	One	Two	Three	Four	Five	Six	Seven	Eight	Nine	Ten
RI	0	0	0.58	0.90	1.12	1.24	1.32	1.41	1.45	1.49

The value $CR < 0.1$ confirms the comparison matrix consistency, while otherwise the reason for inconsistency should be found and calculations repeated [77].

Step 4. The fuzzification process.

Using the triangular fuzzy numbers from the comparison matrix $\tilde{D} = (\tilde{d}_{ij})_{n \times n'}$ applying

$$A = \sum_{i=1}^{n}\sum_{j=1}^{n} \tilde{d}_{ij} = \sum_{i=1}^{n}\sum_{j=1}^{n} (l_{ij}, m_{ij}, u_{ij}), \quad (12)$$

and

$$A^{-1} = \left(\sum_{i=1}^{n}\sum_{j=1}^{n} \tilde{d}_{ij}\right)^{-1} = \left(\frac{1}{\sum_{i=1}^{n}\sum_{j=1}^{n} l_{ij}}, \frac{1}{\sum_{i=1}^{n}\sum_{j=1}^{n} m_{ij}}, \frac{1}{\sum_{i=1}^{n}\sum_{j=1}^{n} u_{ij}}\right), \quad (13)$$

the value of the fuzzy synthetic extent is obtained as follows [64]:

$$\tilde{S}_i = \sum_{j=1}^{n} \tilde{d}_{ij} \otimes A^{-1} = \sum_{j=1}^{n} (l_{ij}, m_{ij}, u_{ij}) \otimes A^{-1}, \quad i = \overline{1, n}. \quad (14)$$

Step 5. The defuzzification process.

Next, in this step, using

$$w_i = I_T^\lambda(\widetilde{S}_i) = \frac{1}{2}(\lambda u_i + m_i + (1-\lambda)m_i), \lambda \in [0,1], i = \overline{1,n}, \qquad (15)$$

the total integral value for the TFNs $\widetilde{S}_i$ is calculated [78].

Step 6. Normalization of weight vector w and obtaining the vector for each criterion. Using

$$w_i^* = w_i \left(\sum_{i=1}^n w_i\right)^{-1}, \qquad (16)$$

the weights for all criteria are obtained.

Step 7. Ranking the weights for all sub-criteria.

The weights for each sub-criterion are obtained by multiplying the weights of the criteria and sub-criteria. Then, arranging the obtained weights, the sub-criteria ranking is received.

These steps can also be presented in algorithm form [79], shown below in Algorithm 1.

Algorithm 1 Steps in the FAHP process.

1: Establish the main goal
2: Identify Xi, Xij ▷ Criteria and sub-criteria
3: Construct **D** ▷ Fuzzy correlation matrix
4: Calculate CR
5: **if** $CR \geq 0.1$ **then**
6:    Adjust values
7:    **go to** 3
8: **else**
9:    Fuzzification, calculate $\widetilde{S}_i$
10:    Defuzzification, calculate w_i
11:    Calculate w_i^* ▷ Normalization vector
12:    Xij ranking
13: **end if**

One of the main general drawbacks of the AHP methods (FAHP included) is the existence of incomparable criteria. This shortcoming may be overcome using the network-like presented ANP, where all the criteria, sub-criteria, and alternatives are presented as nodes, grouped in clusters, enabling them to be compared to each other as long as an interrelation exists there. In this paper, we have chosen the FAHP method only, due to the fact that it enables the expert to decompose a complex problem into a few simplified steps. We have, however, extended the model to include five points of view instead of the usual three. The decision maker can hence easily express their opinion using descriptive grades, and these linguistic values can be further explained with a mathematical approach.

4. Results and Discussion

We firstly discuss the main criteria ranking, both for AHP and FAHP, with three points of view (pessimistic, balanced, and optimistic). Afterwards, we rank individual sub-criteria. Finally, we conduct the ranking of all nineteen sub-criteria using the extended FAHP, with semi-pessimistic and semi-optimistic points of view, and test our ranking using the Spearman rank correlation coefficient [80].

In the FAHP process, we have firstly calculated a fuzzy comparison matrix and weights for the main five criteria, as shown in Table 3, and since $CR = 0.008117 < 0.1$, the matrix is consistent.

Table 3. Fuzzy comparison matrix and weights for the criteria. ($CI = 0.009091$, $CR = 0.008117$).

	X3	X1	X4	X2	X5	AHP	FAHP $\lambda = 0$	FAHP $\lambda = 0.5$	FAHP $\lambda = 1$
X3	1	AW	EW	VW	VW	0.412883117	0.400411317	0.375637961	0.365636296
X1	1/AW	1	AW	EW	EW	0.257090909	0.248161536	0.268051255	0.276081266
X4	1/EW	1/AW	1	AW	AW	0.15387013	0.163961943	0.165933156	0.166728987
X2	1/VW	1/EW	1/AW	1	E	0.088077922	0.098157381	0.105917923	0.109051062
X5	1/VW	1/EW	1/AW	1/E	1	0.088077922	0.089307823	0.084459704	0.082502389

In addition, the ranking of main criteria for both AHP and pessimistic, balanced, and optimistic FAHP points of view (with corresponding $\lambda = 0$, $\lambda = 0.5$ and $\lambda = 1$, respectively) is presented in Figure 4. In both AHP and all three FAHP cases, criteria X3-Service Quality ranked highest, while criteria X5 (customer support) ranked lowest. This is somewhat expected, as Quality of Service, and its superset Quality of Experience, are increasing factors in the Internet presence of B2C websites. This corresponds to the finding of [42] for the pandemic shopping trends. In AHP ranking, our results show that X5 and X2 have the same rank, while in all three cases of FAHP, no two criteria are ranked the same. Using FAHP, a decision-maker can fine-tune their actions to increase an aspect of their B2C website.

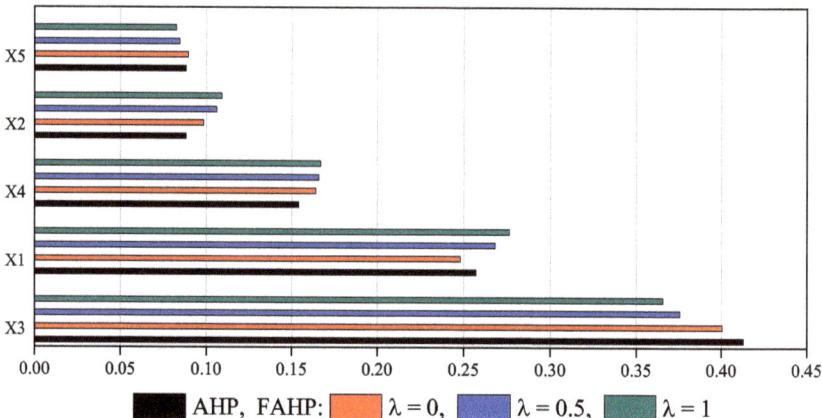

Figure 4. Ranking of main criteria.

Comparing points of view for main criteria, we can observe that a optimistic point of view (i.e., $\lambda = 1$) does not always yield a higher rank when compared to the pessimistic view. For instance, for X3 and X5, the highest and lowest criteria, the pessimistic point of view ranked higher when compared to the corresponding optimistic view.

The ranking of sub-criteria is firstly conducted in the same manner as the ranking of the main criteria, and fuzzy comparison matrices are given in Tables 4–8. The results show that all matrices are consistent. Similar to the main criteria comparison, the AHP method yields equal ranking in some cases, namely, in X2-Information. Out of five sub-criteria, we have two pairs of equal rankings, in the highest and second highest rank. This can also be observed in the triangular fuzzy numbers for X2 in Figure 5. Sub-criteria X21 and X22, corresponding to Comparison and Search functions, respectively, have equal ranking. These two sub-criteria both require customer input, and a B2C website with a better user-friendly design would most certainly aid in these functions. The second highest ranking pair, X23 and X25, referring to contact information and multilingual options, respectively, do not require user input like the previous case but rather serve to increase customers' trust in the company. Both groups are very important in the post-COVID world as e-trust, as stated in the introductory section, is an ever-increasing factor for B2C websites.

Similar to the main criteria case, FAHP distinguishes between sub-criteria; their rankings are unique, regardless of point of view.

Table 4. Fuzzy comparison matrix for the sub-criteria X1. ($CI = 0.01935734$, $CR = 0.033374725$).

X1	X11	X12	X13	AHP	FAHP $\lambda = 0$	FAHP $\lambda = 0.5$	FAHP $\lambda = 1$
X11	1	EW	FW	0.63334572	0.599820738	0.591656755	0.588533901
X12	1/EW	1	EW	0.260497956	0.282085188	0.300366108	0.307358852
X13	1/FW	1/EW	1	0.106156324	0.118094074	0.107977137	0.104107247

Table 5. Fuzzy comparison matrix for the sub-criteria X2. ($CI = 0.006617$, $CR = 0.005908$).

X2	X21	X22	X23	X25	X24	AHP	FAHP $\lambda = 0$	FAHP $\lambda = 0.5$	FAHP $\lambda = 1$
X21	1	E	EW	EW	VW	0.339857789	0.332148452	0.337465904	0.339522834
X22	1/E	1	EW	EW	VW	0.339857789	0.323512873	0.316376598	0.313616098
X23	1/EW	1/EW	1	E	AW	0.12354234	0.137948347	0.148733854	0.152905973
X25	1/EW	1/EW	1/E	1	AW	0.12354234	0.129312769	0.127644548	0.126999237
X24	1/VW	1/VW	1/AW	1/AW	1	0.073199741	0.07707756	0.069779096	0.066955858

Table 6. Fuzzy comparison matrix for the sub-criteria X3. ($CI = 0.017122$, $CR = 0.019024$).

X3	X31	X32	X34	X33	AHP	FAHP $\lambda = 0$	FAHP $\lambda = 0.5$	FAHP $\lambda = 1$
X31	1	AW	EW	FW	0.470859052	0.423579259	0.432912498	0.436834883
X32	1/AW	1	AW	VW	0.284012522	0.312661857	0.289935851	0.280385026
X34	1/EW	1/AW	1	EW	0.171482932	0.184139706	0.202744493	0.210563335
X33	1/FW	1/VW	1/EW	1	0.073645495	0.079619178	0.074407158	0.072216756

Table 7. Fuzzy comparison matrix for the sub-criteria X4. ($CI = 0.01529$, $CR = 0.016989$).

X4	X42	X43	X41	X44	AHP	FAHP $\lambda = 0$	FAHP $\lambda = 0.5$	FAHP $\lambda = 1$
X42	1	AW	EW	VW	0.45962704	0.444670919	0.432519768	0.427562099
X43	1/AW	1	AW	EW	0.294498834	0.276962234	0.291258588	0.297091501
X41	1/EW	1/AW	1	AW	0.157249417	0.175428777	0.176823909	0.177393123
X44	1/VW	1/EW	1/AW	1	0.088624709	0.10293807	0.099397735	0.097953278

Table 8. Fuzzy comparison matrix for the sub-criteria X5. ($CI = 0.009168629$, $CR = 0.01580798$).

X5	X51	X52	X53	AHP	FAHP		
					$\lambda = 0$	$\lambda = 0.5$	$\lambda = 1$
X51	1	EW	VW	0.623224728	0.598898685	0.602150325	0.603699288
X52	1/EW	1	AW	0.239487608	0.253851464	0.262713775	0.266935459
X53	1/VW	1/AW	1	0.137287664	0.147249851	0.1351359	0.129365254

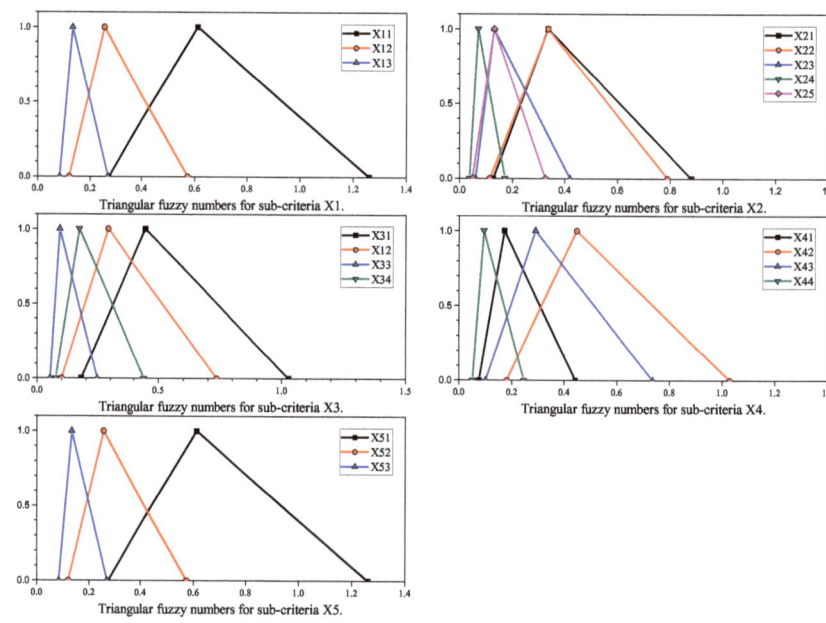

Figure 5. Triangular fuzzy numbers for criteria X.

Finally, we extend the process of FAHP by adding the semi-pessimistic ($\lambda = 0.25$) and semi-optimistic ($\lambda = 0.75$) points of view. The final ranking sub-criteria is given in Figure 6. We observe that while the sub-criteria from X3, namely X31, still ranked highest; however, the remaining sub-criteria from Service Quality, X32, X34, and X33 ranked third, fifth, and eleventh, respectively. Furthermore, the highest ranked sub-criteria from customer support, namely, X51, corresponding to item tracking, ranked seventh overall, is 2.6 times higher than X52 and 4.5 times higher for the AHP case and about 2.301 and 4.395 times higher in the FAHP case (averaged over all points of view). The high overall ranking of tracking and tracing reflects the shift in online transactions, which includes item delivery during the pandemic and, more importantly, in the post-COVID world.

We have applied different solving techniques in this paper, which can, in general, lead to inconsistencies or disagreement. For the purpose of estimation and analysis of ranking similarities applying the AHP and the Extended FAHP to all sub-criteria influencing e-commerce platforms, we have conducted fifteen different rankings using the Spearman rank correlation coefficient: [80]:

$$r_s = 1 - \frac{6 \sum_{k=1}^{n} \left(R_{x_k} - R_{y_k} \right)^2}{n(n^2 - 1)}, \quad (17)$$

where n is the number of elements in the ranking and R_{x_k} and R_{y_k} represent the ranks of the k-th element in the compared rankings. By applying Equation (17), all compared results are presented in Figure 7, and since min $\{r_s\} = 0.964912$, it can be concluded that all rankings have high similarity [81].

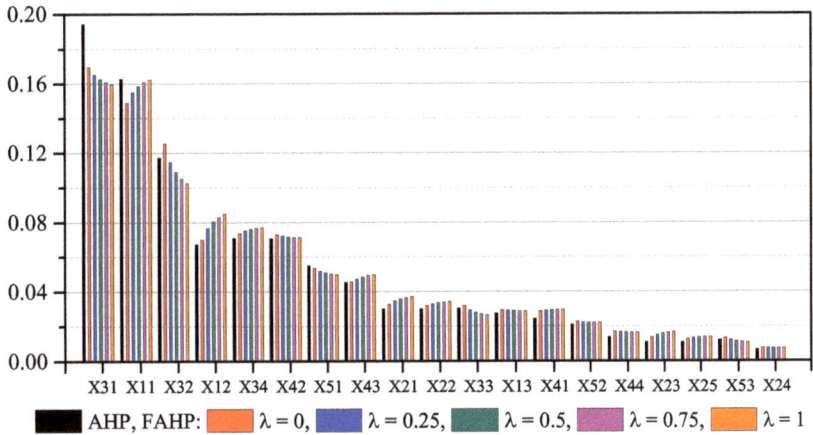

Figure 6. Final ranking of sub-criteria.

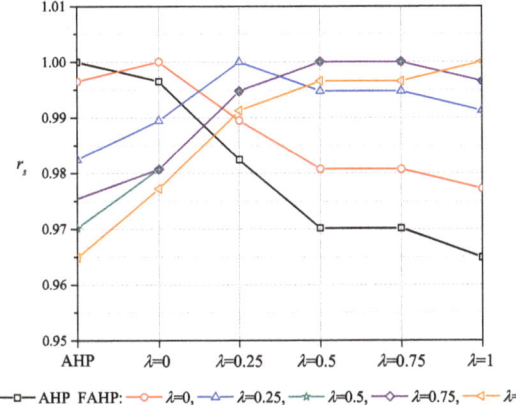

Figure 7. Ranking similarity.

5. Conclusions

Due to the ongoing pandemic, the previous two years have made a significant impact in all aspects of life—everyday activities, education, healthcare, security, economy, and trade, and have hence acclimated people to a new form of reality. Certain situations, such as lockdowns, paved the way for the ever-growing online presence. The struggle of small and medium enterprises to compete on the market therefore heavily relied on their shift towards online commerce. Reports that show multiple increments of online sales are an indicator that the trend of online commerce will continue to exist and grow in the post-COVID world.

The paper has investigated the problem of e-commerce management and the influence of various different factors. Indicators associated with digital platforms have been divided into five groups, involving security, information, quality, design, and support aspects. Using AHP and Extended FAHP, nineteen sub-criteria were ranked to determine the preferred ones in the process of e-commerce evaluation. The obtained results indicated that the proposed methods are entirely capable of estimating the influence of factors and sub-factors on online trade commerce. Considering the obtained weights for each sub-criteria and all five values of λ in the FAHP case, factors such as trust and loyalty, safe payment, exchange or return, and account security have the most significant effect on successful e-commerce platform design, while the FAQs, multilingual option, and contact information deemed the least significant. In the AHP case, the same sub-criteria from the service quality and security, privacy, and authority are ranked highest, while those from the information sector are of least importance.

Although our proposed method gives insight into several advantages and potentials in the field of B2C e-commerce, there are limitations to this work. However, these limitations might lead to future possibilities and steps forwards in our future research. Our use of AHP, because of its top-down direction structure and comparisons of criteria from one level with all criteria from the upper level, can lead to incomparable sub-criteria. This challenge can be overcome utilizing ANP, which allows clusters and elements, as well as interactions between the elements of hierarchy. This approach can further lead to more accurate results in the sub-criteria comparisons.

Another limitation presents the impossibility to examine the market solely from the customers' point of view, which was the main reason for conducting interviews with experts in management and sales from companies with a range of up to two million clients. Based on their experience in e-commerce companies, we have obtained the requirements and experts' judgments related to e-commerce businesses similar to those given by their clients.

The findings in this paper present a starting point for our continual research in the e-business area. Depending on the type of e-business and/or e-trade, we plan to add or remove certain factors or sub-factors. Furthermore, an extension to this research could focus on the practical application for the ranking of the alternatives of given websites. Finally, various MCDM methods, such as AHP, TOPSIS, and VIKOR, could be applied with fuzzy logic, Pythagorean fuzzy numbers, Intuitionictic fuzzy numbers, z-Numbers, and/or Spherical fuzzy numbers.

Author Contributions: Conceptualization: D.J.S. and N.Z., Methodology: D.J.S. and N.Z. and N.O.V., Software: D.J.S., Validation: N.O.V. and N.Z., Formal analysis: N.Z. and D.J.S., Investigation D.J.S. and N.O.V., Resources: N.O.V. and D.J.S., Data curation: N.Z. and D.J.S., Writing—original draft preparation: N.Z. and N.O.V., Writing—review and editing: N.O.V. and D.J.S., Visualization: D.J.S. and N.Z., Supervision: N.Z., N.O.V. and D.J.S., Project administration: D.J.S. and N.O.V., Funding acquisition: N.Z., N.O.V. and D.J.S. All authors have read and agreed to the published version of the manuscript.

Funding: This research received no external funding.

Data Availability Statement: Data sharing not applicable.

Acknowledgments: The first author would like to express his sincere gratitude to Mimica R. Milošević and Dušan M. Milošević for introducing him to the field of MCDM and for their constant advice and support. This paper was supported in part by the Blockchain Technology Laboratory at Belgrade Metropolitan University, Belgrade, Serbia and in part by the Serbian Ministry of Education, Science and Technological Development through Mathematical Institute of the Serbian Academy of Sciences and Arts.

Conflicts of Interest: The authors declare no conflict of interest.

References

1. Hoffman, D.; Novak, T.P. A new marketing paradigm for electronic commerce. *Inf. Soc.* **1997**, *13*, 43–54.
2. DeLone, W.H.; McLean, E.R. Measuring e-commerce success: Applying the DeLone & McLean information systems success model. *Int. J. Electron. Commer.* **2004**, *9*, 31–47.
3. Liang, T.P.; Turban, E. Introduction to the special issue social commerce: A research framework for social commerce. *Int. J. Electron. Commer.* **2011**, *16*, 5–14. [CrossRef]
4. E-Commerce and E-Business. *Information and Communication Technology in Organizations: Adoption, Implementation, Use and Effects*; Saga Publications: London, UK, 2012; pp. 139–162.
5. Shaw, M.J. Electronic commerce: State of the art. In *Handbook on Electronic Commerce*; Springer Science & Business Media: Berlin/Heidelberg, Germany, 2000; pp. 3–24.
6. Bhasin, H. *Top E-Commerce Companies in the World*; Marketing 91: Mumbai, India, 2019.

7. Ashraf, A.R.; Thongpapanl, N.T.; Spyropoulou, S. The connection and disconnection between e-commerce businesses and their customers: Exploring the role of engagement, perceived usefulness, and perceived ease-of-use. *Electron. Commer. Res. Appl.* **2016**, *20*, 69–86. [CrossRef]
8. Ribbink, D.; Van Riel, A.C.; Liljander, V.; Streukens, S. Comfort your online customer: Quality, trust and loyalty on the internet. *Manag. Serv. Qual. Int. J.* **2004**, *14*, 446–456. [CrossRef]
9. Hong, I.B.; Cho, H. The impact of consumer trust on attitudinal loyalty and purchase intentions in B2C e-marketplaces: Intermediary trust vs. seller trust. *Int. J. Inf. Manag.* **2011**, *31*, 469–479. [CrossRef]
10. Gurung, A.; Raja, M. Online privacy and security concerns of consumers. *Inf. Comput. Secur.* **2016**, *24*, 348–371. [CrossRef]
11. Ratnasingam, P.; Pavlou, P.A. Technology trust in internet-based interorganizational electronic commerce. *J. Electron. Commer. Organ. (JECO)* **2003**, *1*, 17–41. [CrossRef]
12. Choi, Y.; Mai, D.Q. The sustainable role of the e-trust in the B2C e-commerce of Vietnam. *Sustainability* **2018**, *10*, 291. [CrossRef]
13. Kim, D.J.; Song, Y.I.; Braynov, S.B.; Rao, H.R. A multidimensional trust formation model in B-to-C e-commerce: A conceptual framework and content analyses of academia/practitioner perspectives. *Decis. Support Syst.* **2005**, *40*, 143–165. [CrossRef]
14. Holsapple, C.W.; Sasidharan, S. The dynamics of trust in B2C e-commerce: A research model and agenda. *Inf. Syst.-Bus. Manag.* **2005**, *3*, 377–403. [CrossRef]
15. Aydin, S.; Kahraman, C. Evaluation of e-commerce website quality using fuzzy multi-criteria decision making approach. *IAENG Int. J. Comput. Sci.* **2012**, *39*, 64–70.
16. Wang, C.N.; Dang, T.T.; Hsu, H.P.; Nguyen, N.A.T. Evaluating sustainable last-mile delivery (LMD) in B2C E-commerce using two-stage fuzzy MCDM approach: A case study from Vietnam. *IEEE Access* **2021**, *9*, 146050–146067. [CrossRef]
17. Milošević, D.M.; Milošević, M.R.; Simjanović, D.J. Implementation of adjusted fuzzy AHP method in the assessment for reuse of industrial buildings. *Mathematics* **2020**, *8*, 1697. [CrossRef]
18. Kutlu Gündoğdu, F.; Kahraman, C. Spherical fuzzy sets and spherical fuzzy TOPSIS method. *J. Intell. Fuzzy Syst.* **2019**, *36*, 337–352. [CrossRef]
19. Zhang, Y.; Deng, X.; Wei, D.; Deng, Y. Assessment of E-Commerce security using AHP and evidential reasoning. *Expert Syst. Appl.* **2012**, *39*, 3611–3623. [CrossRef]
20. Lee, Y.; Kozar, K.A. Investigating the effect of website quality on e-business success: An analytic hierarchy process (AHP) approach. *Decis. Support Syst.* **2006**, *42*, 1383–1401. [CrossRef]
21. Chen, C.F. Applying the analytical hierarchy process (AHP) approach to convention site selection. *J. Travel Res.* **2006**, *45*, 167–174. [CrossRef]
22. Chiu, W.Y.; Tzeng, G.H.; Li, H.L. Developing e-store marketing strategies to satisfy customers' needs using a new hybrid gray relational model. *Int. J. Inf. Technol. Decis. Mak.* **2014**, *13*, 231–261. [CrossRef]
23. Triantaphyllou, E.; Lin, C.T. Development and evaluation of five fuzzy multiattribute decision-making methods. *Int. J. Approx. Reason.* **1996**, *14*, 281–310. [CrossRef]
24. Sanayei, A.; Mousavi, S.F.; Yazdankhah, A. Group decision making process for supplier selection with VIKOR under fuzzy environment. *Expert Syst. Appl.* **2010**, *37*, 24–30. [CrossRef]
25. Ostovare, M.; Shahraki, M.R. Evaluation of hotel websites using the multicriteria analysis of PROMETHEE and GAIA: Evidence from the five-star hotels of Mashhad. *Tour. Manag. Perspect.* **2019**, *30*, 107–116. [CrossRef]
26. Chmielarz, W.; Zborowski, M. The Selection and Comparison of the Methods Used to Evaluate the Quality of E-Banking Websites: The Perspective of Individual Clients. *Procedia Comput. Sci.* **2020**, *176*, 1903–1922. [CrossRef]
27. Abdullah, L.; Ramli, R.; Bakodah, H.O.; Othman, M. Developing a causal relationship among factors of e-commerce: A decision making approach. *J. King Saud-Univ.-Comput. Inf. Sci.* **2020**, *32*, 1194–1201. [CrossRef]
28. Wu, W.W.; Lee, Y.T. Developing global managers' competencies using the fuzzy DEMATEL method. *Expert Syst. Appl.* **2007**, *32*, 499–507. [CrossRef]
29. Nisar, T.M.; Prabhakar, G. What factors determine e-satisfaction and consumer spending in e-commerce retailing? *J. Retail. Consum. Serv.* **2017**, *39*, 135–144. [CrossRef]
30. Zameer, H.; Wang, Y.; Yasmeen, H. Reinforcing green competitive advantage through green production, creativity and green brand image: Implications for cleaner production in China. *J. Clean. Prod.* **2020**, *247*, 119119. [CrossRef]
31. Kaya, T. Multi-attribute evaluation of website quality in E-business using an integrated fuzzy AHPTOPSIS methodology. *Int. J. Comput. Intell. Syst.* **2010**, *3*, 301–314.
32. Aggarwal, A.G.; Aakash. Multi-criteria-based prioritisation of B2C e-commerce website. *Int. J. Soc. Syst. Sci.* **2018**, *10*, 201–222. [CrossRef]
33. Yu, X.; Guo, S.; Guo, J.; Huang, X. Rank B2C e-commerce websites in e-alliance based on AHP and fuzzy TOPSIS. *Expert Syst. Appl.* **2011**, *38*, 3550–3557. [CrossRef]
34. Liang, R.; Wang, J.; Zhang, H. Evaluation of e-commerce websites: An integrated approach under a single-valued trapezoidal neutrosophic environment. *Knowl.-Based Syst.* **2017**, *135*, 44–59. [CrossRef]
35. Del Vasto-Terrientes, L.; Valls, A.; Slowinski, R.; Zielniewicz, P. ELECTRE-III-H: An outranking-based decision aiding method for hierarchically structured criteria. *Expert Syst. Appl.* **2015**, *42*, 4910–4926. [CrossRef]
36. Dey, S.; Jana, B.; Gourisaria, M.K.; Mohanty, S.; Chatterjee, R. Evaluation of Indian B2C E-shopping websites under multi criteria decision-making using fuzzy hybrid technique. *Int. J. Appl. Eng. Res.* **2015**, *10*, 24551–24580.

37. Chou, W.C.; Cheng, Y.P. A hybrid fuzzy MCDM approach for evaluating website quality of professional accounting firms. *Expert Syst. Appl.* **2012**, *39*, 2783–2793. [CrossRef]
38. Kang, D.; Jang, W.; Park, Y. Evaluation of e-commerce websites using fuzzy hierarchical TOPSIS based on ES-QUAL. *Appl. Soft Comput.* **2016**, *42*, 53–65. [CrossRef]
39. Ong, C.E.; Teh, D. Redress procedures expected by consumers during a business-to-consumer e-commerce dispute. *Electron. Commer. Res. Appl.* **2016**, *17*, 150–160. [CrossRef]
40. Wang, C.N.; Dang, T.T.; Nguyen, N.A.T.; Le, T.T.H. Supporting better decision-making: A combined grey model and data envelopment analysis for efficiency evaluation in e-commerce marketplaces. *Sustainability* **2020**, *12*, 10385. [CrossRef]
41. Li, R.; Sun, T. Assessing Factors for Designing a Successful B2C E-Commerce Website Using Fuzzy AHP and TOPSIS-Grey Methodology. *Symmetry* **2020**, *12*, 363. [CrossRef]
42. E-Commerce Rising Stars of the Western Balkans. Available online: https://www.intellinews.com/e-commerce-rising-stars-of-the-western-balkans-205556/ (accessed on 8 August 2021).
43. Badre, A.N. Shaping Web usability: Interaction design in context. *Ubiquity* **2002**, *2002*, 1. [CrossRef]
44. Eastlick, M.A.; Lotz, S.L.; Warrington, P. Understanding online B-to-C relationships: An integrated model of privacy concerns, trust, and commitment. *J. Bus. Res.* **2006**, *59*, 877–886. [CrossRef]
45. Zhou, L.; Wang, W.; Xu, J.D.; Liu, T.; Gu, J. Perceived information transparency in B2C e-commerce: An empirical investigation. *Inf. Manag.* **2018**, *55*, 912–927. [CrossRef]
46. Zhang, P.; Von Dran, G.M. Satisfiers and dissatisfiers: A two-factor model for website design and evaluation. *J. Am. Soc. Inf. Sci.* **2000**, *51*, 1253–1268. [CrossRef]
47. Özkan, B.; Özceylan, E.; Kabak, M.; Dağdeviren, M. Evaluating the websites of academic departments through SEO criteria: A hesitant fuzzy linguistic MCDM approach. *Artif. Intell. Rev.* **2020**, *53*, 875–905. [CrossRef]
48. SEVİM, N. The Effect of E-service Quality, E-trust and E-satisfaction on Formation Online Customer Loyalty. *Bus. Manag. Stud. Int. J.* **2018**, *6*, 107. [CrossRef]
49. Zhu, D.S.; Kuo, M.J.; Munkhbold, E. Effects of e-customer satisfaction and e-trust on e-loyalty: Mongolian online shopping behavior. In Proceedings of the 2016 5th IIAI International Congress on Advanced Applied Informatics (IIAI-AAI), Kumamoto, Japan, 10–14 July 2016; pp. 847–852.
50. Leung, K.; Choy, K.L.; Siu, P.K.; Ho, G.T.; Lam, H.; Lee, C.K. A B2C e-commerce intelligent system for re-engineering the e-order fulfilment process. *Expert Syst. Appl.* **2018**, *91*, 386–401. [CrossRef]
51. Kim, J.; Jin, B.; Swinney, J.L. The role of etail quality, e-satisfaction and e-trust in online loyalty development process. *J. Retail. Consum. Serv.* **2009**, *16*, 239–247. [CrossRef]
52. Cunningham, M. *Smart Things to Know about E-Commerce*; Capstone: Oxford, UK, 2002.
53. Ivory, M. *Automated Web Site Evaluation: Researchers' and Practitioners' Perspectives*; Kluwer Academic Publishers: London, UK, 2003.
54. Oppenheim, C.; Ward, L. Evaluation of web sites for B2C e-commerce. In *Aslib Proceedings*; Emerald Group Publishing Limited: Bingley, UK, 2006.
55. Rahhal, W. The effects of service quality dimensions on customer satisfaction: An empirical investigation in Syrian mobile telecommunication services. *Int. J. Bus. Manag. Invent.* **2015**, *4*, 81–89.
56. Lin, H.F. The impact of website quality dimensions on customer satisfaction in the B2C e-commerce context. *Total Qual. Manag. Bus. Excell.* **2007**, *18*, 363–378. [CrossRef]
57. Abedi, F.; Zeleznikow, J.; Bellucci, E. Universal standards for the concept of trust in online dispute resolution systems in e-commerce disputes. *Int. J. Law Inf. Technol.* **2019**, *27*, 209–237. [CrossRef]
58. Van der Merwe, R.; Bekker, J. A framework and methodology for evaluating e-commerce web sites. *Internet Res.* **2003**, *13*, 330–341. [CrossRef]
59. Zadeh, L.A. The concept of a linguistic variable and its application to approximate reasoning—I. *Inf. Sci.* **1975**, *8*, 199–249. [CrossRef]
60. Zadeh, L.A. The concept of a linguistic variable and its application to approximate reasoning—II. *Inf. Sci.* **1975**, *8*, 301–357. [CrossRef]
61. Zadeh, L.A. The concept of a linguistic variable and its application to approximate reasoning—III. *Inf. Sci.* **1975**, *9*, 43–80. [CrossRef]
62. Dimić, V.; Milošević, M.; Milošević, D.; Stević, D. Adjustable model of renewable energy projects for sustainable development: A case study of the Nišava district in Serbia. *Sustainability* **2018**, *10*, 775. [CrossRef]
63. Sun, C.C. A performance evaluation model by integrating fuzzy AHP and fuzzy TOPSIS methods. *Expert Syst. Appl.* **2010**, *37*, 7745–7754. [CrossRef]
64. Chang, D.Y. Applications of the extent analysis method on fuzzy AHP. *Eur. J. Oper. Res.* **1996**, *95*, 649–655. [CrossRef]
65. Wang, W.M.; Lee, A.H.; Chang, D.T. An integrated FA-FEAHP approach on the social indicators of Taiwan's green building. *Glob. Bus. Econ. Rev.* **2009**, *11*, 304–316. [CrossRef]
66. Kulak, O.; Durmuşoğlu, M.B.; Kahraman, C. Fuzzy multi-attribute equipment selection based on information axiom. *J. Mater. Process. Technol.* **2005**, *169*, 337–345. [CrossRef]
67. Satty, T.L. *The Analytic Hierarchy Process*; McGraw-Hill International: New York, NY, USA, 1980.

68. Waas, T.; Hugé, J.; Block, T.; Wright, T.; Benitez-Capistros, F.; Verbruggen, A. Sustainability assessment and indicators: Tools in a decision-making strategy for sustainable development. *Sustainability* **2014**, *6*, 5512–5534. [CrossRef]
69. Yager, R.R. Uncertainty modeling using fuzzy measures. *Knowl.-Based Syst.* **2016**, *92*, 1–8. [CrossRef]
70. Li, D.F. An approach to fuzzy multiattribute decision making under uncertainty. *Inf. Sci.* **2005**, *169*, 97–112. [CrossRef]
71. Kahraman, C.; Cebeci, U.; Ruan, D. Multi-attribute comparison of catering service companies using fuzzy AHP: The case of Turkey. *Int. J. Prod. Econ.* **2004**, *87*, 171–184. [CrossRef]
72. Srdjevic, B.; Medeiros, Y.D.P. Fuzzy AHP assessment of water management plans. *Water Resour. Manag.* **2008**, *22*, 877–894. [CrossRef]
73. Miloševic, D.; Milošević, M.; Stanojevic, A.; Dimic, V.; Miloševic, A. Application of FAHP Method in the Process of Building Construction from the Aspect of Energy Efficiency. In Proceedings of the 4th International Conference Mechanical Engineering in XXI Century, Niš, Serbia, 19–20 April 2018; pp. 19–20.
74. Chou, T.Y.; Chen, Y.T. Applying fuzzy AHP and TOPSIS method to identify key organizational capabilities. *Mathematics* **2020**, *8*, 836. [CrossRef]
75. Ghorui, N.; Ghosh, A.; Algehyne, E.A.; Mondal, S.P.; Saha, A.K. AHP-TOPSIS inspired shopping mall site selection problem with fuzzy data. *Mathematics* **2020**, *8*, 1380. [CrossRef]
76. Milošević, M.R.; Milošević, D.M.; Stević, D.M.; Stanojević, A.D. Smart city: Modeling key indicators in Serbia using IT2FS. *Sustainability* **2019**, *11*, 3536. [CrossRef]
77. Milošević, M.R.; Milošević, D.M.; Stanojević, A.D.; Stević, D.M.; Simjanović, D.J. Fuzzy and Interval AHP Approaches in Sustainable Management for the Architectural Heritage in Smart Cities. *Mathematics* **2021**, *9*, 304. [CrossRef]
78. Liou, T.S.; Wang, M.J.J. Ranking fuzzy numbers with integral value. *Fuzzy Sets Syst.* **1992**, *50*, 247–255. [CrossRef]
79. Milošević, A.; Milošević, M.; Milošević, D.; Selimi, A. AHP multi-criteria method for sustainable development in construction. In Proceedings of the 4th International Conference Contemporary Achievements in Civil Engineering, Građevinski Fakultet Subotica, Subotica, Srbija, 22 April 2016; pp. 929–938.
80. Ceballos, B.; Lamata, M.T.; Pelta, D.A. A comparative analysis of multi-criteria decision-making methods. *Prog. Artif. Intell.* **2016**, *5*, 315–322. [CrossRef]
81. Vinogradova-Zinkevič, I.; Podvezko, V.; Zavadskas, E.K. Comparative Assessment of the Stability of AHP and FAHP Methods. *Symmetry* **2021**, *13*, 479. [CrossRef]

Article

Interval Type-3 Fuzzy Aggregation of Neural Networks for Multiple Time Series Prediction: The Case of Financial Forecasting

Oscar Castillo [1,*], Juan R. Castro [2] and Patricia Melin [1]

1. Division of Graduate Studies and Research, Tijuana Institute of Technology, Tijuana 22414, Mexico; pmelin@tectijuana.mx
2. School of Engineering, UABC University, Tijuana 22500, Mexico; jrcastror@uabc.edu.mx
* Correspondence: ocastillo@tectijuana.mx

Abstract: In this work, we present an approach for fuzzy aggregation of neural networks for forecasting. The interval type-3 aggregator is used to combine the outputs of the networks to improve the quality of the prediction. This is carried out in such a way that the final output is better than the outputs of the individual modules. In our approach, a fuzzy system is used to estimate the prediction increments that will be assigned to the output in the process of combining them with a set of fuzzy rules. The uncertainty in the process of aggregation is modeled with an interval type-3 fuzzy system, which, in theory, can outperform type-2 and type-1 fuzzy systems. Publicly available data sets of COVID-19 cases and the Dow Jones index were utilized to test the proposed approach, as it has been stated that a pandemic wave can have an effect on the economies of countries. The simulation results show that the COVID-19 data does have, in fact, an influence on the Dow Jones time series and its use in the proposed model improves the forecast of the Dow Jones future values.

Keywords: interval type-3 fuzzy logic; fuzzy aggregation; time series prediction

MSC: 03B52; 03E72; 62P30

1. Introduction

Fuzzy logic has become very important in different disciplines of study, and one of the areas is the main focus of this work, which is the time series prediction area. It has also been shown in the literature that the use of type-1 fuzzy logic helps to improve the results in many problems [1,2]. Later, type-1 evolved into type-2 fuzzy systems with the work of Mendel and others in 2001 [3,4]. Initially, interval type-2 fuzzy systems were studied and applied to several problems [5]. Later, these systems were applied to many problems in areas, such as robotics, control, diagnosis, and others [6]. Simulation and experimental results show that interval type-2 outperforms type-1 fuzzy systems in situations with higher levels of noise, dynamic environments, or in highly nonlinear problems [6–8]. Later, general type-2 fuzzy systems were considered to manage higher levels of uncertainty, and good results have been achieved in several application areas [9–11]. Recently, it has become apparent that type-3 fuzzy systems could help solve even more complex problems [12–14]. For this reason, in this paper, we propose the basic constructs of type-3 fuzzy systems by extending the ideas of type-2 fuzzy systems, and then applying them to a prediction problem.

It has been shown in several previous works that individual neural networks have the ability to outperform statistical methods (in particular for nonlinear problems) and ensembles (formed by sets of networks) can outperform individual neural networks. So, for this reason, we concentrated our efforts on the aggregation part of the ensemble [15–17]. In particular, we focused on fuzzy aggregation, showing that by utilizing type-3 fuzzy logic in the aggregation phase, we are able to outperform type-2 and type-1 fuzzy logic in time series prediction.

Recently, the very rapid propagation of COVID-19 occurred, including several waves, and spreading to all continents of the world. In particular, in the case of Europe, several countries, such as Italy, Spain, and France, were hit hard with the spread of the COVID-19 virus, with a significant number of confirmed cases and deaths [18–23]. In the case of the American continent, the United States, Canada, and Brazil have also experienced a significant number of cases due to the rapid spread of COVID-19 [24–26]. There are also several recent works on the prediction and modeling of COVID-19 behavior in space and time [27–29]. In addition, it has been recognized that the COVID-19 waves have affected the economy (such as the Dow Jones in the USA). For this reason, we consider both time series to test the proposed model.

The main goal of this paper is the proposal of a prediction method based on an ensemble of neural networks with an interval type-3 fuzzy aggregator to combine the predictions of the modules. We believe that the proposed method has the potential to work for any complex time series and the reasoning behind this statement is as follows: It has been shown that individual neural networks can outperform other methods in prediction and ensembles of neural networks can outperform individual networks by having a set of predictors (such as a group of experts) to achieve the prediction of complex time series problems. Of course, to ensure an ensemble produces the best results, an aggregator for combining the outputs of the modules is needed. In this case, a fuzzy system is used. In particular, a type-3 fuzzy system is utilized to manage the uncertainty in combining the prediction of the modules, and, in this way, the best results are obtained. In this work, we test the proposal with an ensemble relating the prediction of COVID-19 data with the Dow Jones time series, but other time series could be tested in the future with the same approach.

The key contribution is the proposal of mathematical definitions of interval type-3 fuzzy theory, which were obtained by applying the extension principle to the type-2 fuzzy theory definitions. In addition, the utilization of interval type-3 fuzzy theory in the aggregation of neural network outputs (of an ensemble) for prediction has not been previously presented in the literature. This paper shows that interval type-3 fuzzy theory has the potential to be better than other methods in the literature for this task. We consider that these are important contributions to the frontier knowledge in soft computing and its applications.

The structure of this article is defined as follows: Section 2 introduces the basic terminology of interval type-3 fuzzy sets, Section 3 describes the proposed type-3 prediction method, Section 4 summarizes the results, and Section 5 outlines the conclusions and future works.

2. Interval Type-3 Fuzzy Logic

Interval type-3 fuzzy logic can be viewed as an extension of the type-2 models. We describe the basic terminology of type-3 fuzzy sets to show how it differs from its type-2 counterpart.

Definition 1. A type-3 fuzzy set (T3 FS) [30–33], denoted by $A^{(3)}$, is represented by the plot of a trivariate function, called the membership function (MF) of $A^{(3)}$, in the Cartesian product $X \times [0,1] \times [0,1]$ in $[0,1]$, where X is the universe of the primary variable of $A^{(3)}$. The MF of $\mu_{A^{(3)}}$ is formulated by $\mu_{A^{(3)}}(x,u,v)$ (or $\mu_{A^{(3)}}$ for short) and it is called a type-3 membership function (T3 MF) of the T3 FS:

$$\mu_{A^{(3)}}: X \times [0,1] \times [0,1] \to [0,1]$$
$$A^{(3)} = \{(x, u(x), v(x,u), \mu_{A^{(3)}}(x,u,v)) \mid x \in X,\ u \in U \subseteq [0,1], v \in V \subseteq [0,1]\} \quad (1)$$

where U is the universe for the secondary variable u and V is the universe for the tertiary variable v. If the tertiary MF is uniformily equal to 1, then we have an interval type-3 fuzzy set (IT3 FS) with interval type-3 MF (IT3MF).

Figure 1 illustrates IT3 FS with IT3MF $\tilde{\mu}(x,u)$, where $\underline{\mu}(x,u)$ is the LMF and $\overline{\mu}(x,u)$ is the UMF. The embedded secondary T1 MFs in x' of $\underline{A}$ and $\overline{A}$ are $\underline{f}_{x'}(u)$ and $\overline{f}_{x'}(u)$.

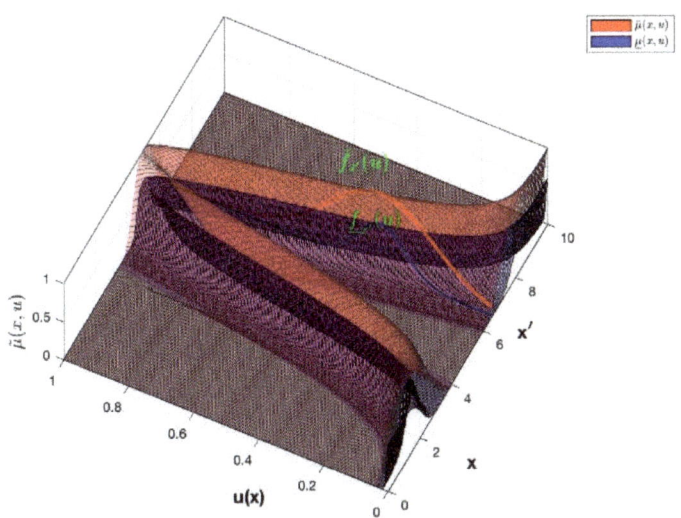

Figure 1. Fuzzy set with an IT3 MF $\tilde{\mu}(x, u)$.

In this case, we utilize interval type-3 MFs that are scaled Gaussians in the primary and secondary, respectively. This function can be represented as, $\tilde{\mu}_\mathbb{A}(x, u)$ = ScaleGaussScaleGauss IT3MF, with a Gaussian footprint of uncertainty $FOU(\mathbb{A})$, characterized by the parameters $[\sigma, m]$ (UpperParameters) for the upper membership function (UMF) and the parameters λ (LowerScale) and ℓ (LowerLag) for the lower membership function (LMF) to form the $DOU = [\underline{\mu}(x), \overline{\mu}(x)]$. The vertical cuts $\mathbb{A}_{(x)}(u)$ characterize the $FOU(\mathbb{A})$, and are IT2 FSs with Gaussian IT2 MFs, $\mu_{\mathbb{A}(x)}(u)$ with parameters $[\sigma_u, m(x)]$ for the UMF and LMF λ (LowerScale), ℓ (LowerLag) The IT3 MF, $\tilde{\mu}_\mathbb{A}(x, u)$ = ScaleGaussScaleGaussIT3MF(x,{{[σ, m]}, λ, ℓ}) is described with the following equations:

$$\overline{u}(x) = exp\left[-\frac{1}{2}\left(\frac{x-m}{\sigma}\right)^2\right] \tag{2}$$

$$\underline{u}(x) = \lambda \cdot exp\left[-\frac{1}{2}\left(\frac{x-m}{\sigma^*}\right)^2\right] \tag{3}$$

where $\sigma^* = \sigma \sqrt{\frac{\ln(\ell)}{\ln(\varepsilon)}}$ and ε is the machine epsilon. If $\ell = 0$, then $\sigma^* = \sigma$. Then, $\overline{u}(x)$ and $\underline{u}(x)$ are the upper and lower limits of the DOU. The range $\delta(u)$ and radius σ_u of the FOU are:

$$\delta(u) = \overline{u}(x) - \underline{u}(x) \tag{4}$$

$$\sigma_u = \frac{\delta(u)}{2\sqrt{3}} + \varepsilon \tag{5}$$

The apex or core, $m(x)$, of the IT3 MF $\tilde{\mu}(x, u)$ is defined by the expression:

$$m(x) = exp\left[-\frac{1}{2}\left(\frac{x-m}{\rho}\right)^2\right] \tag{6}$$

where $\rho = (\sigma + \sigma^*)/2$. Then, the vertical cuts with IT2 MF, $\mu_{\mathbb{A}(x)}(u) = \left[\underline{\mu}_{\mathbb{A}(x)}(u), \overline{\mu}_{\mathbb{A}(x)}(u)\right]$, are described by the equations:

$$\overline{\mu}_{\mathbb{A}(x)}(u) = exp\left[-\frac{1}{2}\left(\frac{u - u(x)}{\sigma_u}\right)^2\right] \tag{7}$$

$$\underline{\mu}_{\mathbb{A}(x)}(u) = \lambda \cdot exp\left[-\frac{1}{2}\left(\frac{u-u(x)}{\sigma_u^*}\right)^2\right] \quad (8)$$

where $\sigma_u^* = \sigma_u \sqrt{\frac{\ln(\ell)}{\ln(\varepsilon)}}$. If $\ell = 0$, then $\sigma_u^* = \sigma_u$. Then, $\overline{\mu}_{\mathbb{A}(x)}(u)$ and $\underline{\mu}_{\mathbb{A}(x)}(u)$ are the UMF and LMF of the IT2 FSs of the vertical cuts of the secondary IT2MF of the IT3 FS.

The interval type-3 fuzzy logic system (IT3 FLS) structure contains the same main components (fuzzifier, rule base, inference machine and, in the final stage, an output processing unit) as its analogous T2 FLSs. While in the case of T2 FLSs the final stage consists of the process of type reduction to T1 FS + defuzzification, in the case of an IT3 FLS, the output processor consists of type reduction to IT2 FS + defuzzification. The fuzzy operators of the inference machine of an IT3 FLS and the type reduction methods are equivalent to a T2 FLS, except that in the inputs and outputs, we have IT3 FSs in an IT3 FLS.

3. Proposed Method

The method consists of utilizing two neural networks and then combining their outputs with an interval type-3 fuzzy system to obtain a revised and improved forecast of one of the time series by taking into account the influence of the other series. Figure 2 illustrates the architecture of the proposed method, where we can appreciate that two time series enter the two modules (neural networks NN_1 and NN_2) and individual predictions P_1 and P_2 are obtained with corresponding increments ΔP_1 and ΔP_2, respectively. Then, these increments are the inputs to the fuzzy system for aggregation, which are obtained after the inference process and increment for the time series number 1, and, finally, the prediction is computed.

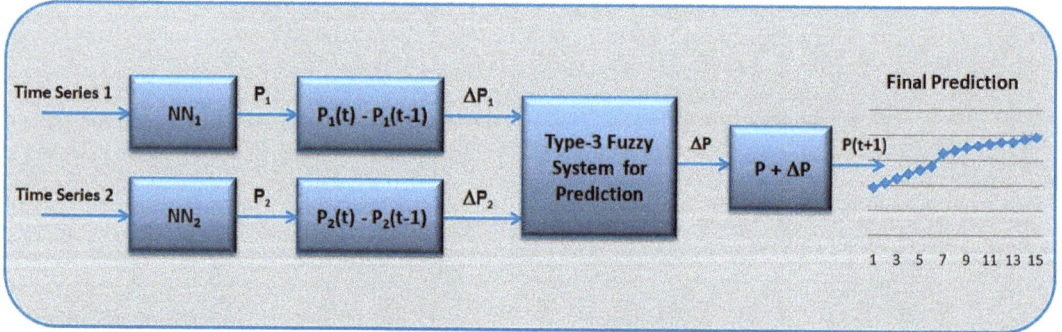

Figure 2. Architecture of the proposed ensemble with type-3 fuzzy response aggregation.

The fuzzy rules for the aggregation of the results with two modules are:
1. If (ΔP_1 is high) and (ΔP_2 is low), then (ΔP is positive).
2. If (ΔP_1 is high) and (ΔP_2 is medium), then (ΔP is negative small).
3. If (ΔP_1 is high) and (ΔP_2 is high), then (ΔP is negative large).
4. If (ΔP_1 is medium) and (ΔP_2 is low), then (ΔP is positive).
5. If (ΔP_1 is medium) and (ΔP_2 is medium), then (ΔP is negative small).
6. If (ΔP_1 is medium) and (ΔP_2 is high), then (ΔP is negative large).
7. If (ΔP_1 is low) and (ΔP_2 is low), then (ΔP is positive).
8. If (ΔP_1 is low) and (ΔP_2 is medium), then (ΔP is negative small).
9. If (ΔP_1 is low) and (ΔP_2 is high), then (ΔP is negative large).

The design of the fuzzy rules is based on general knowledge of training neural networks with time series data. It is known that when two different time series are related, their prediction can be improved by taking into account their interrelations. The fuzzy rules are established based on this general knowledge, so that they reflect that when the time series number two increases, this makes the time series one decrease and the vice versa. This general knowledge was used in proposing the fuzzy rules. The interval type-3 system (seen in Figure 3) has as input the increment in the prediction values of each neural network, P_1 and P_2, respectively. After the defuzzification, the type-3 system has as output the corresponding increment in the time series number 1. The proposed approach is tested using two time series that are supposed to be related; if we combine their information, the prediction can be improved. In particular, we consider the Dow Jones index as the first time series, and the time series of COVID-19 cases as the second one; considering their relation, the prediction of the Dow Jones can be improved.

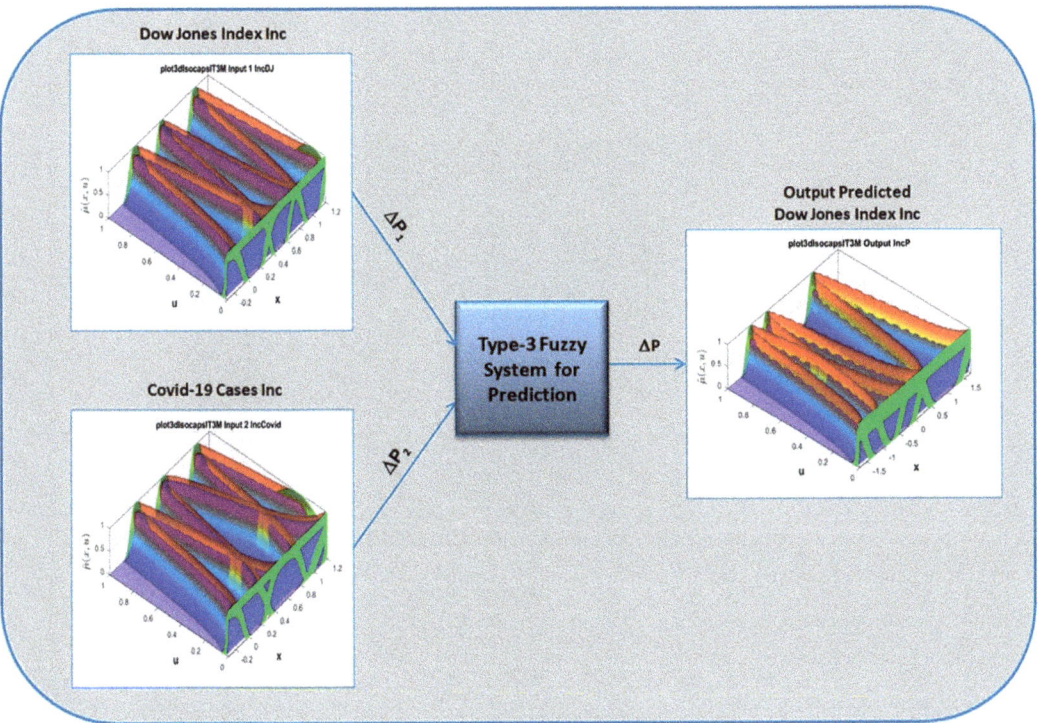

Figure 3. Interval type-3 system to compute the weights.

We note that although the previous explanation and description of the applies to two time series, this approach could be generalized or extended to any number of related time series. Of course, the number of neural modules and the number of fuzzy rules will increase accordingly. In this situation, a metaheuristic could be utilized to automate the process of generating the structure and rules for particular situations.

In Table 1, we show the specific parameters of the MFs, which were found by trial and error, and could be optimized in the future with metaheuristics to achieve even better results. Basically, Table 1 shows the centers and standard deviations of the Gaussian MFs.

Regarding the lower scale (λ) and lower lag (ℓ) parameters, after experimentation to achieve better results, they were found to be 0.9 and 0.2 for the inputs, respectively. On the other hand, for the outputs, they were found to be 0.8 and 0.2, respectively. These values could be optimized with a metaheuristic to further improve the results.

In Figures 4 and 5, we show the input MFs for both errors, respectively. In Figure 6, we illustrate the output MFs, respectively. The actual IT3 MFs are three dimensional, but in these figures, a view on the plane is shown for simplicity.

Table 1. Parameter values for the Gaussian MFs used in the linguistic values (center and standard deviations).

Variable	Membership Function	σ	m
Input 1	small	0.127	0.00
Input 1	medium	0.13	0.50
Input 1	high	0.25	1.00
Input 2	small	0.20	0.00
Input 2	medium	0.15	0.50
Input 2	high	0.30	1.00
Output 1	low	0.15	−1.00
Output 1	medium	0.18	−0.50
Output 1	high	0.25	1.00

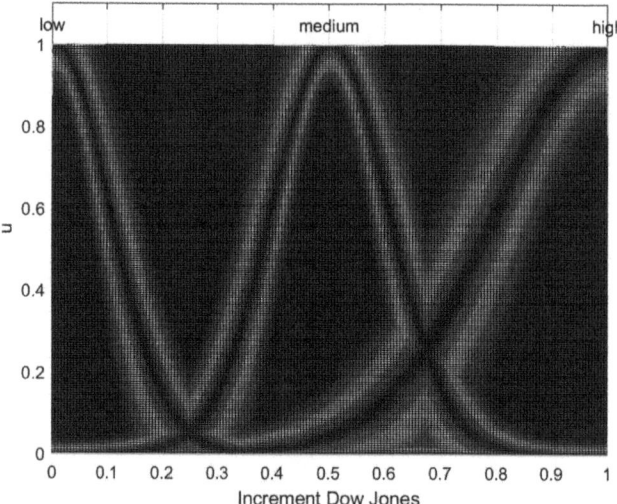

Figure 4. MFs of the input increment in Dow Jones.

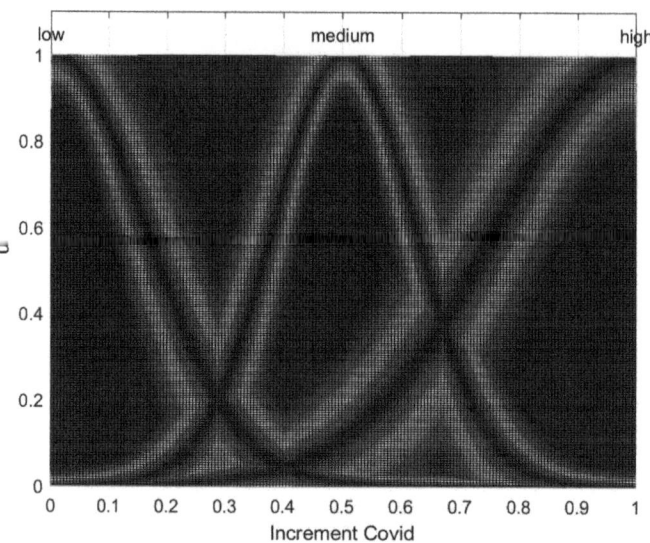

Figure 5. MFs of the input increment in COVID-19.

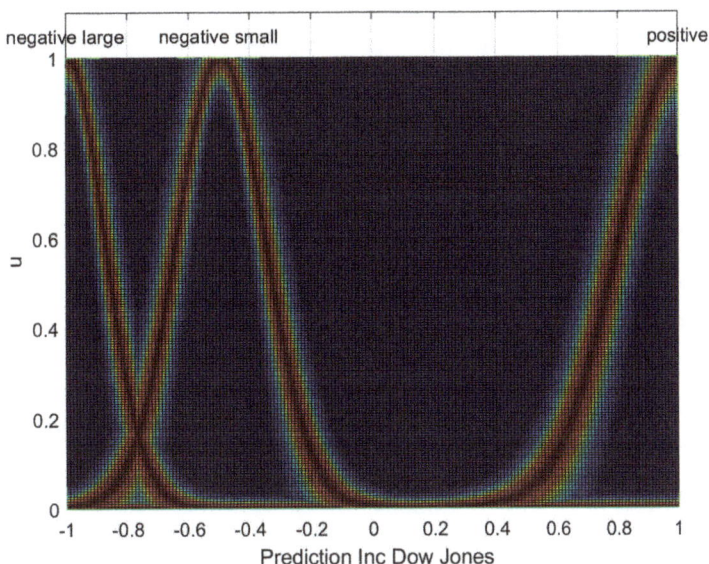

Figure 6. MFs of the output prediction in the increment Dow Jones.

In Figure 7, we show one view of the nonlinear surface representing the fuzzy model, representing the relation of w_1 with respect to the errors e_1 and e_2.

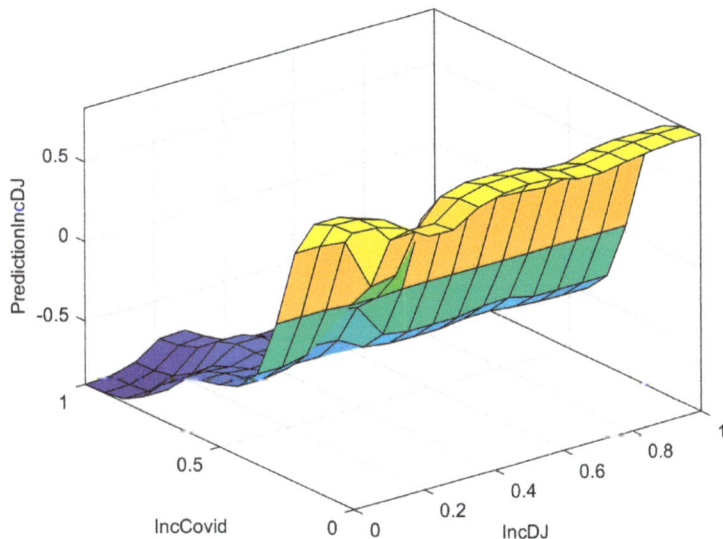

Figure 7. Surface representing the type-3 fuzzy model for prediction.

In Figure 8, we illustrate the inference for a particular value of one of the inputs, and in Figure 9, the type-reduction and defuzzification are shown. We implemented the operations corresponding with type-3 to achieve these results using the computer programs in Matlab.

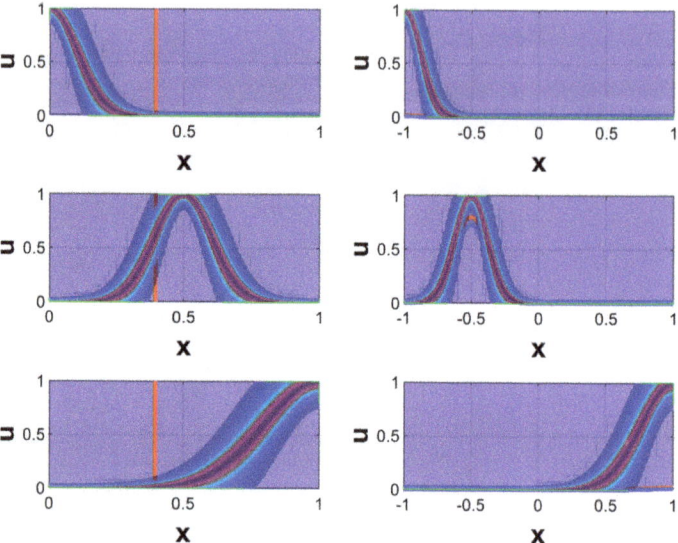

Figure 8. Inference process for a particular value of x.

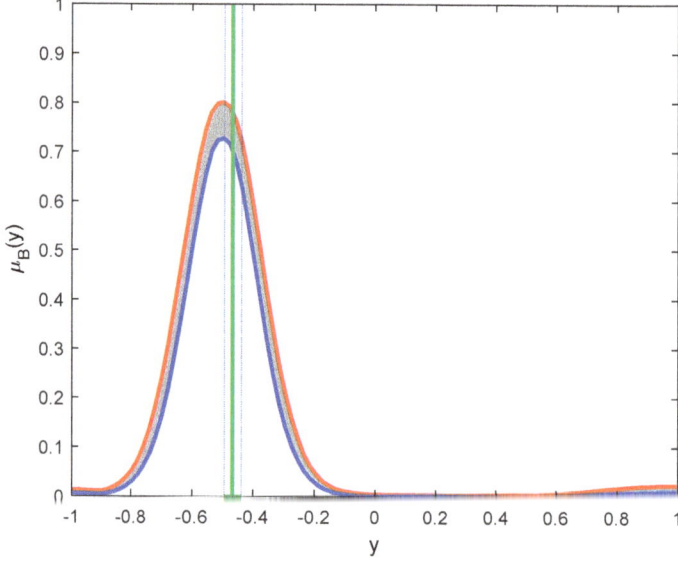

Figure 9. Type reduction and defuzzification for a particular x value.

4. Simulation Results

The experiments were performed with a dataset from the Humanitarian Data Exchange (HDX) [18], which includes COVID-19 data from countries of cases that occurred from January of 2020 to May, 2021 In addition, the Dow Jones time series for the same period of time was collected for use in the experiments [34]. Three different periods of 15 days were used for the testing stage. The first period is from 4 July to 18 July of 2021, the second period is 25 September to 9 October of 2021, and the third one is from 13 January to 27 January of 2022. The main idea is that the Dow Jones forecast can be improved by taking into account the influence of the COVID-19 time series for the USA, as the pandemic affected the economies of countries. The fuzzy aggregator is used to combine the information of the prediction of both time series to obtain a revised and improved prediction of the Dow Jones.

The two modules of the neural network were trained with the COVID-19 time series and Dow Jones data from January of 2020 to May, 2021, respectively. Recurrent neural networks were used, with 3 delays, 300 epochs of training, and backpropagation with momentum learning and an adaptive learning rate. Three layers were used in each of the networks.

Table 2 shows the forecasts of the two neural networks (Dow Jones NN and COVID NN), and the obtained increments of both time series (Inc Dow Jones and Inc COVID), which are the inputs to the type-3 fuzzy system. Finally, the forecast obtained with the type-3 fuzzy aggregator is shown (Dow Jones IT3) and the real value of the Dow Jones for comparison. In Figure 10, we illustrate the prediction with the interval type-3 and neural networks compared with the real data of the Dow Jones for this first testing period from 4 to 18 July 2021. Table 3 shows the forecasts, in the same way, for the second period from 25 September to 9 October of 2021, and Figure 11 illustrates a comparison of the prediction compared and the real values. Finally, Table 4 shows the Dow Jones forecast for the third period from 13 January to 27 January of 2022 and Figure 12 illustrates the prediction.

Table 2. Forecasts of the neural networks and aggregation by the interval type-3 fuzzy system for the period of 4 July to 18 July of 2021.

Dow Jones NN	Inc Dow Jones	COVID NN	Inc COVID	Dow Jones IT3	Dow Jones Real
34,349.25	0.0664	33,849,760	0.0007	34,948.49	34,421.93
34,137.63	0.2917	33,861,363	0.0973	35,536.12	34,870.16
34,477.83	0.4690	33,895,756	0.2887	35,113.13	34,996.18
34,665.86	0.2592	33,921,173	0.2133	34,697.25	34,888.79
34,598.99	0.0921	33,946,079	0.2090	35,257.75	34,933.23
34,614.08	0.0208	34,015,922	0.5863	34,894.75	34,987.02
34,664.91	0.0700	34,015,183	0.0062	34,247.86	34,687.85
34,422.15	0.3347	34,023,764	0.0720	33,628.03	33,962.04
33,696.86	1.0000	34,068,368	0.3744	33,999.74	34,511.99
34,055.52	0.4945	34,101,607	0.2790	34,436.44	34,798.00
34,419.24	0.5014	34,141,916	0.3383	34,820.19	34,823.35
34,494.41	0.1036	34,182,819	0.3433	34,439.27	35,061.55
34,695.49	0.2772	34,301,941	1.0000	34,862.25	35,144.31
34,803.33	0.1486	34,297,819	0.0346	35,488.40	35,058.52
34,748.02	0.0762	34,317,020	0.1611	34,927.89	34,930.93

Table 3. Forecasts of the neural networks and aggregation by the interval type-3 fuzzy system for the period of 25 September to 9 October of 2021.

Dow Jones NN	Inc Dow Jones	COVID NN	Inc COVID	Dow Jones IT3	Dow Jones Real
35,846.72	0.3971	42,945,142	0.9286	35,759.14	36,053.09
35,937.04	0.5319	42,956,944	0.0585	35,911.26	36,157.02
36,012.04	0.4416	42,963,958	0.0347	36,063.11	36,124.66
36,010.28	0.0103	43,165,597	1.0000	36,045.81	36,329.07
36,106.41	0.5661	43,282,333	0.5789	35,960.82	36,431.39
36,182.72	0.4494	43,384,050	0.5044	35,875.72	36,320.50
36,144.14	0.2272	43,485,767	0.5044	35,790.21	36,079.54
36,007.92	0.8022	43,648,660	0.8078	35,712.82	35,921.24
35,884.66	0.7259	43,652,130	0.0172	35,851.73	36,100.37
35,954.61	0.4119	43,655,554	0.0169	36,002.58	36,087.98
35,975.10	0.1206	43,841,478	0.9220	35,980.98	36,144.13
36,001.28	0.1541	43,938,298	0.4801	35,895.52	35,931.52
35,896.29	0.6183	44,035,711	0.4831	35,743.67	35,871.34
35,826.56	0.4106	44,129,867	0.4669	35,658.40	35,602.18
35,656.76	1.0000	44,263,637	0.6634	35,573.42	35,619.26

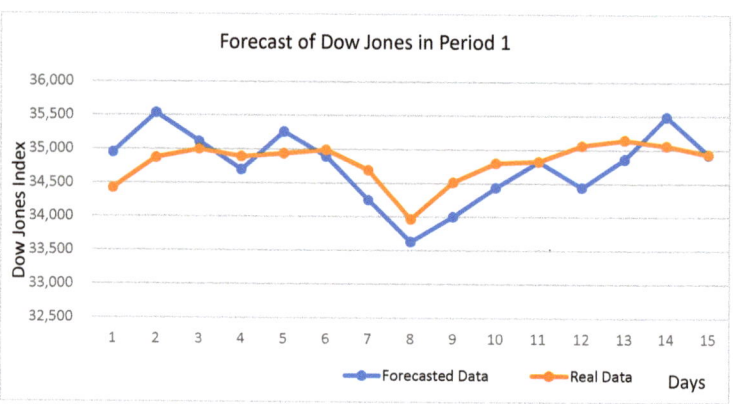

Figure 10. Forecast of Dow Jones for the first period.

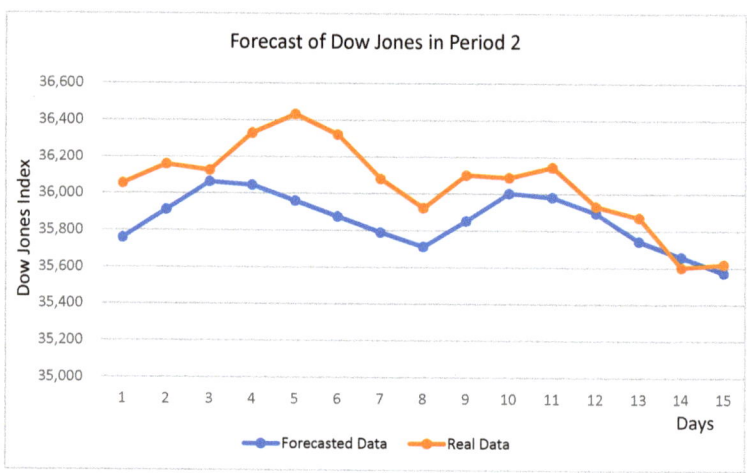

Figure 11. Forecast of Dow Jones for the second period.

Table 4. Forecasts of the neural networks and aggregation by the interval type-3 fuzzy system for the period of 13 January to 27 January of 2022.

Dow Jones NN	Inc Dow Jones	COVID NN	Inc COVID	Dow Jones IT3	Dow Jones Real
35,708.46	1.0000	61,193,732	0.4173	35,951.24	36,231.53
35,690.59	0.0560	61,059,007	0.8109	35,705.81	36,067.75
35,578.43	0.2083	62,512,122	0.5981	35,459.80	36,251.7
35,666.52	0.1796	62,608,798	0.0886	35,868.95	36,290.71
35,714.28	0.0973	62,857,485	0.2280	36,225.59	36,114.94
35,612.50	0.2075	63,468,896	0.5607	35,979.53	35,911.28
35,455.57	0.3200	64,559,291	1.0000	35,903.62	35,369.39
35,040.59	0.8462	65,381,414	0.7539	35,670.02	35,029.17
34,671.35	0.7530	65,738,705	0.3276	35,394.68	34,714.14
34,333.13	0.6897	66,300,125	0.5148	35,147.79	34,265.50
33,853.37	0.9784	66,301,034	0.0008	34,707.74	34,366.67
33,844.16	0.0187	66,423,477	0.1122	34,273.53	34,296.74
33,799.14	0.0918	67,335,050	0.8360	34,519.54	34,166.84
33,656.33	0.2912	67,698,546	0.3333	34,241.95	34,160.51
33,617.53	0.0791	68,105,464	0.3731	34,598.59	34,396.39

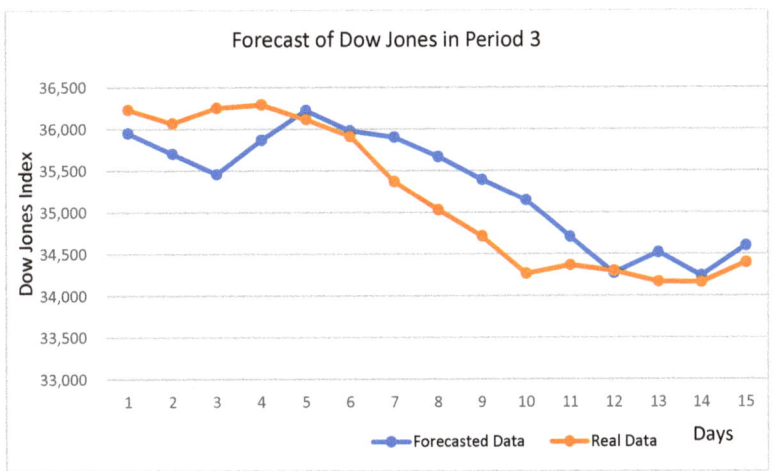

Figure 12. Forecast of Dow Jones for the third period.

Additionally, we consider another simulation set up by changing the lower scale (λ) and lower lag (ℓ) parameter values in all MFs, which are now considered to be 0.8 and 0.3, respectively. In Table 5, a comparison of the prediction results for the 15 days with the previous parameter values (0.9 and 0.2) shown in Tables 2–4, and the new results with the new parameters (0.8 and 0.3) for the three periods are shown. It can be appreciated that the results only show slight changes, showing the robustness of the proposed method.

Table 5. Comparison of the results for the three periods with different parameter values.

	Period 1			Period 2			Period 3		
Day	Forecast $\lambda = 0.9$ $\ell = 0.2$	Forecast $\lambda = 0.8$ $\ell = 0.3$	Real Values of Period 1	Forecast $\lambda = 0.9$ $\ell = 0.2$	Forecast $\lambda = 0.8$ $\ell = 0.3$	Real Values of Period 2	Forecast $\lambda = 0.9$ $\ell = 0.2$	Forecast $\lambda = 0.8$ $\ell = 0.3$	Real Values of Period 3
1	34,948.49	34,951.46	34,421.93	35,759.14	35,759.92	36,053.09	35,951.24	35,951.78	36,231.53
2	35,536.12	35,537.21	34,870.16	35,911.26	35,912.87	36,157.02	35,705.81	35,706.35	36,067.75
3	35,113.13	35,113.78	34,996.18	36,063.11	36,065.49	36,124.66	35,459.80	35,460.24	36,251.70
4	34,697.25	34,698.92	34,888.79	36,045.81	36,048.92	36,329.07	35,868.95	35,872.34	36,290.71
5	35,257.75	35,275.60	34,933.23	35,960.82	35,963.95	36,431.39	36,225.59	36,238.39	36,114.94
6	34,894.75	34,912.66	34,987.02	35,875.72	35,878.85	36,320.50	35,979.53	35,992.23	35,911.28
7	34,247.86	34,262.80	34,687.85	35,790.21	35,793.29	36,079.54	35,903.62	35,918.28	35,369.39
8	33,628.03	33,640.26	33,962.04	35,712.82	35,716.08	35,921.24	35,670.02	35,684.29	35,029.17
9	33,999.74	34,010.26	34,511.99	35,851.73	35,854.36	36,100.37	35,394.68	35,409.05	34,714.14
10	34,436.44	34,449.64	34,798.00	36,002.58	36,005.85	36,087.98	35,147.79	35,161.91	34,265.50
11	34,820.19	34,831.28	34,823.35	35,980.98	35,985.07	36,144.13	34,707.74	34,719.66	34,366.67
12	34,439.27	34,452.54	35,061.55	35,895.52	35,899.73	35,931.52	34,273.53	34,282.26	34,296.74
13	34,862.25	34,875.96	35,144.31	35,743.67	35,747.12	35,871.34	34,519.54	34,528.37	34,166.84
14	35,488.40	35,504.43	35,058.52	35,658.40	35,661.95	35,602.18	34,241.95	34,251.03	34,160.51
15	34,927.89	34,927.75	34,930.93	35,573.42	35,576.98	35,619.26	34,598.59	34,617.08	34,396.39

From the previous tables, we can conclude that the prediction with the interval type-3 fuzzy approach for the aggregation of neural networks is a good alternative in the prediction of complex time series, such as COVID-19 and the Dow Jones. In particular, for the third period, the prediction error of the Dow Jones is less than 1% on most days of the period, with some days with errors in the range of 0.3 to 0.6%. We note that previous studies with type-2 and type-1 fuzzy or even stand-alone neural networks could not achieve these values. The proposed approach can be extended to problems with multiple time series by using more neural networks and utilizing a fuzzy aggregator with more fuzzy rules.

5. Conclusions

In this work a new approach for type-3 fuzzy aggregation of neural networks was outlined. The main idea is to combine the predictions of related time series to improve the final predictions. In our approach, a fuzzy system is utilized to consider the predictions of neural networks as the inputs in the combination process to obtain a revised and improved prediction. The uncertainty in the process of aggregation is modeled with the interval type-3 fuzzy system as, theoretically, it should handle this better than the type-2 and type-1 fuzzy systems. The simulation results of the Dow Jones and COVID-19 time series showed the potential of the approach to outperform other methods. As future work, we plan to use our approach in other applications, such as the ones discussed in [35,36]. Moreover, we plan to optimize the type-3 system using metaheuristics to improve the results. In addition, we will formulate a general method to consider the problems of multiple time series (more than two), where we could automate the generation of the optimal fuzzy system (rules and parameters). Finally, we plan to combine type-3 with other intelligent techniques to build strong hybrid models and consider other time series prediction problems.

Author Contributions: Conceptualization, creation on main idea, writing—review and editing, O.C.; formal analysis, J.R.C.; methodology and validation, P.M. All authors have read and agreed to the published version of the manuscript.

Funding: This research received no external funding.

Data Availability Statement: Not applicable.

Acknowledgments: We would like to thank TecNM and Conacyt for their support during the realization of this research.

Conflicts of Interest: The authors declare no conflict of interest.

References

1. Zadeh, L.A. Knowledge representation in Fuzzy Logic. *IEEE Trans. Knowl. Data Eng.* **1989**, *1*, 89. [CrossRef]
2. Zadeh, L.A. Fuzzy Logic. *Computer* **1998**, *1*, 83–93.
3. Mendel, J.M. *Uncertain Rule-Based Fuzzy Logic Systems: Introduction and New Directions*; Prentice-Hall: Upper-Saddle River, NJ, USA, 2001.
4. Mendel, J.M. *Uncertain Rule-Based Fuzzy Logic Systems: Introduction and New Directions*, 2nd ed.; Springer: Berlin/Heidelberg, Germany, 2017.
5. Karnik, N.N.; Mendel, J.M. Operations on Type-2 Fuzzy Sets. *Fuzzy Sets Syst.* **2001**, *122*, 327–348. [CrossRef]
6. Moreno, J.E.; Sanchez, M.A.; Mendoza, O.; Rodríguez-Díaz, A.; Castillo, O.; Melin, P.; Castro, J.R. Design of an interval Type-2 fuzzy model with justifiable uncertainty. *Inf. Sci.* **2020**, *513*, 206–221. [CrossRef]
7. Mendel, J.M.; Hagras, H.; Tan, W.-W.; Melek, W.W.; Ying, H. *Introduction to Type-2 Fuzzy Logic Control*; Wiley and IEEE Press: Hoboken, NJ, USA, 2014.
8. Olivas, F.; Valdez, F.; Castillo, O.; Melin, P. Dynamic parameter adaptation in particle swarm optimization using interval type-2 fuzzy logic. *Soft Comput.* **2016**, *20*, 1057–1070. [CrossRef]
9. Sakalli, A.; Kumbasar, T.; Mendel, J.M. Towards Systematic Design of General Type-2 Fuzzy Logic Controllers: Analysis, Interpretation, and Tuning. *IEEE Trans. Fuzzy Syst.* **2021**, *29*, 226–239. [CrossRef]
10. Ontiveros, E.; Melin, P.; Castillo, O. High order α-planes integration: A new approach to computational cost reduction of General Type-2 Fuzzy Systems. *Eng. Appl. Artif. Intell.* **2018**, *74*, 186–197. [CrossRef]
11. Castillo, O.; Amador-Angulo, L. A generalized type-2 fuzzy logic approach for dynamic parameter adaptation in bee colony optimization applied to fuzzy controller design. *Inf. Sci.* **2018**, *460–461*, 476–496. [CrossRef]
12. Cao, Y.; Raise, A.; Mohammadzadeh, A.; Rathinasamy, S.; Band, S.S.; Mosavi, A. Deep learned recurrent type-3 fuzzy system: Application for renewable energy modeling/prediction. *Energy Rep.* **2021**, *7*, 8115–8127. [CrossRef]
13. Mohammadzadeh, A.; Castillo, O.; Band, S.S.; Mosavi, A. A Novel Fractional-Order Multiple-Model Type-3 Fuzzy Control for Nonlinear Systems with Unmodeled Dynamics. *Int. J. Fuzzy Syst.* **2021**, *23*, 1633–1651. [CrossRef]
14. Qasem, S.N.; Ahmadian, A.; Mohammadzadeh, A.; Rathinasamy, S.; Pahlevanzadeh, B. A type-3 logic fuzzy system: Optimized by a correntropy based Kalman filter with adaptive fuzzy kernel size. *Inform. Sci.* **2021**, *572*, 424–443. [CrossRef]

15. Khalilpourazari, S.; Doulabi, H.H.; Çiftçioglu, A.Ö.; Weber, G.W. Gradient-based grey wolf optimizer with Gaussian walk: Application in modelling and prediction of the COVID-19 pandemic. *Expert Syst. Appl.* **2021**, *177*, 114920. [CrossRef]
16. Kuvvetli, Y.; Deveci, M.; Paksoy, T.; Garg, H. A predictive analytics model for COVID-19 pandemic using artificial neural networks. *Decis. Anal. J.* **2021**, *1*, 100007. [CrossRef]
17. Liu, D.; Ding, W.; Dong, Z.S.; Pedrycz, W. Optimizing deep neural networks to predict the effect of social distancing on COVID-19 spread. *Comput. Ind. Eng.* **2022**, *166*, 107970. [CrossRef]
18. The Humanitarian Data Exchange (HDX). Available online: https://data.humdata.org/dataset/novel-coronavirus-2019-ncov-cases. (accessed on 31 March 2020).
19. Shereen, M.A.; Khan, S.; Kazmi, A.; Bashir, N.; Siddique, R. COVID-19 infection: Origin, transmission, and characteristics of human coronaviruses. *J. Adv. Res.* **2020**, *24*, 91–98. [CrossRef]
20. Sohrabi, C.; Alsafi, Z.; O'neill, N.; Khan, M.; Kerwan, A.; Al-Jabir, A.; Iosifidis, C.; Agha, R. World Health Organization declares global emergency: A review of the 2019 novel coronavirus (COVID-19). *Int. J. Surg.* **2020**, *76*, 71–76. [CrossRef]
21. Apostolopoulos, I.D.; Bessiana, T. COVID-19: Automatic detection from X-Ray images utilizing Transfer Learning with Convolutional Neural Networks. *arXiv* **2020**, arXiv:2003.11617. [CrossRef]
22. Sarkodie, S.A.; Owusu, P.A. Investigating the Cases of Novel Coronavirus Disease (COVID-19) in China Using Dynamic Statistical Techniques. *Heliyon* **2020**, *6*, e03747. [CrossRef]
23. Beck, B.R.; Shin, B.; Choi, Y.; Park, S.; Kang, K. Predicting commercially available antiviral drugs that may act on the novel coronavirus (SARS-CoV-2) through a drug-target interaction deep learning model. *Comput. Struct. Biotechnol. J.* **2020**, *18*, 784–790. [CrossRef]
24. Zhong, L.; Mu, L.; Li, J.; Wang, J.; Yin, Z.; Liu, D. Early Prediction of the 2019 Novel Coronavirus Outbreak in the Mainland China based on Simple Mathematical Model. *IEEE Access.* **2020**, *8*, 51761–51769. [CrossRef]
25. Kamel Boulos, M.N.; Geraghty, E.M. Geographical tracking and mapping of coronavirus disease COVID-19/severe acute respiratory syndrome coronavirus 2 (SARS-CoV-2) epidemic and associated events around the world: How 21st century GIS technologies are supporting the global fight against outbreaks and epidemics. *Int. J. Health Geogr.* **2020**, *19*, 8. [CrossRef]
26. Gao, P.; Zhang, H.; Wu, Z.; Wang, J. Visualising the expansion and spread of coronavirus disease 2019 by cartograms. *Environ. Plan. A Econ. Space* **2020**, *52*, 698–701. [CrossRef]
27. Srinivasa Rao, A.; Vazquez, J. Identification of COVID-19 can be quicker through artificial intelligence framework using a mobile phone-based survey in the populations when Cities/Towns are under quarantine. *Infect. Control. Hosp. Epidemiol.* **2020**, *41*, 826–830. [CrossRef]
28. Melin, P.; Monica, J.C.; Sanchez, D.; Castillo, O. Analysis of Spatial Spread Relationships of Coronavirus (COVID-19) Pandemic in the World using Self Organizing Maps. *Chaos Solitons Fractals* **2020**, *138*, 109917. [CrossRef]
29. Melin, P.; Monica, J.C.; Sanchez, D.; Castillo, O. Multiple Ensemble Neural Network Models with Fuzzy Response Aggregation for Predicting COVID-19 Time Series: The Case of Mexico. *Healthcare* **2020**, *8*, 181. [CrossRef]
30. Rickard, J.T.; Aisbett, J.; Gibbon, G. Fuzzy subsethood for fuzzy sets of type-2 and generalized type-n. *IEEE Trans. Fuzzy Syst.* **2009**, *17*, 50–60. [CrossRef]
31. Mohammadzadeh, A.; Sabzalian, M.H.; Zhang, W. An interval type-3 fuzzy system and a new online fractional-order learning algorithm: Theory and practice. *IEEE Trans. Fuzzy Syst.* **2020**, *28*, 1940–1950. [CrossRef]
32. Liu, Z.; Mohammadzadeh, A.; Turabieh, H.; Mafarja, M.; Band, S.S.; Mosavi, A. A New Online Learned Interval Type-3 Fuzzy Control System for Solar Energy Management Systems. *IEEE Access* **2021**, *9*, 10498–10508. [CrossRef]
33. Castillo, O.; Castro, J.R.; Melin, P. *Interval Type-3 Fuzzy Systems: Theory and Design*; Springer: Cham, Switzerland, 2022.
34. Dow Jones Time Series Data. Available online: https://m.mx.investing.com/indices/us-30-historical-data (accessed on 31 March 2022).
35. Cervantes, L.; Castillo, O. Type-2 Fuzzy Logic Aggregation of Multiple Fuzzy Controllers for Airplane Flight Control. *Inf. Sci.* **2015**, *324*, 247–256. [CrossRef]
36. Castillo, O.; Castro, J.R.; Melin, P. A Rodriguez-Diaz, Application of interval type-2 fuzzy neural networks in non-linear identification and time series prediction. *Soft Comput.* **2014**, *18*, 1213–1224. [CrossRef]

Article

Comparing Regional Attitudes toward Immigrants in Six European Countries

Alessandro Indelicato [1,*], Juan Carlos Martín [1] and Raffaele Scuderi [2]

1. Institute of Tourism and Sustainable Economic Development, University of Las Palmas de Gran Canaria, 35017 Las Palmas de Gran Canaria, Spain; jcarlos.martin@ulpgc.es
2. Faculty of Economics and Law, Kore University of Enna, 94100 Enna, Italy; raffaele.scuderi@unikore.it
* Correspondence: alessandro.indelicato101@alu.ulpgc.es

Abstract: Many immigrants have risked their lives searching for a better future by crossing the Mediterranean Sea or the Atlantic Ocean. The Canary Islands became the centre of another emerging humanitarian and human rights crisis at Europe's frontier in 2020. The study aims to analyse whether attitudes towards immigrants are affected by territories close to these humanitarian crises. To this end, the study is based on previous studies using a Fuzzy-Hybrid TOPSIS method to analyse attitudes toward immigrants. The synthetic indicator will be built upon a set of eight indicators that proxy the ethnic, economic, cultural, and religious threats experienced by the citizens. The International Social Survey Program (ISSP) dataset for the year 2013 for six countries, namely Belgium, Germany, Spain, France, United Kingdom, and Portugal, will be used. Results show that the attitude toward immigrants is affected by the territorial dimension as classified by the nomenclature of territorial units for statistics at NUTS2 and NUTS3 levels, and that attitudes are very different between those of some of the archipelagos and islands considered in the study. In particular, our results point out a sort of duality between the Balearic Islands—the most open territory toward immigrants, and Corse—the least open territory toward immigrants.

Keywords: attitudes toward immigrants; Europe; island regions; International Social Survey Program (ISSP); Fuzzy-Hybrid TOPSIS

MSC: 03E72

Citation: Indelicato, A.; Martín, J.C.; Scuderi, R. Comparing Regional Attitudes toward Immigrants in Six European Countries. *Axioms* **2022**, *11*, 345. https://doi.org/10.3390/axioms11070345

Academic Editor: Amit K. Shukla

Received: 28 June 2022
Accepted: 18 July 2022
Published: 19 July 2022

Publisher's Note: MDPI stays neutral with regard to jurisdictional claims in published maps and institutional affiliations.

Copyright: © 2022 by the authors. Licensee MDPI, Basel, Switzerland. This article is an open access article distributed under the terms and conditions of the Creative Commons Attribution (CC BY) license (https://creativecommons.org/licenses/by/4.0/).

1. Introduction

In recent years, migration flows have been growing in the Mediterranean Sea and the Atlantic Ocean. Southern European islands have increasingly been a port of arrival for migrants [1,2]. This phenomenon has developed an important public and academic debate on the attitude towards immigrants. Many scholars argue that the anti-immigrant sentiment can depend on the country and socioeconomic characteristics [3–5].

Despite the scientific academic advances in the study of attitudes towards immigrants (ATI) and their related methods, the literature confirms that Confirmatory Factor Analysis (CFA) and Structural Equation Modelling (SEM) have been the most frequently adopted approaches to study immigration attitudes. These methods are based on measurement models in which latent variables are obtained using econometric models adapted to the observed elements [6,7].

However, other methodological approaches that have been used in different fields are less common. This study aims to introduce one of these less-common methods in the field of social sciences, the Fuzzy-Hybrid TOPSIS. The approach has been applied in other disciplines, leading to interesting findings [8–10]. The data are extracted from the International Social Survey Program (ISSP) and the analysis of the attitudes toward immigration was conducted for six European countries, considering the regions at NUTS2 and NUTS3 levels. First, country-level research is conducted. Then, the paper analyses ATI across different socioeconomic characteristics, such as religion, age, income, citizenship, gender, education, work status, and political orientation. As a last step, ATI across regional territories is analysed in order to detect which areas present more positive attitudes toward immigrants.

The paper complements other studies [11–15] using a new approach in the field that has not been commonly used. Therefore, our study will serve as a guideline to apply a new quantitative method based on fuzzy logic and expand the literature of studies on attitudes toward immigrants at the territorial level.

2. Theorical Background

The anti-immigration and exclusionary sentiment of immigrants derives from a perception of the threat to the natives. This threat affects the social, cultural, and institutional status of a country's society [3,16].

Scholars have attributed negative attitudes towards immigrants to various individual factors, such as religion, political orientation, citizenship, or economic status [3,4,15–17]. Martín and Indelicato [1,5] affirm that openness toward immigrants can depend on the socio-economic characteristics of citizens. They focused on a division of Europe into the most open countries to immigration, i.e., those of central and northern Europe, and those that have shown more hostility to immigration (Eastern Europe). Furthermore, they found religion, education, and age as the main determinants of attitudes towards immigrants. At the country level, Davidov and Semyonov [18] argue that anti-immigration sentiments are shaped by terrorist events, the social and political climate of institutions, number of immigrants, and integration policies.

In the global context of immigration, studying the phenomenon at a regional level is arousing much interest among scholars [12–15,19]. Dirksmeier (2021) states that although regionalism per se does not influence the feeling of hostility towards immigrants, local economic disparities may accentuate a trend of negative attitudes towards immigrants.

On the other hand, Markaki and Longhi [14] affirm that anti-immigrant sentiment is a regional factor rather than a national one. They focus on the study of attitudes towards immigrants in a local context, analysing the impact of regional characteristics on anti-immigrant sentiment. They conclude that regional unemployment and high levels of immigration from outside the EU negatively affect natives' attitudes towards immigrants. Although the economic level does not particularly determine anti-immigrant sentiment among regions, the characteristics of immigrant populations are a critical factor in the construction of these sentiments [14].

The relationship between ethnic regional sentiment and anti-immigrant attitudes has been studied by Escandell and Ceobanu [15]. They explain that at the aggregate level, the results show that where there are high levels of feeling of regionalism, there are often high levels of exclusion of immigrants. Thus, they trace individual prejudice to the collective values of specific regions. Similarly, Sanjay Jeram et al. [20] find that hostile attitudes towards immigration can be masked under the umbrella of regionalism or regional identity.

Eger and Breznau [11] shifted the focus of the analysis from national-level attitudes towards immigration to the impact of immigration on regional-level welfare allocation attitudes. In other words, while the literature focuses on a transnational analysis of anti-immigration attitudes, Eger and Breznau [11] examine the contextual determinants of anti-immigrant sentiment in European regions. In particular, they address whether and to what extent the size of the region's foreign-born population has reduced support for national welfare state programs. They analysed 114 regions and concluded that although the percentage of immigrants in the region has reduced support for generous welfare state policies, immigration itself has not increased its opposition to the social rights of immigrants in the regions [18]. Karreth et al. [13] show that locals living in regions with traditionally high levels of immigration tend to be more open to immigrants. However, recent increases in immigration and immigration levels in socially "racially diverse" and economically less developed regions of Europe are generally associated with a lower acceptance of immigration, but only among natives who vote for right-wing parties [13].

Dalle Nogare et al. [19] presented a cross-country analysis across Italian territories and found that the increase in the population support to some anti-immigration parties may be negatively correlated with the presence of public policies that are addressed to immigrants' integration, such as free or discounted access to museums.

Thus, anti-immigrant sentiment has increased in the last few years in a regional context. Researchers have also focused on the peculiar context of island regions [21–23]. For example, in recent years, there have been demonstrations against the "invasion" of immigrants in the Canary Islands. The motto of these demonstrations proclaimed the islanders' right to have their own territory "free of blood" and to "be saved from invasion" [23]. Similarly, in Corsica, the population feels a loss of identity and accuses the institutions of this loss as they feel abandoned because of the massive immigration from North Africa. This fact has fuelled in the Corsican islanders an ever-larger increase in the negative attitudes toward immigrants [22]. The author attributes the Corsican anti-immigrant sentiment to a crumbling economic and social situation, which is correlated with a loss of identity and generates an increase in racism and xenophobia.

On the contrary, after years of emigration, in recent years, the Balearic Islands in Spain have experienced a significant increase in new citizens. Immigrants come from central and northern European countries and do not seek economic stability, and they are not even fleeing a war. Following Provenzano [24], there is a nexus between migration and tourism flows. Immigrants to the Balearic Islands are often citizens that at a first glance were attracted by the archipelago because of tourism and then have returned as immigrants. Therefore, this has not caused economic and cultural instability, and consequently, the Balearic attitudes towards immigrants are positive [21].

3. Data

This study uses the International Social Survey Program (ISSP) dataset for 2013. ISSP is a cross-national study on diverse topics relevant to social sciences. Many scholars have adopted the ISSP dataset to study attitudes toward immigrants [11,12,25]. The data we consider cover six European countries, namely Belgium, Germany, Spain, France, the UK, and Portugal. Due to the different regional level of the data provided by the ISSP dataset (2013), Belgium, Germany, Portugal, and Spain will be analysed at the NUTS2 level; France at the NUTS3 level; and the UK at the NUTS1 level. The choice of countries allows for analysing the differences between continental regions and islands in Europe, in line with the main objective. In addition, countries including separatist territories were selected to broaden the comparison.

Nine thousand sixty-six was the total number of individuals interviewed, distributed across countries as reported in Table 1. There were more females (51.67%) than males (48.24%). The vast majority of the sample was represented by natives (92.69%) compared to foreign citizens (6.43%). Almost 50% of the sample was in paid work, while only 4.47% was studying. Twenty-four-year-old or younger citizens represented the smallest age group in the sample (7.70%), whereas the 45–54 age group represented the biggest one (18.94%). The sample was almost equally distributed across medium incomes, and the highest and lowest income categories represented only 0.87% and 2.10% of the sample, respectively. More than 60% of the sample preferred that newcomers adapt to the traditions of the larger society. From the political views side, more than 55% was moderate, in which conservatives represented 21.97%, left-centre citizens 23.90%, and liberals 9.20% and the extremist wings, far-left and far-right, 4.40% and 2.69%, respectively. Finally, the majority of the respondents were Catholic (44.50%) or agnostic (31.50%).

Table 1. Descriptive statistics [1].

Country	N	%	Traditions	N	%
Belgium	2202	24.29	Maintain trad.	1768	19.50
France	2017	22.25	Adapt	5453	60.15
Germany	1717	18.94	**Citizenship**	**N**	**%**
Portugal	1001	11.04	Natives	8403	92.69
Spain	1225	13.51	Foreigner	583	6.43
UK	904	9.97	**Income**	**N**	**%**
Education	**N**	**%**	Lowest. Bottom	190	2.10
No formal edu	222	2.45	Income2	238	2.63
Primary school	761	8.39	Income3	478	5.27
Lower secondary	2383	26.29	Income4	771	8.50
Upper secondary	1741	19.20	Income5	1811	19.98
Post-secondary	1201	13.25	Income6	1685	18.59
Lower-level tertiary	1293	14.26	Income7	1371	15.12
Upper-level tertiary	1326	14.63	Income8	761	8.39
Main status	**N**	**%**	Income9	130	1.43
In paid work	4516	49.81	Highest. Top	79	0.87
Unemployed	775	8.55	**Political Orientation**	**N**	**%**
In education	405	4.47	Far left	399	4.40
Apprentice or trainee	77	0.85	Left	2167	23.90
Permanently sick or disabled	176	1.94	Center. Liberal	834	9.20
Retired	2479	27.34	Right	1992	21.97
Domestic work	494	5.45	Far right	244	2.69
Other	107	1.18	Other	414	4.57
Gender	**N**	**%**	**Religion**	**N**	**%**
Male	4373	48.24	No religion	2856	31.50
Female	4684	51.67	Catholic	4042	44.58
Age	**N**	**%**	Protestant	877	9.67
24 years or under	698	7.70	Orthodox	40	0.44
25–34 years	1343	14.81	Other Christian	629	6.94
35–44 years	1463	16.14	Jewish	24	0.26
45–54 years	1717	18.94	Islamic	290	3.20
55–64 years	1587	17.50	Other religion	124	1.37
65–74 years	1301	14.35			
75 years or over	941	10.38			

[1] Some categories do not add to 100 because the variable contains some missing values.

The ISSP National Identity module contains eight items that concern the immigration issue. As in [26], the items chosen to measure the attitudes toward immigrants (ATI) are:

1. Immigrants increase crime rates;
2. Immigrants take jobs away from people born in [Country];
3. Legal immigrants should have the same rights;
4. Immigrants are generally good for the economy;
5. Immigrants bring new ideas and cultures;
6. Immigrants undermine the culture;
7. Illegal immigrants should be excluded;
8. Legal immigrants should have equal access to education.

Each of the items were evaluated through a 5-point Likert scale, where one refers to "Agree strongly" and five to "Disagree strongly". Items three, four, five, and eight were recoded reversely in order to obtain that the higher scores express a positive attitude towards immigrants.

4. Methodology

4.1. Fuzzy-Hybrid TOPSIS Approach

In this study, a hybrid method based on a fuzzy approach and technique of similarity to ideal solution (TOPSIS) is used to measure the citizens' attitudes toward immigrants. This approach has had a growing interest in many fields, such as the hotel industry [27], education [8], green energy [28], logistics [29], social sciences [30], agriculture [31], and healthcare [31].

The vagueness associated with subjective assessments is a problem when researchers look for a way to synthesize information for the sake of applying econometric or mathematical models. Fuzzy logic models are an appropriate tool for partially solving such vagueness, which is related with linguistic terms [32,33]. These models handle ambiguous information by deconstructing the concept of objective information to a degree of different strengths. The degree of intensity is conceptualized by a membership function, also called characteristic functions, discriminant functions, or indicator functions [34].

Let X be a set of real numbers ($\mathbb{R}$), that is, $X = \{x_1, x_2, \ldots, x_n\} \in \mathbb{R}$; a fuzzy set $\tilde{A} = \{(x, \mu_A(x)) | x \in X\}$ in X is a set of ordered pairs, where $\mu_A(x)$ is a membership function; and $\mu_A(x) : X \to [0,1]$. Thus, the membership function $\mu_A(x)$ is used as a proxy for the relative truth that exists in the statements $x \in A$ [35,36]. The set X is known as the universe of discourse of the fuzzy set theory and emerged as a generalization of the classical set theory.

Fuzzy TOPSIS consists of 6 consecutive steps. First, the ISSP's answers will be converted into Triangular Fuzzy Numbers (TFNs). As in Salih et al. [37], it has been considered that TFNs are valid tools to deal with the vagueness and uncertainty of information.

Thus, a triplet (a_1, a_2, a_3) of real numbers is considered to assign each scale point to a TFN, as follows:

$$\mu_A(x) = \begin{cases} \frac{x-a_1}{a_2-a_1} & a_1 \leq x \leq a_2 \\ \frac{x-a_3}{a_2-a_3} & a_2 \leq x \leq a_3 \\ 0 & \text{otherwise} \end{cases} \quad (1)$$

The information provided by the scale will be converted into TFNs in a universe of discourse within the interval [0, 100]. In order to perform no-loss generalization and clarity information, 5 intervals were chosen to represent the original 5-scale points: (1) Disagree strongly (0, 0, 30); (2) Disagree (20, 30, 40); (3) Neither agree nor disagree (30, 50, 70); (4) Agree (60, 70, 80); and (5) Agree strongly (70, 100, 100). For each country and for each region, the information has been aggregated through the Fuzzy Set Logic Algebra, and the average fuzzy number is given by:

$$\tilde{A} = (a_1, a_2, a_3) = \left(\frac{1}{n}\right) \otimes \left(\tilde{A}_1 \oplus \tilde{A}_2 \oplus \ldots \oplus \tilde{A}_n\right) = \left(\frac{\sum_{i=1}^{n} a_1^{(i)}}{n}, \frac{\sum_{i=1}^{n} a_2^{(i)}}{n}, \frac{\sum_{i=1}^{n} a_3^{(i)}}{n}\right) \quad (2)$$

where $\otimes$ stand for the multiplication of a scalar and a TFN, $\oplus$ the internal addition of TFNs [38]. Thus, we obtain a matrix of TFNs of each analysed group, which contains a lot of information that is difficult to analyse. Therefore, in agreement with Kumar [27], the matrix is defuzzified into a matrix of real and clear information since the uncertainty and vagueness of the information have been adequately managed. Crisp values are then obtained through the weighted average of the 3-tuple calculated as follows:

$$V_{\tilde{A}} = \frac{(a_1 + 2a_2 + a_3)}{4} \quad (3)$$

4.2. TOPSIS Steps

Once the matrix of crisp values has been obtained, the following steps concern the calculation of the TOPSIS index, which measures attitudes towards immigrants (ATI). Following Hwang and Yoon [39], the ideal positive and negative solutions are calculated as follows:

$$A_j^+ = \{(\max V_{ij}), \; j = 1, 2, \ldots, J\}, \; i = 1, 2, \ldots m$$
$$A_j^- = \{(\min V_{ij}), \; j = 1, 2, \ldots, J\}, \; i = 1, 2, \ldots m \quad (4)$$

where $i = 1$ to m (groups), $j = 1$ to J (criteria), and V_{ij} are crisp values. Therefore, the positive ideal solution indicates the maximum value of the observations indicated by the sample, while the negative ideal solution is the minimum value. All criteria are considered as benefit criteria, as higher values represent more positive values of ATI [40].

The next step is the measurement of the distance of each group with the ideal solutions. To this end, the Euclidean distance between each observation group and the ideal solutions are computed as follows:

$$S_i^+ = \sqrt{\sum_{j=1}^{J} \left(A_j^+ - V_{ij}\right)^2}$$

$$S_i^- = \sqrt{\sum_{j=1}^{J} \left(A_j^- - V_{ij}\right)^2} \quad (5)$$

The ATI indicator, which measures the attitudes of citizens towards immigrants, is given by the ratio of the negative Euclidean distance and the sum of the positive and negative Euclidean distances. Mathematically, this ratio is given by:

$$ATI_i = \frac{S_i^-}{S_i^+ + S_i^-} \rightarrow [0, 1] \quad (6)$$

The group observation is more open toward immigrants when ATI is closer to one. Therefore, the groups are classified using the values obtained from the indicator, in descending order, to find which population group has the most positive attitudes towards immigrants. The ATI indicator logic is clear: the higher the indicator is, the closer it is to the positive ideal solution and the further away from the negative one [41].

Finally, the elasticity of the index for each group j concerning each of the eight criteria i included in ATI is calculated. These values measure the sensitivity of ATI for each of the groups studied to each variation of each criterion. Elasticity, therefore, provides a measure of how each criterion shapes the indicator. Mathematically, elasticities are given by:

$$\eta_{ij} = \frac{\Delta\% ATI_j}{\Delta\% V_{ij}} \quad (7)$$

5. Results

In this section, we detail the results provided by the Fuzzy Hybrid approach. First, the groups that represent the positive ideal solution and the negative ideal solution will be described. Then, the ATI at the country level will be detailed. Finally, the section ends by showing the ATI at the regional level, with a particular focus on comparing the differences between capital regions and island territories.

5.1. Attitudes toward Immigrants

The aforementioned methodology was applied to ISSP data for the categories described in Table 1 and at the territorial level (NUTS2 and NUT3) for the six countries considered. The positive and negative ideal solutions, respectively, indicate the groups with the maximum and minimum crisp values for each ISSP indicator. This means that each group that represents the positive ideal solutions shows the maximum defuzzified value. The contrary happens for groups that are in the negative ideal solutions.

Table 2 shows the results of the ideal solutions for each indicator included in the ATI latent variable. Generally, both for positive and negative ideal solutions, the ideal solutions are represented by territories and political orientations. Residents of the French district of Calvados represent those who do not associate immigration with the crime rate, whereas far-right citizens idealize that the immigrant increases the criminal threat. The inhabitants of the French Occitan province of Gers do not perceive the immigrant as a threat to their job, while in the province of Correze, the immigrant is perceived as a threat to the labour market. The Spanish community of Navarre represents the group of those who support the equality of rights between natives and immigrants. At the same time, the French of Lot prefer that immigrants have fewer rights than natives. In the province of Hautes-Pyrenees, the immigrant is considered a benefit to the economy, while far-right citizens associate immigration with an economic downfall.

Table 2. Ideal solutions.

Indicator	PIS *	Group	NIS **	Group
Immigrants increase crime rates	66.61	Calvados	21.49	Far right
Immigrants take jobs away from people born in [Country]	75.63	Gers	25.71	Correze
Legal immigrants should have same rights	85.17	Navarra	19.64	Lot
Immigrants are generally good for economy	70.00	Hautes-Pyrenees	27.32	Far right
Immigrants bring new ideas and cultures	71.36	Orthodox	28.05	Far right
Immigrants undermine culture	73.75	Tarn-et-Garonne	24.76	Far right
Illegal immigrants should be excluded	55.63	Ariege	7.50	Ardennes
Legal immigrants should have equal access to education	92.50	Ardennes	50.00	Lozere

* positive ideal solution; ** negative ideal solution.

Furthermore, citizens who vote for right-wing parties support the idea that immigrants do not bring ideas and undermine the culture of the country, unlike the Orthodox and the residents of Tarn-et-Garonne. Residents of the northern French province of Ardennes represent those who prefer legal immigration and are opposed to illegal immigration. They prefer legal immigrants having access to education as much as natives, but they would like to expel illegal immigrants. On the contrary, the French from Ariege are more open to illegal immigrants, and those from Lozere are not in favour of educational equality between natives and immigrants.

Once the ideal solutions have been obtained, the distances between the groups of observations and the ideal solutions are measured. Thus, ATI for each group has been calculated (Table 3). At the country level, the results show that the Iberian Peninsula shows more positive attitudes towards immigrants than the other countries in the group under analysis. On the contrary, the UK and Belgium show negative attitudes towards immigrants. France and Germany represent both the intermediate ATI.

At a subsequent step, the ATI for some socio-economic characteristics have been measured. The results show that citizens with more positive attitudes toward immigrants are foreign ones, whereas natives are less open toward immigrants. Those who prefer newcomers to adapt to the traditions of the country show negative ATI values. Instead, the citizens who support the power of the European Union are more open to immigrants. Religion is a determinant of the attitudes toward immigrants too. Muslims and Orthodox show a more positive ATI, whereas Christian religions show low values of attitudes towards immigrants. Levels of education, employment status, age, and political orientation are also decisive in being associated with attitudes towards immigrants. Those with a master's or doctorate, in student status, younger age groups, and far-left voters show a more positive attitude. On the other hand, individuals with primary or lower educational levels, retirees or the disabled, older age groups, and citizens of a conservative or far-right political orientation are less open toward immigrants. Finally, the results are less conclusive with respect to other variables, such as country pride, gender, work status, attendance at religious events, and income.

Table 3. Attitudes toward immigrants.

Group	ATI	Group	ATI	Group	ATI
Country		Religion		Age	
Spain	0.65	Islamic	0.84	25–34 years	0.60
Portugal	0.60	Orthodox	0.80	24 years or under	0.60
Germany	0.59	Other religion	0.64	35–44 years	0.59
France	0.52	Jewish	0.60	45–54 years	0.54
Belgium	0.46	No religion	0.56	55–64 years	0.51
Great Britain	0.39	Protestant	0.52	65–74 years	0.46
Traditions		Catholic	0.51	75 years or over	0.42
Maintain	0.73	Other Christian	0.40	Assiduousness	
Adapt	0.46	Education		Frequently	0.59
Proud		Upper-level tertiary	0.71	Occasionally	0.52
Somewhat proud	0.54	Lower-level tertiary	0.60	Never	0.52
Not very proud	0.53	Upper secondary	0.55	Income	
Not proud at all	0.51	Post-secondary	0.50	Income7	0.58
Very proud	0.46	Primary school	0.48	Income4	0.56
Citizenship		Lower secondary	0.43	Income9	0.56
Native	0.80	No formal education	0.43	Income8	0.56
Foreigner	0.52	Work status		Income5	0.55
Ancestors		Currently in paid work	0.56	Income6	0.55
Neither parent	0.78	Never had paid work	0.56	Highest	0.53
Only father	0.59	Currently not in paid work	0.49	Income2	0.52
Only mother	0.56	Main status		Income3	0.52
Both were citizens	0.50	In education	0.67	Lowest	0.49
EU power		Other	0.66	Political orientation	
More	0.62	Unemployed	0.59	Far left	0.71
Much more	0.62	Apprentice or trainee	0.57	Left. centre left	0.63
As much	0.59	In paid work	0.56	Liberal	0.51
Less	0.47	Domestic work	0.51	Other	0.49
Much less	0.34	Retired	0.44	Right. conservative	0.41
Gender		Permanently sick or disabled	0.42	Far right	0.11
Female	0.54				
Male	0.55				

5.2. Differences across Territories

Table 4 shows the results of the ATI at the regional and provincial levels (NUTS2 and NUTS3) of the countries analysed. The results are sorted in descending order to rank the ATI at the regional level. Thus, the regions or provinces in the first positions of the first column on the left of the table are the areas with the most positive attitudes towards immigrants. Meanwhile, the territories with more negative attitudes toward immigrants are in the last positions of the last column on the right.

Table 4. Regional ATI.

Region		ATI	Region		ATI	Region		ATI
Islas Baleares	ES	0.81	Finistere	FR	0.56	Liege	BE	0.43
Hautes-Pyrenees	FR	0.74	Castilla-La Mancha	ES	0.56	Pas-de-Calais	FR	0.43
Navarra	ES	0.74	Maine-et-Loire	FR	0.56	Aisne	FR	0.43
Berlin-Ost	DE	0.73	Extremadura	ES	0.56	Scotland (GB)	GB	0.43
Ville de Paris	FR	0.72	Belfort	FR	0.55	Var	FR	0.43
Hautes-Alpes	FR	0.71	Rheinland-Pfalz	DE	0.55	Sarthe	FR	0.43
Berlin-West	DE	0.70	Sachsen-Anhalt	DE	0.55	Flemish Brabant	BE	0.43
Hauts-de-Seine	FR	0.70	Schleswig-Holstein	DE	0.55	Limburg	BE	0.43
Cataluña	ES	0.70	Bremen	DE	0.55	Luxemburg	BE	0.43
Madrid	ES	0.70	Gironde	FR	0.55	Loiret	FR	0.42
Hamburg	DE	0.69	Indre-et-Loire	FR	0.55	Deux-Sevres	FR	0.42
Gers	FR	0.69	Oise	FR	0.55	Brabant Walloon	BE	0.42
Creuse	FR	0.69	Haute-Garonne	FR	0.54	West, East Midlands (GB)	GB	0.42
Murcia	ES	0.68	Ain	FR	0.54	Cher	FR	0.41
País Vasco	ES	0.68	Algarve	PT	0.54	Vosges	FR	0.41
Cotes-d'Armor	FR	0.68	Indre	FR	0.53	Dordogne	FR	0.40
Alpes-Hte	FR	0.68	Brandenburg	DE	0.53	Jura	FR	0.40
Lisbon	PT	0.68	Seine-et-Marne	FR	0.53	Drome	FR	0.40
Cantabria	ES	0.67	Aube	FR	0.52	Aude	FR	0.40
Saarland	DE	0.66	Morbihan	FR	0.52	Nord	FR	0.40
Ariege	FR	0.66	Puy-de-Dome	FR	0.52	Antwerp	BE	0.39
Calvados	FR	0.65	Alpes-Maritimes	FR	0.52	East Anglia, South-West, South-East (GB)	GB	0.39
Galicia	ES	0.65	Seine-Maritime	FR	0.51	Charente-Maritime	FR	0.38
Brussels Capital	BE	0.65	Valenciana	ES	0.51	East Flanders	BE	0.38
Aragón	ES	0.65	Eure	FR	0.51	Hainaut	BE	0.37
Andalucía	ES	0.64	Bas-Rhin	FR	0.51	Vaucluse	FR	0.36
Hessen	DE	0.64	Savoie	FR	0.51	Cote-d'Or	FR	0.36
La Rioja	ES	0.64	Meuse	FR	0.51	Orne	FR	0.36
Val-de-Marne	FR	0.64	Mecklenburg-Vorpommern	DE	0.50	North, North-West, Yorkshire Humbershire (GB)	GB	0.34
Tarn-et-Garonne	FR	0.64	Allier	FR	0.50	Loir-et-Cher	FR	0.34
Asturias	ES	0.64	Greater London (GB)	GB	0.50	Lozere	FR	0.33
Niedersachsen	DE	0.63	Gard	FR	0.50	Vienne	FR	0.33
Nordrhein-Westfalen	DE	0.62	Sachsen	DE	0.50	West Flanders	BE	0.33
Bayern	DE	0.62	Doubs	FR	0.49	Moselle	FR	0.30
Haute-Loire	FR	0.62	Charente	FR	0.49	Ardennes	FR	0.29
Herault	FR	0.61	Loire-Atlantique	FR	0.49	Wales (GB)	GB	0.27
Val-d'Oise	FR	0.61	Vendee	FR	0.48	Lot	FR	0.25
Tarn	FR	0.60	Bouche-du-Rhone	FR	0.48	Eure-et-Loire	FR	0.24
Yvelines	FR	0.60	Ardeche	FR	0.48	Correze	FR	0.23
Castilla-León	ES	0.60	Marne	FR	0.48	Cantal	FR	0.20
Seine-Saint-Denis	FR	0.60	Haute-Vienne	FR	0.48	Corse	FR	0.19
Nievre	FR	0.59	Mayenne	FR	0.48			
Islas Canarias	ES	0.59	Namur	BE	0.48			
Alentejo	PT	0.59	Meurthe-et-Moselle	FR	0.47			
Isere	FR	0.59	Haute-Marne	FR	0.47			
Baden-Wuerttemberg	DE	0.58	Ille-et-Vilaine	FR	0.47			
Haute-Saone	FR	0.58	Yonne	FR	0.47			
Haute-Savoie	FR	0.57	Pyrenees-Orientales	FR	0.46			
Essone	FR	0.57	Aveyron	FR	0.46			
Pyrenees-Atlantiques	FR	0.57	Manche	FR	0.46			
North	PT	0.57	Somme	FR	0.45			
Thueringen	DE	0.57	Haut-Rhin	FR	0.45			
Loire	FR	0.57	Lot-et-Garonne	FR	0.45			
Rhone	FR	0.56	Landes	FR	0.44			
Centre	PT	0.56	Saone-et-Loire	FR	0.44			

Own elaboration. DE: Germany; ES: Spain; FR: France; PT: Portugal; GB: United Kingdom; BE: Belgium.

At the regional level, the Spanish territories are located in the first part of Table 4, that is, among those with the most positive attitude. The Balearic Islands and the community of Navarre are the first two regions in the ATI ranking of all the regions and provinces considered in this study. There are also the Catalans, Madrid, Murcia, and the Basque country among the most open to immigrants. Therefore, the regions with a strong regional identity feeling have the highest ATI values. Even if the Spanish regions are all in the first half of the ATI ranking, the Valencian community is the region with the worst value of attitudes towards immigrants compared to other compatriots.

Although Portugal has high ATI values at the country level, the Portuguese territories are not present in the top positions of the ATI ranking at NUTS2 and NUTS3 levels. The French provinces are the most heterogeneous ones. The territories most open to immigrants are the southwestern French provinces and the territories close to Paris. Citizens residing in Hautes-Pyrenees, Hautes-Alpes, Hauts-de-Seine, and Creuse are the French with a better perception of immigrants. At the same time, the central and northern provinces, Eure-et-Loire, Correze, and Cantal, show a more negative attitude towards immigrants. Despite this, no reference patron divides the territories among France, even if the results reveal that the territories with regionalist movements, such as Brittany and the French area of the Basque country, present more positive attitudes toward immigrants.

German regions are divided into two macro areas: the former East Germany and the former West Germany. It is evident from the results that the formerly socialist territories are more hostile to immigrants than the former Federal Republic of Germany. The results show that the most economically advanced regions report the most positive ATI values, such as Hessen, Saarland, and Hamburg. The regions adverse to immigration are the eastern regions of Brandenburg, Sachsen, and Mecklenburg.

The results show that the Belgian and British regions have the lowest ATI values. The Belgian case shows that the western Flamenco region (West-Vlaanderen) is the territory with the lowest ATI value in Belgium. All the other Belgian regions are hostile towards immigrants, except for the Namur region and the capital region. Even more hostile are the British towards immigrants. The northern regions of England and Wales have the worst indicators of attitudes toward immigrants in the UK. The only region with slightly more positive attitudes toward immigrants is the capital region of London.

Furthermore, Table 4 also focuses on the capital regions of our six countries under analysis. The results have been summarised in Table 5 to study the capital effect more easily. In this context, it is evident that there could be a capital effect between the regions analysed, as their ATI indicator is always above the respective national average. The value of Berlin's attitude towards immigrants is at least 11 points above the German ATI (11 for West Berlin and 14 for East Berlin). The seat of the French government, Paris, has an ATI of 0.72, even 20 points higher than the national ATI. Madrid's Spanish capital has an ATI value of 0.70, only two points above the national average, while Lisbon is eight points above the ATI Portuguese average. Brussels is much more open to immigrants than other Belgian regions, with ATI values of 0.65, 21 points above the ATI of Belgium. The last capital in the order of ATI is London, the capital region most hostile to immigrants. Thus, it is in line with the rest of the country, although compared to the British average, it ranks 11 points above.

Table 5. ATI Capital regions.

Group	Country	ATI	Country ATI
Berlin-East	DE	0.73	0.59
Ville de Paris	FR	0.72	0.52
Berlin-West	DE	0.70	0.59
Madrid	ES	0.70	0.65
Lisbon	PT	0.68	0.60
Brussels	BE	0.65	0.46
Greater London	GB	0.50	0.39

Own elaboration. DE: Germany; ES: Spain; FR: France; PT: Portugal; GB: United King-dom; BE: Belgium.

We now want to provide a comparison between island regions and continental regions. Regarding island regions, Table 6 summarises the values of the attitudes towards immigrants from the Balearic Islands, the Canary Islands, and Corsica. The regions have been sorted in order of ATI values. Regional data on the number of immigrants in the regions were extracted from the respective national statistical institutes (Spain: INE; France: INSEE) to provide a broader overview of ATI in insular territories. The Balearic Islands are the island region with both the highest indicators, and it has a high immigration rate (20%) and the best ATI value of all regions. The Canary Islands have more moderate openness towards immigrants and an immigration rate of 14%. The results highlight a dual behaviour between the Balearic Islands and Corsica. These two island regions exhibit an opposite behaviour, as Corsica has the lowest immigration rate and a high hostility towards immigrants.

Table 6. ATI and immigration rate in Corsica, Balearic, and Canary Islands.

Group	Country	ATI	Immigration
Balearic Islands	ES	0.81	221.406 (20%) *
Canary Islands	ES	0.59	301.234 (14%) *
Corsica	FR	0.19	32.661 (10.2%) **

* INE; ** INSEE. ES: Spain; FR: France.

Finally, the elasticities of ATI by Islands regions and capital regions were calculated (Table 7). The elasticity analysis was studied because it provides interesting insights into the criteria that affect more ATI in each territory. In this study, the elasticities for each item of the capital and island regions were calculated. The ATI of the Balearic Islands is quite inelastic to all criteria, even if the criteria concerning equality of rights and access to education between natives and immigrants have a more significant impact than other criteria. The same behaviour is repeated in the Canary Islands, but the criterion concerning the equality of rights has the most significant impact. The competition in the labour market, the perception of the economic threat of immigrants, and the equal access to education between natives and immigrants are criteria that have a significant impact on the Corsican ATI, and, interestingly, these three values are part of the five most elastic values that are analysed. The ATI is inelastic concerning all attributes as far as the capital regions are concerned. The criterion with the highest elasticity is the same rights between natives and immigrants, especially for Berlin-West and Paris.

Table 7. Elasticities.

	C1	C2	C3	C4	C5	C6	C7	C8
Balearic Islands	0.0972	0.2744	0.3137	0.1479	0.1094	0.1236	0.0577	0.3037
Canary Islands	0.1752	0.2106	0.3267	0.1803	0.1876	0.2151	0.1197	0.2497
Corse	0.1305	0.9151	0.2598	0.5688	0.0851	0.1015	0.0554	1.0876
Brussels	0.1822	0.2259	0.3285	0.1810	0.1910	0.2165	0.1487	0.2600
Berlin-E	0.1820	0.1952	0.3306	0.1347	0.0818	0.1803	0.0876	0.2719
Berlin-W	0.1798	0.2151	0.3311	0.1562	0.1389	0.1657	0.1149	0.2454
Madrid	0.1406	0.2408	0.2407	0.1478	0.1731	0.1645	0.1423	0.2393
Paris	0.1656	0.1623	0.3382	0.1525	0.1749	0.1407	0.1422	0.2180
London	0.2231	0.2247	0.2878	0.2396	0.2506	0.2503	0.1301	0.2645
Lisbon	0.1654	0.2347	0.2937	0.1427	0.1542	0.1811	0.1329	0.2513

C1: Immigrants increase crime rates; C2: Immigrants take jobs away from people born in [Country] C3: Legal immigrants should have the same rights C4: Immigrants are generally good for economy; C5: Immigrants bring new ideas and cultures C6: Immigrants undermine the culture; C7: Illegal immigrants should be excluded; C8: Legal immigrants should have equal access to education.

The five most inelastic pairs also show that three are observed in insular territories (Corse and Balearic Islands) and two in Berlin-East. The criteria involved were those of bringing new ideas and cultures, and illegal immigrants should be excluded.

6. Discussion

Now, the results presented above will be discussed highlighting that the more open citizens toward immigrants depend on some socioeconomic characteristics. This section explains which individual characteristics can have a positive or negative influence on ATI. Thus, an overview of why some regions are more or less open toward immigrants than others will be further discussed.

6.1. Pro-Immigrants Profiles

Previous studies have analysed the attitudes of citizens towards immigrants by country, religion, age, income, and education [1,3,5,11,13,18,42]. The socio-economic characteristics of individuals are seen as proxies of factors that affect anti-immigrant sentiments.

The study introduced a methodology not commonly used in the social sciences. The Fuzzy-Hybrid TOPSIS approach was recently introduced in attitudes toward immigrants by Martín and Indelicato [1]. The methodology is effective, as the results replicate other studies [18,26,43,44].

The analysis of the positive and negative ideal solutions shows that the maximum and minimum values expressed for each criterion are mainly represented by French territories and the political orientation of the extreme right. In particular, the criteria concerning the crime rate, the economy, and culture are negatively represented by the political orientation of the far right. In agreement with Creighton et al. [45], financial and economic crises, such as in the first decade of the 2000s, immediately impacted anti-immigrant sentiment. Especially among far-right citizens, the perception of economic and country safety threats arises when immigration increases [46,47].

At the country level, three areas of attitudes towards immigrants have been detected. The Iberian Peninsula is the most open territory towards immigrants; civic nationalist countries, France and Germany, present moderate attitudes towards immigrants; and, finally, the UK and Belgium represent the group of countries with anti-immigrant sentiments. Following McLaren and Johnson's [48] work, what worries the British citizens is the impact of immigration on society. In this regard, the key factors requiring specific attention are the economy, crime, and symbols of British identity. Brits are concerned that immigration threatens the jobs of their compatriots, which in turn affects how attitudes towards immigrants are shaped. Furthermore, the British are concerned about the symbolic and cultural threats arising from mass immigration, such as perceived religious threats to emphasise non-British values and end communities outside the UK and threats to shared customs and lifestyles [48,49].

Religion is an essential determinant of anti-immigrant attitudes. The results show that citizens who profess minority religions in the countries analysed show more positive attitudes towards immigrants. For example, Muslims are the ones most in favour of immigration. This issue can be explained because Muslims are the ethnic minority and the largest share of immigrants to European countries. According to Marfouk [50], anti-immigrant sentiment is a more Islamophobic sentiment. Therefore, it is easy to think that Muslims show more positive attitudes toward immigration as solidarity.

On the contrary, Catholics display negative attitudes towards immigrants. According to Kerwin and Alulema [51], many Catholics do not align with Christian teachings, as they have negative feelings and attitudes towards immigrants. Following Ambrosini's [52] work the charitable activities of Catholics do not include activities toward immigrants because according to the priorities of many Catholics, the protection of migrants and refugees is a secondary or lower priority [51].

6.2. Capital Regions and Islands

Attitudes towards immigrants at the territorial level have been summarised in Figure 1. The first result that the study confirms is the capital effect of the six countries, which can be explained by the fact that European capitals are multicultural societies. The literature shows that multiculturalism tends to have beneficial effects on immigrant attitudes, but it can also be a detonator against immigration [53,54]. According to Mahfud et al. [55], multiculturalism is related to more positive attitudes towards immigration. They have shown that in the condition of multiculturalism, citizens perceive low feelings of threat and, therefore, less prejudice. Research among majority group members has shown that multiculturalism can promote positive relationships between groups, evoke resistance, and hinder harmony between groups [55]. This last result is supported by the findings of the British regions, as multiculturalism has resulted in an increased perception of the threat to Britain [48].

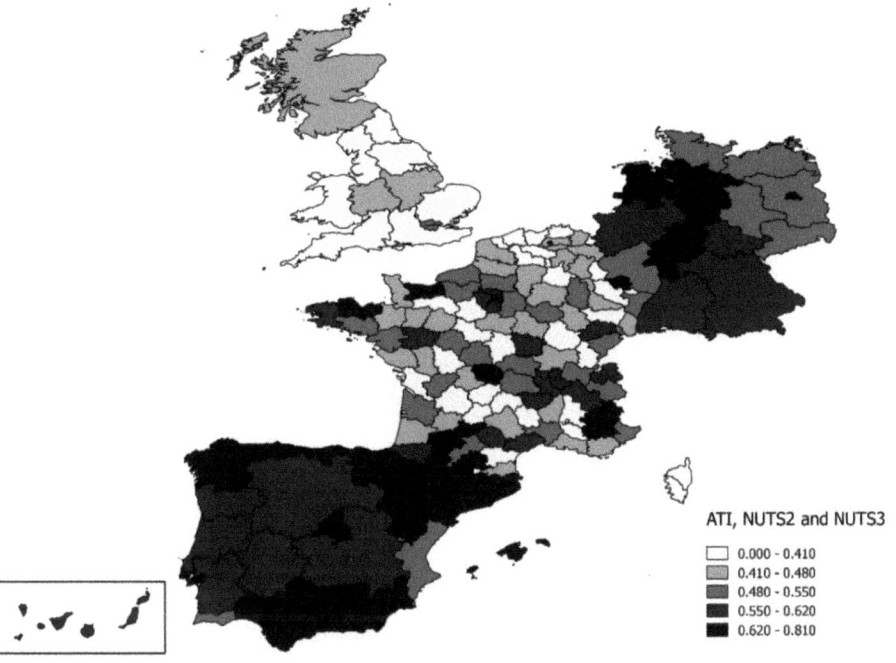

Figure 1. ATI at the territorial level—our own elaboration.

This study obtains significant results at the island region level. There is a perfect duality between Corsica and the Balearic Islands, as the French island shows negative attitudes towards immigrants and the Balearics are more open to immigrants. One explanation may be the difference in the level of multiculturalism between the two regions, as the immigrant population in the Balearic Islands is 20%, while in Corsica, immigrants do not exceed 10%. In addition, it can be explained through the nexus between immigration and tourism [24,56,57].

Provenzano [24] shows that the tourist flow between the two countries is affected by the migration rate and vice versa. His findings suggest a positive relationship between tourism and immigration. In other words, the greater the number of migrants from one country to another, the greater the flow of tourists from the first country to the second. Therefore, the duality between the Balearic Islands and Corsica can be dictated by the differences in tourism policies. Provenzano [24] shows that the islands are characterized by a tourism development model that has favoured the construction of large hotels with a high average number of beds per structure, thus creating important and prominent tourist destinations. According to Capó et al. [56] and Ruggieri and Cal [57], the Balearic Islands is an archipelago that invests more in tourism, creating infrastructures and promoting tourist activity, while Corsica is an island region with the lowest levels of tourism. Thus, the differences between the Balearic Islands and Corsica can be explained by the fact that high levels of tourism cause high rates of immigration [24]. Thus, high levels of immigration build multicultural societies, which are societies that show more positive attitudes towards immigrants [55].

7. Conclusions

Attitudes towards immigrants (ATI) is a very studied topic at the academic level [3–5]. The issue of immigration is still a very hot topic in political and social debate. Researchers studying the ATI commonly use Confirmatory Factor Analysis (CFA) and Structural Equation Models (SEM), which have proven to be valid methodologies that are confirmed as efficient tools [11,26,42]. Despite this, the research does not seem to advance on a methodological level.

The study aimed to introduce a new methodology in this field of studies, namely the Fuzzy-Hybrid TOPSIS, which is not commonly used in the social sciences. The advantage of this approach is that it deals with the vague information provided by the Likert scale commonly used in social science questionnaires. The 2013 ISSP data from the National Identity form were extracted. Eight items were chosen to measure attitudes towards immigrants (ATI), such as Immigrants increase crime rates; Immigrants take jobs away from people born in [Country]; Legal immigrants should have the same rights; Immigrants are generally good for the economy; Immigrants bring new ideas and cultures; Immigrants undermine culture; Illegal immigrants should be excluded; and Legal immigrants should have equal access to education. The analysis was carried out at the country and territorial levels (NUTS2 and NUTS3).

The results confirm previous studies in the literature, giving an innovative approach by applying the methodology based on the fuzzy set theory. At the country level, the countries showing the highest ATI values are the countries of the Iberian Peninsula and Germany. At the same time, the United Kingdom and Belgium represent the group of countries with negative attitudes towards immigrants. At the territorial level, a capital effect is highlighted, as the capitals of the countries analysed tend to have more positive ATI than the average of the respective country. Finally, a duality between the Balearic Islands and Corsica has been pointed out. The Spanish archipelago, driven by the nexus between tourist and migratory flows [24], has built a multicultural society tolerant of immigrants [55], while Corsica, which has invested less in tourism, presents more hostile attitudes.

As with any other study, future research is needed to overcome some limitations such as: (1) a small number of countries were chosen; (2) only 2013 was considered; and (3) the analysis was carried out at an aggregate level, although the methodology allows the study at an individual level. Future research should first aim to introduce new ISSP versions after those of 2013 in the analysis providing more insights into the dynamic of ATI. Furthermore, second, it would be interesting to provide a more complete overview of Europe, introducing countries such as Italy, Austria, and other Eastern European countries. Thus, it will be possible to obtain interesting insights with respect to whether the territorial differences obtained in the study are more or less reinforced using a wide sample of countries between the North, West, East, and South of Europe. In addition, other econometrics models could be used to detect if some socioeconomic variables are important drivers or not on ATI formation.

Author Contributions: Conceptualization, J.C.M., A.I. and R.S.; methodology, J.C.M.; software, J.C.M., A.I. and R.S.; validation, J.C.M., A.I. and R.S.; investigation, J.C.M., A.I. and R.S; data curation, J.C.M. and A.I.; writing—original draft preparation, J.C.M., A.I. and R.S.; writing—review and editing, J.C.M., A.I. and R.S. All authors have read and agreed to the published version of the manuscript.

Funding: This research received no external funding.

Institutional Review Board Statement: Not applicable.

Informed Consent Statement: Informed consent was obtained from all subjects involved in the study.

Data Availability Statement: Data available on http://www.issp.org/data-download/by-topic/ (accessed on 15 June 2021).

Conflicts of Interest: The authors declare no conflict of interest.

References

1. Martín, J.C.; Indelicato, A. A fuzzy-hybrid analysis of citizens' perception toward immigrants in Europe. *Qual. Quant.* **2022**. [CrossRef]
2. King, R.; DeBono, D. Irregular Migration and the "Southern European Model" of Migration. *J. Mediterr. Stud.* **2013**, *22*, 1–31.
3. Czymara, C.S. Attitudes toward Refugees in Contemporary Europe: A Longitudinal Perspective on Cross-National Differences. *Soc. Forces* **2021**, *99*, 1306–1333. [CrossRef]
4. De Vreese, C.H. How changing conditions make us reconsider the relationship between immigration attitudes, religion, and EU attitudes. *Eur. Union Polit.* **2017**, *18*, 137–142. [CrossRef] [PubMed]
5. Martín, J.C.; Indelicato, A. A DEA MCDM Approach Applied to ESS8 Dataset for Measuring Immigration and Refugees Citizens' Openness. *J. Int. Migr. Integr.* **2021**. [CrossRef]
6. Meuleman, B.; Billiet, J. Measuring attitudes toward immigration in Europe: The cross–cultural validity of the ESS immigration scales. *Ask. Res. Methods* **2012**, *21*, 5–29.
7. Thomsen, J.P.F.; Rafiqi, A. When does superficial intergroup contact reduce anti-foreigner sentiment? Negative contact as an essential condition. *Int. J. Comp. Sociol.* **2018**, *59*, 25–43. [CrossRef]
8. Di Nardo, E.; Simone, R. A model-based fuzzy analysis of questionnaires. *Stat. Methods Appl.* **2019**, *28*, 187–215. [CrossRef]
9. Palczewski, K.; Sałabun, W. The fuzzy TOPSIS applications in the last decade. *Procedia Comput. Sci.* **2019**, *159*, 2294–2303. [CrossRef]
10. Cantillo, J.; Martin, J.C.; Román, C. A hybrid-fuzzy TOPSIS method to analyze the consumption and buying behavior of fishery and aquaculture products (FAPs) in the EU28. *Br. Food J.* **2020**, *122*, 3403–3417. [CrossRef]
11. Eger, M.A.; Breznau, N. Immigration and the welfare state: A cross-regional analysis of European welfare attitudes. *Int. J. Comp. Sociol.* **2017**, *58*, 440–463. [CrossRef]
12. Dirksmeier, P. The impact of regionalism on anti-immigrant attitudes: A multilevel international comparative study. *Territ. Polit. Gov.* **2021**, *9*, 1–21. [CrossRef]
13. Karreth, J.; Singh, S.P.; Stojek, S.M. Explaining Attitudes toward Immigration: The Role of Regional Context and Individual Predispositions. *West Eur. Polit.* **2015**, *38*, 1174–1202. [CrossRef]
14. Markaki, Y.; Longhi, S. What determines attitudes to immigration in European countries? An analysis at the regional level. *Migr. Stud.* **2013**, *1*, 311–337. [CrossRef]
15. Escandell, X.; Ceobanu, A.M. Nationalisms and anti-immigrant sentiment in Spain. *South Eur. Soc. Polit.* **2010**, *15*, 157–179. [CrossRef]
16. Sides, J.; Citrin, J. European opinion about immigration: The role of identities, interests and information. *Br. J. Polit. Sci.* **2007**, *37*, 477–504. [CrossRef]
17. Dekeyser, E.; Freedman, M. Elections, Party Rhetoric, and Public Attitudes Toward Immigration in Europe. *Polit. Behav.* **2021**. [CrossRef]
18. Davidov, E.; Semyonov, M. Attitudes toward immigrants in European societies. *Int. J. Comp. Sociol.* **2017**, *58*, 359–366. [CrossRef]
19. Dalle Nogare, C.; Scuderi, R.; Bertacchini, E. Immigrants, voter sentiment, and local public goods: The case of museums. *J. Reg. Sci.* **2021**, *61*, 1087–1112. [CrossRef]
20. Jeram, S.; van der Zwet, A.; Wisthaler, V. Friends or Foes? Migrants and Sub-state Nationalists in Europe Sanjay. *J. Ethn. Migr. Stud.* **2016**, *42*, 1229–1241. [CrossRef]
21. Salvà-Tomàs, P.A. Tourist development and foreign immigration in Balearic Islands. *Rev. Eur. Migr. Int.* **2002**, *18*, 87–101. [CrossRef]
22. Vincenzini, N. Racisme Corse anti-maghrébin. *Multitudes* **2004**, *19*, 85. [CrossRef]
23. Engelken-Jorge, M. The anti-immigrant discourse in tenerife: Assessing the lacanian theory of ideology. *J. Polit. Ideol.* **2010**, *15*, 69–88. [CrossRef]
24. Provenzano, D. The migration–tourism nexus in the EU28. *Tour. Econ.* **2020**, *26*, 1374–1393. [CrossRef]
25. Ceobanu, A.M.; Escandell, X. Comparative Analyses of Public Attitudes Toward Immigrants and Immigration Using Multinational Survey Data: A Review of Theories and Research. *Annu. Rev. Sociol.* **2010**, *36*, 309–328. [CrossRef]
26. Grigoryan, L.K.; Ponizovskiy, V. The three facets of national identity: Identity dynamics and attitudes toward immigrants in Russia. *Int. J. Comp. Sociol.* **2018**, *59*, 403–427. [CrossRef]
27. Kumar, H. Some recent defuzzification methods. *Theor. Pract. Adv. Fuzzy Syst. Integr.* **2017**, 31–48. [CrossRef]
28. Mohsin, M.; Zhang, J.; Saidur, R.; Sun, H.; Sait, S.M. Economic assessment and ranking of wind power potential using fuzzy-TOPSIS approach. *Environ. Sci. Pollut. Res.* **2019**, *26*, 22494–22511. [CrossRef]
29. Liu, Y.; Li, L.; Tu, Y.; Mei, Y. Fuzzy topsis-ew method with multi-granularity linguistic assessment information for emergency logistics performance evaluation. *Symmetry* **2020**, *12*, 1331. [CrossRef]
30. Indelicato, A.; Martín, J.C. Two Approaches to Analyze Whether Citizens' National Identity Is Affected by Country, Age, and Political Orientation—A Fuzzy Eco-Apostle Model. *Appl. Sci.* **2022**, *12*, 3946. [CrossRef]
31. Cagri Tolga, A.; Basar, M. The assessment of a smart system in hydroponic vertical farming via fuzzy MCDM methods. *J. Intell. Fuzzy Syst.* **2022**, *42*, 2–12. [CrossRef]

32. Martínez, M.P.; Cremasco, C.P.; Gabriel Filho, L.R.A.; Braga Junior, S.S.; Bednaski, A.V.; Quevedo-Silva, F.; Correa, C.M.; da Silva, D.; Moura-Leite Padgett, R.C. Fuzzy inference system to study the behavior of the green consumer facing the perception of greenwashing. *J. Clean. Prod.* **2020**, *242*, 116064. [CrossRef]
33. Behdioğlu, S.; Acar, E.; Burhan, H.A. Evaluating service quality by fuzzy SERVQUAL: A case study in a physiotherapy and rehabilitation hospital. *Total Qual. Manag. Bus. Excell.* **2019**, *30*, 301–319. [CrossRef]
34. Martin, J.C.; Bustamante-Sánchez, N.S.; Indelicato, A. Analyzing the Main Determinants for Being an Immigrant in Cuenca (Ecuador) Based on a Fuzzy Clustering Approach. *Axioms* **2022**, *11*, 74. [CrossRef]
35. Mamdani, E.H.; Assilian, S. An experiment in linguistic synthesis with a fuzzy logic controller. *Int. J. Hum. Comput. Stud.* **1999**, *51*, 135–147. [CrossRef]
36. Zadeh, L.A. Information and control. *Fuzzy Sets* **1965**, *8*, 338–353.
37. Salih, M.M.; Zaidan, B.B.; Zaidan, A.A.; Ahmed, M.A. Survey on fuzzy TOPSIS state-of-the-art between 2007 and 2017. *Comput. Oper. Res.* **2019**, *104*, 207–227. [CrossRef]
38. Buckley, J.J. Fuzzy hierarchical analysis. *Fuzzy Sets Syst.* **1985**, *17*, 233–247. [CrossRef]
39. Hwang, C.-L.; Yoon, K. Methods for Information on Attribute Given. In *Multiple Attribute Decision Making*; Springer: Berlin/Heidelberg, Germany, 1981; pp. 58–191.
40. Behzadian, M.; Khanmohammadi Otaghsara, S.; Yazdani, M.; Ignatius, J. A state-of the-art survey of TOPSIS applications. *Expert Syst. Appl.* **2012**, *39*, 13051–13069. [CrossRef]
41. Martín, J.C.; Moreira, P.; Román, C. A hybrid-fuzzy segmentation analysis of residents' perception towards tourism in Gran Canaria. *Tour. Econ.* **2020**, *26*, 1282–1304. [CrossRef]
42. Löw, A.; Puzić, S.; Matić Bojić, J. Anti-immigrant prejudice in a post-socialist context: The role of identity-based explanations. *Ethn. Racial Stud.* **2022**, *45*, 113–132. [CrossRef]
43. Storm, I. When does religiosity matter for attitudes to immigration? The impact of economic insecurity and religious norms in Europe. *Eur. Soc.* **2018**, *20*, 595–620. [CrossRef]
44. Bail, C.A. The configuration of symbolic boundaries against immigrants in Europe. *Am. Sociol. Rev.* **2008**, *73*, 37–59. [CrossRef]
45. Creighton, M.J.; Jamal, A.; Malancu, N.C. Has Opposition to Immigration Increased in the United States after the Economic Crisis? An Experimental Approach. *Int. Migr. Rev.* **2015**, *49*, 727–756. [CrossRef]
46. Boateng, F.D.; McCann, W.S.; Chenane, J.L.; Pryce, D.K. Perception of Immigrants in Europe: A Multilevel Assessment of Macrolevel Conditions. *Soc. Sci. Q.* **2021**, *102*, 209–227. [CrossRef]
47. Melossi, D. The Processes of Criminalization of Migrants and the Borders of 'Fortress Europe. In *Borders and Crime*; McCulloch, J., Pickering, S., Eds.; Palgrave Macmillan UK: London, UK, 2012; pp. 17–34, ISBN 978-1-137-28382-5.
48. McLaren, L.; Johnson, M. Resources, group conflict and symbols: Explaining anti-immigration hostility in Britain. *Polit. Stud.* **2007**, *55*, 709–732. [CrossRef]
49. Evans, G. In search of tolerance. *Br. Soc. Attitudes* **2002**, *57*, 213–228.
50. Marfouk, A. I'm neither racist nor xenophobic, but: Dissecting European attitudes towards a ban on Muslims' immigration. *Ethn. Racial Stud.* **2019**, *42*, 1747–1765. [CrossRef]
51. Kerwin, D.; Alulema, D. The CRISIS Survey: The Catholic Church's Work with Immigrants in a Period of Crisis. *J. Migr. Hum. Secur.* **2021**, *9*, 271–296. [CrossRef]
52. Ambrosini, M. Protected but separate: International immigrants in the Italian Catholic Church. In *Migration, Transnationalism and Catholicism*; Springer: Berlin/Heidelberg, Germany, 2016; pp. 317–335.
53. Deaux, K.; Verkuyten, M. The social psychology of multiculturalism: Identity and intergroup relations. In *The Oxford Handbook of Multicultural Identity*; Benet-Martínez, V., Hong, Y.-Y., Eds.; Oxford University Press: Oxford, UK, 2014; pp. 118–138.
54. Rattan, A.; Ambady, N. Diversity ideologies and intergroup relations: An examination of colorblindness and multiculturalism. *Eur. J. Soc. Psychol.* **2013**, *43*, 12–21. [CrossRef]
55. Mahfud, Y.; Badea, C.; Verkuyten, M.; Reynolds, K. Multiculturalism and Attitudes Toward Immigrants: The Impact of Perceived Cultural Distance. *J. Cross Cult. Psychol.* **2018**, *49*, 945–958. [CrossRef]
56. Capó, J.; Font, A.R.; Nadal, J.R. Dutch disease in tourism economies: Evidence from the Balearics and the Canary Islands. *J. Sustain. Tour.* **2007**, *15*, 615–627. [CrossRef]
57. Ruggieri, G.; Cal, P. Tourism Dynamics and Sustainability: A Comparative Analysis between Mediterranean Islands—Evidence for Post-COVID-19 Strategies. *Sustainability* **2022**, *14*, 4183. [CrossRef]

Article

Brain Tumor Classification Using Dense Efficient-Net

Dillip Ranjan Nayak [1], Neelamadhab Padhy [1], Pradeep Kumar Mallick [2], Mikhail Zymbler [3] and Sachin Kumar [3,*]

1 School of Engineering and Technology (CSE), GIET University, Gunupur 765022, India; dilipranjan.nayak@giet.edu (D.R.N.); dr.neelamadhab@giet.edu (N.P.)
2 School of Computer Engineering, Kalinga Institute of Technology, Deemed-to-Be-University, Bhubaneswar 751024, India; pradeep.mallickfcs@kiit.ac.in
3 Department of Computer Science, South Ural State University, 454080 Chelyabinsk, Russia; mzym@susu.ru
* Correspondence: sachinagnihotri16@gmail.com

Abstract: Brain tumors are most common in children and the elderly. It is a serious form of cancer caused by uncontrollable brain cell growth inside the skull. Tumor cells are notoriously difficult to classify due to their heterogeneity. Convolutional neural networks (CNNs) are the most widely used machine learning algorithm for visual learning and brain tumor recognition. This study proposed a CNN-based dense EfficientNet using min-max normalization to classify 3260 T1-weighted contrast-enhanced brain magnetic resonance images into four categories (glioma, meningioma, pituitary, and no tumor). The developed network is a variant of EfficientNet with dense and drop-out layers added. Similarly, the authors combined data augmentation with min-max normalization to increase the contrast of tumor cells. The benefit of the dense CNN model is that it can accurately categorize a limited database of pictures. As a result, the proposed approach provides exceptional overall performance. The experimental results indicate that the proposed model was 99.97% accurate during training and 98.78% accurate during testing. With high accuracy and a favorable F1 score, the newly designed EfficientNet CNN architecture can be a useful decision-making tool in the study of brain tumor diagnostic tests.

Keywords: brain tumor; confusion matrix; EfficientNet; CNN; MRI; fuzzy logic

1. Introduction

The brain has billions of active cells, making analysis very difficult. Today, one of the leading causes of childhood and adult death is brain tumors. Primary brain tumors affect about 250,000 individuals worldwide each year and account for less than 2% of all malignancies. In total, 150 different kinds of brain tumors may be seen in humans. Among them are: (i) benign tumors; and (ii) malignant tumors. Benign tumors spread within the brain. Typically, malignant tumors are referred to as brain cancer since they may spread outside of the brain [1]. Early diagnosis and true grading of brain tumors are vital to save the life of human beings. The manual technique is very difficult because of the significant density of brain tumors. Thus, an automated computer-based method is very beneficial for tumor detection [2]. Today, things are very different. Using machine learning and deep learning to improve brain tumor detection algorithms [3] enables radiologists to quickly locate tumors without requiring surgical intervention. Recent advances in deep neural network modeling have resulted in the emergence of a novel technology for the study, segmentation, and classification of brain tumors [4,5].

Brain tumor classification is possible with the help of the fully automated CNN model to make fast and accurate decisions by researchers. However, achieving high accuracy is still an endless challenge in brain image classification due to vagueness. The objective of this paper is to designate fully automatic CNN models with min-max normalization for multi-classification of the brain tumors using publicly available datasets. We have

proposed a dense EfficientNet network for three-class brain tumor classification to obtain better accuracy. It is focused on data augmentation with min-max normalization combined with dense EfficientNet to enhance the quicker training accuracy with higher depth of the network. It contains separable convolution layers in-depth to reduce to a smaller extent the parameters and computation. However, to segment brain tumors, the EfficientNet model must be further expanded via the use of dense chain blocks. Thus, dense EfficientNet can also achieve excellent classification accuracy. It obtains deep image information and reconstructs dense segmentation masks for brain tumor classification of three tumor kinds. It was evaluated on T1-weighted contrast-enhanced magnetic resonance imaging. The performance of the network was tested using pre-processing, augmentation, and classification. A novel dense depth classifier is presented based on a deep convolutional neural network. The suggested approach has higher classification accuracy compared to existing deep learning methods. The suggested approach provides excellent performance with a smaller number of training samples as is demonstrated in the confusion matrix. The issue of overfitting is minimized with reduced classification error owing to dropout layers.

This paper is split into several sections: the next part deals with the various related work about tumor segmentation; suggested methodology is described in Section 3; additionally, Section 4 emphasizes the findings using confusion matrix analysis; and finally, Section 5 provides the conclusion derived from the study output and the scope of the potential development.

2. Related Work

Medical image segmentation for detection and classification of brain tumor from the magnetic resonance (MR) images is a very important process for deciding the right therapy at the right time. Many techniques have been proposed for classification of brain tumors in MRI. Shelhamer et al. [6] proposed a dual path CNN skipping architecture that combines deep, coarse layer with fine layer to find accurate and detailed segmentation of brain cancer. Brain tumor cells have soaring baleful fluid which has very high vigor and is vague. Therefore, min-max normalization is a better pre-processing tool to classify tumors into different grades [7]. Today, there are several image processing methodologies used for classifying MR images [8,9]. Karunakaran created a technique for detecting meningioma brain tumors utilizing fuzzy-logic-based enhancement and a co-active adaptive neuro-fuzzy inference system, as well as U-Net convolutional neural network classification algorithms. The suggested method for detecting meningioma tumors includes the following stages: enhancement, feature extraction, and classification. Fuzzy logic is used to improve the original brain picture, and then a dual tree-complex wavelet transform is performed on the augmented image at various scale levels. The deconstructed sub-band pictures are used to calculate the features, which are then categorized using the CAN FIS classification technique to distinguish meningioma brain images from non-meningioma brain images. The projected meningioma brain's performance sensitivity, specificity, segmentation accuracy, and dice coefficient index with detection rate are all evaluated for the tumor detection and segmentation system [10]. Recent advances in deep learning ideas have increased the accuracy of computer-aided brain tumor analysis on tumors with significant fluctuation in form, size, and intensity. Cheng et al. [11] used T1-MRI data to investigate the three-class brain tumor classification issue. This method employs image dilation to enlarge the tumor area, which is then divided into progressively fine ring-form sub-regions. Badza and Barjaktarovic [12] presented a novel CNN architecture based on the modification of an existing pre-trained network for the categorization of brain tumors using T1-weighted contrast-enhanced magnetic resonance images. The model's performance is 96.56 percent, and it is composed of two 10-fold cross-validation techniques using augmented pictures. Mzough et al. [13] used a pre-processing method based on intensity normalization and adaptive contrast enhancement to propose a completely automated 3D CNN model for glioma brain tumor categorization into low-grade and high-grade glioma. They obtained validation accuracy of 96.49 percent overall when utilizing the Brats-2018 dataset. A hybrid technique: Hashemzehi et al. [14] evaluated the detection of brain cancers from MRI images using a hybrid model CNN and NADE. They used 3064 T1-weighted contrast-enhanced images. They evaluated in order to identify three distinct kinds of brain cancers with a 96 percent accuracy rate. Diaz-Pernas et al. [15] presented a completely automated brain tumor segmentation and classification algorithm based on MRI scans of meningioma, glioma, and pituitary tumors. They utilized CNN to implement the idea of a multi-scale approach inherent in human functioning. They achieved 97 percent accuracy on a 3064-slice imaging collection from 233 patients. Sultan et al. [16] utilized a CNN structure comprising 16 convolution layers, pooling and normalizing, and a dropout layer before the fully linked layer. They discovered a 96 percent accuracy rate when 68 percent of the pictures were used for training and the remaining images were used for validation and testing. Abd et al. [17] conducted their experiment on 25,000 brain magnetic resonance imaging (MRI) pictures using a differential deep-CNN to identify various kinds of brain tumor. They achieved outstanding total performance with an accuracy of 99.25 percent in training. Sajja et al. [18] conducted their research on Brat's dataset which includes 577 T1-weighted brain tumors for classifying malignant and benign tumors using the VGG16 network. They performed their performance with 96.70 inaccuracy. Das et al. [19] identified various kinds of brain cancers, such as glioma tumor, meningioma tumor, and pituitary tumor using a convolutional neural network which includes 3064 T1-weighted contrast-enhanced MRI pictures. The CNN model was trained to utilize several convolutional and pooling procedures. They obtained 94 percent accuracy by resizing the convolutional network based on convolutional filters/kernels of variable size.

3. Proposed Methodology

In this paper, the authors have applied min-max normalization and data augmentation techniques on a large dataset of 3260 different types of brain MRI images [20]. The image database includes 3064 T1-weighted contrast-enhanced MRI images collected from Kaggle.com. These are mainly three kinds of brain tumors: one is meningioma which contains 708 pictures; the second is glioma which contains 1426 pictures; and lastly there is pituitary tumor which contains 930 pictures. All pictures were collected from 233 patients in three planes: sagittal (1025 photos), axial (994 photos), and coronal (1045 photos). The authors divided the dataset into three distinct parts for training, validation, and testing. The suggested model is composed of different stages which are illustrated in Figure 1.

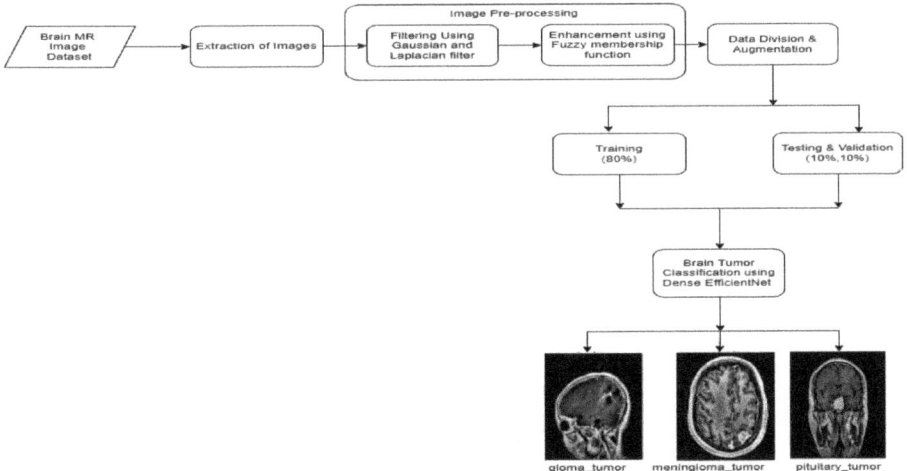

Figure 1. Overview of proposed dense EfficientNet methodology.

3.1. Image Pre-Processing

The brain tumor images have low quality due to noises and low illumination. The proposed method converts the low pixel value images to brighter ones using data normalization and using the min-max normalization function method followed by Gaussian and Laplacian filter. Initially, the authors added Gaussian blur to the original images and then subtracted the blurred image by adding a weighted portion of the mask to obtain the de-blurred image. Then they used a Laplacian filter with kernel size 3 × 3 for smoothing the images which are shown in Figure 2.

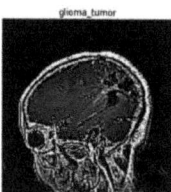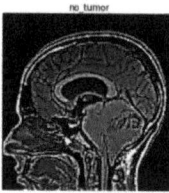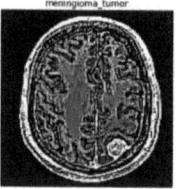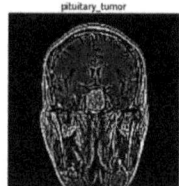

Figure 2. T1- contrast MR images of each label after filtration.

The MRI image as obtained from the patient's database is unclear. These images also contain a certain amount of uncertainty. Therefore, brain images need to be normalized before further processing. Usually, MRI images look like grey scale images. Hence, the images are easily normalized to improve the image quality and reduce miscalculation. Nayak et al. [21] applied L membership function with the morphology concept to detect brain tumors. The membership function used in the study is as follows:

$$r = \frac{d - mn}{mx - mn} \tag{1}$$

where d = double (image), mn = min (min (image)), mx = max (max (image)), and r = normalized image.

This membership function is mainly used to normalize the image for enhancement with the range 0 to 1. Thus, it is also called the max-min normalization method.

The resultant image after applying the normalization is shown in Figure 3.

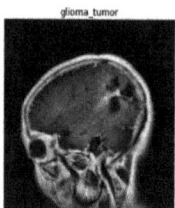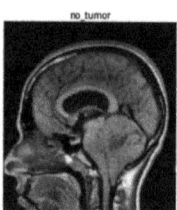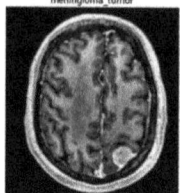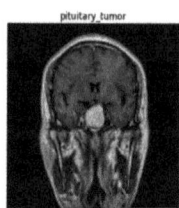

Figure 3. T1-contrast MR images of each label after fuzzification.

3.2. Data Division and Augmentation

The deep neural network needs large datasets for better results but our dataset is limited. Our dataset contains 3260 brain images, further divided into 80% for training, which remains for testing and validation purposes. So, data augmentation is needed to change in the minor. The authors have applied rotation, width-shift, height-shift, and the zoom—range for the data requirement. They augmented the original data 21 times for better training. This will enhance the amount of training data, allowing the model to learn more effectively. This may assist in increasing the quantity of relevant data. It contributes to the reduction of overfitting and enhances generalization. Data augmentation (DA) is the process of creating additional samples to supplement an existing dataset via transformation. Dropout through augmentation, practical solutions such as dropout regularization, and batch normalization are performed on the original dataset. By data warping or oversampling, this augmentation exaggerated the size of the training dataset.

3.3. Dense EfficientNet CNN Model

A novel dense CNN model is presented in this article, which is a mix of pre-trained EfficientNetB0 with dense layers. EfficientB0 has 230 layers and 7 MBConv blocks [22,23]. It features a thick block structure consisting of four tightly linked layers with a development rate of 4. Each layer in this structure uses the output feature maps of the preceding levels as the input feature maps. The dense block concept is composed of convolution layers of the same size as the input feature maps in EfficientNet. Dense block takes advantage of the preceding convolution layers' output feature maps to generate more feature maps with fewer convolution kernels. This CNN model retrieved 150 × 150 enhanced MRI image data. The dense EfficientNet network has an alternate dense and drop-out layer. A dense layer is the basic layer which feeds all outputs from the previous layer to all its neurons, each neuron providing one output to the next layer. The drop-out layer is used to reduce the capacity or thin the network during training and avoids the overfitting. We begin by adding a pooling layer, followed by four dense layers and three drop-out layers to ensure the model runs smoothly. The numbers of neurons in the dense units are 720, 360, 360, and 180, respectively. The drop-out values are 0.25, 0.25, and 0.5, respectively. Finally, the authors have used a dense layer composed of four fully connected neurons in conjunction with a Softmax output layer to compute and classify the probability score for each class. Figure 4 illustrates the structure of the proposed EfficientNet in detail.

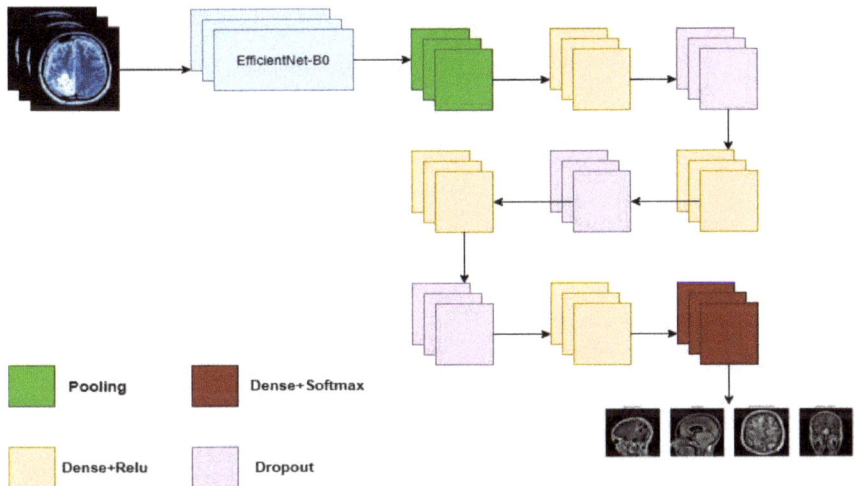

Figure 4. Proposed dense EfficientNet CNN model architecture.

4. Results and Discussion

Numerous experimental assessments have been conducted to determine the suggested dense CNN model's validity. All the experimental evaluations have been conducted using a Python programming environment with GPU support. First, pre-processing is performed to enhance the contrast in MRI images using max-min normalization and then the images are augmented for training. The proposed dense-CNN model activated the augmented tumors for better accuracy. The proposed model showed 99.97% accuracy on training data and 98.78% accuracy on the testing dataset which is plotted in Figure 5.

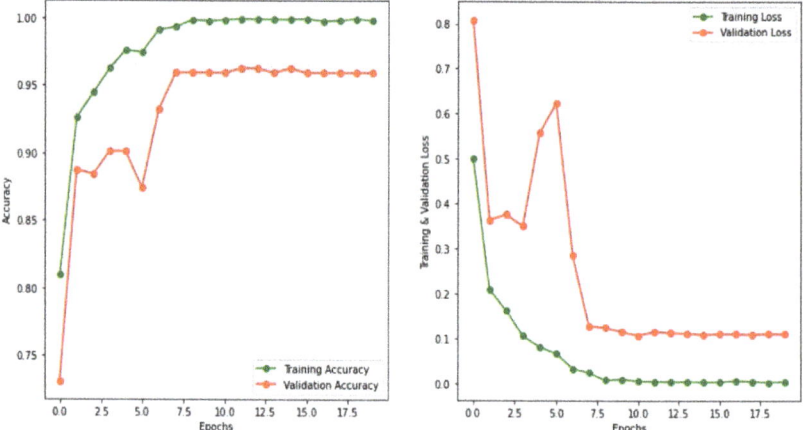

Figure 5. Graph representing model accuracy and model loss for training and validation set using the dense EfficientNet approach.

The experiment has been performed in 20 epochs. A batch size of 32, image size 150, and verbose 1 have been considered for the experiment. In the accuracy model, initial validation accuracy is below 0.75 but after one epoch the validation accuracy suddenly increases to nearly 0.88. In the same manner, the initial validation loss is above 0.8 but after one epoch the loss decreases below 0.4. As shown in Figure 5, there is a positive trend toward improving accuracy and reducing loss. At first, validation accuracy is low, but it progressively improves to almost 97.5 percent. The succeeding part of the measure was accomplished on the ResNet50 model, MobileNet, and the MobileNetV2 model, which are shown in Figure 6, Figure 7, and Figure 8, respectively.

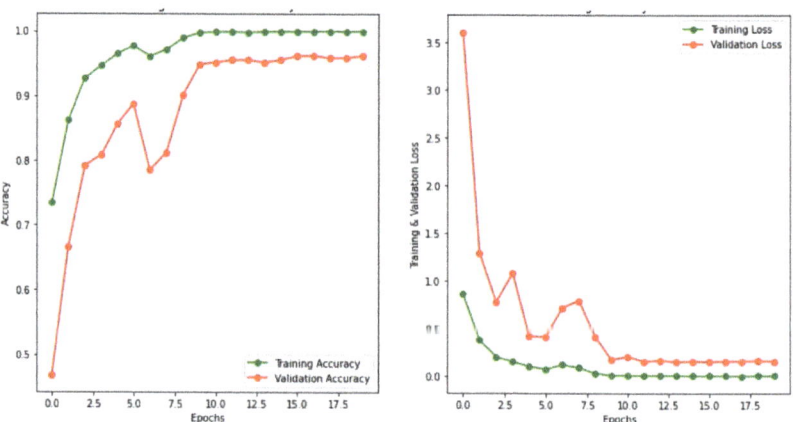

Figure 6. Graph representing model accuracy and model loss for training and validation set using the ResNet50 approach.

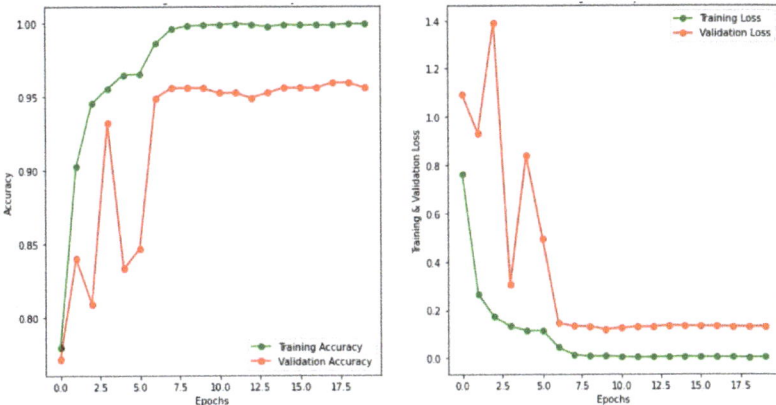

Figure 7. Graph representing model accuracy and model loss for training and validation set using the MobileNet approach.

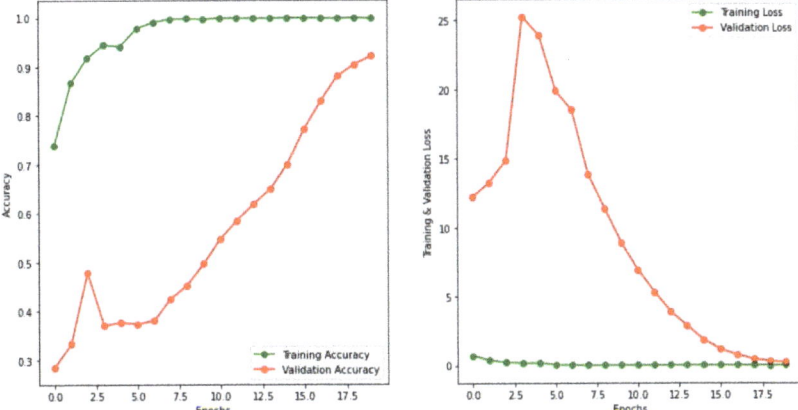

Figure 8. Graph representing model accuracy and model loss for training and validation set using the MobileNetV2 approach.

From the above model accuracy and model loss graphs, the authors concluded that in the case of the mobile net case, the graph is disordered, and the difference between loss and accuracy is very high. So, the accuracy value of MobileNetV2 is lower than the others. The accuracy and loss graphs of dense EfficientNet, ResNet, and MobileNet are almost nearly equal. The testing accuracy and testing loss of dense EfficientNet is 98.78% and 0.0645, respectively, whereas the accuracy and loss in the case of MobileNetV2 is 96.94% and 0.2452, respectively. The testing accuracy acquired using the MobileNet model is 96.94% and the test loss is 0.1339 whereas the accuracy and loss value of ResNet is just less than MobileNet. The detailed comparison of test accuracy, as well as loss of different models, is shown in Table 1, and performance analysis is shown in Figure 9.

Table 1. Comparison of accuracy and loss among different pre-trained deep-learning-based techniques.

Model	Dataset	Testing Loss	Testing Accuracy
Proposed dense EfficientNet	T1 contrast brain tumors	0.0645	98.78%
ResNet50	T1 contrast brain tumors	0.1337	96.33%
MobileNet	T1 contrast brain tumors	0.1339	96.94%
MobileNetV2	T1 contrast brain tumors	0.2452	94.80%

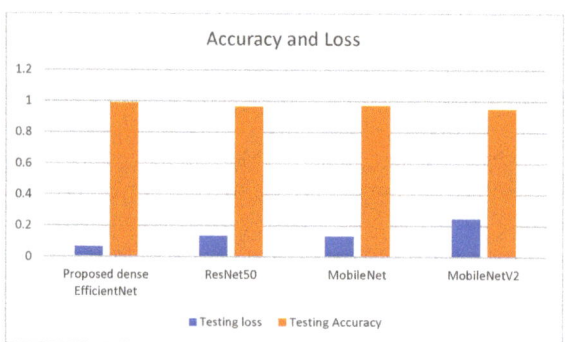

Figure 9. Comparison of accuracy and loss among different pre-trained deep-learning-based techniques.

Different performance measures, such as accuracy, precision, recall, and F1-score, were utilized to compare the suggested model's performance. These parameters are evaluated using the confusion matrix. The details were also examined using the confusion matrix which is shown in Figure 10. The confusion matrix presents misclassifications as a consequence of overfitting using 10% of testing data obtained from the original dataset of 3260. From the matrix it is observed that the misclassified tumors in the proposed dense EfficientNet model have 04, the ResNet50 model has 12, MobileNet has 10, and MobileNetV2 has 15 out of 326 testing images/ Due to lesser amounts of misclassified data, the accuracy of the proposed model is higher than the others. The confidence level of the pituitary in the case of MobileNetV2 is the worst in comparison to other tumors. All CNN models perform the classification of meningioma tumor very well. The majority of the misclassified samples belong to the "glioma" class which cannot learn as effectively as the other three.

For comparison of different techniques, three important measures have been considered: precision, recall, and F1-score. All the assessment metrics for all the CNN models were evaluated from Table 2 and are displayed in Figure 11. All these measures are based on the following parameters:

True positive (TP) = classified as +ve and sample belongs to the tumor;
True negative (TN) = classified as −ve and sample belongs to healthy;
False positive (FP) = classified as +ve and sample belongs to healthy;
False negative (FN) = classified as −ve and sample belongs to a tumor.

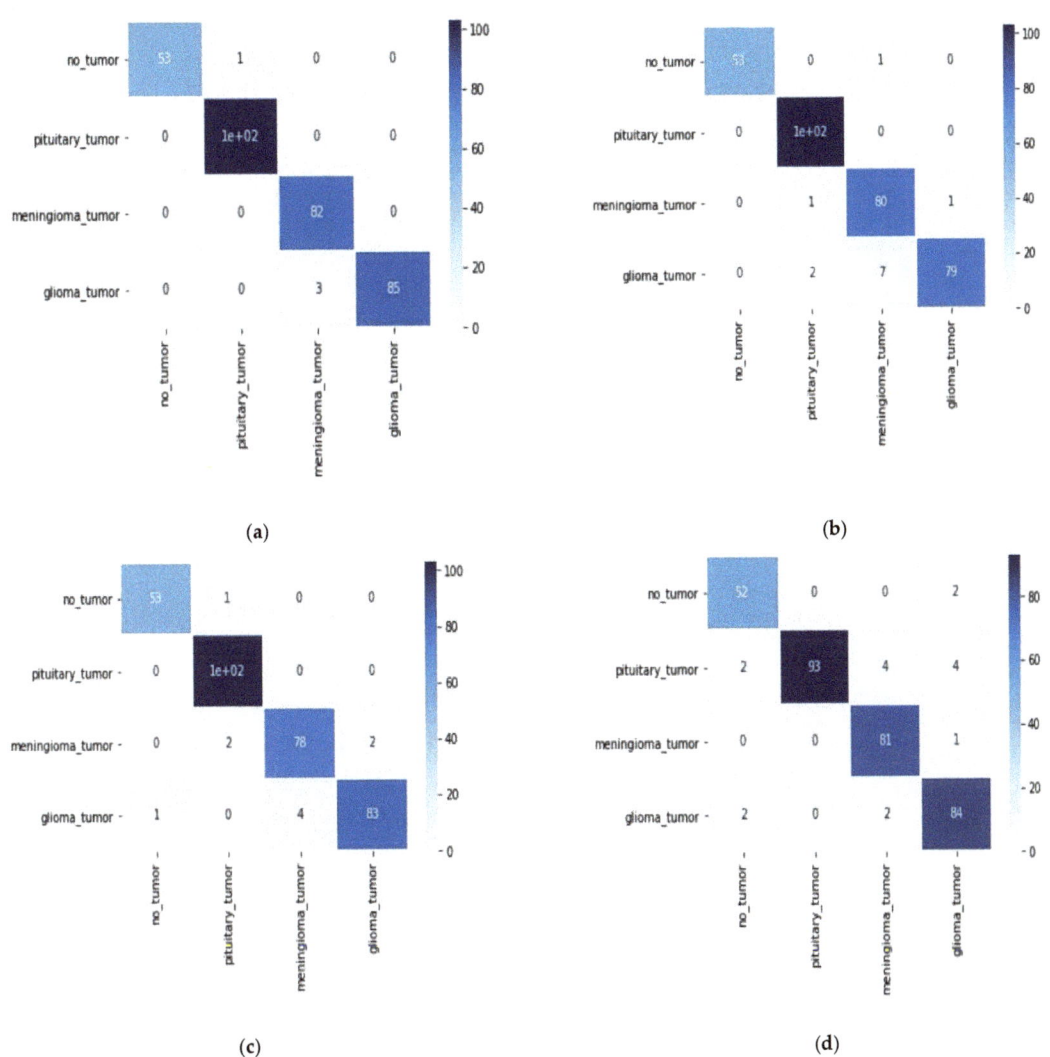

Figure 10. Confusion matrix of: (**a**) proposed dense EfficientNet model; (**b**) ResNet50 model; (**c**) MobileNet model; (**d**) MobileNetV2 model.

Table 2. Class-specific evaluation of brain tumors using different CNN.

Types of CNN	Dense EfficientNet			ResNet50			MobileNet			MobileNetV2		
Different types of tumors	Precision	Recall	F1-Score	Precision	Recall	F1-Score	Precision	Recall	F1-Score	Precision	Recall	F1-Score
No tumor	1	0.98	0.99	1	0.98	0.99	0.98	0.98	0.98	0.93	0.96	0.95
Pituitary tumor	0.99	1	1	0.97	1	0.99	0.97	1	0.99	1	0.9	0.95
Meningioma	0.96	1	0.98	0.91	0.98	0.94	0.95	0.95	0.95	0.93	0.99	0.96
Glioma tumor	1	0.97	0.98	0.99	0.9	0.94	0.98	0.94	0.96	0.92	0.95	0.94

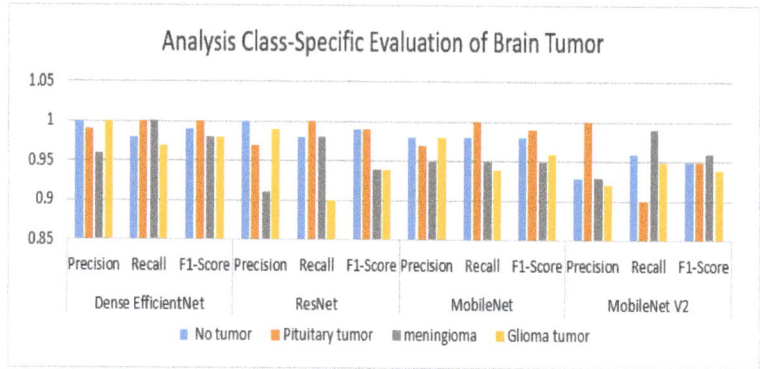

Figure 11. Analysis: class-specific evaluation of brain tumor using different CNN.

These parameters are calculated from the confusion matrix, which is shown in Figure 10. Hence, the different measures can be defined as follows:

$$Accuracy = \frac{(TP+TN)}{(TP+FP+TN+FN)} \quad (2)$$

$$Sensitivity = \frac{TP}{(TP+FN)} \quad (3)$$

$$Specificity = \frac{TN}{(TN+FP)} \quad (4)$$

$$Precision = \frac{TP}{(TP+FP)} \quad (5)$$

$$F1\ Score = \frac{2*(Recall)*(Precision)}{(Recall+Precision)} \quad (6)$$

where *Recall* is the same as *Sensitivity* as shown in Equation (2).

It is observed from Table 2 and the analysis graph in Figure 11 that dense EfficientNet has the highest precision, recall, and F1-score when compared to the other three models. The pituitary tumor has the best performance in all measurements when compared to other types of tumors. All the values of precision, recall, and F1-score of pituitary tumors are quite good. The overall results of dense EfficientNet are excellent. For comparison purposes, the authors have also considered the recent performance of modified CNN structure by the different researchers, which is shown in Table 3 analysis and is displayed in Figure 12. The accuracy, precision, and F1-score of the proposed method are 98.78%, 98.75%, and 98.75%, respectively, which is better than other comparison methods. As shown in Table 3, the proposed deep learning segmentation algorithm outperforms state-of-the-art techniques. Based on Table 3, the authors conclude that dense EfficientNet outperforms other techniques because deep-learning-based approaches are more efficient and capable of handling large amounts of data for classification.

Table 3. Comparison of performance among different deep-learning-based techniques.

Authors	Year	Dataset	Model	Accuracy	Precision	F1-Score
Badza et al. [12]	2020	T1 contrast brain tumors	CNN	96.56%	94.81%	94.94%
Mizoguchi et al. [13]	2020	Brats-2018	3D CNN	96.49%	-	-
Hashemzehi et al. [14]	2020	T1 contrast brain tumors	CNN and NAND	96.00%	94.49%	94.56%
Díaz-Pernas et al. [15]	2021	T1 contrast brain tumors	Multi-scale CNN	97.00%	95.80%	96.07%
Sajja et al. [18]	2021	T1 contrast brain tumors	Deep-CNN	96.70%	97.05%	97.05%
Proposed method	Present	T1 contrast brain tumors	Dense EfficientNet	98.78%	98.75%	98.75%

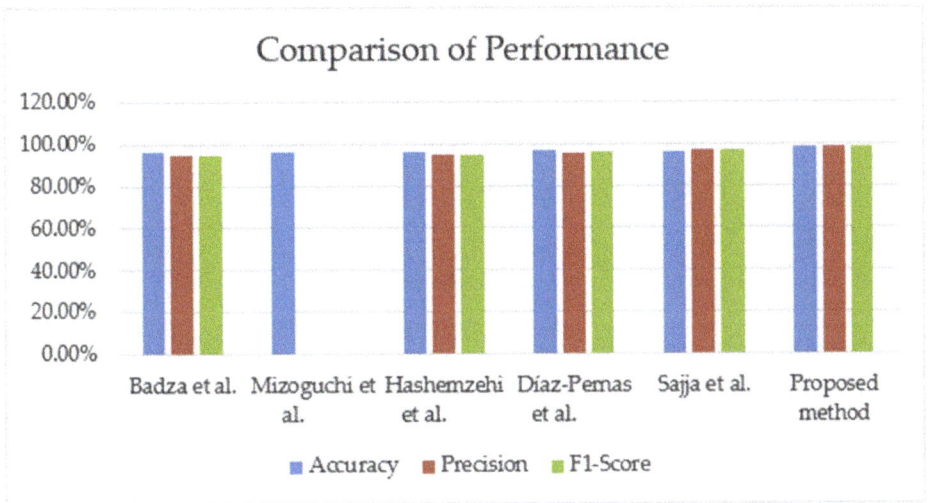

Figure 12. Comparison of performance among different deep-learning-based techniques. Data from [12–15,18].

Figure 12 illustrates that all mentioned authors used contrast brain tumors for their experiments. The proposed dense EfficientNet method has higher accuracy, at nearly 99%, than the others do.

5. Conclusions

In this paper, the authors have used dense EfficientNet with min-max normalization that is suitable to classify the different types of brain tumors with 98.78% accuracy, which is better than other related work using the same dataset. The suggested technique outperforms existing deep learning methods in terms of accuracy, precision, and F1-score. This proposed idea can play a prognostic role in detecting tumors in the brain. It has been observed that glioma has the lowest detection rate with an F1-score of 98% and pituitary has the highest rate with an F1-score of 100%. Among deep learning methods, dense CNN has performed more rapidly, with higher classification accuracy. This method is suitable to locate and detect tumors easily.

Further, a better pre-processing technique can be applied with fuzzy thresholding concept or nature-based algorithms for early diagnosis of dangerous medical imaging disease by adapting more layers to segment the different medical image segmentation. Our future research will concentrate on minimizing the number of parameters and computing time required to run the suggested model without sacrificing performance.

Author Contributions: Writing—original draft preparation, D.R.N., N.P., P.K.M., M.Z. and S.K. Writing—review and editing, D.R.N., N.P., P.K.M., M.Z. and S.K. All authors have read and agreed to the published version of the manuscript.

Funding: This research received no external funding.

Data Availability Statement: Data is contained within the article.

Acknowledgments: This work is supported by the Ministry of Science and Higher Education of the Russian Federation (Government Order FENU-2020-0022).

Conflicts of Interest: There is no such conflict of interest disclosed by the authors in relation to the content of the work.

References

1. Pradhan, A.; Mishra, D.; Das, K.; Panda, G.; Kumar, S.; Zymbler, M. On the Classification of MR Images Using "ELM-SSA" Coated Hybrid Model. *Mathematics* **2021**, *9*, 2095. [CrossRef]
2. Reddy, A.V.N.; Krishna, C.P.; Mallick, P.K.; Satapathy, S.K.; Tiwari, P.; Zymbler, M.; Kumar, S. Analyzing MRI scans to detect glioblastoma tu-mor using hybrid deep belief networks. *J. Big Data* **2020**, *7*, 35. [CrossRef]
3. Nayak, D.R.; Padhy, N.; Mallick, P.K.; Bagal, D.K.; Kumar, S. Brain Tumour Classification Using Noble Deep Learning Approach with Parametric Optimization through Metaheuristics Approaches. *Computers* **2022**, *11*, 10. [CrossRef]
4. Mansour, R.F.; Escorcia-Gutierrez, J.; Gamarra, M.; Díaz, V.G.; Gupta, D.; Kumar, S. Ar-tificial intelligence with big data analytics-based brain intracranial hemorrhage e-diagnosis us-ing CT images. *Neural Comput. Appl.* **2021**. [CrossRef]
5. Rehman, A.; Naz, S.; Razzak, M.I.; Akram, F.; Imran, M.A. Deep learning-based framework for automatic brain tumors classification using transfer learning. *Circuits Syst. Signal Processing* **2020**, *39*, 757–775. [CrossRef]
6. Long, J.; Shelhamer, E.; Darrell, T. Fully convolutional networks for semantic segmentation. In Proceedings of the IEEE Conference on Computer Vision and Pattern Recognition, Boston, MA, USA, 7–12 June 2015; pp. 3431–3440.
7. Ozyurt, F.; Sert, E.; Avci, D. An expert system for brain tumor detection, Fuzzy C-means with super-resolution and convolutional neural network with extreme learning machine. *Med. Hypotheses* **2020**, *134*, 109433. [CrossRef] [PubMed]
8. Hu, M.; Zhong, Y.; Xie, S.; Lv, H.; Lv, Z. Fuzzy System Based Medical Image Processing for Brain Disease Prediction. *Front. Neurosci.* **2021**, *15*, 714318. [CrossRef] [PubMed]
9. Maqsood, S.; Damasevicius, R.; Shah, F.M. An Efficient Approach for the Detection of Brain Tumor Using Fuzzy Logic and U-Net CNN Classification. In *Lecture Notes in Computer Science*; Springer: Berlin/Heidelberg, Germany, 2021; Volume 12953.
10. Ragupathy, B.; Karunakaran, M. A fuzzy logic-based meningioma tumor detection in magnetic resonance brain images using CANFIS and U-Net CNN classification. *Int. J. Imaging Syst. Technol.* **2021**, *31*, 379–390. [CrossRef]
11. Cheng, J.; Huang, W.; Cao, S.; Yang, R.; Yang, W.; Yun, Z.; Wang, Z.; Feng, Q. Correction, enhanced performance of brain tumor classification via tumor region augmentation and partition. *PLoS ONE* **2015**, *10*, e0144519. [CrossRef] [PubMed]
12. Badža, M.M.; Barjaktarović, M.Č. Classification of brain tumors from MRI images using a convolutional neural network. *Appl. Sci.* **2020**, *10*, 1999. [CrossRef]
13. Mzoughi, H.; Njeh, I.; Wali, A.; Slima, M.B.; BenHamida, A.; Mhiri, C.; Mahfoudhe, K.B. Deep multi-scale 3D convolutional neural network (CNN) for MRI gliomas brain tumor classification. *J. Digit. Imaging* **2020**, *33*, 903–915. [CrossRef] [PubMed]
14. Hashemzehi, R.; Mahdavi, S.J.S.; Kheirabadi, M.; Kamel, S.R. Detection of brain tumors from MRI images base on deep learning using hybrid model CNN and NADE. *Biocybern. Biomed. Eng.* **2020**, *40*, 1225–1232. [CrossRef]
15. Díaz-Pernas, F.J.; Martínez-Zarzuela, M.; Antón-Rodríguez, M.; González-Ortega, D. A deep learning approach for brain tumor classification and segmentation using a multiscale convolutional neural network. *Healthcare* **2021**, *9*, 153. [CrossRef] [PubMed]
16. Sultan, H.H.; Salem, N.M.; Al-Atabany, W. Multi-classification of brain tumor images using deep neural network. *IEEE Access* **2019**, *7*, 69215–69225. [CrossRef]
17. Abd El Kader, I.; Xu, G.; Shuai, Z.; Saminu, S.; Javaid, I.; Salim Ahmad, I. Differential deep convolutional neural network model for brain tumor classification. *Brain Sci.* **2021**, *11*, 352. [CrossRef] [PubMed]
18. Sajja, V.R. Classification of Brain tumors using Fuzzy C-means and VGG16. *Turk. J. Comput. Math. Educ. (TURCOMAT)* **2021**, *12*, 2103–2113.
19. Das, S.; Aranya, O.R.; Labiba, N.N. Brain tumor classification using a convolutional neural network. In Proceedings of the 2019 1st International Conference on Advances in Science, Engineering and Robotics Technology (ICASERT), Dhaka, Bangladesh, 3 May 2019; IEEE: New York, NY, USA, 2019; pp. 1–5.
20. Cheng, J. Brain tumor dataset. Figshare. Dataset. 2017, 1512427/5. Available online: https://figshare.com/articles/dataset/brain_tumor_dataset/1512427 (accessed on 12 October 2021).

21. Nayak, D.R.; Padhy, N.; Swain, B.K. Brain Tumor Detection and Extraction using Type-2 Fuzzy with Morphology. *Int. J. Emerg. Technol.* **2020**, *11*, 840–844.
22. Tan, M.; Le, Q.V. EfficientNet, Rethinking Model Scaling for Convolutional Neural Networks. *arXiv* **2019**, arXiv:1905.11946.
23. Available online: https://towardsdatascience.com/complete-architectural-details-of-all-efficientnet-models-5fd5b736142 (accessed on 16 October 2021).

Article

Combining Students' Grades and Achievements on the National Assessment of Knowledge: A Fuzzy Logic Approach

Daniel Doz *, Darjo Felda and Mara Cotič

Faculty of Education, University of Primorska, Cankarjeva 5, 6000 Koper, Slovenia; darjo.felda@pef.upr.si (D.F.); mara.cotic@pef.upr.si (M.C.)
* Correspondence: daniel.doz@upr.si

Abstract: Although the idea of evaluating students' mathematical knowledge with fuzzy logic is not new in the literature, few studies have explored the possibility of assessing students' mathematical knowledge by combining teacher-assigned grades (i.e., school grades) with students' achievements on standardized tests (e.g., national assessments). Thus, the present study aims to investigate the use of fuzzy logic to generate a novel assessment model, which combines teacher-assigned mathematics grades with students' results on the Italian National Assessment of Mathematical Knowledge (INVALSI). We expanded the findings from previous works by considering a larger sample, which included more than 90,000 students attending grades 8, 10, and 13. The results showed that the tested model led to a lower assessment score compared to the traditional grading method based on teacher's evaluation. Additionally, the use of fuzzy logic across the examined school levels yielded similar results, suggesting that the model is adequate among different educational levels.

Keywords: assessment; education; fuzzy logic; INVALSI

MSC: 03B52

1. Introduction

The assessment of students' knowledge is one of the most important components of the pedagogical process [1], as it provides educators, students, and their parents with important feedback information on learners' knowledge, skills, and competencies [2]. In recent decades, several researchers [3–14] have studied the possibility of evaluating students' knowledge with fuzzy logic.

Fuzzy logic is based on the fuzzy set theory introduced by the Iranian mathematician Lofti A. Zadeh in 1965 [15]. This type of logic provides a significant addition to standard logic since its applications are wide-ranging and it offers the possibility of modeling under conditions of imprecision [3,4], for example in engineering [16], science [17], economics [18], medicine [19], and psychology [20]. Despite its name, which may recall an imprecise, hazy, or even false mathematical theory, fuzzy logic operates on the basis of precise and rigorous mathematical rules [21]. In real-life situations, fuzzy logic could be used to construct mathematical solutions of problems, which are expressed in natural language and characterized by a degree of vagueness and/or uncertainty [3]. Fuzzy logic refers to the ability to calculate with words; additionally, it provides mathematical strength to emulate several linguistic attributes associated with human cognition [4].

Precisely because fuzzy logic tackles operating with inaccurate data, some research [3–14] has proposed its use for the purpose of assessing students' knowledge and competencies. In particular, teacher-given grades are usually based on verbal judgements. For instance, in Italy, where grades range from 1 to 10, grade "10" corresponds to "excellent", while grade "6" means "sufficient". In addition, teacher-given grades can include several factors that contribute to the final grading, such as students' academic knowledge [5], their class attendance [8], achievements obtained in different exams [7], students' lab work [6], etc.

Fuzzy logic, therefore, represents a mathematical tool which educators and researchers can use to combine multiple verbal and imprecise variables.

The present paper aims to explore how fuzzy logic can be used to evaluate students' mathematical knowledge, specifically by combining their school grades (i.e., teacher-given grades) with their achievements on a standardized mathematics test, namely the Italian National Assessment of Mathematical knowledge INVALSI. The topic on how to combine teacher-given grades with their performance on standardized tests is still developing. Therefore, with the present paper, we want to contribute to the literature by comparing the traditional method of assessing students' mathematical knowledge (i.e., teacher-given grades) with the fuzzy logic model.

In the paper, we will first present some basic definitions regarding fuzzy logic and then a review of the literature on using fuzzy logic for student's evaluation. A detailed description of the adopted methodology and the obtained results will follow. Finally, the results will be discussed and implication for practice will be presented.

2. Related Works

2.1. Basic Definitions

A basics concept of fuzzy logic is the fuzzy set [9]. A fuzzy set is a set A in a universal set X, defined as a set of pairs $A = \{(x, \mu_A(x)) : x \in X\}$, where $\mu_A : X \to [0,1]$ is a mapping called "membership function" of the fuzzy set A, and $\mu_A(x)$ is the degree of belongingness (or degree of membership) of element $x \in X$ in the fuzzy set A.

Among the most used membership functions, we focus on the triangular, trapezoidal, and Gaussian membership functions. Due to the simple formula and computational efficiency, the triangular and trapezoidal membership functions are among the most popular in fuzzy logic applications [9] and have been widely used in evaluating students' academic achievement [22]. On the other hand, the Gaussian membership function is the most adequate to represent uncertainty in the measurements [23] and some authors [24,25] have suggested that it is the most suitable for improving the reliability and robustness of the evaluation of student systems. The triangular function (for $a < b < c$) is defined as follows [9,22]:

$$\text{Tri}(x, a, b, c) = \begin{cases} 0 & x \leq a,\ x \geq c \\ \frac{x-a}{b-a} & a < x < b \\ \frac{c-x}{c-b} & b \leq x < c \end{cases}. \qquad (1)$$

The trapezoidal membership function (for $a < b < c < d$) is defined as follows [9,17]:

$$\text{Trap}(x, a, b, c, d) = \begin{cases} 0 & x \leq a,\ x \geq d \\ \frac{x-a}{b-a} & a < x \leq b \\ 1 & b < x \leq c \\ \frac{d-x}{d-c} & c < x \leq d \end{cases}. \qquad (2)$$

The Gaussian membership function (for two parameters μ and σ) is defined as follows [18]:

$$\text{Gauss}(x, \mu, \sigma) = e^{-\frac{(x-\mu)^2}{2\sigma^2}}. \qquad (3)$$

Fuzzy logic consists of three main components [3,6,21]: (i) the fuzzification process, (ii) decision-making based on fuzzy rules and (iii) the defuzzification process (Figure 1). Fuzzification is the process in which crisp (i.e., clear) terms and data are transformed into a fuzzy set. This process is determined by the membership functions, which are applied to the crisp values of the variables to determine their membership factor in the fuzzy set. The fuzzification process allows us to express inputs and outputs in linguistic terms. Decision-making (i.e., the inference process) consists in defying the rules, which will determine the fuzzy output information. The inference rules are logical sequences of the IF-THEN form. They are defined by the user based on their experience [25]. The result of the inference phase must be then converted back into crisp data. This process is called defuzzification. There are several ways to defuzzify the data. Among the most used ones, there are the Mean of Maximum (MoM) and the Center of Gravity (CoG) [25]. The MoM method is given by the following:

$$\text{MoM}(A) = \frac{1}{|T|} \times \sum_{x \in T} x, \qquad (4)$$

where T is the set of all elements $x \in X$, for which $\mu_A(x)$ has the maximum degree of membership and $|T|$ is its cardinality. The CoG for continuous values of x is defined as:

$$\text{CoG}(A) = \frac{\int \mu_A(x) \times x \, dx}{\int \mu_A(x) \, dx}. \qquad (5)$$

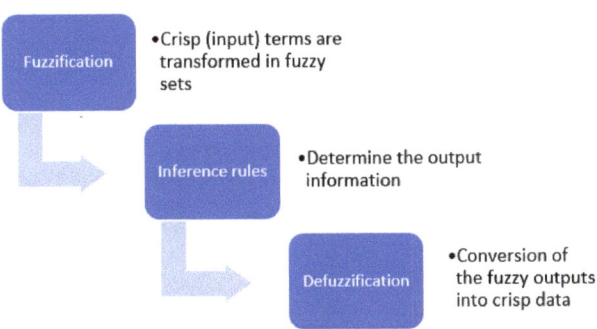

Figure 1. The fuzzy logic process.

2.2. The Usage of Fuzzy Logic in Education

In education, teachers often face a situation of vagueness when evaluating students' knowledge, so fuzzy logic offers many applications to partially solve this issue [3]. Several applications of the fuzzy logic have been proposed in the past. For instance, the study by Sripan and Suksawat [4] aimed to investigate the use of fuzzy logic to evaluate students' knowledge by combining their scores on a test and the time to solve it. They experimented the proposed model with 26 students and found that students' traditional grades and their fuzzy grades were similar, but fuzzy logic represented an effective method for classifying student learning groups based on their performance and real-time implementation.

In the research by Gokmen and colleagues [6], the authors focused on generating students' grades by considering two input values, i.e., their performance in two exams. They tested their model on 20 students and contrary to the previously mentioned study [4], they found a difference in the grades obtained with the classical assessment method and the fuzzy logic method. They concluded that fuzzy logic has greater flexibility, however the evaluation criteria are difficult to explain to students. Similar conclusions are presented by Petrudi and colleagues [7], who aimed to assess students' knowledge by considering the performance on three exams, one of which was practical. The findings revealed that the fuzzy logic evaluation method lowered the grades of better performing students and conversely, increased the grades of lower performing students.

Saliu [26] developed a student knowledge assessment model by considering various factors that could influence students' final performance, such as the originality of students' work. The author tested the model on a sample of 33 students and found no significant differences between the classic evaluation method and the fuzzy logic one.

Namli and Şenkal [9] proposed a model for assessing students' knowledge by considering their grades and class attendance. The researchers found that student assessment with fuzzy logic did not significantly differ from the traditional assessment method.

Very few works have explored the possibility of using fuzzy logic on a larger scale, as for example for assessing students' knowledge by combining academic results with the results obtained in standardized tests. Recently, the work ref. [27] explored the possibility of using fuzzy logic to evaluate students' mathematical knowledge by merging both oral and written students' grades, and their results on the Italian national assessment. There were 2279 students from grade 13 involved in the tested model. The results indicated that students' grades generated by the fuzzy logic method (i.e., a combination of teacher-assigned math grades and students' performance on the INVALSI test) were significantly lower than teacher-given grades. The study explored the differences in students' achievement between the four types of Italian high schools (i.e., scientific high schools, technical schools, vocational schools, and other high schools), finding significant differences in final grades between the four types of schools.

Considering the abovementioned studies, it can be noticed that the literature is ambivalent and contrasting as to whether fuzzy logic is similar to traditional evaluation methods or whether there are substantial differences between these assessment methods. Some papers have found that fuzzy logic produces lower or higher grades than traditional evaluation methods [6,7,27], while others have concluded that there are no significant differences between the two methods [4,9,26]. Furthermore, the previously cited works tested the models on relatively small samples of students and did not consider the possibility that fuzzy logic could have different effects at different school levels, such as secondary or high school. The present empirical research aims to address this gap in the literature by examining the effects that fuzzy logic-based assessment model could have on a larger sample of students considering the different school levels.

2.3. Research Aims

The aim of the current research is to develop and test a model for assessing students' mathematical knowledge which considers both students' academic achievements (i.e., mathematics grades assigned by the teacher) and their performance on the INVALSI national assessment, and comparing it to the traditional assessment method (i.e., teacher-given grades). In doing this, we aimed to broaden the existing studies on the application of fuzzy logic for the assessment of students' mathematical knowledge (e.g., [27]) by testing it among a larger sample of participants, as well as considering different school levels, particularly grades 8, 10, and 13. This would allow us to understand whether fuzzy logic-based assessment method produces similar evaluations at different educational levels and if it is therefore adequate for measuring math knowledge of younger and older students.

Thus, the research questions of the present study are the following:

RQ1: Is there any significant difference between the fuzzy logic evaluation method (which considers the combination of teacher-assigned grades and students' performance on national assessment) of students' math knowledge and the traditional one (based on teacher-assigned grades) in students attending the 8th, 10th, and 13th grade?

RQ2: Is there any significant difference in the evaluation of students' math knowledge based on fuzzy method among school levels of the 8th, 10th, and 13th grade?

3. Materials and Methods

3.1. Methodology

The present study is a quantitative non-experimental empirical study. The nature of the research is descriptive.

The diagram of the methodology is presented in Figure 2. The data about students' teacher-given grades and their achievements on the national assessment of mathematics INVALSI were retrieved from official data sources [28]. The data were then filtered to remove the missing items (see also the Research sample subsection). The remaining data were then combined using the fuzzy logic method, explained in detail in the Procedure subsection. After the combined grade was produced in terms of fuzzy logic, the data were analyzed with statistical tools.

Figure 2. General diagram illustrating the methodology used in the present study. * Data from school year 2018–2019 was used.

3.2. Data Collection

The data were obtained from the official web page of the Statistical Service [28], where the following variables were available:

- Teacher-given grades on oral evaluations in mathematics;
- Teacher-given grades on written evaluations in mathematics;
- Scores on the national assessment INVALSI;
- Students' gender.

We focused solely on these variables, since the aim of the research was to compare the teacher-given grades with the fuzzy grades. The data about gender were used for the description of the sample. Furthermore, since the data were collected directly by the INVALSI Institute, they are considered a reliable source [29,30]. However, despite the attention that the INVALSI institute places on collecting valid and reliable data, it must be noted that there is still an almost negligible probability that these data contain some small errors which could result from inattentive transcription of students' written and oral grades [31].

3.3. Data Filtering

From the official website of the Statistical Service [28], which includes data from all Italian students who completed the INVALSI assessment, three samples of students were retrieved. In particular, a sample of 29,675 students attending grade 8, a sample of 35,802 students from grade 10, and a sample of 36,589 students from grade 13. Students' data referred to school year 2018–2019.

From the original samples, a total of 9801 students (9.6%) were deleted, since they reported missing data on both teacher-given grades (oral and written grade). (Table 1). In particular:

1. Grade 8: 619 students presented missing data on both teacher-given grades and were therefore excluded from the analyses. The remaining sample consisted of students who had at least one teacher-assigned grade (oral or written). We did not make any distinction between oral or written grades, since in Italian middle school educational system, students receive only one grade for mathematics, which refers to both oral and written evaluations;
2. Grade 10: 3008 students were excluded due to missing data. The remaining sample consisted of students who had at least one teacher-assigned grade. For the students who had both oral and written grades, only the oral grade was considered, since it includes a broader range of evaluations;
3. Grade 13: 6174 students presented missing data on both teacher-given grades. The filtering procedure is the same as for grade 10.

Table 1. The three considered samples.

Grade	Original Sample	Final Sample	% of Original Sample
8	29,675	29,056	97.9%
10	35,802	32,794	91.6%
13	36,589	30,415	83.1%

The gender distribution among the final samples is presented in Table 2. The participants' age was not possible to retrieve.

Table 2. The distribution of gender in the three samples.

Grade	Gender	Frequency (f)	Percentage Frequency (%f)
8	Male	14,983	51.6%
	Female	14,073	48.4%
10	Male	15,663	47.8%
	Female	17,131	52.2%
13	Male	14,785	48.6%
	Female	15,630	51.4%

3.3.1. Teacher-Given Grades

In Italian secondary (i.e., middle school; grades 6–8) and high schools (grades 9–13), the grades assigned by teachers are numerical and range from a minimum of 1 to a maximum of 10, with 10 being the highest grade. Grades lower than 6 are "failing grades", while grades greater or equal to 6 are "passing grades" [32]. Several laws [32,33] establish that the teacher of a certain subject suggests students' final grade; however, the class councils (i.e., all schoolteachers who teach in a given class) are in charge of accepting or modifying the proposed grade.

For each subject, students' knowledge can be assessed in three possible ways: (1) through written and oral evaluations, (2) only written evaluations, or (3) only oral evaluations [33]. Written evaluations are obtained through more complex written tests, whereas oral evaluations are assessments that consist of oral examinations, homework, project work, exercises, or other shorter written tests. High school class councils determine the preferred assessing method [32–34], which could result in students obtaining one (oral or written) or two grades (oral and written) in each subject. In contrary, middle school students have only one grade on their report cards (i.e., only one oral or written grade).

3.3.2. The INVALSI Test

Each school year, the INVALSI institute assesses the entire Italian student population in the 2nd (average age 7 years), 5th (10 years old), 8th (13 years old), 10th (15 years old) and from school year 2018–2019 also 13th (18 years old) grades. Students are thus required to take the mandatory national standardized assessment of mathematical knowledge [32]. It is a standardized assessment evaluating students' knowledge of the mathematical contents present in the *National indications for the curriculum in the primary and secondary school* [35] (for secondary schools), and in the *Indications for high schools* [36] (for high schools). These documents cover the themes that math teachers are required to teach in secondary and high schools.

The national assessment INVALSI is composed of several questions, which vary each year (normally around 30–45 items), and which can be closed or open ended. All students in grades 8, 10, and 13 solve the computerized version of the test [32,37]. Moreover, questions are automatically and randomly chosen from a database of questions, which decreases the possibility of cheating. Since the chosen questions are equally difficult, the tests can be considered equivalent and comparable [37]. The results obtained by students in the INVALSI test are measured on a quantitative Rasch scale, where 200 is the mean and the standard deviation is 40 [38,39]; a similar method is used by the PISA [40] and TIMSS [41] evaluations. INVALSI tests are an objective measure of students' knowledge [42].

3.4. Application of Fuzzy Logic

The model proposed for the evaluation of students' mathematical knowledge is presented in Figure 3. The model considers two students' attainments in mathematics, i.e., (1) teacher-given school grades ("School attainments"), and (2) their results on the national assessment of mathematics ("INVALSI"). These crisp data are numerical values: school attainments are ordinal data from 1 to 10, where "10" represents excellent grade, while the INVALSI results are interval data, which are determined with the Rasch method by the institute INVALSI. These data are then fuzzified ("Fuzzification") using the membership functions we present in the following subsection. Fuzzified grades are combined by using inference rules ("Inference rule") which are defined in the following subsections: this permits us to retrieve fuzzified combined grades. Such grades are then defuzzified following the procedure depicted in the following subsections ("Defuzzification") and final grades are produced ("Final grade").

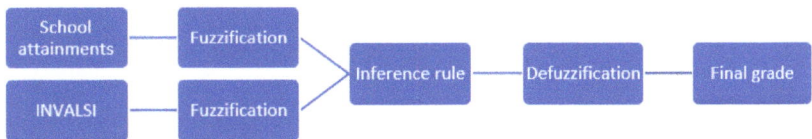

Figure 3. The utilized model for the assessment of students' mathematical knowledge.

3.4.1. Fuzzification of Teacher-Given Grades

The fuzzification of students' school (i.e., teacher-given) grades was performed using input variables (on a discrete scale from a minimum of 1 to a maximum of 10) and their membership functions of fuzzy sets. Each student had one school grade. Each input variable has a triangle or trapezoidal membership functions (Table 3 and Figure 4).

Table 3. The used membership functions for the fuzzification of the teacher-given grades.

Level	Membership Function
Very low (VL)	$Tri(x, 1, 1, 3)$
Low (L)	$Tri(x, 1, 3, 5)$
Medium (M)	$Trap(x, 3, 5, 6, 8)$
High (H)	$Tri(x, 6, 8, 10)$
Very high (VH)	$Tri(x, 8, 10, 10)$

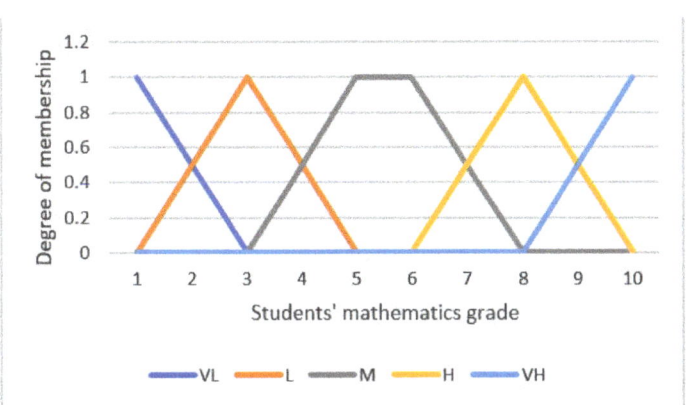

Figure 4. Plots of the membership functions for the fuzzification of crisp grades.

3.4.2. Fuzzification of Students' Attainments on the National Assessment INVALSI

Students' scores on the national assessment of mathematical knowledge INVALSI are interval data, thus the Gaussian membership function was preferred. Since the mean of students' attainments on the test is set to be around 200 and the standard deviation is 40, we considered the Gaussian functions presented in Table 4 and Figure 5 [27].

Table 4. Membership functions for the fuzzification of students' attainments on the INVALSI test.

Level	Membership Function
Very low (VL)	$\text{Gauss}(x, 120, 40)$
Low (L)	$\text{Gauss}(x, 160, 40)$
Medium (M)	$\text{Gauss}(x, 200, 40)$
High (H)	$\text{Gauss}(x, 240, 40)$
Very high (VH)	$\text{Gauss}(x, 280, 40)$

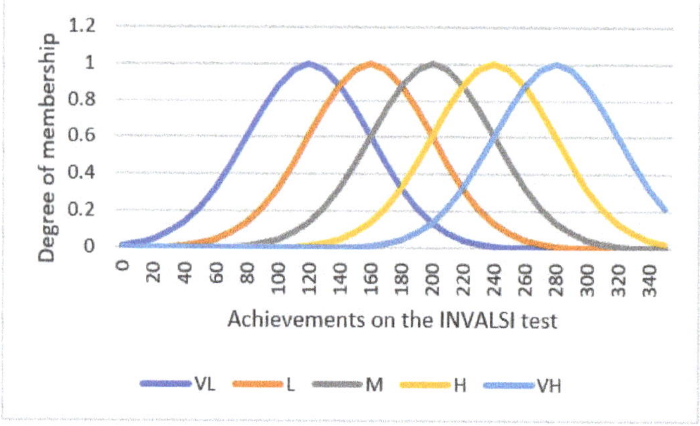

Figure 5. Plots of the membership functions for the fuzzification of crisp test scores.

3.4.3. Rules and Inference

Inference rules are linguistic variables, also entitled "If-Then" rules. In Table 5 we present the inference rules. The inference rules used are the same as in [7] with the following differences [25]:

4. It is possible to have the "Very high" (VH) level only if both tests are very high (VH), so the VH levels of [7] have been adapted to H;
5. High performance (H) on the INVALSI tests can only produce at least medium (M) ratings;
6. The final grade is high (H) only if both ratings are high (H) or one rating is very high (VH) and the other is at least medium (M).

Table 5. Inference rules.

		Teacher-Given Grades				
		VL	L	M	H	VH
INVALSI	VL	VL	VL	L	L	M
	L	VL	L	L	M	M
	M	L	L	M	M	H
	H	M	M	M	H	H
	VH	M	M	H	H	VH

For instance, a student with a high teacher-given grade (H) and a low achievement (L) on the INVALSI test gets a medium (M) final grade (M).

3.4.4. Defuzzification

The output variable, which is the overall students' mathematical achievement, is entitled "Final grade" and has five membership functions (Table 3 and Figure 4). After completing the fuzzy inference, the fuzzy final grade has to be converted into a crisp value through defuzzification. In the present study, the MoM method was applied. The surface of the final grades is presented in Figure 6. All fuzzy grades (i.e., the output data) were rounded to the nearest integer.

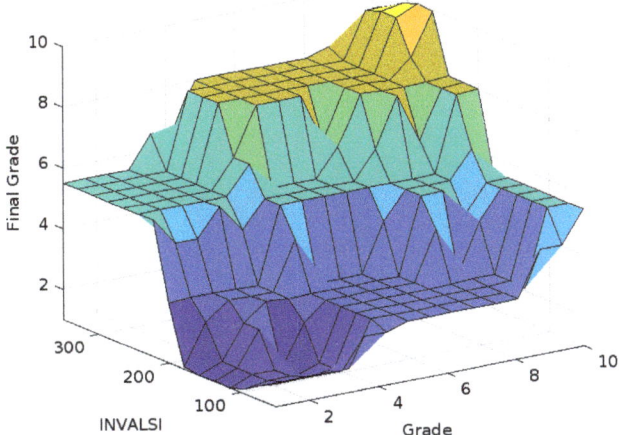

Figure 6. The output surface for the fuzzy inference system, plotting the output variable "Final Grade" against the first two input variables, i.e., "INVALSI" and "Grade".

Figure 6 presents the final grades obtained with the fuzzy logic method ("Final Grade") depending on the teacher-given grades ("Grade") and students' results on the INVALSI test ("INVALSI"). Thus, Figure 6 represents the plot of the function $FinalGrade(Grade, INVALSI)$. For example, a student who has 2 in mathematics (insufficient) but did well in the INVALSI test and got 300 points, has a final grade produced with the fuzzy logic of 5.50: $FinalGrade(2300) = 5.50$, which is then rounded to 6.

3.5. Quantitative Analysis

Fuzzification, inference, and defuzzification were conducted with the "Fuzzy Logic Toolbox" [43,44] (Figure 7) of the MATLAB R2020b [45]. Statistical analyses were performed with the *Jamovi* [46] statistical software.

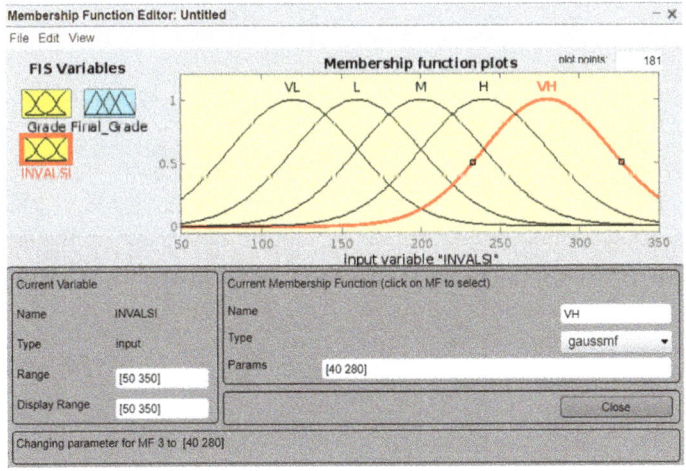

Figure 7. The "Fuzzy Logic Toolbox" in the MATLAB program.

Both descriptive and inferential statistical methods have been applied. Among the descriptive statistical tools, frequencies, means, medians, and standard deviations were computed. The Kolmogorov–Smirnov test was used to check for the normality of data, which is reasonably sensitive to the characteristics of distribution, such as its dispersion, shape, and location [47], and works best if the sample size is more than 50 [48]. Due to the violation of the conditions of normality, non-parametric inference statistical tests were used in order to lower the possibility of Type II error [49]. In particular, we used:

7. The Spearman's ρ coefficient to compute the correlation between data [50,51], e.g., to what extent are teacher-given grades and fuzzy final grades correlated. The requirement is that each variable is measured on at least ordinal scale; the usage of this coefficient does not make any assumption regarding the distribution of the variables.
8. The Wilcoxon W signed-rank test for paired samples to check for differences between two categories [52], e.g., the difference between the traditional and fuzzy final grades. The assumptions of the test are that samples are random samples, which are mutually independent, and that the measurement scale is at least ordinal.
9. The Kruskal–Wallis χ^2-test to check for differences among three or more categories [53] with the Dwass-Steel-Critchlow-Fligner (DSCF) post-hoc test, e.g., whether fuzzy final grades differ among different teacher-given grades. The assumptions are similar to those for the Wilcoxon test.

For the effect sizes, we used the ε^2 coefficient [54] for the Kruskal–Wallis test and the rank biserial correlation coefficient r_{rb} [55] for the Wilcoxon test. Effect sizes lower than 0.10 are considered small, those around 0.25 are considered middle, and those greater than 0.40 are considered large [56,57].

4. Results

4.1. Differences between Classical and Fuzzy Logic Assessment

4.1.1. Grade 8

In Table 6, the descriptive statistics concerning teacher-given grades, students' attainments on the INVALSI test, and the fuzzy grade for students of grade 8 (n = 29,056) are presented.

Table 6. Descriptive statistics for 8th grade students.

	Mathematics Grade	INVALSI	Fuzzy Grade
Mean	6.79	201	5.62
Standard deviation	1.42	38.5	1.78
Median	7	200	6
Minimum	3	66.5	1
Maximum	10	326	10
Skewness (SE)	0.160 (0.0144)	0.247 (0.0144)	−0.0461 (0.0144)
Kurtosis (SE)	−0.693 (0.0287)	−0.0442 (0.0287)	−0.390 (0.0287)

The Kolmogorov–Smirnov test for normality showed that teacher-given grades (KS = 0.128; $p < 0.001$), INVALSI achievements (KS = 0.026; $p < 0.001$) and fuzzy grades (KS = 0.251; $p < 0.001$) violate the assumption of normality. This justifies the use of non-parametric statistical tests.

The Wilcoxon test indicated that fuzzy grades are significantly lower than students' mathematics grades ($W = 1.96 \times 10^8$; $p < 0.001$) with a big effect size (r_{rb} = 0.922).

The correlation analysis indicated that fuzzy grades are highly correlated both with students' mathematics grades ($\rho = 0.693$; $p < 0.001$) and with their scores on the INVALSI test ($\rho = 0.880$; $p < 0.001$).

To have a better insight into how fuzzy grades were distributed among students with different teacher-given mathematics grades, we constructed Table 7. The results indicate that among the 613 students with teacher-given grade 10, only 310 (50.6%) of them would receive the same grade ("10") even if evaluated with the fuzzy logic method. Moreover, 300 students (48.9%) would receive grade 8, while 3 students (0.0%) would get 6. On the other hand, among the 4668 students with teacher-given grade 5, 2860 (61.3%) would get an even lower grade (4), while the remaining 1808 (1792 + 16) students would get a passing grade (i.e., 6 or higher).

Table 7. The distribution of fuzzy grades among students with different school grades.

School Grade	Fuzzy Grades										Total
	1	2	3	4	5	6	7	8	9	10	
3	3	0	9	0	0	0	0	0	0	0	12 (0.0%)
4	0	384	2	202	420	7	0	0	0	0	1015 (3.5%)
5	0	0	2860	0	0	1792	0	16	0	0	4668 (16.1%)
6	0	0	3276	0	0	4274	0	49	0	0	7599 (26.2%)
7	0	0	18	0	2412	4064	0	26	0	0	6520 (22.4%)
8	0	0	35	0	0	2533	0	2710	0	0	5278 (18.2%)
9	0	0	0	0	11	1270	717	0	1353	0	3351 (11.5%)
10	0	0	0	0	0	3	0	300	0	310	613 (2.1%)
Total	3 (0.0%)	384 (1.3%)	6200 (21.3%)	202 (.7%)	2843 (9.8%)	12943 (48.0%)	717 (2.5%)	3101 (10.7%)	1353 (4.7%)	310 (1.1%)	29056 (100.0%)

In Table 8 presents the descriptive statistics for fuzzy grades distinguished among teacher-given grades. The results suggest that students from each teacher-given grade category would get a lower grade if assessed with the fuzzy logic method. For instance, students with teacher-given grade 10 would get grade 9 on average, if assessed with fuzzy logic.

Table 8. Descriptive statistics for fuzzy grades among the levels of teacher-given grades.

Teacher-Given Grade	Fuzzy Grade				
	Mean	Standard Deviation	Median	Minimum	Maximum
3	2.50	0.905	3	1	3
4	3.67	1.36	4	2	6
5	4.17	1.47	3	3	8
6	4.72	1.51	6	3	8
7	5.63	0.523	6	3	8
8	7.01	1.05	8	3	8
9	7.42	1.35	7	5	9
10	9.00	1.02	10	6	10

The Kruskal–Wallis test has shown that fuzzy grades statistically significantly differ among the categories of teacher-given grades ($\chi^2(7) = 15{,}035$; $p < 0.001$; $\varepsilon^2 = 0.517$). The DSCF pairwise comparisons between school grades are all statistically significant ($p < 0.05$), except for the comparison among students with teacher-given grade 3 and 4 ($W = 3.89$; $p = 0.108$).

4.1.2. Grade 10

In Table 9, the descriptive statistics concerning teacher-given grades, students' attainments on the INVALSI test and the fuzzy grade for the students of grade 10 ($n = 32{,}794$) are presented.

Table 9. Descriptive statistics for 10th grade students.

	Mathematics Grade	INVALSI	Fuzzy Grade
Mean	6.15	206	5.54
Standard deviation	1.45	39.1	1.60
Median	6	203	6
Minimum	1	72.3	1
Maximum	10	314	10
Skewness (SE)	0.004 (0.0135)	0.226 (0.0135)	−0.293 (0.0135)
Kurtosis (SE)	−0.233 (0.0271)	−0.053 (0.0271)	0.009 (0.0271)

The Kolmogorov–Smirnov test for normality showed that teacher-given grades ($KS = 0.148$; $p < 0.001$), INVALSI achievements ($KS = 0.023$; $p < 0.001$), and fuzzy grades ($KS = 0.228$; $p < 0.001$) violate the assumption of normality. This justifies the use of non-parametric statistical tests.

The Wilcoxon test indicated that fuzzy grades are significantly lower than students' mathematics grades ($W = 1.88 \times 10^8$; $p < 0.001$) with a medium effect size ($r_{rb} = 0.600$).

The correlation analysis indicated that fuzzy grades are correlated both with students' mathematics grades ($\rho = 0.572$; $p < 0.001$) and highly correlated with their scores on the INVALSI test ($\rho = 0.825$; $p < 0.001$).

To have a better insight into how fuzzy grades were distributed among students with different teacher-given mathematics grades, we constructed Table 10, which shows that 69 (39.9%) students with school grade 10 would get the same grade if assessed with the method of fuzzy logic, while the remaining 104 (98 + 6) students would get a lower grade. On the contrary, if we consider students with the teacher-given grade 5 (insufficient), we note that 3861 (3652 + 209) students (62.9%) would get a passing grade, while 2282 (37.1%) students would get a much lower grade.

Table 10. The distribution of fuzzy grades among students with different school grades.

School Grade	Fuzzy Grades										Total
	1	2	3	4	5	6	7	8	9	10	
1	3	0	0	0	0	0	0	0	0	0	3 (0.0%)
2	3	89	0	14	11	1	0	0	0	0	118 (0.4%)
3	102	0	683	0	0	51	0	0	0	0	835 (2.5%)
4	0	519	0	536	1951	227	0	0	0	0	3233 (9.9%)
5	0	0	2282	0	0	3652	0	209	0	0	6143 (18.7%)
6	0	0	2550	0	0	6560		566	0	0	9676 (29.5%)
7	0	0	17	0	2008	4654	0	180	0	0	6859 (20.9%)
8	0	0	17	0	0	1745	0	2362	0	0	4124 (12.6%)
9	0	0	0	0	8	634	202	0	785	0	1629 (5.0%)
10	0	0	0	0	0	6	0	98	0	69	173 (0.5%)
Total	108 (0.3%)	608 (1.9%)	5549 (16.9%)	550 (1.7%)	3978 (12.1%)	17539 (53%)	202 (0.6%)	3415 (10.4%)	785 (2.4%)	69 (0.2%)	32794 (100.0%)

In Table 11, the descriptive statistics for fuzzy grades distinguished among the teacher-given grades are presented. The results showed that on average, some categories of students, such as excellent (10) and very good (9) students would get a lower grade if assessed with the method of fuzzy logic.

Table 11. Descriptive statistics for fuzzy grades among the levels of teacher-given grades.

Teacher-Given Grade	Fuzzy Grade				
	Mean	Standard Deviation	Median	Minimum	Maximum
1	1.00	.000	1	1	1
2	2.53	1.10	2	1	6
3	2.94	1.02	3	1	6
4	4.42	1.16	5	2	6
5	4.95	1.54	6	3	8
6	5.33	1.47	6	3	8
7	5.75	.599	6	3	8
8	7.13	1.02	8	3	8
9	7.56	1.42	7	5	9
10	8.73	1.10	8	6	10

The Kruskal–Wallis test has shown that fuzzy grades statistically significantly differ among the categories of teacher-given grades ($\chi^2(9) = 13{,}150$; $p < 0.001$; $\varepsilon^2 = 0.401$). The DSCF pairwise comparisons between school grades are all statistically significant ($p < 0.05$), except for the comparison among students with teacher-given grade 6 and 7 ($W = 4.43$; $p = 0.055$).

4.1.3. Grade 13

In Table 12, the descriptive statistics concerning teacher-given grades, students' attainments on the INVALSI test, and the fuzzy grade for the students of grade 13 ($n = 30415$) are presented.

Table 12. Descriptive statistics for 13th grade students.

	Mathematics Grade	INVALSI	Fuzzy Grade
Mean	6.33	204	5.54
Standard deviation	1.46	39.8	1.62
Median	6	201	6
Minimum	1	69.5	1
Maximum	10	341	10
Skewness (SE)	−0.005 (0.014)	0.211 (0.014)	−0.205 (0.014)
Kurtosis (SE)	−0.215 (0.0281)	−0.177 (0.0281)	−0.053 (0.0281)

The Kolmogorov–Smirnov test for normality showed that teacher-given grades ($KS = 0.140$; $p < 0.001$), INVALSI achievements ($KS = 0.021$; $p < 0.001$) and fuzzy grades ($KS = 0.199$; $p < 0.001$) violate the assumption of normality. This justifies the use of non-parametric statistical tests.

The Wilcoxon test indicated that fuzzy grades are significantly lower than students' mathematics grades ($W = 1.85 \times 10^8$; $p < 0.001$) with a medium effect size ($r_{rb} = 0.690$).

The correlation analysis revealed that fuzzy grades are correlated with students' mathematics grades ($\rho = 0.552$; $p < 0.001$) and highly correlated with their scores on the INVALSI test ($\rho = 0.824$; $p < 0.001$).

To have a better insight into how fuzzy grades were distributed among students with different teacher-given mathematics grades, we constructed Table 13. The results highlight that among the students with an excellent school grade (10), only 141 (48.6%) would get the same grade if assessed with the method of fuzzy logic; the remaining 149 (51.4%) students would get a lower grade. On the contrary, among the 5109 students with the teacher-given grade 5, 3085 (2907 + 178; 60.4%) would still get a passing grade, while the remaining 2024 (39.6%) would get an even lower grade.

Table 13. The distribution of fuzzy grades among students with different school grades.

School Grade	Fuzzy Grades										Total
	1	2	3	4	5	6	7	8	9	10	
1	4	0	1	0	0	0	0	0	0	0	5 (0.0%)
2	1	50	0	13	12	2	0	0	0	0	78 (0.3%)
3	59	0	534	0	0	68	0	0	0	0	661 (2.4%)
4	0	449	0	320	1458	228	0	0	0	0	2455 (10.5%)
5	0	0	2024	0	0	2907	0	178	0	0	5109 (16.8%)
6	0	0	2889	0	0	5500	0	506	0	0	8895 (29.2%)
7	0	0	22	0	2379	4141	0	416	0	0	6688 (22.0%)
8	0	0	42	0	0	2062	0	2141	0	0	4245 (14.0%)
9	0	0	0	0	18	877	298	13	783	0	1989 (6.5%)
10	0	0	0	0	0	5	0	134	10	141	290 (1.0%)
Total	64 (.2%)	499 (1.6%)	5512 (18.1%)	333 (1.1%)	3867 (12.7%)	15790 (51.9%)	298 (1.0%)	3118 (10.3%)	793 (2.6%)	141 (0.5%)	30415 (100.0%)

In Table 14, the descriptive statistics for fuzzy grades distinguished among the teacher-given grades are presented.

Table 14. Descriptive statistics for fuzzy grades among the levels of teacher-given grades.

Teacher-Given Grade	Fuzzy Grade				
	Mean	Standard Deviation	Median	Minimum	Maximum
1	1.40	0.894	1	1	3
2	2.88	1.31	2	1	6
3	3.13	1.13	3	1	6
4	4.41	1.24	5	2	6
5	4.88	1.57	6	3	8
6	5.14	1.55	6	3	8
7	5.68	0.608	6	3	8
8	6.98	1.07	8	3	8
9	7.33	1.40	7	5	9
10	8.97	1.05	9	6	10

The Kruskal–Wallis test has shown that fuzzy grades statistically significantly differ among the categories of teacher-given grades ($\chi^2(9) = 11{,}351$; $p < 0.001$; $\varepsilon^2 = 0.373$). The DSCF pairwise comparisons between school grades are all statistically significant ($p < 0.05$), except for the comparison among students with teacher-given grade 1 and 2 ($W = 4.37$; $p = 0.063$).

4.2. Differences in Fuzzy Logic Assessment among Students of Grade 8, 10, and 13

Students' fuzzy achievements statistically significantly differ among grades ($\chi^2(2) = 51.2$; $p < 0.001$), although the effect size is extremely low ($\varepsilon^2 = 5.55 \times 10^{-4}$). The DSCF test has shown that there are statistically significant differences in fuzzy grades between the 8th and 10th grade students ($W = -8.572$; $p < 0.001$), as well as between the 8th and 13th grade students ($W = -8.983$; $p < 0.001$). However, there are no statistically significant differences between the 10th and 13th grade students ($W = -0.824$; $p = 0.830$). Due to the low effect size, results indicate that students' fuzzy achievements are hardly dependent on students' classes. Moreover, high school students have similar fuzzy achievements, thus fuzzy grades are almost uniformly distributed in all grades.

5. Discussion

The idea of evaluating students' knowledge with fuzzy logic is not entirely new, as it has been studied by several researchers [3–14,22,26,27], mainly because the grades awarded by teachers are based on verbal descriptions of students' knowledge. Moreover, students' assessment is an imprecise construct and fuzzy logic seems to be suitable for such variables [3,4]. The international literature has proposed different models for assessing students' knowledge, i.e., combining test scores and the time taken to solve them [4], combining two or more test/exam outcomes [6,7], combining student achievement and class attendance [9], etc. Among those studies which investigated the difference between traditional assessing method and fuzzy logic based one, the findings are relatively inconsistent: some researchers found no difference between fuzzy grades and traditional grades [4,9,26], while others found that fuzzy grades were lower or higher than those of the teachers [6,7,27].

Therefore, the main aim of the present work was to clarify these inconsistencies by comparing the traditional (based on teacher-given grades) math knowledge assessing method to the fuzzy logic one, which combines teacher-assigned grades with students' performance on a standardized math test (i.e., the INVALSI). Moreover, extending previous literature, we were interested in exploring whether there are differences in the fuzzy logic evaluation method among different school levels (grades 8, 10, and 13).

To answer the first research question, we compared traditional grades to the fuzzy ones in students attending the 8th, 10th, and 13th grade in Italy. In all school levels, students' traditional grades were statistically higher than their fuzzy grades; the effect sizes were medium to large, suggesting that the fuzzy logic evaluation method yields lower overall ratings. Therefore, combining teacher-given grades with students' results obtained from the national assessment using fuzzy logic reduces their final grades. This result is consistent with previous research [27]; we have shown that the affirmation is valid for all considered school levels.

A deeper look at the distribution of fuzzy grades across categories of teacher-assigned grades reveals that fuzzy grades within the same teacher-assigned grades are sparse. This consequently means that students with the same grade assigned by the teacher could get a different grade when assessed with the proposed fuzzy model. This finding also raises questions regarding the validity and reliability of teachers' grades [2]: students who have excellent academic results could get lower grades if the INVALSI standardized test is also considered. This could have important consequences, especially considering the labor market [58] and the possibility of being accepted to higher education institutions, such as universities. For example, the present study showed that 5 students who had an excellent grade on their report cards (i.e., a 10), would obtain a lower grade (i.e., a 6), if evaluated by the fuzzy logic method proposed. On the other hand, there have been some students who received an insufficient grade by the teacher (e.g., 5), but would have obtained a sufficient grade (e.g., 6 or more) if evaluated with the system of logic fuzzy. Therefore, although the academic results of some excellent students may indeed be excellent, their results on the INVALSI test could demonstrate that these students do not master all the mathematics topics assessed by the national standardized test. In the document ref. [37] it is stated that the INVALSI test cannot evaluate the non-cognitive and metacognitive factors involved in math learning, such as the students' attitude toward the subject, therefore, considering merely the students' performance on the INVALSI test might not give a complete picture of students' math competencies. Thus, the proposed fuzzy logic method for assessing students' mathematical knowledge and skills could provide educators, students, and their parents with a clearer picture of students' mathematical skills [2].

The importance of predicting students' grades and developing a sustainable learning environment was recently studied by Kanetaki and colleagues [59]. They identified and quantified the factors affecting mechanical engineering students' outcomes (e.g., classroom fatigue, understanding of the concept of planes, insecurity, computer skills, etc.,) when classes were held online or in a hybrid learning environment due to the COVID-19 outbreak. The proposed model is a valid model that can be used to predict students' failure of promotion in a hybrid or online learning environment. Although the model predicted the promotion of some students who then failed (and therefore, the model overestimated their achievements), the model still has a non-negligible importance from an educational point of view, as it could help educators and especially learners to have a clearer picture of students' knowledge and competencies. Our work can be placed within the effort made by Kanetaki et al. [59] and could be used by educators to implement sustainable assessment, i.e., giving students skills to become lifelong learners [60]. In particular, students would gain self-awareness and would be able to self-assess [60], since they might constantly monitor their performances by receiving additional feedback information from the standardized INVALSI tests. Future research could seek to develop a model for predicting the grades that students would receive if the INVALSI test results were also considered, so that students could self-assess their mathematics knowledge, improving and possibly changing their way of learning mathematics. The model could be tested as suggested by [59] and used by students to obtain real-time feedback on their knowledge and competencies in mathematics.

The second aim of the research was to explore possible differences in fuzzy scores between 8th, 10th, and 13th grade students. We found that among high school students (i.e., grades 10 and 13), there are no significant differences in fuzzy scores, while there are some significant differences between secondary (i.e., grade 8) and high school students. However, the differences found have an almost negligible effect size, meaning that the proposed method produces similar results at all levels of education. This fact therefore underlines that the evaluation method with fuzzy logic is solid and produces very similar outcomes, even when used at different educational levels. Further research could extend the proposed model to primary schools and verify whether the fuzzy logic assessment model produces comparable grades to those found in this study. In particular, the fact that the obtained results do not significantly differ among school levels contributes to a further validation of the model proposed in the present study.

The present study has some relevant implications for educators. For instance, the assessment method based on teacher-assigned grades and performance on standardized tests (such as national assessment) has been suggested by some authors as a possible solution to grade inflation [61], i.e., the phenomenon of assigning students higher grades than they deserve or that they would obtain if they were evaluated with a sort of standardized evaluation [62]. The proposed fuzzy logic method could serve the purpose of lowering excessively high mathematics grades while also offering a clearer picture of students' mathematical knowledge. Furthermore, as already mentioned, the model could help students develop self-assessment skills and therefore, sustainable learning and assessment [59,60]. In addition, the existence of different evaluation methodologies can influence the improvement of teaching policies. In particular, teachers who consider other methods of assessing students' knowledge and competencies can verify how much their grades differ from students' achievements in other forms of assessment, such as standardized tests [63]. Additionally, educators need to know about different data sources [64] and use multiple assessment strategies, including criterion-referenced methods and standardized tests [65]. Recent research on the impacts the INVALSI test has on teachers' practices [66] has shown that some teachers (1) enhanced activities aimed at improving students' skills in problem-solving and critical thinking; (2) changed the teaching method by using more examples of the applications of mathematics to reality; and (3) implemented the curriculum by anticipating the order of the topics covered. Another aspect that was highlighted in the same research is the fact that a critical analysis of the INVALSI tests has led teachers to reflect on their teaching methodologies and try developing argumentative skills in students. Moreover, some argued that standardized tests are promising tools for the evaluation of the effectiveness of different instructional practices [67], therefore, by using the fuzzy logic model teachers would be able to monitor the effectiveness of their teaching practices and implement them.

The present empirical research should be considered in light of some limitations. First, the results obtained through fuzzy logic depend on the techniques used, on fuzzification, on the definition and the granularity of fuzzy rules, and on defuzzification. Membership functions and inferential rules were chosen by the researchers based on previous studies [7] and based on their experiences as educators [25]. Changing the functions and inference rules would lead to potentially very different results. Future research should address the question of how fuzzy grades would change if different membership functions or defuzzification methods were used. Second, in the present work, we assumed the proposed model to be better than considering solely teacher-given grades. In particular, teacher-given grades and standardized assessment scores measure slightly different aspects of achievement and achievement-related behavior [68]. Considering both measures of students' knowledge and competencies is important to improve student achievement [69] and give educators, students, and parents more complete information regarding students' achievements [2]. However, we did not compare the proposed model with other assessing models. Future studies could therefore evaluate the validity of the proposed model by comparing it with other methods. Lastly, in this study, we did not consider some factors which could affect students' achievement, such as their gender, socio-economic status, and geographic origin. Future studies could therefore explore the role these factors play in the fuzzy logic model proposed in this paper. There are also practical limitations in applying the methodology described in this work. Indeed, teachers may not be familiar with fuzzy logic, so the transition from traditional to fuzzy assessing model may not be smooth. Teachers should thus receive specific training and knowledge on the fuzzy logic itself before the model could be used in everyday teaching practice.

6. Conclusions

Although teacher-given grades are often reported numerically, the grades awarded by teachers are based on verbal descriptions of students' knowledge and competencies. To work with variables that are based on descriptions and verbal judgments and characterized by a degree of vagueness, it is recommended to use the fuzzy logic [3]. Moreover, the teachers' approach to evaluation in classrooms may not coincide with the approach taken in INVALSI tests. Indeed, in classrooms, the tests have a concentrated focus on the subject content which is studied (e.g., tests assess solely students' knowledge of equations), while in the INVALSI tests, the focus is usually more multidisciplinary (i.e., several mathematics topics are assessed). The aim of the present work was to investigate how to combine teacher-given grades with students' results in the standardized INVALSI test in order to create a novel assessing method, based on fuzzy logic, and how it differs from the traditional assessment method.

From the obtained results we can deduce that in the considered samples, the fuzzy assessment method reduces students' grades. Therefore, the evaluation method with fuzzy logic is stricter than the traditional one. Furthermore, we have shown that the level of schooling has an almost negligible effect on students' fuzzy grades.

Although this research has considered solely secondary and high school students, future research is needed to test the possibility of evaluating students' mathematical knowledge also in lower schools, namely elementary schools. Therefore, more research is needed to explore the possibility of extending the proposed model of assessing students' mathematical knowledge across grades. In the present research, we used students' achievement on the Italian national assessment of mathematics knowledge INVALSI, while future research could investigate the combination of student grades with their results in other standardized tests, such as the PISA or TIMSS. Additionally, the proposed model, although it has been tested only for mathematics, can also be extended to other subjects, for which there are standardized national or international tests (e.g., the INVALSI institute also assesses the knowledge of Italian and English language).

Author Contributions: Conceptualization, D.D., D.F. and M.C.; methodology, D.D.; software, D.D.; validation, D.F. and M.C.; resources, D.D., D.F. and M.C.; data curation, D.D., D.F. and M.C.; writing—original draft preparation, D.D. and D.F.; writing—review and editing, D.D. and M.C.; supervision, M.C. All authors have read and agreed to the published version of the manuscript.

Funding: This research received no external funding.

Institutional Review Board Statement: Not applicable.

Informed Consent Statement: Not applicable.

Data Availability Statement: Not applicable.

Conflicts of Interest: The authors declare no conflict of interest.

References

1. Gao, X.; Li, P.; Shen, J.; Sun, H. Reviewing assessment of student learning in interdisciplinary STEM education. *Int. J. STEM Educ.* **2020**, *7*, 24. [CrossRef]
2. Mellati, M.; Khademi, M. Exploring teachers' assessment literacy: Impact on learners' writing achievements and implications for teacher development. *Austr. J. Teach. Educ.* **2018**, *43*, 1–18. [CrossRef]
3. Voskoglou, M.G. Fuzzy logic as a tool for assessing students' knowledge and skills. *Educ. Sci.* **2013**, *3*, 208–221. [CrossRef]
4. Sripan, R.; Suksawat, B. Propose of fuzzy logic-based students' learning assessment. In Proceedings of the ICCAS 2010, Gyeonggi-do, Korea, 27–30 October 2010; IEEE: Manhattan, NY, USA, 2010; pp. 414–417.
5. Krouska, A.; Troussas, C.; Sgouropoulou, C. Fuzzy logic for refining the evaluation of learners' performance in online engineering education. *Eur. J. Eng. Sci. Tech.* **2019**, *4*, 50–56.
6. Gokmen, G.; Akinci, T.Ç.; Tektaş, M.; Onat, N.; Kocyigit, G.; Tektaş, N. Evaluation of student performance in laboratory applications using fuzzy logic. *Procedia Soc.* **2010**, *2*, 902–909. [CrossRef]
7. Petrudi, S.H.J.; Pirouz, M.; Pirouz, B. Application of fuzzy logic for performance evaluation of academic students. In Proceedings of the 2013 13th Iranian Conference on Fuzzy Systems (IFSC), Qazvin, Iran, 27–29 August 2013; IEEE: Manhattan, NY, USA, 2013; pp. 1–5.
8. Namli, N.A.; Şenkal, O. Using the fuzzy logic in assessing the programming performance of students. *Int. J. Assess. Tool. Educ.* **2018**, *5*, 701–712. [CrossRef]
9. Yadav, R.S.; Soni, A.K.; Pal, S. A study of academic performance evaluation using Fuzzy Logic techniques. In Proceedings of the 2014 International Conference on Computing for Sustainable Global Development (INDIACom), New Delhi, India, 5–7 March 2014; IEEE: Manhattan, NY, USA, 2014; pp. 48–53.
10. Ivanova, V.; Zlatanov, B. Application of fuzzy logic in online test evaluation in English as a foreign language at university level. In Proceedings of the 45th International Conference on Application of Mathematics in Engineering and Economics (AMEE'19), Sozopol, Bulgaria, 7–13 June 2019; AIP Publishing: Long Island, NY, USA, 2019; Volume 2172, p. 040009.
11. Eryılmaz, M.; Adabashi, A. Development of an intelligent tutoring system using bayesian networks and fuzzy logic for a higher student academic performance. *Appl. Sci.* **2020**, *10*, 6638. [CrossRef]
12. Ivanova, V.; Zlatanov, B. Implementation of fuzzy functions aimed at fairer grading of students' tests. *Educ. Sci.* **2019**, *9*, 214. [CrossRef]
13. Amelia, N.; Abdullah, A.G.; Mulyadi, Y. Meta-analysis of student performance assessment using fuzzy logic. *Indones. J. Sci. Technol.* **2019**, *4*, 74–88. [CrossRef]
14. Chrysafiadi, K.; Troussas, C.; Virvou, M. Combination of fuzzy and cognitive theories for adaptive e-assessment. *Expert Syst. Appl.* **2020**, *161*, 113614. [CrossRef]
15. Zadeh, L.A. Fuzzy sets. *Inf. Control* **1965**, *8*, 338–353. [CrossRef]
16. Bissey, S.; Jacques, S.; Le Bunetel, J.C. The fuzzy logic method to efficiently optimize electricity consumption in individual housing. *Energies* **2017**, *10*, 1701. [CrossRef]
17. Liu, H.; Jeffery, C.J. Moonlighting Proteins in the Fuzzy Logic of Cellular Metabolism. *Molecules* **2020**, *25*, 3440. [CrossRef] [PubMed]
18. Thalmeiner, G.; Gáspár, S.; Barta, Á.; Zéman, Z. Application of Fuzzy Logic to Evaluate the Economic Impact of COVID-19: Case Study of a Project-Oriented Travel Agency. *Sustainability* **2021**, *13*, 9602. [CrossRef]
19. Khalil, S.; Hassan, A.; Alaskar, H.; Khan, W.; Hussain, A. Fuzzy Logical Algebra and Study of the Effectiveness of Medications for COVID-19. *Mathematics* **2021**, *9*, 2838. [CrossRef]
20. Xue, Z.; Dong, Q.; Fan, X.; Jin, Q.; Jian, H.; Liu, J. Fuzzy Logic-Based Model That Incorporates Personality Traits for Heterogeneous Pedestrians. *Symmetry* **2017**, *9*, 239. [CrossRef]
21. Zadeh, L.A.; Aliev, R.A. *Fuzzy Logic Theory and Applications: Part I and Part II*; World Scientific Publishing: Singapore, 2018.
22. Yadav, R.S.; Singh, V.P. Modeling academic performance evaluation using soft computing techniques: A fuzzy logic approach. *Int. J. Comput. Sci. Eng.* **2011**, *3*, 676–686.
23. Azam, M.H.; Hasan, M.H.; Hassan, S.; Abdulkadir, S.J. Fuzzy type-1 triangular membership function approximation using fuzzy C-means. In Proceedings of the 2020 International Conference on Computational Intelligence (ICCI), Bandar Seri Iskandar, Malaysia, 8–9 October 2020; IEEE: Manhattan, NY, USA, 2020; pp. 115–120.
24. Bakar, N.A.; Rosbi, S.; Bakar, A.A. Robust estimation of student performance in massive open online course using fuzzy logic approach. *Int. J. Eng. Technol.* **2020**, editor issue. 143–152.
25. Bai, Y.; Wang, D. Fundamentals of fuzzy logic control—fuzzy sets, fuzzy rules and defuzzifications. In *Advanced Fuzzy Logic Technologies in Industrial Applications*; Bai, Y., Zhuang, H., Wang, D., Eds.; Springer: London, UK, 2006; pp. 17–36.
26. Saliu, S. Constrained subjective assessment of student learning. *J. Sci. Educ. Technol.* **2005**, *14*, 271–284. [CrossRef]
27. Doz, D.; Felda, D.; Cotič, M. Assessing Students' Mathematical Knowledge with Fuzzy Logic. *Educ. Sci.* **2022**, *12*, 266. [CrossRef]
28. INVALSI. Servizio Statistico. Available online: https://invalsi-serviziostatistico.cineca.it/ (accessed on 1 June 2022).

29. INVALSI. Rapproto Prove INVALSI 2019. Available online: https://invalsi-areaprove.cineca.it/docs/2019/rapporto_prove_invalsi_2019.pdf (accessed on 1 June 2022).
30. Cardone, M.; Falzetti, P.; Sacco, C. INVALSI Data for School System Improvement: The Value Added. Available online: https://www.invalsi.it/download2/wp/wp43_Falzetti_Cardone_Sacco.pdf (accessed on 1 June 2022).
31. INVALSI. Istruzioni Informazioni Contest Scuola Secondaria Secondo Grado. Available online: https://invalsi-areaprove.cineca.it/docs/2020/02_2020_Istruzioni_informazioni_contesto_Scuola_secondaria_secondo%20_grad.pdf (accessed on 1 June 2022).
32. DLgs 62/2017. Available online: https://www.gazzettaufficiale.it/eli/id/2017/05/16/17G00070/sg (accessed on 1 June 2022).
33. RD 653/1925. Available online: https://www.normattiva.it/uri-res/N2Ls?urn:nir:stato:legge:1925-05-04;653 (accessed on 1 June 2022).
34. DLgs 297/1994. Available online: https://www.gazzettaufficiale.it/eli/id/1994/05/19/094G0291/sg (accessed on 1 June 2022).
35. D 254/2012. Available online: https://www.gazzettaufficiale.it/eli/id/2013/02/05/13G00034/sg (accessed on 1 June 2022).
36. DPR 89/2010. Available online: https://www.gazzettaufficiale.it/eli/id/2010/06/15/010G0111/sg (accessed on 1 June 2022).
37. INVALSI. Quadro di Riferimento 2018. Available online: https://invalsi-areaprove.cineca.it/docs/file/QdR_MATEMATICA.pdf (accessed on 1 June 2022).
38. INVALSI. Rapproto Prove INVALSI 2018. Available online: https://www.invalsi.it/invalsi/doc_evidenza/2018/Rapporto_prove_INVALSI_2018.pdf (accessed on 1 June 2022).
39. INVALSI. Rapproto Prove INVALSI 2017. Available online: https://www.invalsi.it/invalsi/doc_eventi/2017/Rapporto_Prove_INVALSI_2017.pdf (accessed on 1 June 2022).
40. Organization for Economic Co-Operation and Development [OECD]. Technical Report PISA 2018. Available online: https://www.oecd.org/pisa/data/pisa2018technicalreport/Ch.09-Scaling-PISA-Data.pdf (accessed on 1 June 2022).
41. Trends in International Mathematics and Science Study [TIMSS]. Scaling Methodology. Available online: https://timssandpirls.bc.edu/timss2019/methods/pdf/T19_MP_Ch11-scaling-methodology.pdf (accessed on 2 June 2022).
42. Pastori, G.; Pagani, V. What do you think about INVALSI tests? School directors, teachers and students from Lombardy describe their experience. *J. Educ. Cult. Psychol. Stud.* **2016**, *13*, 97–117. [CrossRef]
43. Thukral, S.; Rana, V. Versatility of fuzzy logic in chronic diseases: A review. *Med. Hypotheses* **2019**, *122*, 150–156. [CrossRef] [PubMed]
44. MATLAB. Fuzzy Logic Toolbox. Available online: https://it.mathworks.com/products/fuzzy-logic.html (accessed on 2 June 2022).
45. MATLAB. Breve Riepilogo su R2020b. Available online: https://it.mathworks.com/products/new_products/release2020b.html (accessed on 2 June 2022).
46. The Jamovi Project. Jamovi (Version 2.2.5) [Computer Software]. Available online: https://www.jamovi.org (accessed on 1 June 2022).
47. Arnastauskaitė, J.; Ruzgas, T.; Bražėnas, M. An Exhaustive Power Comparison of Normality Tests. *Mathematics* **2021**, *9*, 788. [CrossRef]
48. Gerald, B. A brief review of independent, dependent and one sample t-test. *Int. J. Appl. Math. Theor. Phys.* **2018**, *4*, 50–54. [CrossRef]
49. Hopkins, S.; Dettori, J.R.; Chapman, J.R. Parametric and nonparametric tests in spine research: Why do they matter? *Glob. Spine J.* **2018**, *8*, 652–654. [CrossRef] [PubMed]
50. Schober, P.; Boer, C.; Schwarte, L.A. Correlation coefficients: Appropriate use and interpretation. *Anesth. Analg.* **2018**, *126*, 1763–1768. [CrossRef]
51. Akoglu, H. User's guide to correlation coefficients. *Turk. J. Emerg. Med.* **2018**, *18*, 91–93. [CrossRef]
52. Grzegorzewski, P.; Śpiewak, M. The sign test and the signed-rank test for interval-valued data. *Int. J. Itell. Syst.* **2019**, *34*, 2122–2150. [CrossRef]
53. Johnson, R.W. Alternate Forms of the One-Way ANOVA F and Kruskal–Wallis Test Statistics. *J. Stat. Data Sci. Educ.* **2022**, *30*, 82–85. [CrossRef]
54. Albers, C.; Lakens, D. When power analyses based on pilot data are biased: Inaccurate effect size estimators and follow-up bias. *J. Exp. Soc. Psychol.* **2018**, *74*, 187–195. [CrossRef]
55. Liu, X.S.; Carlson, R.; Kelley, K. Common language effect size for correlations. *J. Gen. Psychol.* **2019**, *146*, 325–338. [CrossRef] [PubMed]
56. Lovakov, A.; Agadullina, E.R. Empirically derived guidelines for effect size interpretation in social psychology. *Eur. J. Soc. Psychol.* **2021**, *51*, 485–504. [CrossRef]
57. Funder, D.C.; Ozer, D.J. Evaluating effect size in psychological research: Sense and nonsense. *Adv. Methods Pract. Psychol. Sci.* **2019**, *2*, 156–168. [CrossRef]
58. Quadlin, N. The mark of a woman's record: Gender and academic performance in hiring. *Am. Sociol. Rev.* **2018**, *83*, 331–360. [CrossRef]
59. Kanetaki, Z.; Stergiou, C.; Bekas, G.; Jacques, S.; Troussas, C.; Sgouropoulou, C.; Ouahabi, A. Grade Prediction Modeling in Hybrid Learning Environments for Sustainable Engineering Education. *Sustainability* **2022**, *14*, 5205. [CrossRef]
60. Chung, S.J.; Choi, L.J. The development of sustainable assessment during the COVID-19 pandemic: The case of the English language program in South Korea. *Sustainability* **2021**, *13*, 4499. [CrossRef]
61. Bowers, A.J. Towards measures of different and useful aspects of schooling: Why schools need both teacher-assigned grades and standardized assessments. In *Classroom Assessment and Educational Measurement*; Routledge: New York, NY, USA, 2019; pp. 209–223.

62. Gershenson, S.; Thomas, B.; Fordham Institute. Grade Inflation in High Schools (2005–2016). Available online: https://files.eric.ed.gov/fulltext/ED598893.pdf (accessed on 16 June 2022).
63. Herppich, S.; Praetorius, A.K.; Förster, N.; Glogger-Frey, I.; Karst, K.; Leutner, D.; Behrmann, L.; Böhmer, M.; Ufer, S.; Klug, J.; et al. Teachers' assessment competence: Integrating knowledge-, process-, and product-oriented approaches into a competence-oriented conceptual model. *Teach. Teach. Educ.* **2018**, *76*, 181–193. [CrossRef]
64. Marsh, J.A.; Farrell, C.C. How leaders can support teachers with data-driven decision making: A framework for understanding capacity building. *Educ. Manag. Adm. Leadersh.* **2015**, *43*, 269–289. [CrossRef]
65. Stronge, J.H.; Tucker, P.D. *Handbook on Teacher Evaluation: Assessing and Improving Performance*; Routledge: New York, NY, USA, 2020.
66. Ferretti, F.; Funghi, S.; Martignone, F. How Standardised Tests Impact on Teacher Practices: An Exploratory Study of Teachers' Beliefs. In *Theorizing and Measuring Affect in Mathematics Teaching and Learning*; Springer: Cham, Germany, 2020; pp. 139–146.
67. Eriksson, K.; Helenius, O.; Ryve, A. Using TIMSS items to evaluate the effectiveness of different instructional practices. *Instr. Sci.* **2019**, *47*, 1–18. [CrossRef]
68. Westphal, A.; Vock, M.; Kretschmann, J. Unraveling the relationship between teacher-assigned grades, student personality, and standardized test scores. *Front. Psychol.* **2021**, *12*, 627440. [CrossRef]
69. Bergbauer, A.B.; Hanushek, E.A.; Woessmann, L. Testing. Available online: https://www.nber.org/system/files/working_papers/w24836/w24836.pdf (accessed on 14 July 2022).

Article

Explainable Fuzzy AI Challenge 2022: Winner's Approach to a Computationally Efficient and Explainable Solution

Sunny Mishra [1], Amit K. Shukla [2,*] and Pranab K. Muhuri [1]

1 Department of Computer Science, South Asian University, New Delhi 110021, India
2 Faculty of Information Technology, University of Jyvaskyla, P.O. Box 35 (Agora), 40014 Jyvaskyla, Finland
* Correspondence: amit.k.shukla@jyu.fi or amitkshukla@live.com

Abstract: An explainable artificial intelligence (XAI) agent is an autonomous agent that uses a fundamental XAI model at its core to perceive its environment and suggests actions to be performed. One of the significant challenges for these XAI agents is performing their operation efficiently, which is governed by the underlying inference and optimization system. Along similar lines, an Explainable Fuzzy AI Challenge (XFC 2022) competition was launched, whose principal objective was to develop a fully autonomous and optimized XAI algorithm that could play the Python arcade game "Asteroid Smasher". This research first investigates inference models to implement an efficient (XAI) agent using rule-based fuzzy systems. We also discuss the proposed approach (which won the competition) to attain efficiency in the XAI algorithm. We have explored the potential of the widely used Mamdani- and TSK-based fuzzy inference systems and investigated which model might have a more optimized implementation. Even though the TSK-based model outperforms Mamdani in several applications, no empirical evidence suggests this will also be applicable in implementing an XAI agent. The experimentations are then performed to find a better-performing inference system in a fast-paced environment. The thorough analysis recommends more robust and efficient TSK-based XAI agents than Mamdani-based fuzzy inference systems.

Keywords: explainable AI; fuzzy systems; AI agents; Mamdani inference system; TSK; 03B52

MSC: 03B52

1. Introduction

An explainable artificial intelligence [1] (or XAI) is an artificial intelligence (AI) where humans can easily understand and analyze the actions performed by the AI. The idea behind using XAI is that the results given by AI models would be more acceptable to the end-user if the results have an explanation in layman's terms associated with them [2]. The recent advances in machine learning algorithms can produce an AI that can learn, decide, and act independently without any supervision. However, these AI systems cannot explain their output and actions to human users [1]. It is challenging to apply these models to high-stakes or government-regulated domains such as insurance, loans, mortgages, portfolio rebalancing, power plant operations, etc. XAI provides much-needed explanations for AI applications in such domains [3]. It tries to improve by providing reasoning behind the decisions made by an AI system.

Recent research has shown that rule-based fuzzy systems work well in implementing XAI models because fuzzy rules consist of words and IF–ELSE statements that contribute to the overall explainability of the AI model [3,4]. Autonomous XAI agents can be built using rule-based fuzzy systems that can work in a fast-paced environment. However, one of the major concerns while implementing XAI agents using rule-based fuzzy systems is the associated performance penalty. Along similar lines, an Explainable Fuzzy AI Challenge (XFC 2022) competition was launched, whose principal objective was to develop a fully autonomous and optimized XAI algorithm that could play the Python arcade game "Asteroid Smasher" [5]. In the game, a 2-dimensional spacecraft moves around in an asteroid field, and the goal of the XAI agent is to terminate all the asteroids while avoiding collision with them.

This paper introduces a computationally efficient and most explainable solution to the competition, where we implement XAI agents using rule-based fuzzy systems. This recent work motivated us to explore the feasibility and performance of such XAI implementations, which use rule-based fuzzy inference systems at their core in a fast-paced environment [6,7]. Further, we wanted to explore which type-1 fuzzy inference system would be most efficient and perform better for such explainable artificial intelligence implementations.

In this research work, we tried to answer the following questions

- Can an AI agent be implemented using the fuzzy inference system and later be explained logically?
- Which type-1 fuzzy inference system is most computationally efficient and performs better in such an implementation?
- How does such an inference system help to attain higher efficiency?
- Are the generated explanations sensible and understandable to the end-user?

To answer these research questions, we took the implementation of an explainable AI system provided by the competition [5]. The game environment changes at 60 frames per second; hence, the XAI agent needs to perform its calculation within that time. Simply, the XAI agent code needs to complete its execution in less than 0.016 s to control the spacecraft efficiently. Further, we compared and experimented with the two most popular type-1 fuzzy inference systems, Mamdani and Takagi–Sugeno–Kang (TSK). We implemented the same XAI agent using both Mamdani and TSK inference systems to perform a fair comparison. We then benchmarked both implementations to determine which fuzzy inference system performs better and is computationally efficient.

The major contribution of the manuscript is as follows:

1. An XAI agent to work in a fast-paced environment using fuzzy inference systems is designed.
2. The objective is to find a computationally efficient and feasible way to implement these XAI agents using rule-based fuzzy systems.
3. The actions of the agents are explained in IF–ELSE statements, which are easier for an average user to understand without any technical expertise.
4. The proposed fuzzy-inference-systems-based XAI agent achieved an accuracy of 85.45%.

This paper is organized in the following way. Section 2 provides quick background material for the related methodologies used in this competition. Section 3 provides a step-by-step flow of the proposed approach, which includes the components of the competition and the utilized methodology. The results are also compiled in this section. Section 4 concludes the paper by presenting a detailed discussion of the outcomes and future works.

2. Literature Survey

There have been no past works in this area apart from the XFC competition in 2021 [8]. However, we provide a short literature study for the ready reference of the readers, which will also help them understand the methodologies behind the approaches used in the competition.

To start with, Mendel and Bonissone [3] have discussed why rule-based fuzzy inference systems are suitable for XAI implementation. The authors further presented a way to explain the output of rule-based fuzzy inference systems by taking an association of antecedents of the rule-base. They stated that triangular or trapezoidal membership functions for rule antecedents were more suitable for XAI implementation than Gaussian membership functions because the former partitioned the state space more unambiguously than the latter. Hagras [2] discussed the need for XAI and the efforts that are currently being researched to realize XAI or Whitebox/Transparent models. He also discussed the feasibility of using Type-1 and Type-2 fuzzy inference systems to implement XAI because a layman user can easily understand the output of such fuzzy inference systems.

Gunning and Aha [1] discussed the DARPA's XAI program for developing and evaluating a wide variety of new ML techniques. The study included deep learning models, learning explainable features, creating more structured and interpretable models, and model induction techniques that can infer an explainable model from any black-box model. Chimatapu et al. [9] studied several approaches to implementing XAI and compared them in terms of accuracy and interpretability. They also proposed an alternate method of implementing XAI using fuzzy rule-based systems, which use IF–ELSE rules and are easy to understand for an average end-user. This alternate approach allows us to create AI systems that have a good balance between accuracy and interpretability. Ferreyra et al. [10] proposed a concise and incremental framework for developing XAI solutions in the telecommunication workforce allocation domain. They used type-2 fuzzy inference systems [11] to model the decision-making process in the workforce allocation domain, particularly for a goal-driven solution. The framework proposed also contained an intuitive explanatory user interface to depict the developed application's understanding.

Potie et al. [12] performed a case study on predicting lung cancer by implementing XAI using evolutionary fuzzy systems; it combined the good degree of understanding, comprehensibility, and explainability associated with fuzzy rule-based systems with the potential of evolutionary algorithms as the optimization technique for improving fuzzy rule-based systems. Experiments done by the author have shown that evolutionary fuzzy systems can be a very feasible solution as they achieve the highest test accuracy and the best explainable features. Kiani et al. [13] discussed the implementation of an XAI system using a type-2 fuzzy inference system for analyzing the fNIRS dataset to get a better insight into how a developing child's brain responds to different stimuli. The authors chose the type-2 fuzzy inference system because of its unique ability to model uncertainty in the input data, which was paramount in this work. Poli et al. [14] worked on semantic image annotation by modeling the problem as a fuzzy constraint satisfaction problem [15]. The authors also proposed an algorithm for semantic image annotation. The XAI system they developed also gives explanations for each annotation that, according to the survey conducted by them, are easy for an average end-user to understand.

As for the background of the 2021 competition, there was only a single agent and no restriction on the execution time [8]. However, in the present competition [7], we have multiple agents, and a time limit of 0.016 s is imposed. For each execution, if the controller takes more time than this, the controller's output is ignored. Further, in this study, we discuss why rule-based fuzzy inference systems are optimal for implementing explainable AI systems.

3. Proposed Approach, Competition Scenarios, and Outcomes

This section covers the step-by-step details of the competition framework and our (winning) proposed approach to providing an efficient solution. The following procedure is depicted in Figure 1.

Step 1: *Agent Environment*

At first, we explore and analyze the agent environment to determine what inputs the environment provides and the actions the agent is allowed to perform. We use the Python implementation of a classic arcade game called fuzzy asteroids [16].

A two-dimensional spacecraft moves in the game environment to avoid collisions with numerous asteroids that appear. The asteroids have different shapes, sizes, and velocities. The spacecraft also has a weapon that can shoot straight ahead. If the projectiles emitted reach any target asteroids, they break into smaller pieces. The smallest asteroid pieces disappear after being hit by a bullet. The environment is 800 pixels high by 1000 pixels wide, with object wrapping enabled on the corners, i.e., a ship or asteroid that goes out of the game screen space will come back into it from the opposite side.

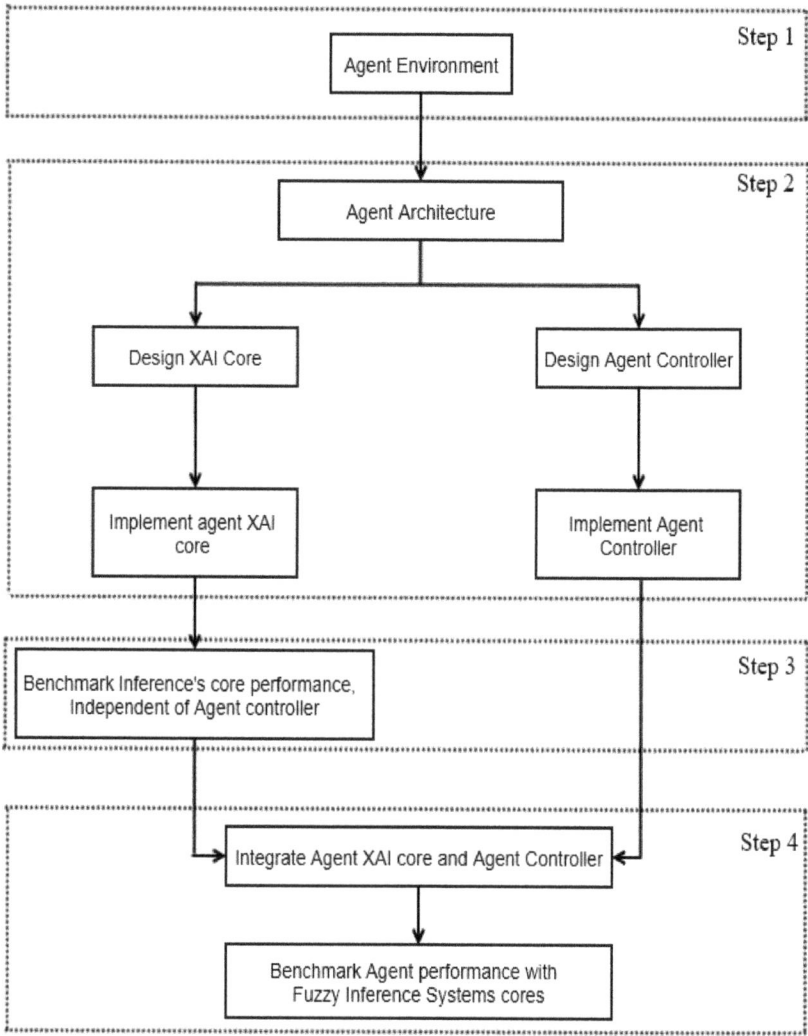

Figure 1. Flowchart of the competition framework and proposed methodology.

The agent environment provides the XAI agent with information about the ship and all the asteroids currently in the agent environment. The agent can control the ship's velocity, the ship's turning speed, and the ship's gun to fire bullets. Tables 1–3 summarize the inputs and available actions for the XAI agent.

Table 1. Available inputs for each asteroid on the screen.

Input Name	Description
position	Absolute position of the asteroid on the screen in a tuple (x-coordinate, y-coordinate).
velocity	Current velocity of the asteroids in a tuple (x-velocity, y-velocity) in meters/second.
size	The size of the asteroid.
angle	The angle at which the asteroid is moving.

Table 2. Available inputs for the ship.

Input Name	Description
is_respawning	Boolean variable, which tells if the ship is currently spawning or not.
position	The absolute position of the ship on the screen in a tuple (x-coordinate, y-coordinate).
velocity	Current velocity of the ship in a tuple (x-velocity, y-velocity) in meters/second.
angle	The angle at which the ship is moving.

Table 3. Available actions XAI agent can perform to control the ship.

Action Name	Description and Possible Values
thrust	The XAI agent can set this variable's value to change the ship's acceleration between −480 and 480 to accelerate backward or forward, respectively.
turning_rate	The XAI agent can set this variable's value to change the ship's turning speed between −180.0 and 180.0 to rotate the ship anti-clockwise or clockwise, respectively.
shoot	The XAI agent can call this method to make the ship shoot a bullet.

Step 2: *Agent Design and Implementation*

The next step is to design the architecture of the XAI agent. The main challenge in designing the agent architecture would be to keep the XAI core separate as an independent module so that we can swap the fuzzy inference system XAI cores easily while performing the required experiments. We will be working independently on designing the XAI core and agent controller to keep these two primary components of our XAI agent independent. We will design the XAI core for a rule-based fuzzy inference system and then implement the XAI core using both Mamdani and TSK fuzzy inference systems. Another crucial component is to design and implement the agent controller such that it can treat the XAI core like an independent module. The agent controller will give specific inputs to the XAI core and then expect a particular output from the XAI core, which it will use to make certain decisions regarding the functioning of the XAI agent.

To simplify, the XAI agent consists of two components (see Figure 2); the first component is the XAI agent controller, and the second component is the XAI core. The XAI agent controller component is responsible for interfacing with the environment and making decisions based on the outputs of the XAI core. The XAI agent controller first gets the inputs from the agent environment and performs the required calculations. It passes the calculated values to the XAI core and returns the output from the XAI core. Then, it decides on the actions to take based on the result of the XAI core. In the end, it conveys the steps to be taken by the ship to the agent environment.

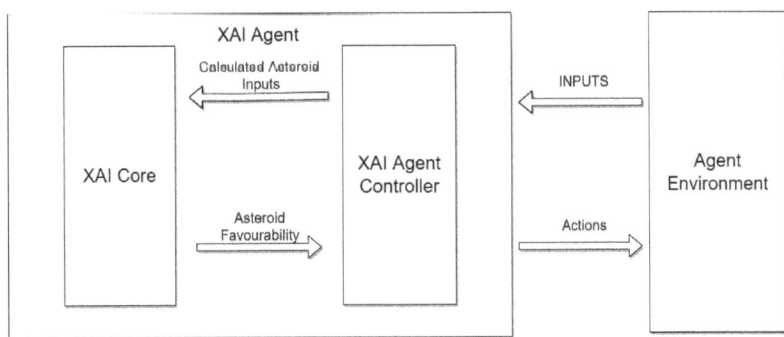

Figure 2. XAI agent block diagram.

The XAI core component is responsible for calculating the asteroid favorability values. Asteroid favorability is a numeric value assigned to each asteroid in the agent environment to signify the importance of targeting that particular asteroid by the XAI agent controller. The higher the asteroid's favorability, the more critical it is to target that asteroid at that moment. The value of asteroid favorability depends on two factors in the following order of importance:

1. How much of a threat does the asteroid currently pose to the ship?
2. How easy is it to target that particular asteroid at this moment?

XAI Agent Controller Design

Firstly, the agent controller uses the output of the XAI core to calculate which asteroid is currently the best target in the agent environment. The agent controller gets all the inputs from the agent environment and calculates the three inputs (see Table 4) for the XAI core to function. After calculating the inputs needed, the agent controller passes the information to the XAI core to obtain asteroid favorability. The controller selects the asteroid with the maximum favorability as the target asteroid.

Table 4. XAI core inputs.

Input	Description
asteroid distance	The distance between the asteroid and the ship.
asteroid size	The size of the asteroid.
asteroid orientation	The asteroid's orientation relative to the ship.

Then, the agent controller divides the agent environment into three zones to decide the agent's behavior (see Figure 3). The first zone (depicted in red) is the threat zone; if an asteroid is in the threat zone, the agent goes into defensive mode and tries to either shoot down the closest asteroid or move away from the closest asteroid. The second zone (depicted in yellow) is the targeting zone; if an asteroid is in the targeting zone, the agent goes into attack mode, selects the best asteroid to target, and shoots it down. The third zone (depicted in green) is the "search and destroy" zone; if an asteroid is in this zone, the agent goes into "search and destroy" mode and moves towards the best asteroid to target and shoots it down.

After finding out which asteroid is best to target and the behavior the agent needs to perform, the agent controller follows Algorithm 1 to decide on what actions to perform when the agent is in defensive mode, attacking mode, or "search and destroy" mode.

XAI Core Design and Implementation using Rule-Based Fuzzy Inference Systems

The XAI core (see Figure 4) takes three inputs, as shown in Table 4. The output of the XAI core is the asteroid favorability value that the agent controller uses. The process of calculating the asteroid favorability is not specified in the XAI core design, and it is decided while implementing the XAI core. The fuzzy inference system (see Figure 5) takes three inputs, as specified in the XAI core design. First, it fuzzifies the input values into their respective fuzzy sets (see Table 5) and uses their respective membership functions (see Figures 6–8).

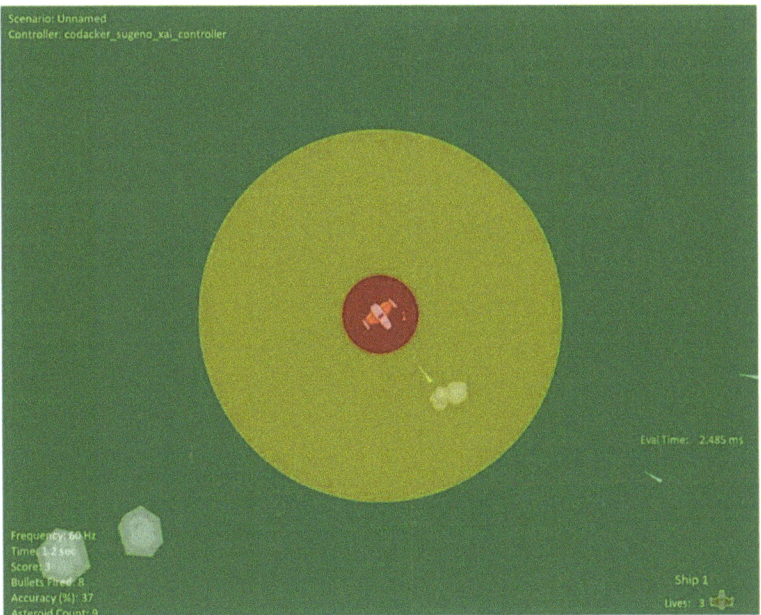

Figure 3. Agent zones and environment.

Algorithm 1: *Decide Agent's Action*

Input: agent_mode, target_asteroid
Output: action

1 **if** agent_mode = defensive **then**
2   **if** agent is facing the target_asteroid **then**
3   action ← fire bullet
4   **end**
5   **else**
6   action ← move away from the target_asteroid
7   **end**
8 **end**
9 **else if** agent_mode = attacking **then**
10   **if** ship is facing the target_asteroid **then**
11   action ← fire bullet
12   **end**
13   **else**
14   action ← turn towards the target_asteroid
15   **end**
16 **end**
17 **else if** agent_mode = search and destroy **then**
18   **if** ship is facing the target_asteroid **then**
19   action ← move towards the target_asteroid
20   **end**
21   **else**
22   action ← turn towards the target_asteroid
23   **end**
24 **end**

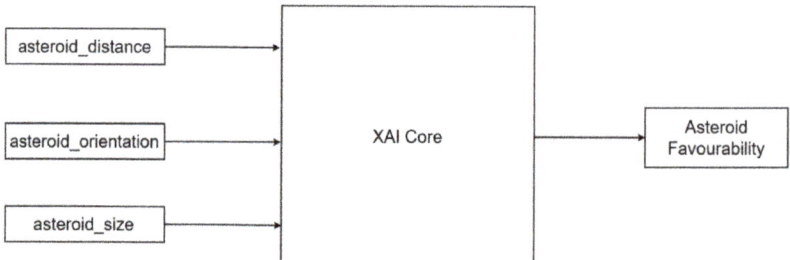

Figure 4. XAI Core block diagram.

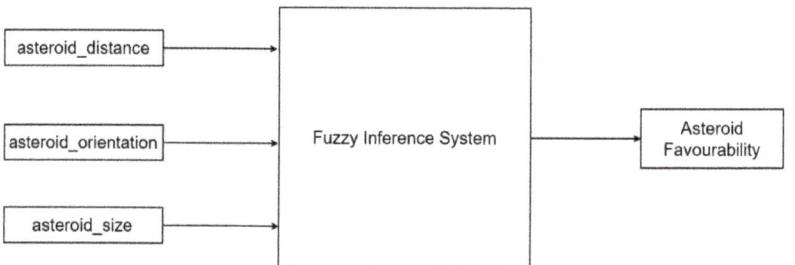

Figure 5. FIS block diagram.

Table 5. Fuzzy inference system inputs.

Input	Fuzzy Sets
asteroid distance	Near, Close, Far
asteroid size	Small, Medium, Large
asteroid orientation	In Sight, Normal, Out of Sight

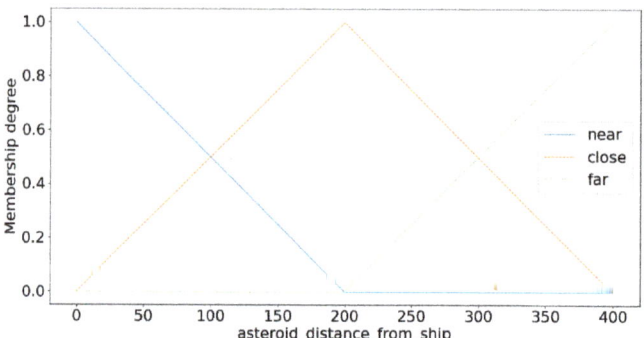

Figure 6. Asteroid distance fuzzy set.

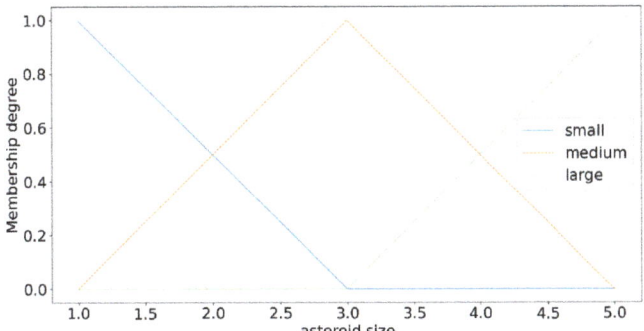

Figure 7. Asteroid size fuzzy set.

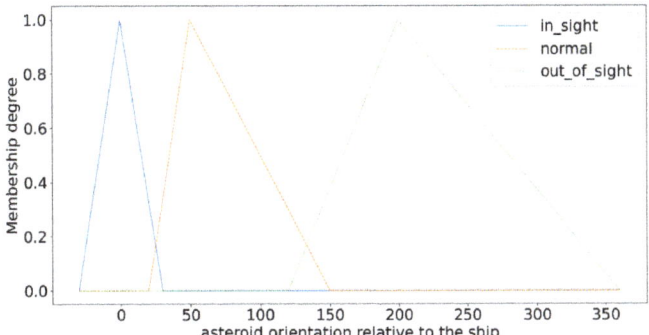

Figure 8. Asteroid orientation fuzzy set.

Trapezoidal and triangular (a special case of trapezoidal membership function) functions have been widely used in the literature for XAI implementation. They partition the state space more unambiguously than any other membership function [6]. Therefore, for our current implementation, we have used triangular membership functions. After conducting several experiments empirically, we identified the following rule-base to be the most efficient for our XAI core implementation using rule-based fuzzy inference systems.

1. IF (asteroid_size IS small) THEN (favorability IS high)
2. IF (asteroid_size IS medium) THEN (favorability IS medium)
3. IF (asteroid_size IS large) THEN (favorability IS low)
4. IF (asteroid_orientation IS insight) THEN (favorability IS high)
5. IF (asteroid_orientation IS normal) THEN (favorability IS medium)
6. IF (asteroid_orientation IS outofsight) THEN (favorability IS low)
7. IF (asteroid_distance IS near) THEN (favorability IS high)
8. IF (asteroid_distance IS close) THEN (favorability IS medium)
9. IF (asteroi_distance IS far) THEN (favorability IS low).

The first three rules are for asteroid size. If we hit a giant asteroid, it will split into multiple asteroids, increasing the number of asteroids in the agent environment. When the number of asteroids increases in the agent environment, the agent takes more time for its execution, reducing our computational performance. Hence, it is better to favor the smaller asteroids first and the large asteroids last.

The following three rules deal with asteroid orientation relative to the ship, i.e., how much we need to rotate our ship to face the ship's gun towards the asteroid. Therefore, it makes sense to favor the asteroid that is in sight (requires less rotation) first and the one that is out of sight (requires more rotation) last.

The last three rules deal with the asteroid's distance from the ship. An asteroid near the ship poses a more significant threat than one that is far away; therefore, it makes sense to favor the asteroid that is near first and the asteroid that is far last.

The fuzzy inference system calculates the asteroid favorability output by applying the fuzzy rule base to the input values. The output values are different for Mamdani and TSK inference systems. In Mamdani, the output is a fuzzy variable with defined membership functions (see Figure 9); in TSK, the output values are real numbers, as defined in Table 6. The Mamdani output calculation requires defuzzification on the fuzzy output value to get a real value. We use the center of area defuzzification method to get a concrete value between 1 and 10 for asteroid favorability. In the case of TSK, we calculate the output by taking a weighted average of the consequent of each rule, which is a real value by default; hence, no defuzzification is required.

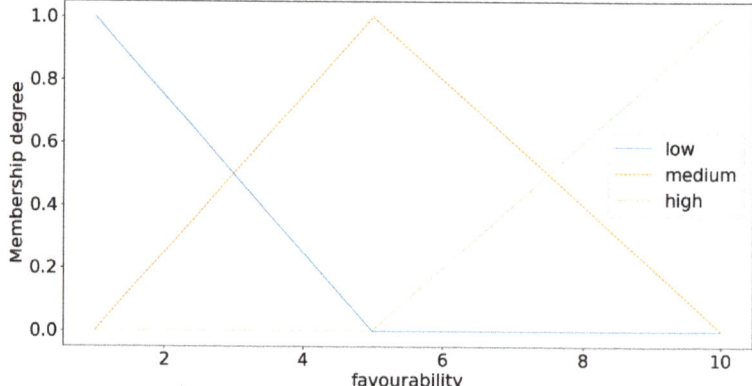

Figure 9. Asteroid favorability fuzzy set.

Table 6. Asteroid favorability output for Mamdani and TSK inference systems.

Asteroid Favorability	Mamdani Output Fuzzy Set	TSK Output Value
Low	Triangular function (1, 1, 5)	1
Medium	Triangular function (1, 5, 10)	5
High	Triangular function (5, 10, 10)	10

Step 3: Benchmarking FIS's core performance

For the next step, we will benchmark the performance of the Mamdani and TSK XAI cores independent of the agent controller to find empirical evidence of which implementation is more computationally efficient for such implementations using Algorithm 2. Figure 10 shows the benchmark result, and clearly, TSK outperforms Mamdani in terms of execution time.

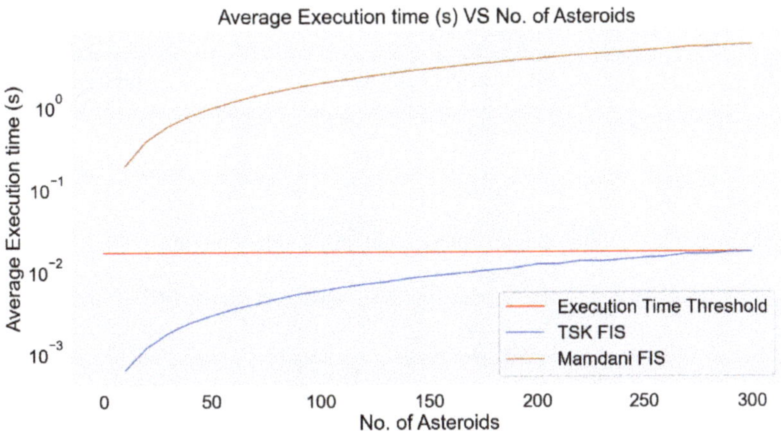

Figure 10. Mamdani vs. TSK execution time benchmark.

Algorithm 2: *XAI Core Execution Time Benchmark*

Input: xai_core, N
Output: execution_time_metrics

1 i ← 1
2 execution_time_metrics ← new array()
3 **while** i < N **do**
4   xai_core_input_vector ← generate_random_inputs(i)
5   t1 ← time.now()
6   result ← xai_core.evaluate(xai_core_input_vector)
7   evaluation_time ← time.now() − t1
8   execution_time_metrics.append((i, evaluation_time))
9 **end**
10 return execution_time_metrics

Algorithm 3: *XAI Core Noise Benchmark*

Input: xai_core, N
Output: noisy_metrics

1 variances ← [0.00001, 0.0001, 0.001, 0.01, 0.1, 1]
2 noisy_metrics ← new array()
3 **for** variance in variances **do**
4   xai_core_input_vector ← generate_random_inputs(N)
5   original_outputs ← xai_core.evaluate(xai_core_input_vector)
6   noise ← generate_random_noise(mean = 0, variance = variance, shape = xai_core_input_vector.shape)
7   noisy_input_vector ← xai_core_input_vector + noise
8   noisy_outputs ← xai_core.evaluate(noisy_input_vector)
9   mean_squared_error ← calculate_mean_squared_error(original_outputs, noisy_outputs)
10   noisy_metrics.append(variance, mean_squared_error)
11 **end**
12 return noisy_metrics

Step 4: *Integrate Agent XAI core and controller and benchmarking*

In the next step, we will integrate the XAI core and agent controller such that the XAI cores are easily swappable for easy experimentation. We will then run benchmarks to evaluate agent performance for Mamdani and TSK implementations of XAI cores using Algorithm 3.

This benchmark was to identify which fuzzy inference system performs better when there is noise in the input data. Figure 11 shows the benchmark results, and here, both Mamdani and TSK fuzzy inference system XAI core implementations have a mean squared error of less than 10^{-1}. However, when the variance reaches 1, TSK output values changes by a significant factor, showing that TSK is sensitive when the input values are out of the noisy range. It depicts an actual change in the input values, which is a good thing for us as the change of 1 in the asteroid size input should be able to create a big difference in favorability value.

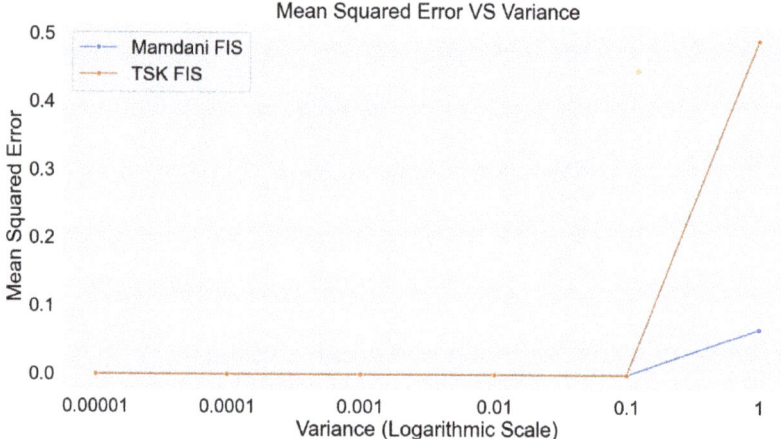

Figure 11. Mamdani vs. TSK noise benchmark.

We wanted to benchmark the agent's performance in the environment after integrating the XAI core implemented using rule-based fuzzy inference systems with the agent controller. We benchmarked the agent's performance using Algorithm 4 with both TSK and Mamdani XAI core implementations. The metrics obtained by this benchmark are summarized in Table 7. Clearly, in this benchmark, the TSK fuzzy-inference-system-based XAI core implementation outperforms the Mamdani fuzzy-inference-system-based XAI core implementation.

Table 7. Mamdani vs TSK agent performance.

Performance Metric	Mamdani-Based XAI Agent	TSK-Based XAI Agent
Number of deaths	76	43
Number of asteroids destroyed	227	8427
Number of bullets fired	322	110,313
Average accuracy	57.27%	85.45%
Average execution time	0.0510 s	0.0016 s

Algorithm 4: *XAI Agent Benchmark using a given XAI core*

Input: xai_core
Output: agent_performance_metrics

1 scores ← new array()
2 scenarios ← get_predefined_scenarios()
3 N ← scenarios.length
4 execution_time_metrics ← new array()
5 xai_agent ← new agent(core = xai_core)
6 **for** i ← 0, i < N, i + + **do**
7   environment ← new environment(scenario = scenarios[i], agent = xai_agent)
8   agent_score ← environment.run()
9   scores.append(agent_score)
10 **end**
11 agent_performance_metrics ← summarize_scores(scores)
12 return agent_performance_metrics

Based on our results and game performance, the proposed approach has been awarded the most computationally efficient and explainable solution in the XFC 2022 competition. The results of the competition were presented at the 2022 North American Fuzzy Information Processing Society Conference [17]. The results are available to the readers online [18].

4. Discussion, Conclusion, and Future Work

In this work, we have designed an XAI agent to work in a fast-paced environment using both Mamdani and TSK fuzzy inference systems at its XAI core to prove the feasibility of using rule-based fuzzy systems for XAI agent implementations. We further conducted experiments to gather empirical evidence to determine which type-1 fuzzy inference system performs better in a fast-paced environment. The Mamdani fuzzy inference system output calculation process contains an extra step for the defuzzification of the output values from the fuzzy output. The defuzzification process includes complex mathematical operations and is very time-consuming even for computers to perform. In the TSK output calculation process, there is no need for the defuzzification step, which gives an edge to TSK in terms of computational efficiency. Due to this extra edge in computational efficiency, the TSK-based XAI core implementation performs marginally better than the Mamdani-based XAI core implementation.

For each execution during the gameplay, the XAI agent outputs timestamped explanations for the action it chooses (see Figure 12). The output of the XAI core is the favorability value governed by the set of rules currently being applied for the calculations. In Figure 12, we can see the applicability or firing rate of each rule currently applicable in calculating the favorability value. For example, consider the output *"Targeting asteroid at (752.34, 486.60) because of rules: ['Rule 1': 1.0, 'Rule 4': 0.48, 'Rule 8': 0.86, 'Rule 9': 0.14]"*. Here, this output tells us that Rule 1 was 100% applicable, Rule 4 was 0.48% applicable, Rule 8 was 86% applicable, and Rule 9 was 14% applicable. Now, cross-referring the rule-base in Section 3, we can understand the decision taken by the XAI module to target this asteroid. With the timestamped recording of the gameplay and these timestamped explanations, anyone can analyze the explanations and find out exactly why the agent decided to act at any given time. The explanation behind choosing a target asteroid is explained in terms of the applicability of each rule from the fuzzy rule base, which is just a set of IF–ELSE statements and is easy for an average user to understand without any technical expertise required.

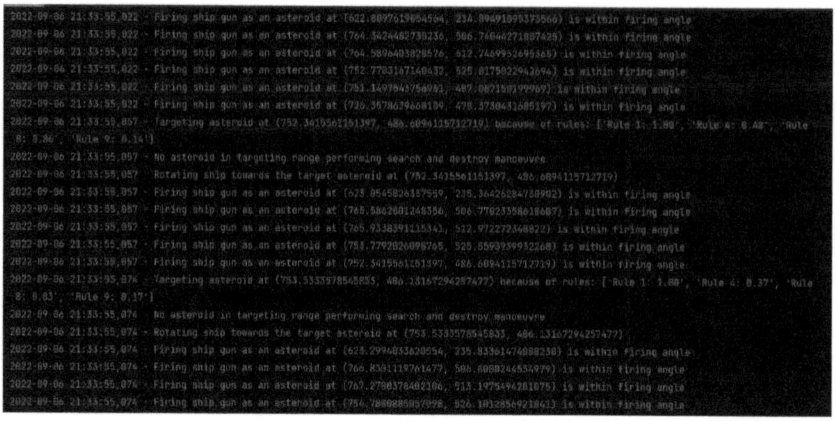

Figure 12. XAI agent explanations.

Further, the experiments showed that the TSK-based XAI agent performed 30 times better than the Mamdani-based XAI agent in computational efficiency. Regarding the agent's performance, the TSK-based XAI agent had an accuracy of 85.45%, while the Mamdani-based XAI agent had an accuracy of 57.27%. The number of deaths for the TSK-based XAI agent was 43. In contrast, the Mamdani-based XAI agent died 75 times. The TSK-based XAI agent was able to destroy 8427 asteroids, while the Mamdani-based XAI agent could only destroy 227 asteroids. The empirical evidence that we have gathered shows that it is better to use TSK fuzzy inference systems for rule-based XAI core implementations whenever the XAI application requires time-critical execution and better performance simultaneously. We further show that the actions taken by the XAI agent using a rule-based fuzzy inference system at its XAI core implementation could easily be explained in plain English using IF–ELSE rules. It is easier for an average user to understand without any technical expertise as a prerequisite.

This work faced several challenges that are to be considered during implementation. One of the major challenges was writing efficient code so that it would not become a bottleneck for the XAI system. Further, it was essential to design the XAI module flexibly so that we could plug and play different implementations of the XAI and perform benchmarks on them. In addition, it was also challenging to maintain consistency between the interface of the XAI module and the rest of the controller so that XAI implementations would follow the guidelines for the interface.

To conclude, this work helps those new to explainable AI and fuzzy inference systems to understand the concepts in a fun, hands-on learning manner. Further, the experimental approach that we have used can be used as a baseline to compare the efficiency and performance of various XAI agent implementations and find empirical evidence of which XAI implementation performs better.

In this research work (based on competition), we have only explored rule-based fuzzy inference system XAI core implementations. However, the proposed experimental approach and benchmarking algorithms can be used to perform experiments to compare rule-based fuzzy inference system XAI core implementations with any other XAI core implementation to find out which implementation is best in terms of performance and explainability.

In the outcome of this study, the XAI explanations are only text-based. These explanations can be extended further to show visual explanations in real-time for the agent's actions, which will further add to the explainability of the agent as visual explanations are much easier to analyze than textual explanations for an average human being.

Author Contributions: Conceptualization: A.K.S. and P.K.M.; Methodology: S.M. and A.K.S.; Validation: S.M.; Resources: S.M. and A.K.S.; Data curation: S.M. and A.K.S.; Writing—S.M. and A.K.S.;

Writing—review and editing: A.K.S. and P.K.M.; Supervision: A.K.S. and P.K.M. All authors have read and agreed to the published version of the manuscript.

Funding: This research received no external funding.

Data Availability Statement: The data and codes are provided by the organizers of XFC 2022. It is Available online: https://xfuzzycomp.pythonanywhere.com/ (accessed on 28 July 2022). Available online: https://pypi.org/project/fuzzy-asteroids/ (accessed on 28 July 2022). Available online: https://ceas.uc.edu/academics/departments/aerospace-engineering-mechanics/artificial-intelligence-competition/archive.html (accessed on 28 July 2022).

Acknowledgments: We are grateful to the organizers of the Explainable Fuzzy AI Challenge (XFC 2022) and North American Fuzzy Information Processing Society for presenting the problem and related material. The regular tutorials and slack discussions helped in clarifications of the problem.

Conflicts of Interest: The authors declare no conflict of interest.

References

1. Gunning, D.; Aha, D. DARPA's explainable artificial intelligence (XAI) program. *AI Mag.* **2019**, *40*, 44–58.
2. Hagras, H. Toward human-understandable, explainable AI. *Computer* **2018**, *51*, 28–36. [CrossRef]
3. Mendel, J.M.; Bonissone, P.P. Critical thinking about explainable ai (XAI) for rule- based fuzzy systems. *IEEE Trans. Fuzzy Syst.* **2021**, *29*, 3579–3593. [CrossRef]
4. Shukla, A.K.; Smits, G.; Pivert, O.; Lesot, M.J. Explaining data regularities and anomalies. In Proceedings of the 2020 IEEE International Conference on Fuzzy Systems (FUZZ-IEEE), Glasgow, UK, 19–24 July 2020; IEEE: Piscataway, NJ, USA; pp. 1–8.
5. Available online: https://ceas.uc.edu/academics/departments/aerospace-engineering-mechanics/artificial-intelligence-competition.html (accessed on 28 July 2022).
6. Yang, L.H.; Liu, J.; Ye, F.F.; Wang, Y.M.; Nugent, C.; Wang, H.; Martínez, L. Highly explainable cumulative belief rule-based system with effective rule-base modeling and inference scheme. *Knowl. Based Syst.* **2022**, *240*, 107805. [CrossRef]
7. Mamdani, E.H.; Assilian, S. An experiment in linguistic synthesis with a fuzzy logic controller. *Int. J. Hum. Comput. Stud.* **1999**, *51*, 135–147. [CrossRef]
8. Available online: https://ceas.uc.edu/academics/departments/aerospace-engineering-mechanics/artificial-intelligence-competition/archive.html (accessed on 28 July 2022).
9. Chimatapu, R.; Hagras, H.; Starkey, A.; Owusu, G. Explainable AI and fuzzy logic systems. In *Theory and Practice of Natural Computing, Proceedings of the 7th International Conference, TPNC 2018, Dublin, Ireland, 12–14 December 2018*; Springer: Cham, Switzerland, 2018; pp. 3–20.
10. Ferreyra, E.; Hagras, H.; Kern, M.; Owusu, G. Depicting Decision-Making: A Type-2 Fuzzy Logic Based Explainable Artificial Intelligence System for Goal-Driven Simulation in the Workforce Allocation Domain. In Proceedings of the 2019 IEEE International Conference on Fuzzy Systems (FUZZ-IEEE), New Orleans, LA, USA, 23–26 June 2019; IEEE: Piscataway, NJ, USA, 2019; pp. 1–6.
11. Shukla, A.K.; Banshal, S.K.; Seth, T.; Basu, A.; John, R.; Muhuri, P.K. A bibliometric overview of the field of type-2 fuzzy sets and systems [discussion forum]. *IEEE Comput. Intell. Mag.* **2020**, *15*, 89–98. [CrossRef]
12. Potie, N.; Giannoukakos, S.; Hackenberg, M.; Fernandez, A. On the need of interpretability for biomedical applications: Using fuzzy models for lung cancer prediction with liquid biopsy. In Proceedings of the 2019 IEEE international conference on fuzzy systems (FUZZ-IEEE), New Orleans, LA, USA, 23–26 June 2019; IEEE: Piscataway, NJ, USA, 2019; pp. 1–6.
13. Kiani, M.; Andreu-Perez, J.; Hagras, H.; Filippetti, M.L.; Rigato, S. A Type-2 Fuzzy Logic Based Explainable Artificial Intelligence System for Developmental Neuroscience. In Proceedings of the 2020 IEEE International Conference on Fuzzy Systems (FUZZ-IEEE), Glasgow, UK, 19–24 July 2020; IEEE: Piscataway, NJ, USA, 2020; pp. 1–8.
14. Poli, J.P.; Ouerdane, W.; Pierrard, R. Generation of textual explanations in XAI: The case of semantic annotation. In Proceedings of the 2021 IEEE International Conference on Fuzzy Systems (FUZZ-IEEE), Luxembourg, Luxembourg, 11–14 July 2021; IEEE: Piscataway, NJ, USA, 2021; pp. 1–6.
15. Lin, K.; Liu, Y.; Lu, P.; Yang, Y.; Fan, H.; Hong, F. Fuzzy constraint-based agent negotiation framework for doctor-patient shared decision-making. *BMC Med. Inform. Decis. Mak.* **2022**, *22*, 218. [CrossRef] [PubMed]
16. Available online: https://pypi.org/project/fuzzy-asteroids/ (accessed on 26 July 2022).
17. Available online: https://nafips2022.cs.smu.ca/ (accessed on 28 July 2022).
18. Available online: https://xfuzzycomp.pythonanywhere.com/ (accessed on 30 July 2022).

Article

Research Agenda on Multiple-Criteria Decision-Making: New Academic Debates in Business and Management

Fernando Castelló-Sirvent [1,2,*] and Carlos Meneses-Eraso [3]

[1] Department of Economics and Finance, ESIC Business & Marketing School, 46021 Valencia, Spain
[2] Business Organization Department, Universitat Politècnica de València, 46022 Valencia, Spain
[3] Escuela de Economía, Universidad Sergio Arboleda, Bogotá 110221, Colombia
* Correspondence: fernando.castello@esic.edu

Citation: Castelló-Sirvent, F.; Meneses-Eraso, C. Research Agenda on Multiple-Criteria Decision-Making: New Academic Debates in Business and Management. *Axioms* **2022**, *11*, 515. https://doi.org/10.3390/axioms11100515

Academic Editors: Amit K. Shukla and Darjan Karabašević

Received: 19 August 2022
Accepted: 24 September 2022
Published: 29 September 2022

Publisher's Note: MDPI stays neutral with regard to jurisdictional claims in published maps and institutional affiliations.

Copyright: © 2022 by the authors. Licensee MDPI, Basel, Switzerland. This article is an open access article distributed under the terms and conditions of the Creative Commons Attribution (CC BY) license (https://creativecommons.org/licenses/by/4.0/).

Abstract: Systemic disruptions are becoming more continuous, intense, and persistent. Their effects have a severe impact on the economy in volatile, uncertain, complex, and ambiguous (VUCA) environments that are increasingly transversal to productive sectors and activities. Researchers have intensified their academic production of multiple-criteria decision-making (MCDM) in recent years. This article analyzes the research agenda through a systematic review of scientific articles in the Web of Science Core Collection according to the Journal Citation Report (JCR), both in the Social Sciences Citation Index (SSCI) and in the Science Citation Index Expanded (SCIE). According to the selected search criteria, 909 articles on MCDM published between 1979 and 2022 in Web of Science journals in the business and management categories were located. A bibliometric analysis of the main thematic clusters, the international collaboration networks, and the bibliographic coupling of articles was carried out. In addition, the analysis period is divided into two subperiods (1979–2008 and 2009–2022), establishing 2008 as the threshold, the year of the Global Financial Crisis (GFC), to assess the evolution of the research agenda at the beginning of systemic disruptions. The bibliometric analysis allows the identification of the motor, basic, specialized, and emerging themes of each subperiod. The results show the similarities and differences between the academic debate before and after the GFC. The evidence found allows academics to be guided in their high-impact research in business and management using MCDM methodologies to address contemporary challenges. An important contribution of this study is to detect gaps in the literature, highlighting unclosed gaps and emerging trends in the field of study for journal editors.

Keywords: bibliometric analysis; research agenda; multiple-criteria decision-making (MCDM); complexity; VUCA; VOSviewer; SciMAT

MSC: 90B50; 91B06; 60A86; 94D05; 68V30

1. Introduction

In recent decades, systemic events that have accelerated the speed of economic, social, and political shocks have become widespread and frequent. Increasingly radical and intense disruptions impact society and companies by generating global challenges and affecting the stability of the economic system. Some examples of these shocks in recent years, such as the Global Financial Crisis, (GFC), sustainability challenges of the 2030 Agenda, COVID-19, war in Ukraine, sanctions against Russia, European energy crisis, risks of reversal of globalization, and political and military tensions with China, should be noted. This dynamic economic environment forces companies, governments, and investors to make increasingly agile decisions to try to eliminate bias in decision-making and minimize risks in professional endeavors. Advanced decision-making methods have been gaining popularity among managers and analysts in an increasingly common VUCA environment. The context of implicit uncertainty has changed the analysis paradigm, affecting management sciences [1–7] and creating a need to articulate efficient mechanisms for decision-making in multiple fields [8–15].

The first radical shock of the contemporary era was the GFC that began after the bankruptcy of Lehman Brothers [16–18], a situation that created a need to develop better and more sophisticated methods for decision-making in such fields as finance, investment, and policymaking, among others. Society was transformed at great speed and academics progressively altered its predominant interests, as the generalization of VUCA environments transformed the archetypes of researchers and their priorities. Some emerging issues in the academic debate after 2008 are specified in the green strategies of the Sustainable Development Goals (SDG) [19–28], evaluation of decision-making systems based on the urgency and effectiveness of the applied models [23,29–37], and the impact disruptions in VUCA environments on global value chains [3,4,19,26,38–42].

The motivation for this research article is a drive to describe the structure of the academic agenda in detail and to identify the opportunities for high-impact publications related to MCDC. This study analyzes the academic discourse on multiple-criteria decision-making (MCDM) within the business and management areas before and after 2008. In addition, the change in the research agenda produced after the intensification of disruptions in VUCA environments is evaluated, and context is offered to understand the driving and emerging issues that articulate the new debate after 2008. The goal of this article is to present an overview and evolution of the research agenda, allowing academics to learn about new emerging trends, gaps not closed in the literature, and high-impact publication opportunities in the MCDM field of research. In addition, the findings of this study should provide a guide and a roadmap for journal editors to the evolution of the research agenda, facilitating the design of editorial lines and the preparation of special issues that may be thematically oriented to a more mainstream scope among scholars. The article is structured as follows. First, the materials and methods section is presented. Next, the results and discussion with a special focus on the opportunities detected for high-impact publications are reported. Finally, the conclusions of the study are formulated.

2. Materials and Methods

The objective of this research article was to develop a comprehensive bibliometric analysis on the methodologies of multiple-criteria decision-making (MCDM). As per Zupic and Čater [43], the study followed this sequence: (1) design of the research; (2) collection of bibliometric data; (3) analysis and reporting of results; and (4) discussion of the findings. The search strategy for the literature review was an analysis of articles published in the Web of Science Core Collection (WoS-CC).

Based on the quality standards established by this study and the purpose of intertemporal comparison between periods, the WoS-CC was chosen, focusing the analysis on journals in the areas of business and management indexed in the Social Sciences Citation Index (SSCI) and the Scientific Citation Index Expanded (SCIE). Journals indexed in the Emerging Sources Citation Index (ESCI) were discarded. The use of Scopus was also ruled out, since the object of analysis began before the creation of Scopus and the inclusion of articles from this database would cause sample biases that would invalidate the analysis and conclusions of this research [44–47]. Thus, the WoS-CC was chosen as a source of robust bibliometric information [48,49], for its coverage [50] and its homogeneous availability throughout the period analyzed. The search discarded chapters, books and proceedings, and focused on articles. Based on the high heterogeneity of terms available to analyze the focus determined by the study, the first step taken was to identify the search terms and operators that would allow the identification of the relevant published studies. The PRISMA statement [51,52], widely used in systematic reviews in business and management research, was used [42,53–57]. In addition, the methodology proposed by Tavares Thomé et al. [58], which suggests that researchers should perform searches both backwards and forwards in order to reinforce the robustness of their studies and through this same practice eliminate the risk of search and/or approach biases, was followed. In this way, the main research topics published on MCDM or MCDA in business and management journals—according to Web of Science categories—indexed in Journal Citation Reports® (JCR) were identified. Figure 1 shows the selection criteria and the Boolean search string applied to topic (TS), according to the information provided by title (TI), abstract (AB), author keywords (AK) or Keyword Plus® (KP). Figure 2 presents the flow diagram for new systematic reviews and reports the details of the search strategy according to each stage defined by the PRISMA statement [51].

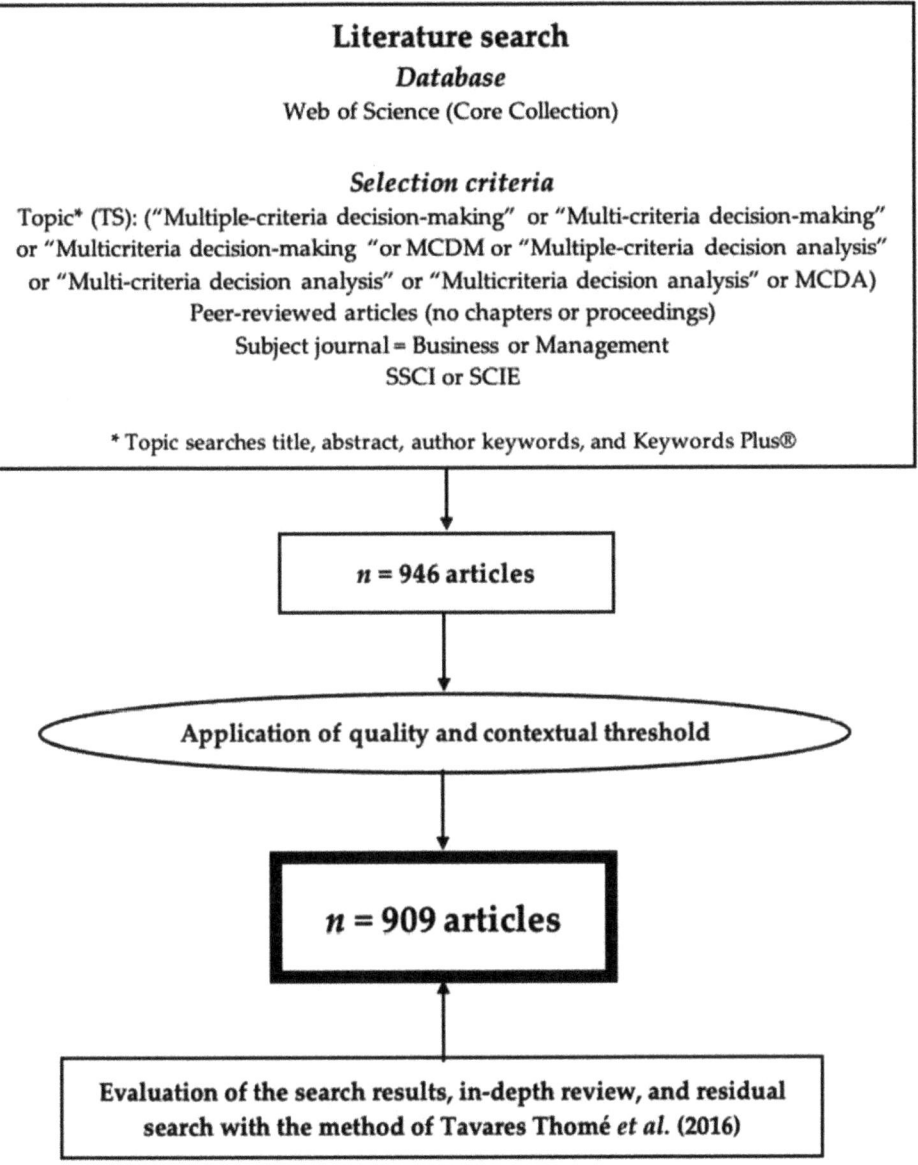

Figure 1. Systematic literature review strategy [58].

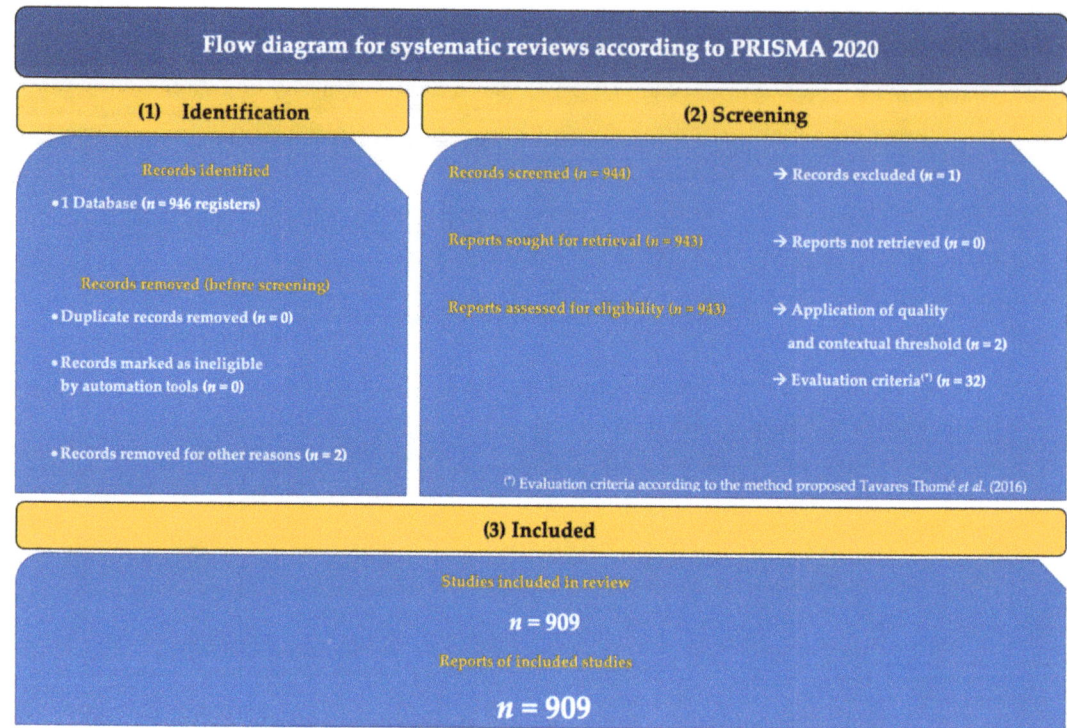

Figure 2. PRISMA 2020 flow diagram. Own elaboration according to Page et al. (2021) [51], Tavares Thomé et al. (2016) [58].

The resulting database was analyzed from a static approach for the total period available according to the criteria reported from the first record located (1Q 1979) and until the last available according to the date of the investigation (2Q 2022). In addition, two subperiods (1979–2008 and 2009–2022) were constructed for the comparative analysis of the academic discourse and the evolution of the scientific debate in the field. The year 2008 was chosen as it established important conjunctural and systemic changes, which were exemplified by the occurrence of the GFC. In addition, since 2008, academic production has increased based on a strong evolution of academic interest, and new fuzzy-related journals have been created [59].

The complexity of the world has been increasing progressively from 2008. In this year, there was an important financial event that began in September 2008 with the bankruptcy of Lehman Brothers [17] and the resulting consequences for the world's main economies (e.g., deep financial crisis in the United States and debt crisis in the Eurozone, quantitative easing of the Federal Reserve and the European Central Bank) [16,18,60–63], a subsequent period of high interdependence of economic agents and global value chains began, the continuing effects of which are further evidence of the fact that the process of generalization of VUCA environments is accelerating [1–3,6,64,65]. Bibliometric studies have analyzed academic discourse in comparative terms for two periods [66]. Based on its relevance, the 2008 cutoff threshold has been used to analyze changes in trends in bibliometric terms [67–69].

According to the specific criteria selected, the applied method reports 909 articles published between Q1 1979 and Q2 2022, corresponding to journals indexed in JCR. Based on the size asymmetry of the two constructed subperiods (30 years vs. 13 years) and the limitations that this asymmetry represents for a measurement of the academic impact of scientific production, the normalized impact per year (NIY) method was used, in accordance with Castelló-Sirvent [70]. This method calls for the weighing of total academic impact as measured by a count of citations and dividing this number by the number of years elapsed from the publication of an article to the date of completion of this study. Thus, the NIY highlights the most relevant information since it brings to the surface papers that mark an accelerated academic interest of a topic at a certain moment. This facilitates the process of comparing articles published in different subperiods. In this study, the NIY is used for the analysis of articles, and the NIY average for the analysis of the academic production of journals or subperiods.

A citations per document (CpD) ratio was also calculated [70] as an indicator of academic efficiency that divides the total citation count by the number of articles published in a period, or by an author, university, country or journal. In addition, the dynamic comparison of the top 25 articles by total citations and the top 25 articles by NIY for the same subperiod offers information on the articles that quickly become more interesting for researchers, particularly in shorter and more recent subperiods [70]. These types of articles were indicated in this research under the term "strong trend" (ST) and were shown in the results corresponding to the top 25 articles with the greatest impact of citations per year (NIY). This allowed this article to highlight research that did not manage to be placed in the top 25 articles with the greatest impact by total citations. In other words, the articles marked as ST are mainstream articles that arouse growing academic interest based on the trend accelerator that the NIY represents. [71]. The detailed analysis and evaluation of ST articles is likely to serve as an indicator of "hot topics" in the research agenda of a field of study [70,71]. Similarly, this research also applied the ST analysis to the main journals of both subperiods to identify "hot journals" as defined by having the greatest impact in comparative terms. ST analysis is a tool that enables academics to more easily select mainstream topics and journals, so that their research will be oriented to the emerging and most active topics in the area of study. It also helps researchers by offering an in-depth discussion on high-impact publication opportunities. [70,71].

The bibliometric software used was VOSviewer 1.6.17 [72,73] and SciMAT 1.1.04. [74]. VOSviewer enabled the analysis of international collaboration networks in MCDM research and the bibliographic coupling of articles. SciMAT showed the strategic diagrams of the two subperiods analyzed, identifying driving, basic, specialized and emerging themes. According to Cobo et al. [74–77], following Callon's preliminary approaches [78], the bibliometric analysis of topics with SciMAT identifies the thematic clusters in a two-dimensional plane that represents the centrality and density of the academic discourse, in order to know the academic field architecture [77] and visualize and evaluate its space–time path [75]. In this way, it is possible to identify the groups (clusters) of analyzed elements and their links with other related elements [73], according to the relative importance of the elements reviewed with respect to the academic corpus under study [79].

In this way, strategic diagrams built with SciMAT show four quadrants that are configured at the intersection of the X and Y axes, with the topics included in each quadrant being characterized in a specific way. The driving themes show high density and high centrality and, consequently, contribute in a relevant way to research and maintain links with their thematic networks, helping to articulate the research agenda. On the other hand, the emerging themes register low density and low centrality, since they are poorly developed, both in the area and in other areas. In the intermediate positions, the basic topics are shown, characterized by their low density and high centrality, reporting a limited development, although they suppose important contributions in other areas of knowledge. Specialized topics have a high density and low centrality, as they are well developed in the area, but in isolation from other areas.

SciMAT was used to know the typologies of themes for both subperiods and to understand the dynamic evolution of the discourse of academia on MCDM. For the analysis, the equivalence index [78] was used without network reduction, with association strength [80], based on the simple centers algorithm (min. 5; max. 12). In addition, core mapper, inclusion index and Jaccard's index [81] were reported.

3. Results and Discussion

This section is structured as follows. First, an overview of the academic production linked to the study area is reported, both for the total period analyzed and for the two proposed subperiods. Second, the main authors, universities, and international collaboration networks identified are named. Third, the coupling clusters of articles generated in order to understand the construction of the academic debate are shown. Fourth, a general analysis of the dynamic evolution of the research agenda is carried out through the use of overlapping and evolution maps of the transformation process, and then a detailed analysis of this process is presented through strategic diagrams of each subperiod. Fifth, the publication opportunities detected are discussed.

3.1. Academic Production

The results of the longitudinal analysis show an incremental evolution ($R^2 = 0.9293$) of the scientific production on MCDM (Figure 3). As of 2009, an acceleration of the trend, coinciding with the international extension of the GFC is observed. Economic agents, companies and public administrations being forced to make quick and agile decisions in an increasingly interdependent VUCA environment is also evidenced.

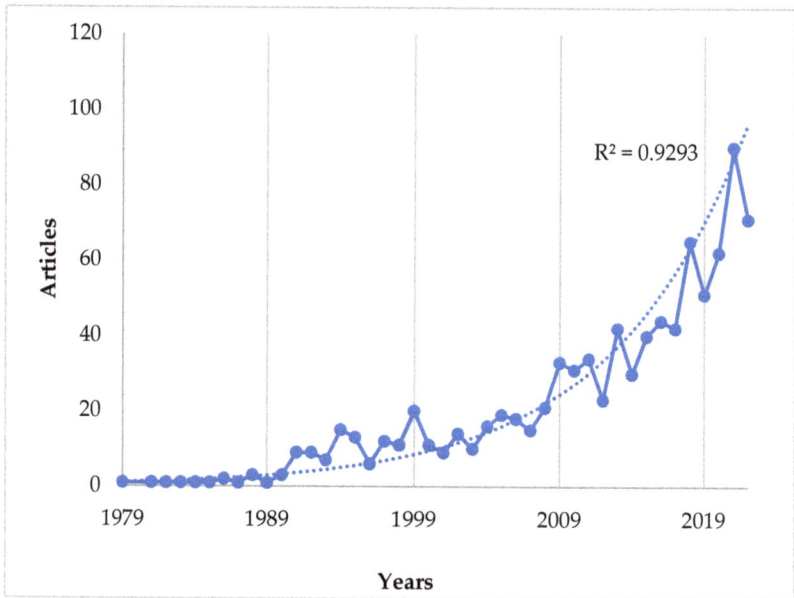

Figure 3. Intertemporal evolution of academic production on MCDM.

In sum, 909 articles published over 43 years (1979–2022) in journals from the business and management areas indexed in JCR were identified and retrieved. The articles generated an impact level of 37,904 citations. The annual averages of the NIY method previously discussed (Figure 4) show that the articles published during the years prior to the GFC (2002 and 2004) achieved greater academic impact per year, and a trend analysis corroborates a change in trend as of 2011. Academic interest in MCDM increased in terms of comparative annual impact.

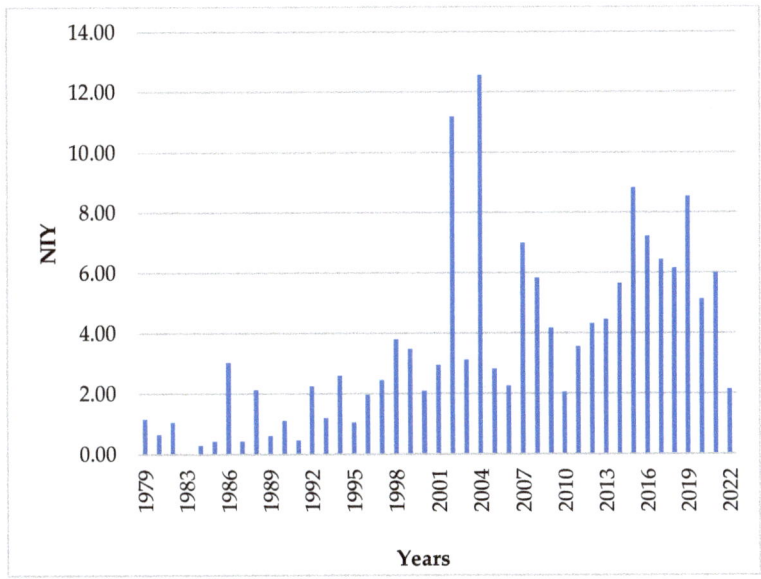

Figure 4. NIY detail analysis. Annual average.

Table 1 shows a comparative analysis for both subperiods. NIY average clearly increases after the GFC. Given the asymmetry of years of the analyzed subperiods, CpD after the GFC is lower than the CpD before the GFC.

Table 1. Published articles, citations and NIY. Detail by subperiods.

Subperiods	Years	Articles	Articles per Year	Total Citations	CpD	NIY Average
Subperiod 1 (1979–2008)	30	251	8.66	20032	80	4.05
Subperiod 2 (2009–2022)	13	658	50.62	17872	27	5.41

Source: Own elaboration.

However, the evidence found corroborates a higher production of articles per year after the GFC, as shown in the bibliometric analysis carried out by Liu [59]. The total number of articles published on MCDM is 2.6 times higher after 2008 and the academic impact of the articles published after 2008 (13 years) is 89% of the academic impact of the articles published before 2008 (30 years).

3.2. Main Authors, Universities and International Collaboration Networks

The main authors with scientific production equal to or greater than 10 articles in MCDM fields are professors Zavdskas, Stewart, Ferreira, Greco, Turskis, Liao, Hashemkhani Zolfani and Ferreira (Table 2). The detailed analysis of academic efficiency reports an excellent performance in the number of citations per document of professors Greco (CpD = 69.2) and Stewart (CpD = 65.82).

On the other hand, Table 3 shows the results of the analysis of universities of those researchers who achieved greater academic efficiency in the publication of MCDM articles from Taiwan (National Chiao Tung University; CpD = 224), Italy (University of Catania; CpD = 76.07) and Portugal (University of Coimbra; CpD = 75.10).

Table 2. Academic production of authors with more than 10 articles.

Rank	Author	Citations	Articles	CpD
1	Zavadskas, Edmundas Kazimieras	1016	26	39.08
2	Stewart, Tj	724	11	65.82
3	Ferreira, Fernando A. F.	717	36	19.92
4	Greco, Salvatore	692	10	69.20
5	Turskis, Zenonas	454	10	45.40
6	Liao, huchang	352	13	27.08
7	Hashemkhani Zolfani, Sarfaraz	321	10	32.10
8	Ferreira, Joao J. M.	311	17	18.29

Source: Own elaboration.

Table 3. Academic production of universities with more than 10 articles.

Rank	Universities	Citations	Articles	CpD
1	Natl. Chiao Tung. Univ.	3808	17	224.00
2	Vilnius Gediminas Tech. Univ.	1413	59	23.95
3	Univ. Catania	1065	14	76.07
4	Univ. Memphis	758	36	21.06
5	Univ. Coimbra	751	10	75.10
6	Kainan Univ.	748	12	62.33
7	Univ. Manchester	672	12	56.00
8	Tech. Univ. Crete	666	18	37.00
9	Univ. Jyvaskyla	625	11	56.82
10	Univ. Inst. Lisbon	588	32	18.38
11	Polish Acad. Sci.	572	12	47.67
12	Poznan Univ. Tech.	541	11	49.18
13	Univ. Portsmouth	474	14	33.86
14	Sichuan Univ.	460	17	27.06
15	Aalto Univ.	421	16	26.31
16	Islamic Azad Univ.	421	25	16.84
17	City Univ. Hong Kong	364	10	36.40
18	Univ. Beira Interior	356	19	18.74
19	Natl. Tech. Univ. Athens	261	10	26.10
20	Univ. Tehran	237	18	13.17

Source: Own elaboration.

Figure 5 reports the connections between countries in international collaboration networks. According to the fractional counting method, the results show five co-authorship clusters between countries for the MCDM area. Cluster 1 (green) includes European countries (Portugal, France, Belgium and Greece) and the American continent (USA, Canada and Brazil). Cluster 2 (blue) includes England and European countries (Italy, Poland, Denmark, Germany). Cluster 3 (pink) links the academic production of countries such as Iran, Lithuania or Malaysia. Cluster 4 (red) shows the way in which European countries (Spain and Netherlands) and the Pacific area (India, Taiwan and Australia) connect their academic production through co-authorships. Cluster 5 (yellow) reports the connection of publication co-authors in MCDM from Finland, Switzerland, Scotland and South Korea.

The evaluation of academic production reports 27 countries with at least 10 articles for the period analyzed (Table 4). The detailed analysis of academic efficiency places Serbia, Netherlands and Denmark above 100 citations per article.

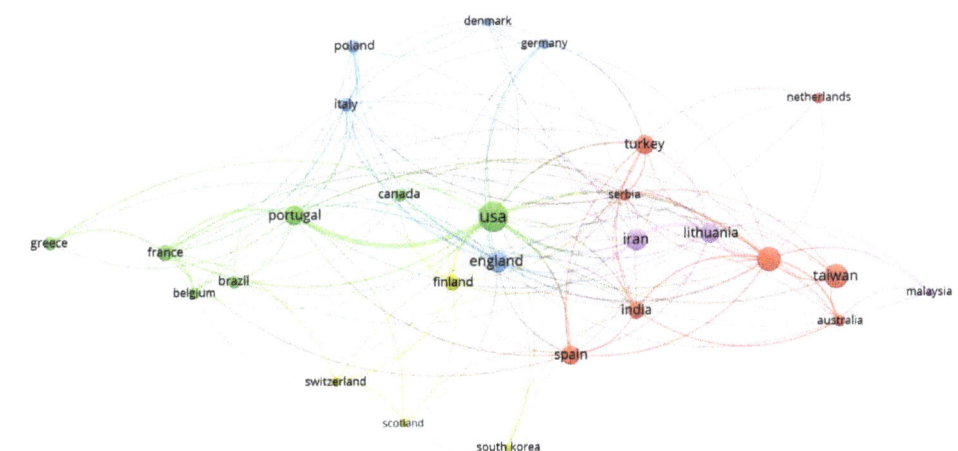

Figure 5. International collaboration networks.

Table 4. Collaboration networks in co-authorship. Countries with more than 10 articles.

Rank	Countries	Citations	Articles	CpD
1	Taiwan	6684	91	73.45
2	USA	5183	151	34.32
3	Serbia	3289	18	182.72
4	China	3184	90	35.38
5	Spain	2426	57	42.56
6	Portugal	2312	66	35.03
7	Netherlands	2163	18	120.17
8	England	2122	68	31.21
9	Finland	1812	43	42.14
10	Iran	1611	81	19.89
11	Poland	1587	30	52.90
12	France	1582	43	36.79
13	Lithuania	1472	64	23.00
14	Germany	1470	20	73.50
15	Italy	1329	32	41.53
16	Denmark	1279	12	106.58
17	Belgium	1211	23	52.65
18	Greece	1055	32	32.97
19	Turkey	1042	59	17.66
20	Canada	1032	27	38.22
21	India	796	48	16.58
22	Brazil	512	27	18.96
23	South Korea	368	13	28.31
24	Australia	308	22	14.00
25	Switzerland	287	15	19.13
26	Malaysia	263	12	21.92
27	Scotland	157	10	15.70

Source: Own elaboration.

Among the countries with the greatest impact, located in positions 1 to 13 in the ranking, the USA, China, Spain, Portugal, England, Finland, France and Lithuania stand out for their low academic efficiency (CpD below average). These are countries that, in order to achieve academic impact, must increase their production of articles, but the average impact per article is low in comparative terms. In contrast, Australia, Scotland, India, Turkey, Brazil, Iran or Switzerland recorded little impact in comparative terms, given their high level of production, with CpD levels of fewer than 20 citations per article.

3.3. Bibliographic Coupling per Documents

The analysis of bibliographic coupling per documents (Figure 6) set a minimum cutoff threshold of 150 citations of a document, establishing four clusters that include 36 central articles.

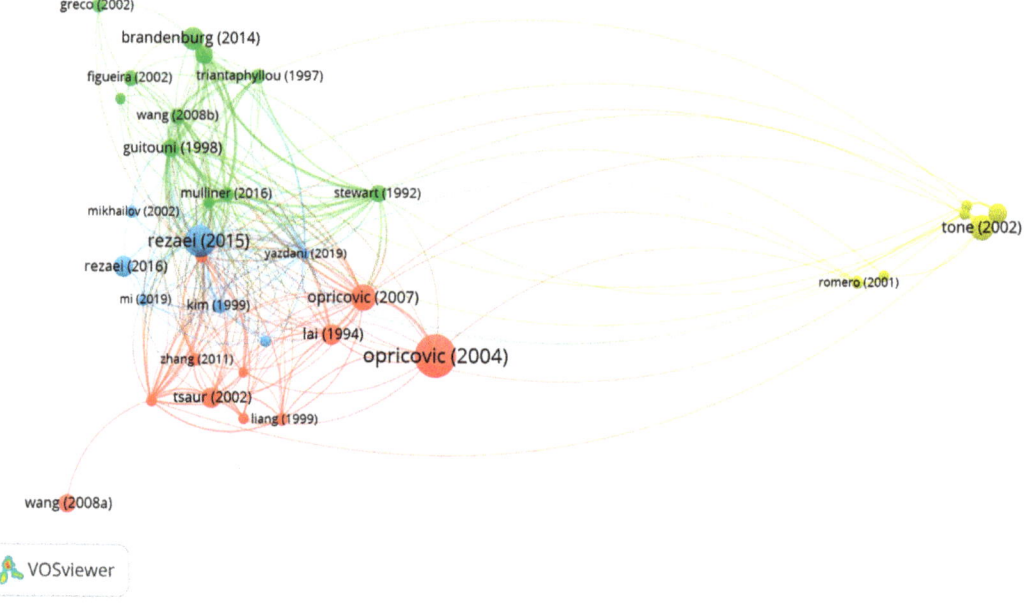

Figure 6. Coupling of articles with at least 150 citations.

Cluster 1 (red) includes articles on the comparison of methods (e.g., VIKOR and TOPSIS) [82,83], Qualiflex [84], Electre I [85], TOPSIS [86], fuzzy AHP [87], fuzzy MCDM [8,88–90], and practical applications based on firm technological innovation capabilities under uncertainty [91] or tourism destination competitiveness [92]. Cluster 2 (green) focuses on supply chain management [19], portfolio optimization [93], social multicriteria evaluations [94] and methodological advances [10–12,20,95–97]. Cluster 3 (blue) focuses on advanced methodological aspects such as geometrical representations [98], combined compromise solutions [99], procedure under incomplete information [100], linear models [29] and worst methods in decision-making [101]. This cluster also includes seminal articles on practical applications of the MCDM methodology to virtual enterprises [102], robust portfolios [103] or port performance [104]. Cluster 4 (yellow) is located at a great distance from the three previous clusters and is made up of Romero's articles on goal programming [105,106], and peripheral articles on ranking methods [9], superefficiency [107], value efficiency [13] and data envelopment analysis [15].

3.4. Dynamic Evolution of the Research Agenda

The analysis of the overlapping map (Figure 7) reports the comparison of the dominant academic production between subperiods. A total of 87 seminal articles articulated the debate before the GFC and 158 after the GFC. After 2008, the new research agenda incorporated 75 new articles that became central to shaping the scientific debate. In fact, in the VUCA era, the 83 articles from the previous period accounted for 51% of the 158 core articles that researchers used to build their references and advance science in fields such as MCDM.

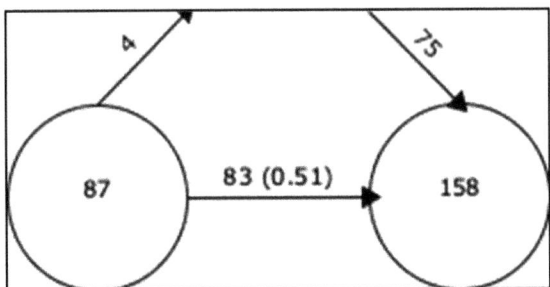

Figure 7. Overlapping map.

Important research that dominated the debate addressed the study of strategic performance [37], sustainable housing affordability [20], tourism policy implementation [108] or urban sewage sludge and transitions for eco-cities [22]. In this sense, the VUCA environments promoted research on blockchain [53,109], green supply chain management [42], new business models based in sharing economy [110], development of smart cities [111–114], mobility systems [115,116], fuzzy and MCDM methodologies to prioritize the best alternatives [90,117,118], wastewater treatment [119] and solution of challenges of water management of developing countries [120,121].

Figures 8 and 9 and Tables 5 and 6 report the results of the analysis carried out with SciMAT for both subperiods. The detailed evaluation based on the compared thematic clusters offers relevant information to guide future research according to the evolution of the research agenda.

Table 5. Cluster information. Subperiod 1 (1979–2008).

Cluster Name	CDC *	CDHI	DAC	CDSC	Centrality	CR	Density	DR
Ranking	17	13	64.18	1091	42.68	1	16.27	0.5
Decision	5	5	59.8	299	26.81	0.67	29.84	0.67
Multiple-criteria-decision-making	39	23	41.67	1625	30.1	0.83	9.18	0.17
Decision-support-systems	8	7	153.5	1228	21.55	0.5	9.19	0.33
Multi criteria decision making	4	4	44.5	178	11.27	0.33	33.77	1
Preference-modelling	2	2	112	224	3.41	0.17	32.5	0.83

* See Acronyms for details of acronyms. Source: Own elaboration.

Emerging themes before 2008, year in which one of the biggest global economic crises broke out (GFC) as seen in Figure 8 and Table 5 were tangentially related to decision support systems [14], and after 2008, Figure 9 and Table 6 new academic debates arise about multi-objective optimization [30,93] and additive value functions [32]. Basic themes also evolved between both subperiods. Before 2008 (Figure 8; Table 5), multiple-criteria decision-making [82,88,89] was the most important basic theme, while after 2008 (Figure 9; Table 6) the theory of the firm [122,123] and the analysis of decision weights [97,124,125] became basic themes. Specialized topics were also transformed after 2008. Before 2008 (Figure 8; Table 5) the preference modeling theme stood out [103] and after 2008 (Figure 9; Table 6) the niche themes that were identified where the preferences [126], distance measures [37,104] and impacts [36,124] themes.

Figure 8. Strategic diagram of subperiod 1 (1979–2008).

Before 2008 (Figure 8; Table 5) were the multiple-criteria decision-making [82,88,89], while after 2008 (Figure 9; Table 6) the theory of the firm [122,123] and the analysis of decision weights [97,124,125] became basic themes (Figure 8; Table 5), the motor themes were decisions and rankings, while the motor themes after 2008 (Figure 9; Table 6) were multicriteria [22,29,34,38,94,99,119,124,125,127,128], environment [41,120,124,129,130] and models [5,19,38,107,108,116]. The strong irruption of the 2030 Agenda in the academic debate is verified. The influence of the SDGs was articulated in a transversal way around the main research topics of the subperiod analyzed after 2008. The understanding of the models and methodologies for multicriteria decision-making in contexts of environmental and social sustainability helped to improve adherence and the impact of their application to reality. Emerging themes before 2008 (Figure 8; Table 5) were tangentially related to decision support systems [14], and after 2008 (Figure 9; Table 6) new academic debates arise about multiobjective optimization [30,93] and additive value functions [32]. The basic themes also evolved between both subperiods. Before 2008 (Figure 8; Table 5) were the multiple-criteria decision-making [82,88,89], while after the GFC (Figure 9; Table 6) the theory of the firm [122,123] and the analysis of weights in decision analysis [97,124,125] became basic topics. Specialized topics were transformed after 2008. Before 2008 (Figure 8; Table 5), preference modeling stood out [103], and after 2008 (Figure 9; Table 6), niche themes were preferences [126], distance measures [37,104], and impacts [36,124].

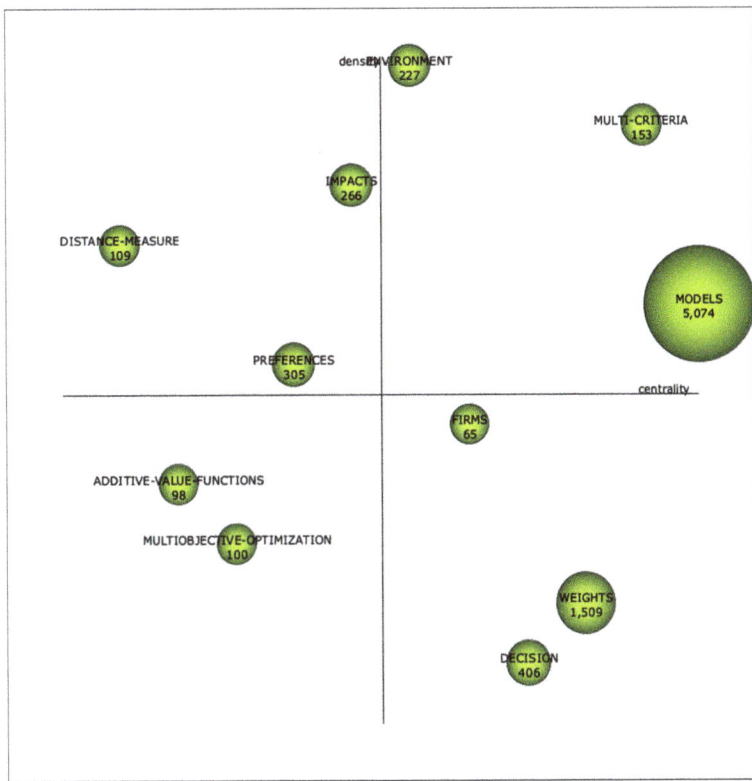

Figure 9. Strategic diagram of subperiod 2 (2009–2022).

Table 6. Clusters information. Subperiod 2 (2009–2022).

Cluster Name	CDC *	CDHI	DAC	CDSC	Centrality	CR	Density	DR
Environment	9	7	25.22	227	20.92	0.6	11.93	1
Models	141	34	35.99	5074	33.08	1	5.98	0.6
Preferences	14	9	21.79	305	19.04	0.4	5.39	0.6
Impacts	11	9	24.18	266	20.79	0.5	8.74	0.8
Multi-criteria	9	6	17	153	29.32	0.9	10.24	0.9
Weights	9	8	167.7	1509	28.11	0.8	3.06	0.2
Decision	12	8	33.83	406	23.58	0.7	1.77	0.1
Firms	7	4	9.29	65	20.95	0.6	4.56	0.5
Multiobjective-optimization	6	5	16.67	100	15.26	0.3	3.79	0.3
Distance-measure	4	3	27.25	109	10.53	0.1	6.67	0.7
Additive-value-functions	5	5	19.6	98	12.26	0.2	3.97	0.4

* See Acronyms for details of acronyms. Source: Own elaboration.

Figure 10 reports the details of the transformation of the academic debate on MCDM after 2008. The evolution map for both subperiods shows the connection of preceding and subsequent themes. Among others, four major conversion nuclei of the academic debate stand out: (a) rankings [9,11] towards models [5,19,38,108,116]; (b) MCDM [8,82,88,89,93] towards models, preferences, weights, decision, firms and distance measure [5,85,104,124–126,131]; (c) decision support systems [14] towards weights analysis [124,125]; (d) preference modeling [13,103] towards multiple criteria [38,95,124–128,132] and additive value functions [32].

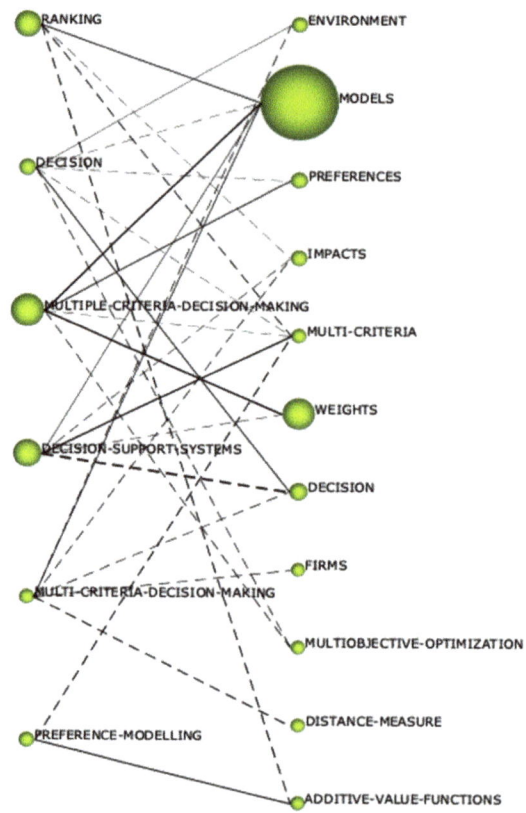

Figure 10. Evolution map. Subperiod 1 (1979–2008) vs. subperiod 2 (2009–2022).

3.5. High-Impact Publishing Opportunities

Proper understanding of the evolving research agenda offers important opportunities for high-impact publishing. There are multiple gaps not yet closed by the literature and in recent years issues have emerged that are of growing interest to scholars. Appendix A reports the top 25 articles and journals. From the perspective of the total impact expressed as the total count of citations for the subperiod prior to 2008 (Appendix A; Table A1), seminal articles on MCDM are located in the index with the highest impact [8–15,82,83,86–89,91,93,94,96–98,100,102,106,107,133], and those that stand out for their high performance expressed in academic efficiency through the normalized impact per year (NIY) method the seminal works of Opricovic and Tzeng [82] on comparative analysis of VIKOR and TOPSIS (NIY = 132,11) and extended VIKOR method in comparison with outranking methods (NIY = 60,27), and Tone [107] on measure of superefficiency (NIY = 46,50). The academic performance of these three articles is markedly superior to the rest of the research indexed in the top 25 articles by citations.

Based on the asymmetry of years included in both subperiods, the NIY analysis for the top 25 articles by citations (Appendix A; Table A2) [19–23,29–37,84,85,92,95,99,101,108,134–137] offers relevant information on "hot topics" for scholars. This evaluation of WHAT research is likely to have a greater impact in the contemporary academic context. Thus, WHAT is determined from the NIY analysis, in order to identify mainstream themes for each of the two subperiods. In particular, the evaluation of the articles included in the top 25 per NIY that were not included in the top 25 articles by citations (Appendix A; Tables A3 and A4; second column: strong trend (ST), shows that before 2008, four very important articles published in the years immediately prior to the 2008 stood out for NIY). These articles addressed topics of academic interest such as robust portfolio modeling [103,138], goal programming models [105] and multiobjective optimization [139]. The articles that are part of the top 25 per NIY after 2008 and that did not achieve enough total impact to be included in the top 25 per citations are articles with high academic efficiency, since they generate many citations in the trade-off per year since posting. Thus, given that subperiod 2 includes only 13 years, a detailed analysis of the "hot topics" allows us to identify mainstream topics in recent years. Given the high level of impact achieved by these articles in just a few years, issues such as linguistic analysis for smart health care emerge [140] and MCDM under uncertainty [141], decision-makers' psychological preferences [142], cognitive mapping [113,143–145], stochastic MCDM [146], big data analytics capabilities and firm performance [147], open innovation in SMEs [145], smart cities [113] and sustainable supplier selection for megaprojects [25,130,148].

The evidence found suggests that the reported topics are presented in the first line of advancement of scientific knowledge. These themes and their semantic connecting detail represent important high-impact publishing opportunities. In this sense, Appendix B (Figures A1–A11) offers detailed information on how to connect the topics based on the clusters of greatest interest in academia, so the "how" shows the connection between the subtopics through the cluster's networks of subperiod 2. These are thematic nuclei required with interest by the journals, and that make up the academic vanguard. Researchers can identify the way in which contemporary discourse is articulated and build their research on the environment (Figure A1), models (Figure A2), preferences (Figure A3), impacts (Figure A4), multiple criteria (Figure A5), weights (Figure A6), decisions (Figure A7), firms (Figure A8), multiobjective optimization (Figure A9), distance measures (Figure A10) and additive value functions (Figure A11).

On the other hand, after analyzing what to research and how to connect the topics to achieve maximum impact, it is necessary to look at where it is most effective to publish high-impact research. Analogously to the previous analysis, evidence is presented for both subperiods. Table A5 (Appendix B) shows the main journals of subperiod 1, ordered by total citations. Before 2008, the 10 journals with the greatest impact on MCDM were the *European Journal of Operational Research, Omega—International Journal of Management Science, Journal of the Operational Research Society, Decision Sciences, Tourism Management, Management Science, Technovation, IEEE Transactions on Engineering Management, Systems Research and Behavioral Science,* and *Group Decision and Negotiation*. The ComD evaluation offers indicators of high academic efficiency for three journals that manage to register at least 100 citations per article: *Tourism Management* (CpD = 544), *Systems Research and Behavioral Science* (CpD = 146), and the *European Journal of Operational Research* (CpD = 103.78).

Table A6 (Appendix A) shows the 25 journals with the greatest academic impact in the second subperiod analyzed, offering a useful guide to determine where to publish research on MCDM. According to the second column of Table A6, according to the strong trend (ST) indication, several journals are evidenced, characterized by their emerging impact within the field in comparative intertemporal terms. After 2008, 16 journals appear in the ranking that were not included in the same top 25 ranking of the previous subperiod. The finding of these journals is a very useful recommendation for scholars on where to direct their research on MCDM within the area of business and management once the systemic change in the research agenda after the 2008 took place. The strong trend (ST) evidence found shows 16 "hot journals" in the field: *Journal of Business Economics and Management, Technological Forecasting and Social Change, International Journal of Strategic Property Management, International Transactions in Operational Research, Journal of Enterprise Information Management, Transformations in Business and Economics, Journal of Business Research, Total Quality Management and Business Excellence, Socio-Economic Planning Sciences, International Journal Of Logistics Management, E a M: Ekonomie a Management, Business Strategy and the Environment, Engineering Construction and Architectural Management, Journal of Purchasing and Supply Management,* and *Tourism Management Perspectives*.

The results of this article should give researchers a better understanding of the structure of research done on MCDM and MCDA. Among the new contributions to the literature that this article represents is the evaluation of new motor topics though the SciMAT software, which permits the visualization of the most current mainstream thematic nuclei of the academic discourse on MCDM and MCDA.

Although the research was not designed or conducted as a meta-analysis, it can be deemed valuable due to the clarity of the information provided. As such, the findings of this study are relevant to the academic community and advance the scientific debate on MCDM. When information is focalized, it constitutes a resource that makes academic interaction more accessible for researchers, allowing for scholarly discussions based on decision-making traditions.

4. Conclusions

The recent succession of economic, social, health, and war crises has generalized the irruption of a continuum of VUCA environments (volatile, uncertain, complex, and ambiguous) that have become global and hegemonic. The existing interdependence among the different systems has a substantial effect on companies, entrepreneurs, and investors, as well as governments and civil society, and forces accurate and rapid decisions to be made. On the other hand, shocks are becoming more frequent, deep, and persistent. In the contemporary era, the first recent systemic crisis that caused major economic and social disruption in most developed countries was the GFC. Since 2008, all kinds of disruptive events have taken place that force managers and governors to make quick and concrete decisions. Following 2008, academic interest in multiple-criteria decision-making (MCDM) or multiple-criteria decision-analysis (MCDA) has clearly increased. Articles published on these topics in scientific journals in the business and management area in recent years have achieved a much higher normalized impact per year (NIY). In addition to the increase in interest from academia, there has been an important paradigm shift causing the transformation of the research agenda. International collaboration networks have intensified, and Taiwan, USA, Serbia, China, and Spain are leaders in total citations. However, academic efficiency measured as citations per document (CpD) is very strong in Serbia, Netherlands, and Denmark and very weak in Australia, Scotland, India, Turkey, Brazil, Iran, and Switzerland. The theme construction of the scientific vanguard and bibliographic coupling per article analysis show four large clusters that contribute to a better understanding of the structure of the academic debate on MCDM.

The dynamic evolution of the research agenda shows a profound transformation of the driving, basic, and emerging issues, offering important recommendations on the construction of the academic debate. The evolution of specialized topics advises scholars on major emerging trends that allow them to increase the impact of their future research. From the perspective of the practical application of the methodologies analyzed, a finding of this study guides future academic production around "hot topics", such as mobility, management of scarce resources, such as water or energy, electrification, and electric vehicles, and new models of business based on blockchain or the sharing economy. In addition, from a particular approach, the evidence found suggests that future research on portfolio modeling, multiobjective optimization, or goal-programming models were emerging topics before 2008, but high-impact publication opportunities are focused on the study of the construction of cognitive maps and a better understanding of the psychological preferences of decision-makers, as well as the application of MCDM methodologies to specific problems, such as smart cities, green supply chain alternatives, open innovation in SMEs, and the impact of big data capabilities on firm performance.

The axes of systematic review and analysis carried out by this research offer new vectors to be explored and developed by scholars. In addition, researchers and journal editors can find in this article a roadmap to be used in the planning, design, and publishing of research in the field. Further value can be found in the identification of "hot topics" and changing trends defined on the basis of the methodologies used. The main contribution of this study is to offer a panoramic view of the field of research published in business and management areas on MCDM, and to help academics in understanding how the research agenda has been transformed. In addition, the identification of the change vectors of the internal structure of the area guides and advises researchers in their future academic production, informing about gaps not closed by the scientific literature. This research provides journal editors with specific guidance on new emerging topics and the forefront of the scientific debate on MCDM, as well as the uses and applications with the greatest academic impact.

A limitation of this study is in the bibliographic methodology used. Future research should complement the scientometric knowledge generated by this research with a qualitative approach that is provided by researchers who are building the cutting edge of science on MCDM. In addition, this research could include a classification of the MCDM methodology that identifies its evolution and its fields of application. Among others, future lines of research should hybridize bibliographic methodologies with others of a qualitative type, such as design and system thinking or focus group, to improve the understanding of the underlying motivations of the researchers, as well as sources of funding, that explain the transformation of the research agenda. Other research should delve into the detailed analysis of specific methodologies used for decision-making, such as fuzzy analytic hierarchy process (F-AHP) or fuzzy-set qualitative comparative analysis (fsQCA), extending the analysis to the construction and selection of sociotechnical transitions designed to achieve the SDGs.

Author Contributions: Conceptualization, F.C.-S.; methodology, F.C.-S.; software, F.C.-S.; validation, F.C.-S. and C.M.-E.; formal analysis, F.C.-S.; investigation, F.C.-S.; resources, F.C.-S.; data curation, F.C.-S.; writing—original draft preparation, F.C.-S.; writing—review and editing, F.C.-S. and C.M.-E.; visualization, F.C.-S. and C.M.-E.; supervision, F.C.-S.; project administration, F.C.-S. All authors have read and agreed to the published version of the manuscript.

Funding: This research received no external funding.

Data Availability Statement: Data sharing not applicable.

Conflicts of Interest: The authors declare no conflict of interest.

Acronyms

AB	abstract
AHP	analytical hierarchy process
AK	author keywords
CDAC	core documents average citations
CDC	core documents count
CDHI	core documents h-index
CR	centrality range
CDSC	core document sum citations
DpY	documents per year
DR	density range
fsQCA	fuzzy-set qualitative comparative analysis
JCR	Journal Citation Reports®
KP	Keyword Plus®
MCDM	multiple-criteria decision-making or multicriteria decision-making
MCDA	multiple-criteria decision analysis or multicriteria decision analysis
NIY	normalized impact per year
SSCI	Social Sciences Citation Index
SCIE	Science Citation Index Expanded
ST	strong trend
TI	title
TS	topic
WoS-CC	Web of Science Core Collection

Appendix F. Top 25 Articles and Journals

Table A1. Top 25 articles by citations. Subperiod 1 (1979–2008).

Rank	Tittle	Authors	Journal	Year	Cites	NIY
1	Compromise solution by MCDM methods: A comparative analysis of VIKOR and TOPSIS [83]	Opricovic, S; Tzeng, GH	European journal of operational research	2004	2378	132.11
2	A slacks-based measure of super-efficiency in data envelopment analysis [107]	Tone, K	European journal of operational research	2002	930	46.50
3	Extended VIKOR method in comparison with outranking methods [83]	Opricovic, S; Tzeng, GH	European journal of operational research	2007	904	60.27
4	Topsis for MODM [86]	Lai, YJ; Liu, TY; Hwang, CL	European journal of operational research	1994	565	20.18
5	The evaluation of airline service quality by fuzzy MCDM [8]	Tsaur, SH; Chang, TY; Yen, CH	Tourism management	2002	544	27.20
6	Review of ranking methods in the data envelopment analysis context [9]	Adler, N; Friedman, L; Sinuany-Stern, Z	European journal of operational research	2002	532	26.60
7	On the extent analysis method for fuzzy AHP and its applications [87]	Wang, YM; Luo, Y; Hua, Z	European journal of operational research	2008	465	33.21
8	Social multi-criteria evaluation: Methodological foundations and operational consequences [94]	Munda, G	European journal of operational research	2004	458	25.44
9	Tentative guidelines to help choosing an appropriate MCDA method [10]	Guitouni, A; Martel, JM	European journal of operational research	1998	446	18.58
10	A critical survey on the status of multiple criteria decision-making theory and practice [96]	Stewart, TJ	Omega-international journal of management science	1992	387	12.90
11	Rough sets methodology for sorting problems in presence of multiple attributes and criteria [133]	Greco, S; Matarazzo, B; Slowinski, R	European journal of operational research	2002	348	17.40
12	Determining the weights of criteria in the ELECTRE type methods with a revised Simos' procedure [97]	Figueira, J; Roy, B	European journal of operational research	2002	337	16.85
13	Ranking irregularities when evaluating alternatives by using some ELECTRE methods [11]	Wang, XT; Triantaphyllou, E	Omega-international journal of Management science	2008	327	23.36
14	A sensitivity analysis approach for some deterministic multi-criteria decision-making methods [12]	Triantaphyllou, E; Sanchez, A	Decision sciences	1997	305	12.20

Table A1. Cont.

Rank	Tittle	Authors	Journal	Year	Cites	NIY
15	Interactive group decision making procedure under incomplete information [100]	Kim, SH; Ahn, BS	European journal of operational research	1999	290	12.61
16	Fuzzy MCDM based on ideal and anti-ideal concepts [88]	Liang, GS	European journal of operational research	1999	231	10.04
17	Fuzzy analytical approach to partnership selection in formation of virtual enterprises [102]	Mikhailov, L	Omega-international journal of Management science	2002	216	10.80
18	Extended lexicographic goal programming: a unifying approach [106]	Romero, C	Omega-international journal of Management science	2001	196	9.33
19	Evaluating firm technological innovation capability under uncertainty [91]	Wang, CH; Lu, IY; Chen, CB	Technovation	2008	178	12.71
20	A value efficiency approach to incorporating preference information in data envelopment analysis [13]	Halme, M; Joro, T; Korhonen, P; Salo, S; Wallenius, J	Management science	1999	176	7.65
21	An MCDM approach to portfolio optimization [93]	Ehrgott, M; Klamroth, K; Schwehm, C	European journal of operational research	2004	172	9.56
22	Decision Support Systems in action: Integrated application in a multicriteria decision aid process [14]	Bana E Costa, CA; Ensslin, L; Correa, EC; Vansnick, JC	European journal of operational research	1999	169	7.35
23	Evaluating sustainable fishing development strategies using fuzzy MCDM approach [89]	Chiou, HK; Tzeng, GH; Cheng, DC	Omega-international journal of management science	2005	168	9.88
24	Geometrical representations for MCDA [98]	Mareschal, B; Brans, JP	European journal of operational research	1988	164	4.82
25	Relationships between data envelopment analysis and multicriteria decision analysis [15]	Stewart, TJ	Journal of the operational research society	1996	162	6.23

Source: Own elaboration.

Table A2. Top 25 articles by citations. Subperiod 2 (2009–2022).

Rank	Title	Authors	Journal	Year	Cites	NIY
1	Best-worst multi-criteria decision-making method [134]	Rezaei, J	Omega-international journal of management science	2015	1263	180.43
2	Quantitative models for sustainable supply chain management: Developments and directions [19]	Brandenburg, M; Govindan, K; Sarkis, J; Seuring, S	European journal of operational research	2014	666	83.25
3	Best-worst multi-criteria decision-making method: Some properties and a linear model [29]	Rezaei, J	Omega-international journal of management science	2016	576	96.00
4	Comparative analysis of MCDM methods for the assessment of sustainable housing affordability [20]	Mulliner, E; Malys, N; Maliene, V	Omega-international journal of management science	2016	225	37.50
5	An extension of the Electre I method for group decision-making under a fuzzy environment [85]	Hatami-Marbini, A; Tavana, M	Omega-international journal of management science	2011	210	19.09
6	The evaluation of tourism destination competitiveness by TOPSIS & information entropy—A case in the Yangtze River Delta of China [92]	Zhang, H; Gu, CL; Gu, LW; Zhang, Y	Tourism management	2011	207	18.82
7	g-dominance: Reference point based dominance for multiobjective metaheuristics [30]	Molina, J; Santana, LV; Hernandez-Diaz, AG; Coello, CAC; Caballero, R	European journal of operational research	2009	179	13.77
8	Generalised framework for multi-criteria method selection [95]	Watrobski, J; Jankowski, J; Ziemba, P; Karczmarczyk, A; Ziolo, M	Omega-international journal of management science	2019	177	59.00
9	The state-of-the-art survey on integrations and applications of the best worst method in decision making: Why, what, what for and what's next? [101]	Mi, XM; Tang, M; Liao, HC; Shen, WJ; Lev, B	Omega-international journal of management science	2019	167	55.67
10	The extended QUALIFLEX method for multiple criteria decision analysis based on interval type-2 fuzzy sets and applications to medical decision making [84]	Chen, TY; Chang, CH; Lu, JFR	European journal of operational research	2013	160	17.78
11	A combined compromise solution (CoCoSo) method for multi-criteria decision-making problems [99]	Yazdani, M; Zarate, P; Zavadskas, EK; Turskis, Z	Management decision	2019	150	50.00
12	Strategic performance measurement in a healthcare organisation: A multiple criteria approach based on balanced scorecard [37]	Grigoroudis, E; Orfanoudaki, E; Zopounidis, C	Omega-international journal of management science	2012	150	15.00
13	FAMCDM: A fusion approach of MCDM methods to rank multiclass classification algorithms [31]	Peng, Y; Kou, G; Wang, GX; Shi, Y	Omega-international journal of management science	2011	150	13.64

Table A2. Cont.

Rank	Tittle	Authors	Journal	Year	Cites	NIY
14	An assessment of sustainable housing affordability using a multiple criteria decision making method [21]	Mulliner, E; Smallbone, K; Maliene, V	Omega-international journal of management science	2013	147	16.33
15	Improving tourism policy implementation—The use of hybrid MCDM models [108]	Liu, CH; Tzeng, GH; Lee, MH	Tourism management	2012	136	13.60
16	An extended TODIM approach with intuitionistic linguistic numbers [135]	Yu, SM; Wang, J; Wang, JQ	International transactions in operational research	2018	135	33.75
17	Building a set of additive value functions representing a reference preorder and intensities of preference: GRIP method [32]	Figueira, JR; Greco, S; Slowinski, R	European journal of operational research	2009	133	10.23
18	Urban sewage sludge, sustainability, and transition for Eco-City: Multi-criteria sustainability assessment of technologies based on best-worst method [22]	Ren, JZ; Liang, HW; Chan, FTS	Technological forecasting and social change	2017	128	25.60
19	Using fuzzy multiple criteria decision making approach to enhance risk assessment for metropolitan construction projects [33]	Kuo, YC; Lu, ST	International journal of project management	2013	123	13.67
20	Hesitant fuzzy Bonferroni means for multi-criteria decision making [34]	Zhu, B; Xu, ZS	Journal of the operational research society	2013	123	13.67
21	Non-additive robust ordinal regression: A multiple criteria decision model based on the Choquet integral [35]	Angilella, S; Greco, S; Matarazzo, B	European journal of operational research	2010	123	10.25
22	An intelligent-agent-based fuzzy group decision making model for financial multicriteria decision support: The case of credit scoring [136]	Yu, L; Wang, SY; Lai, KK	European journal of operational research	2009	120	9.23
23	Application of a novel PROMETHEE-based method for construction of a group compromise ranking to prioritization of green suppliers in food supply chain [23]	Govindan, K; Kadzinski, M; Sivakumar, R	Omega-international journal of management science	2017	116	23.20
24	A modified TOPSIS with a different ranking index [137]	Kuo, T	European journal of operational research	2017	116	23.20
25	The sustainability balanced scorecard as a framework for selecting socially responsible investment: an effective MCDM model [36]	Tsai, WH; Chou, WC; Hsu, W	Journal of the operational research society	2009	114	8.77

Source: Own elaboration.

Table A3. Top 25 articles by NIY. Subperiod 1 (1979–2008).

Rank	ST	Title	Authors	Journal	Year	Cites	NIY
1		Compromise solution by MCDM methods: A comparative analysis of VIKOR and TOPSIS [82]	Opricovic, S; Tzeng, GH	European journal of operational research	2004	2378	132.11
2		Extended VIKOR method in comparison with outranking methods [83]	Opricovic, S; Tzeng, GH	European journal of operational research	2007	904	60.27
3		A slacks-based measure of super-efficiency in data envelopment analysis [107]	Tone, K	European journal of operational research	2002	930	46.50
4		On the extent analysis method for fuzzy AHP and its applications [87]	Wang, YM; Luo, Y; Hua, Z	European journal of operational research	2008	465	33.21
5		The evaluation of airline service quality by fuzzy MCDM [8]	Tsaur, SH; Chang, TY; Yen, CH	Tourism management	2002	544	27.20
6		Review of ranking methods in the data envelopment analysis context [9]	Adler, N; Friedman, L; Sinuany-Stern, Z	European journal of operational research	2002	532	26.60
7		Social multi-criteria evaluation: Methodological foundations and operational consequences [94]	Munda, G	European journal of operational research	2004	458	25.44
8		Ranking irregularities when evaluating alternatives by using some ELECTRE methods [11]	Wang, XT; Triantaphyllou, E	Omega-international journal of Management science	2008	327	23.36
9		TOPSIS FOR MODM [86]	Lai, YJ; Liu, TY; Hwang, CL	European journal of operational research	1994	565	20.18
10		Tentative guidelines to help choosing an appropriate MCDA method [10]	Guitouni, A; Martel, JM	European journal of operational research	1998	446	18.58
11		Rough sets methodology for sorting problems in presence of multiple attributes and criteria [133]	Greco, S; Matarazzo, B; Slowinski, R	European journal of operational research	2002	348	17.40
12		Determining the weights of criteria in the ELECTRE type methods with a revised Simos' procedure [97]	Figueira, J; Roy, B	European journal of operational research	2002	337	16.85
13		A critical survey on the status of multiple criteria decision-making theory and practice [96]	Stewart, TJ	Omega-international journal of Management science	1992	387	12.90
14		Evaluating firm technological innovation capability under uncertainty [91]	Wang, CH; Lu, IY; Chen, CB	Technovation	2008	178	12.71

Table A3. *Cont.*

Rank	ST	Title	Authors	Journal	Year	Cites	NIY
15		Interactive group decision making procedure under incomplete information [100]	Kim, SH; Ahn, BS	European journal of operational research	1999	290	12.61
16		A sensitivity analysis approach for some deterministic multi-criteria decision-making methods [12]	Triantaphyllou, E; Sanchez, A	Decision sciences	1997	305	12.20
17		Fuzzy analytical approach to partnership selection in formation of virtual enterprises [102]	Mikhailov, L	Omega-international journal of management science	2002	216	10.80
18	✓	Preference programming for robust portfolio modeling and project selection [18]	Liesio, J; Mild, P; Salo, A	European journal of operational research	2007	159	10.60
19	✓	Robust portfolio modeling with incomplete cost information and project interdependencies [138]	Liesio, J; Mild, P; Salo, A	European journal of operational research	2008	145	10.36
20		Fuzzy MCDM based on ideal and anti-ideal concepts [88]	Liang, GS	European journal of operational research	1999	231	10.04
21		Evaluating sustainable fishing development strategies using fuzzy MCDM approach [89]	Chiou, HK; Tzeng, GH; Cheng, DC	Omega-international journal of management science	2005	168	9.88
22		An MCDM approach to portfolio optimization [93]	Ehrgott, M; Klamroth, K; Schwehm, C	European journal of operational research	2004	172	9.56
23		Extended lexicographic goal programming: a unifying approach [106]	Romero, C	Omega-international journal of Management science	2001	196	9.33
24	✓	A general structure of achievement function for a goal programming model [105]	Romero, C	European journal of operational research	2004	160	8.89
25	✓	Synchronous approach in interactive multiobjective optimization [139]	Miettinen, K; Makela, MM	European journal of operational research	2006	130	8.13

Source: Own elaboration.

Table A4. Top 25 articles by NIY. Subperiod 1 (2009–2022).

Rank	ST	Title	Authors	Journal	Year	Cites	NIY
1		Best-worst multi-criteria decision-making method [134]	Rezaei, J	Omega-international journal of management science	2015	1263	180.43
2		Best-worst multi-criteria decision-making method: Some properties and a linear model [29]	Rezaei, J	Omega-international journal of management science	2016	576	96.00
3		Quantitative models for sustainable supply chain management: Developments and directions [19]	Brandenburg, M; Govindan, K; Sarkis, J; Seuring, S	European journal of operational research	2014	666	83.25
4		Generalised framework for multi-criteria method selection [95]	Watrobski, J; Jankowski, J; Ziemba, P; Karczmarczyk, A; Ziolo, M	Omega-international journal of management science	2019	177	59.00
5		The state-of-the-art survey on integrations and applications of the best worst method in decision making: Why, what for and what's next? [101]	Mi, XM; Tang, M; Liao, HC; Shen, WJ; Lev, B	Omega-international journal of management science	2019	167	55.67
6		A combined compromise solution (CoCoSo) method for multi-criteria decision-making problems [99]	Yazdani, M; Zarate, P; Zavadskas, EK; Turskis, Z	Management decision	2019	150	50.00
7	✓	Probabilistic double hierarchy linguistic term set and its use in designing an improved VIKOR method: The application in smart healthcare [140]	Gou, XJ; Xu, ZS; Liao, HC; Herrera, F	Journal of the operational research society	2021	41	41.00
8	✓	Generalised probabilistic linguistic evidential reasoning approach for multi-criteria decision-making under uncertainty [141]	Fang, R; Liao, HC; Yang, JB; Xu, DL	Journal of the operational research society	2021	39	39.00
9		Comparative analysis of MCDM methods for the assessment of sustainable housing affordability [20]	Mulliner, E; Malys, N; Maliene, V	Omega-international journal of management science	2016	225	37.50
10		An extended TODIM approach with intuitionistic linguistic numbers [135]	Yu, SM; Wang, J; Wang, JQ	International transactions in operational research	2018	135	33.75
11	✓	Stochastic multicriteria decision-making approach based on SMAA-ELECTRE with extended gray numbers [146]	Zhou, H; Wang, JQ; Zhang, HY	International transactions in operational research	2019	84	28.00
12	✓	Big data analytics capabilities and firm performance: An integrated MCDM approach [147]	Yasmin, M; Tatoglu, E; Kilic, HS; Zaim, S; Delen, D	Journal of business research	2020	56	28.00
13	✓	SMART-C: Developing a Smart City Assessment System Using Cognitive Mapping and the Choquet Integral [113]	Castanho, MS; Ferreira, FAF; Carayannis, EG; Ferreira, JJM	IEEE transactions on engineering management	2021	27	27.00

Table A4. Cont.

Rank	ST	Title	Authors	Journal	Year	Cites	NIY
14	✓	Sustainable Supplier Selection in Megaprojects: Grey Ordinal Priority Approach [130]	Mahmoudi, A; Deng, XP; Javed, SA; Zhang, N	Business strategy and the environment	2021	26	26.00
15		Urban sewage sludge, sustainability, and transition for Eco-City: Multi-criteria sustainability assessment of technologies based on best-worst method [22]	Ren, JZ; Liang, HW; Chan, FTS	Technological forecasting and social change	2017	128	25.60
16	✓	Measuring SMEs Propensity for Open Innovation Using Cognitive Mapping and MCDA [145]	Silva, ARD; Ferreira, FAF; Carayannis, EG; Ferreira, JJM	IEEE transactions on engineering management	2021	25	25.00
17	✓	An integrated method for cognitive complex multiple experts multiple criteria decision making based on ELECTRE III with weighted Borda rule [143]	Liao, HC; Wu, XL; Mi, XM; Herrera, F	Omega-international journal of management science	2020	49	24.50
18		Application of a novel PROMETHEE-based method for construction of a group compromise ranking to prioritization of green suppliers in food supply chain [23]	Govindan, K; Kadzinski, M; Sivakumar, R	Omega-international journal of management science	2017	116	23.20
19		A modified TOPSIS with a different ranking index [137]	Kuo, T	European journal of operational research	2017	116	23.20
20	✓	Probabilistic linguistic multi-criteria decision-making based on evidential reasoning and combined ranking methods considering decision-makers' psychological preferences [142]	Tian, ZP; Nie, RX; Wang, JQ	Journal of the operational research society	2020	44	22.00
21	✓	Selection of a sustainable third-party reverse logistics provider based on the robustness analysis of an outranking graph kernel conducted with ELECTRE I and SMAA [25]	Govindan, K; Kadzinski, M; Ehling, R; Miebs, G	Omega-international journal of management science	2019	62	20.67
22		An extension of the Electre I method for group decision-making under a fuzzy environment [85]	Hatami-Marbini, A; Tavana, M	Omega-international journal of management science	2011	210	19.09
23		The evaluation of tourism destination competitiveness by TOPSIS & information entropy—A case in the Yangtze River Delta of China [92]	Zhang, H; Gu, CL; Gu, LW; Zhang, Y	Tourism management	2011	207	18.82
24	✓	Sustainable Supplier Selection and Order Allocation Under Risk and Inflation Condition [149]	Almasi, M; Khoshfetrat, S; Galankashi, MR	IEEE transactions on engineering management	2021	18	18.00
25		The extended QUALIFLEX method for multiple criteria decision analysis based on interval type-2 fuzzy sets and applications to medical decision making [84]	Chen, TY; Chang, CH; Lu, JFR	European journal of operational research	2013	160	17.78

Source: Own elaboration.

Table A5. Top journals in period 1 (1979–2008) for citations.

Rank	Journal	Citations	Articles	CpD
1	European journal of operational research	14,218	137	103.78
2	Omega-international journal of management science	1829	20	91.45
3	Journal of the operational research society	1136	33	34.42
4	Decision sciences	603	10	60.30
5	Tourism management	544	1	544.00
6	Management science	489	10	48.90
7	Technovation	286	5	57.20
8	IEEE transactions on engineering management	215	6	35.83
9	Systems research and behavioral science	146	1	146.00
10	Group decision and negotiation	144	7	20.57
11	Information systems research	107	3	35.67
12	Information & management	100	3	33.33
13	Interfaces	73	3	24.33
14	Journal of productivity analysis	45	1	45.00
15	Journal of engineering and technology management	25	1	25.00
16	Electronic commerce research and applications	18	1	18.00
17	Operations research	15	1	15.00
18	Canadian journal of administrative sciences-revue canadienne des sciences de l'administration	12	2	6.00
19	Long range planning	9	1	9.00
20	International journal of technology management	7	1	7.00
21	Quality progress	6	1	6.00
22	Management decision	3	1	3.00
23	Journal of management information systems	1	1	1.00
24	Zbornik radova ekonomskog fakulteta u rijeci-proceedings of rijeka faculty of economics	1	1	1.00

Source: Own elaboration.

Table A6. Top 25 journals in period 2 (2009–2022) for citations.

Rank	ST	Journal	Cites	Articles	CpD
1		Omega-international journal of management science	4069	44	92.48
2		European journal of operational research	4015	88	45.63
3		Journal of the operational research society	1297	52	24.94
4	✓	Journal of business economics and management	816	33	24.73
5		Tourism management	782	10	78.20
6	✓	Technological forecasting and social change	748	31	24.13
7		Management decision	637	31	20.55
8	✓	International journal of strategic property management	596	25	23.84
9	✓	International transactions in operational research	489	26	18.81
10		Group decision and negotiation	481	23	20.91
11	✓	Journal of enterprise information management	367	22	16.68
12		IEEE transactions on engineering management	292	37	7.89
13		International journal of project management	287	4	71.75
14	✓	Transformations in business & economics	230	18	12.78
15	✓	Journal of business research	204	9	22.67
16	✓	Total quality management & business excellence	203	4	50.75
17	✓	Socio-economic planning sciences	201	21	9.57
18	✓	International journal of logistics management	154	9	17.11
19	✓	E & M ekonomie a management	138	9	15.33
20	✓	Business strategy and the environment	134	4	33.50
21	✓	Engineering construction and architectural management	111	11	10.09
22	✓	Journal of purchasing and supply management	105	2	52.50
23	✓	Tourism management perspectives	81	3	27.00
24		Operations research	76	2	38.00
25		Electronic commerce research and applications	75	4	18.75

Source: Own elaboration.

Appendix B. Cluster Network for Subperiod 2 (2009–2022)

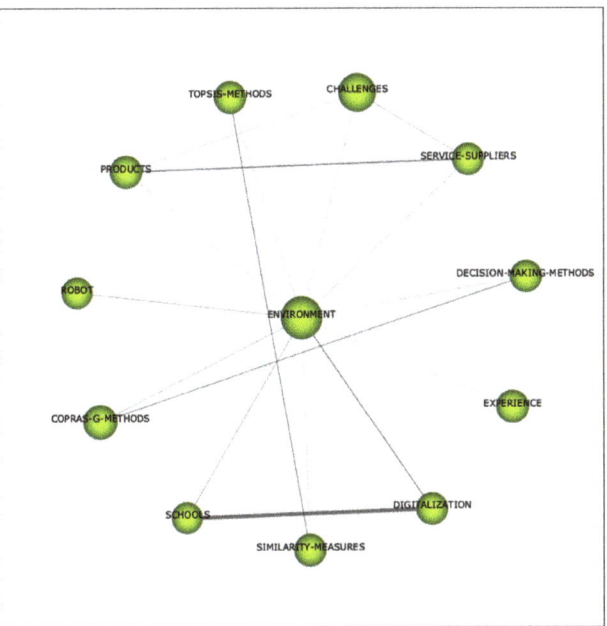

Figure A1. Environment cluster network.

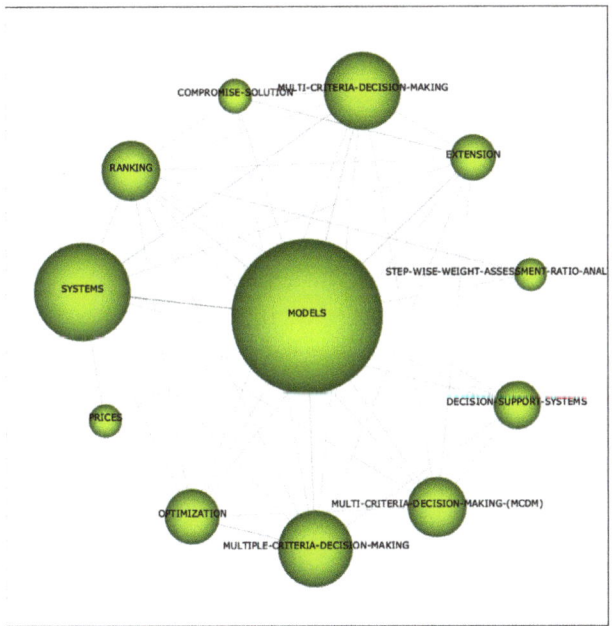

Figure A2. Model cluster network.

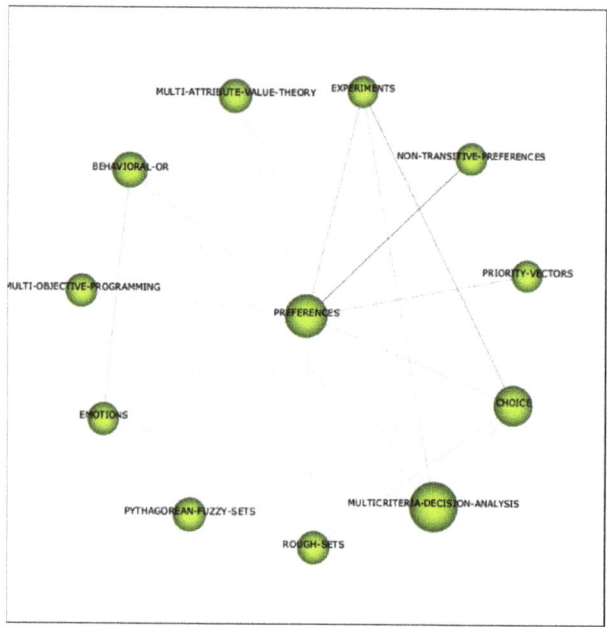

Figure A3. Preference cluster network.

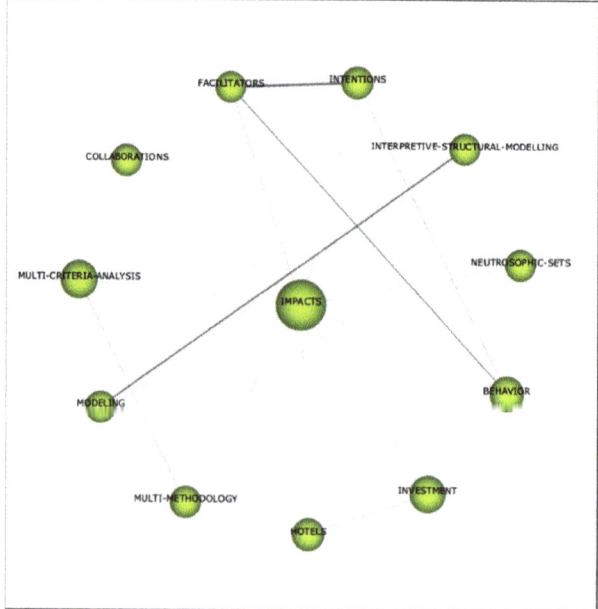

Figure A4. Impact cluster network.

Figure A5. Multi-criteria cluster network.

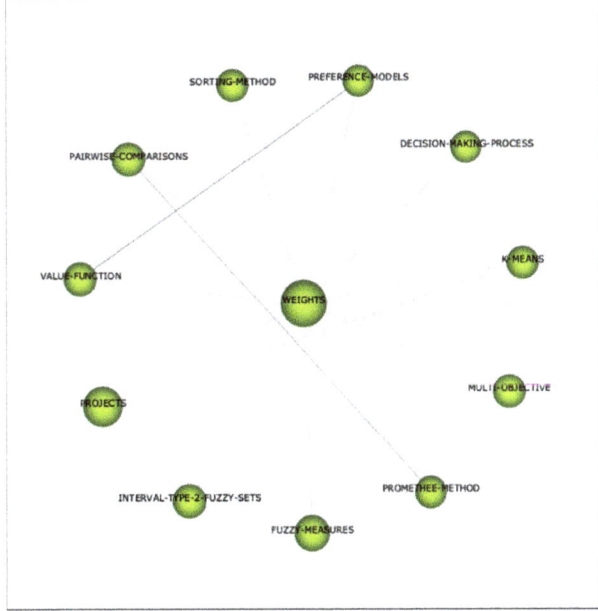

Figure A6. Weight cluster network.

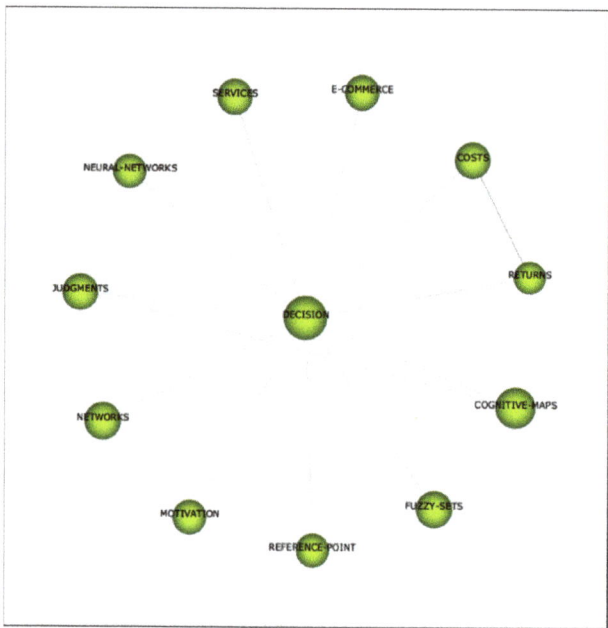

Figure A7. Decision cluster network.

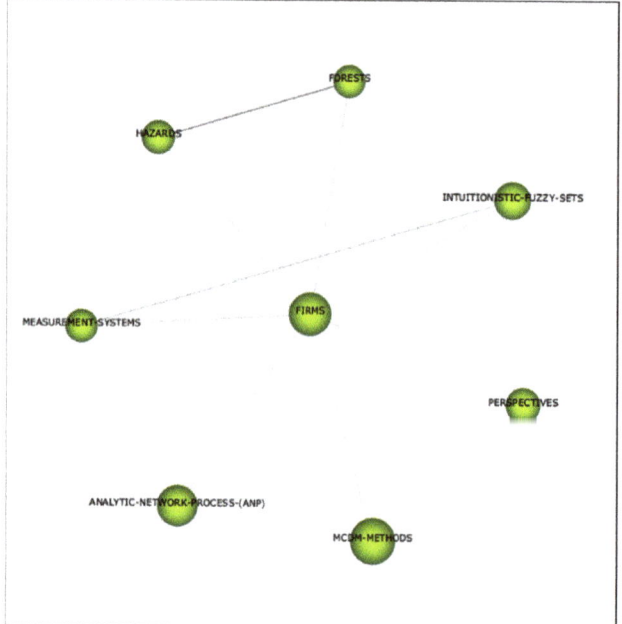

Figure A8. Firm cluster network.

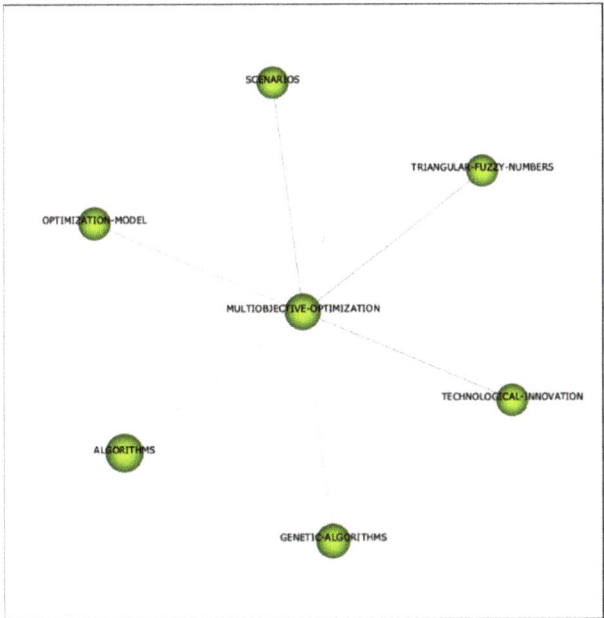

Figure A9. Multiobjective-optimization cluster network.

Figure A10. Distance-measure cluster network.

Figure A11. Additive-value-function cluster network.

References

1. Lepeley, M.-T. Management in the Global VUCA Environment. In *Soft Skills for Human Centered Management and Global Sustainability*; Routledge: New York, NY, USA, 2021.
2. Kuusisto, E. Approaching VUCA Environment with Enterprise Agility in Government Organization: Case Business Finland and COVID-19. Master's Thesis, University of Vaasa, Vaasa, Finland, 2022.
3. Gao, Y.; Feng, Z.; Zhang, S. Managing supply chain resilience in the era of VUCA. *Front. Eng. Manag.* **2021**, *8*, 465. [CrossRef]
4. Mack, O.; Khare, A.; Krämer, A.; Burgartz, T. *Managing in a VUCA World*; Springer: New York, NY, USA, 2015; ISBN 9783319168890.
5. Schoemaker, P.J.H.; Heaton, S.; Teece, D. Innovation, dynamic capabilities, and leadership. *Calif. Manage. Rev.* **2018**, *61*, 15–42. [CrossRef]
6. Dalko, V.; Wang, M.H. Is the Stock Market a VUCA Environment? *J. Appl. Bus. Econ.* **2018**, *20*, 10–19.
7. Bennett, N.; Lemoine, G.J. What a difference a word makes: Understanding threats to performance in a VUCA world. *Bus. Horiz.* **2014**, *57*, 311–317. [CrossRef]
8. Tsaur, S.-H.; Chang, T.-Y.; Yen, C.-H. The evaluation of airline service quality by fuzzy MCDM. *Tour. Manag.* **2002**, *23*, 107–115. [CrossRef]
9. Adler, N.; Friedman, L.; Sinuany-Stern, Z. Review of ranking methods in the data envelopment analysis context. *Eur. J. Oper. Res.* **2002**, *140*, 249–265. [CrossRef]
10. Guitouni, A.; Martel, J.-M. Tentative guidelines to help choosing an appropriate MCDA method. *Eur. J. Oper. Res.* **1998**, *109*, 501–521. [CrossRef]
11. Wang, X.; Triantaphyllou, E. Ranking irregularities when evaluating alternatives by using some ELECTRE methods. *Omega* **2008**, *36*, 45–63. [CrossRef]
12. Triantaphyllou, E.; Sánchez, A. A sensitivity analysis approach for some deterministic multi-criteria decision-making methods. *Decis. Sci.* **1997**, *28*, 151–194. [CrossRef]
13. Halme, M.; Joro, T.; Korhonen, P.; Salo, S.; Wallenius, J. A value efficiency approach to incorporating preference information in data envelopment analysis. *Manag. Sci.* **1999**, *45*, 103–115. [CrossRef]
14. e Costa, C.A.B.; Ensslin, L.; Cornêa, É.C.; Vansnick, J.-C. Decision support systems in action: Integrated application in a multicriteria decision aid process. *Eur. J. Oper. Res.* **1999**, *113*, 315–335. [CrossRef]
15. Stewart, T.J. Relationships between data envelopment analysis and multicriteria decision analysis. *J. Oper. Res. Soc.* **1996**, *47*, 654–665. [CrossRef]
16. Baba, N.; Packer, F. From turmoil to crisis: Dislocations in the FX swap market before and after the failure of Lehman Brothers. *J. Int. Money Financ.* **2009**, *28*, 1350–1374. [CrossRef]

17. Burkhanov, U. The Big Failure: Lehman Brothers' Effects On Global Markets. *Eur. J. Bus. Econ.* **2011**, *2*. [CrossRef]
18. De Haas, R.; Van Horen, N. International shock transmission after the Lehman Brothers collapse: Evidence from syndicated lending. *Am. Econ. Rev.* **2012**, *102*, 231–237. [CrossRef]
19. Brandenburg, M.; Govindan, K.; Sarkis, J.; Seuring, S. Quantitative models for sustainable supply chain management: Developments and directions. *Eur. J. Oper. Res.* **2014**, *233*, 299–312. [CrossRef]
20. Mulliner, E.; Malys, N.; Maliene, V. Comparative analysis of MCDM methods for the assessment of sustainable housing affordability. *Omega* **2016**, *59*, 146–156. [CrossRef]
21. Mulliner, E.; Smallbone, K.; Maliene, V. An assessment of sustainable housing affordability using a multiple criteria decision making method. *Omega* **2013**, *41*, 270–279. [CrossRef]
22. Ren, J.; Liang, H.; Chan, F.T.S. Urban sewage sludge, sustainability, and transition for Eco-City: Multi-criteria sustainability assessment of technologies based on best-worst method. *Technol. Forecast. Soc. Chang.* **2017**, *116*, 29–39. [CrossRef]
23. Govindan, K.; Kadziński, M.; Sivakumar, R. Application of a novel PROMETHEE-based method for construction of a group compromise ranking to prioritization of green suppliers in food supply chain. *Omega* **2017**, *71*, 129–145. [CrossRef]
24. Michailidou, A.V.; Vlachokostas, C.; Moussiopoulos, N. Interactions between climate change and the tourism sector: Multiple-criteria decision analysis to assess mitigation and adaptation options in tourism areas. *Tour. Manag.* **2016**, *55*, 1–12. [CrossRef]
25. Govindan, K.; Kadziński, M.; Ehling, R.; Miebs, G. Selection of a sustainable third-party reverse logistics provider based on the robustness analysis of an outranking graph kernel conducted with ELECTRE I and SMAA. *Omega* **2019**, *85*, 1–15. [CrossRef]
26. Sang, X.; Liu, X. An interval type-2 fuzzy sets-based TODIM method and its application to green supplier selection. *J. Oper. Res. Soc.* **2016**, *67*, 722–734. [CrossRef]
27. Escrig-Olmedo, E.; Muñoz-Torres, M.J.; Fernández-Izquierdo, M.Á.; Rivera-Lirio, J.M. Measuring corporate environmental performance: A methodology for sustainable development. *Bus. Strateg. Environ.* **2017**, *26*, 142–162. [CrossRef]
28. Balcerzak, P.; Bernard, M.P. Digital economy in Visegrad countries. Multiple-criteria decision analysis at regional level in the years 2012 and 2015. *J. Compet.* **2017**, *9*, 5–18. [CrossRef]
29. Rezaei, J. Best-worst multi-criteria decision-making method: Some properties and a linear model. *Omega* **2016**, *64*, 126–130. [CrossRef]
30. Molina, J.; Santana, L.V.; Hernández-Díaz, A.G.; Coello, C.A.C.; Caballero, R. g-dominance: Reference point based dominance for multiobjective metaheuristics. *Eur. J. Oper. Res.* **2009**, *197*, 685–692. [CrossRef]
31. Peng, Y.; Kou, G.; Wang, G.; Shi, Y. FAMCDM: A fusion approach of MCDM methods to rank multiclass classification algorithms. *Omega* **2011**, *39*, 677–689. [CrossRef]
32. Figueira, J.R.; Greco, S.; Słowiński, R. Building a set of additive value functions representing a reference preorder and intensities of preference: GRIP method. *Eur. J. Oper. Res.* **2009**, *195*, 460–486. [CrossRef]
33. Kuo, Y.-C.; Lu, S.-T. Using fuzzy multiple criteria decision making approach to enhance risk assessment for metropolitan construction projects. *Int. J. Proj. Manag.* **2013**, *31*, 602–614. [CrossRef]
34. Zhu, B.; Xu, Z.S. Hesitant fuzzy Bonferroni means for multi-criteria decision making. *J. Oper. Res. Soc.* **2013**, *64*, 1831–1840. [CrossRef]
35. Angilella, S.; Greco, S.; Matarazzo, B. Non-additive robust ordinal regression: A multiple criteria decision model based on the Choquet integral. *Eur. J. Oper. Res.* **2010**, *201*, 277–288. [CrossRef]
36. Tsai, W.-H.; Chou, W.-C.; Hsu, W. The sustainability balanced scorecard as a framework for selecting socially responsible investment: An effective MCDM model. *J. Oper. Res. Soc.* **2009**, *60*, 1396–1410. [CrossRef]
37. Grigoroudis, E.; Orfanoudaki, E.; Zopounidis, C. Strategic performance measurement in a healthcare organisation: A multiple criteria approach based on balanced scorecard. *Omega* **2012**, *40*, 104–119. [CrossRef]
38. Tabatabaei, M.H.; Amiri, M.; Firouzabadi, S.; Ghahremanloo, M.; Keshavarz-Ghorabaee, M.; Saparauskas, J. A new group decision-making model based on bwm and its application to managerial problems. *Transform. Bus. Econ.* **2019**, *18*, 197–214.
39. Deveci, M.; Torkayesh, A.E. Charging type selection for electric buses using interval-valued neutrosophic decision support model. *IEEE Trans. Eng. Manag.* **2021**. [CrossRef]
40. Belhadi, A.; Kamble, S.; Gunasekaran, A.; Mani, V. Analyzing the mediating role of organizational ambidexterity and digital business transformation on industry 4.0 capabilities and sustainable supply chain performance. *Supply Chain Manag. An Int. J.* **2021**. [CrossRef]
41. Vafadarnikjoo, A.; Tavana, M.; Chalvatzis, K.; Botelho, T. A socio-economic and environmental vulnerability assessment model with causal relationships in electric power supply chains. *Socioecon. Plann. Sci.* **2022**, *80*, 101156. [CrossRef]
42. Nekmahmud, M.; Rahman, S.; Sobhani, F.A.; Olejniczak-Szuster, K.; Fekete-Farkas, M. A systematic literature review on development of green supply chain management. *Polish J. Manag. Stud.* **2020**, *22*, 351–370. [CrossRef]
43. Zupic, I.; Čater, T. Bibliometric methods in management and organization. *Organ. Res. Methods* **2015**, *18*, 429–472. [CrossRef]
44. Bartol, T.; Budimir, G.; Dekleva-Smrekar, D.; Pusnik, M.; Juznic, P. Assessment of research fields in Scopus and Web of Science in the view of national research evaluation in Slovenia. *Scientometrics* **2014**, *98*, 1491–1504. [CrossRef]
45. Vieira, E.; Gomes, J. A comparison of Scopus and Web of Science for a typical university. *Scientometrics* **2009**, *81*, 587–600. [CrossRef]
46. Bakkalbasi, N.; Bauer, K.; Glover, J.; Wang, L. Three options for citation tracking: Google Scholar, Scopus and Web of Science. *Biomed. Digit. Libr.* **2006**, *3*, 1–8. [CrossRef] [PubMed]

47. Franceschini, F.; Maisano, D.; Mastrogiacomo, L. Empirical analysis and classification of database errors in Scopus and Web of Science. *J. Informetr.* **2016**, *10*, 933–953. [CrossRef]
48. Yang, K.; Meho, L.I. Citation analysis: A comparison of Google Scholar, Scopus, and Web of Science. *Proc. Am. Soc. Inf. Sci. Technol.* **2006**, *43*, 1–15. [CrossRef]
49. AlRyalat, S.A.S.; Malkawi, L.W.; Momani, S.M. Comparing bibliometric analysis using PubMed, Scopus, and Web of Science databases. *JoVE (J. Vis. Exp.)* **2019**, *152*, e58494. [CrossRef]
50. Martín-Martín, A.; Thelwall, M.; Orduna-Malea, E.; Delgado López-Cózar, E. Google Scholar, Microsoft Academic, Scopus, Dimensions, Web of Science, and OpenCitations' COCI: A multidisciplinary comparison of coverage via citations. *Scientometrics* **2021**, *126*, 871–906. [CrossRef] [PubMed]
51. Page, M.J.; McKenzie, J.E.; Bossuyt, P.M.; Boutron, I.; Hoffmann, T.C.; Mulrow, C.D.; Shamseer, L.; Tetzlaff, J.M.; Akl, E.A.; Brennan, S.E. The PRISMA 2020 statement: An updated guideline for reporting systematic reviews. *Syst. Rev.* **2021**, *10*, 1–11. [CrossRef]
52. Yepes-Nuñez, J.J.; Urrutia, G.; Romero-Garcia, M.; Alonso-Fernandez, S. The PRISMA 2020 statement: An updated guideline for reporting systematic reviews. *Rev. Esp. Cardiol.* **2021**, *74*, 790–799.
53. Frizzo-Barker, J.; Chow-White, P.A.; Adams, P.R.; Mentanko, J.; Ha, D.; Green, S. Blockchain as a disruptive technology for business: A systematic review. *Int. J. Inf. Manag.* **2020**, *51*, 102029. [CrossRef]
54. Mahat, J.; Alias, N.; Yusop, F.D. Systematic literature review on gamified professional training among employees. *Interact. Learn. Environ.* **2022**, 1–21. [CrossRef]
55. Giganti, P.; Falcone, P.M. Strategic Niche Management for Sustainability: A Systematic Literature Review. *Sustainability* **2022**, *14*, 1680. [CrossRef]
56. Flegr, S.; Schmidt, S.L. Strategic management in eSports–a systematic review of the literature. *Sport Manag. Rev.* **2022**, 1–25. [CrossRef]
57. Damasceno, E.; Azevedo, A.; Perez-Cota, M. The State-of-the-Art of Business Intelligence and Data Mining in the Context of Grid and Utility Computing: A PRISMA Systematic Review. In *International Conference on Software Process Improvement*; Springer: Cham, Switzerland, 2021; pp. 83–96.
58. Tavares Thomé, A.M.T.; Scavarda, L.F.; Scavarda, A.J. Conducting systematic literature review in operations management. *Prod. Plan. Control* **2016**, *27*, 408–420. [CrossRef]
59. Liu, W.; Liao, H. A bibliometric analysis of fuzzy decision research during 1970–2015. *Int. J. Fuzzy Syst.* **2017**, *19*, 1–14. [CrossRef]
60. Katsanidou, A.; Lefkofridi, Z. A decade of crisis in the European Union: Lessons from Greece. *JCMS J. Common Mark. Stud.* **2020**, *58*, 160–172. [CrossRef]
61. Drudi, F.; Durré, A.; Mongelli, F.P. The interplay of economic reforms and monetary policy: The case of the eurozone. *JCMS J. Common Mark. Stud.* **2012**, *50*, 881–898. [CrossRef]
62. Pronobis, M. Is monetary policy of ECB the right response to the Eurozone crisis? *Procedia-Soc. Behav. Sci.* **2014**, *156*, 398–403. [CrossRef]
63. Allegret, J.-P.; Raymond, H.; Rharrabti, H. The impact of the Eurozone crisis on European banks stocks contagion or interdependence? *Eur. Res. Stud. J.* **2016**, *19*, 129–148. [CrossRef]
64. Juhro, S.M. Central Bank Policy Mix: Issues, Challenges, and Policy Responses. In *Central Bank Policy Mix: Issues, Challenges, and Policy Responses*; Springer: Singapore, 2022; pp. 17–26.
65. Juhro, S.M. Central Banking Practices in the Digital Era: Salient Challenges, Lessons, and Implications. In *Central Bank Policy Mix: Issues, Challenges, and Policy Responses*; Springer: Singapore, 2022; p. 261.
66. Miyata, Y.; Ishita, E.; Yang, F.; Yamamoto, M.; Iwase, A.; Kurata, K. Knowledge structure transition in library and information science: Topic modeling and visualization. *Scientometrics* **2020**, *125*, 665–687. [CrossRef]
67. Bai, Y.; Li, H.; Liu, Y. Visualizing research trends and research theme evolution in E-learning field: 1999–2018. *Scientometrics* **2021**, *126*, 1389–1414. [CrossRef]
68. Kocak, M.; García-Zorita, C.; Marugan-Lazaro, S.; Çakır, M.P.; Sanz-Casado, E. Mapping and clustering analysis on neuroscience literature in Turkey: A bibliometric analysis from 2000 to 2017. *Scientometrics* **2019**, *121*, 1339–1366. [CrossRef]
69. Castelló-Sirvent, F.; Roger-Monzó, V. Research Agenda on Turnaround Strategies Beyond Systemic Disruptions. *J. Organ. Chang. Manag.* **2022**, in press. [CrossRef]
70. Castelló-Sirvent, F. A Fuzzy-Set Qualitative Comparative Analysis of Publications on the Fuzzy Sets Theory. *Mathematics* **2022**, *10*, 1322. [CrossRef]
71. Garrido-Ruso, M.; Aibar-Guzmán, B.; Monteiro, A.P. Businesses' Role in the Fulfillment of the 2030 Agenda: A Bibliometric Analysis. *Sustainability* **2022**, *14*, 8754. [CrossRef]
72. Van Eck, N.; Waltman, L. Software survey: VOSviewer, a computer program for bibliometric mapping. *Scientometrics* **2010**, *84*, 523–538. [CrossRef]
73. Waltman, L.; Van Eck, N.J.; Noyons, E.C.M. A unified approach to mapping and clustering of bibliometric networks. *J. Informetr.* **2010**, *4*, 629–635. [CrossRef]
74. Cobo, M.J.; López-Herrera, A.G.; Herrera-Viedma, E.; Herrera, F. SciMAT: A new science mapping analysis software tool. *J. Am. Soc. Inf. Sci. Technol.* **2012**, *63*, 1609–1630. [CrossRef]

75. López-Robles, J.R.; Cobo, M.J.; Gutiérrez-Salcedo, M.; Martínez-Sánchez, M.A.; Gamboa-Rosales, N.K.; Herrera-Viedma, E. 30th Anniversary of Applied Intelligence: A combination of bibliometrics and thematic analysis using SciMAT. *Appl. Intell.* **2021**, *51*, 6547–6568. [CrossRef]
76. Cobo, M.J.; López-Herrera, A.G.; Herrera-Viedma, E.; Herrera, F. An approach for detecting, quantifying, and visualizing the evolution of a research field: A practical application to the Fuzzy Sets Theory field. *J. Informetr.* **2011**, *5*, 146–166. [CrossRef]
77. Santana, M.; Cobo, M.J. What is the future of work? A science mapping analysis. *Eur. Manag. J.* **2020**, *38*, 846–862. [CrossRef]
78. Callon, M.; Courtial, J.-P.; Laville, F. Co-word analysis as a tool for describing the network of interactions between basic and technological research: The case of polymer chemsitry. *Scientometrics* **1991**, *22*, 155–205. [CrossRef]
79. Cardella, G.M.; Hernández-Sánchez, B.R.; Sánchez García, J.C. Entrepreneurship and family role: A systematic review of a growing research. *Front. Psychol.* **2020**, *10*, 2939. [CrossRef] [PubMed]
80. Coulter, N.; Monarch, I.; Konda, S. Software engineering as seen through its research literature: A study in co-word analysis. *J. Am. Soc. Inf. Sci.* **1998**, *49*, 1206–1223. [CrossRef]
81. Peters, H.; Van Raan, A. Structuring scientific activities by co-author analysis: An expercise on a university faculty level. *Scientometrics* **1991**, *20*, 235–255. [CrossRef]
82. Opricovic, S.; Tzeng, G.-H. Compromise solution by MCDM methods: A comparative analysis of VIKOR and TOPSIS. *Eur. J. Oper. Res.* **2004**, *156*, 445–455. [CrossRef]
83. Opricovic, S.; Tzeng, G.-H. Extended VIKOR method in comparison with outranking methods. *Eur. J. Oper. Res.* **2007**, *178*, 514–529. [CrossRef]
84. Chen, T.-Y.; Chang, C.-H.; Lu, J.R. The extended QUALIFLEX method for multiple criteria decision analysis based on interval type-2 fuzzy sets and applications to medical decision making. *Eur. J. Oper. Res.* **2013**, *226*, 615–625. [CrossRef]
85. Hatami-Marbini, A.; Tavana, M. An extension of the Electre I method for group decision-making under a fuzzy environment. *Omega* **2011**, *39*, 373–386. [CrossRef]
86. Lai, Y.-J.; Liu, T.-Y.; Hwang, C.-L. Topsis for MODM. *Eur. J. Oper. Res.* **1994**, *76*, 486–500. [CrossRef]
87. Wang, Y.M.; Luo, Y.; Hua, Z. On the extent analysis method for fuzzy AHP and its applications. *Eur. J. Oper. Res.* **2008**, *186*, 735–747. [CrossRef]
88. Liang, G.-S. Fuzzy MCDM based on ideal and anti-ideal concepts. *Eur. J. Oper. Res.* **1999**, *112*, 682–691. [CrossRef]
89. Chiou, H.-K.; Tzeng, G.-H.; Cheng, D.-C. Evaluating sustainable fishing development strategies using fuzzy MCDM approach. *Omega* **2005**, *33*, 223–234. [CrossRef]
90. Wu, Y.; Xu, C.; Zhang, T. Evaluation of renewable power sources using a fuzzy MCDM based on cumulative prospect theory: A case in China. *Energy* **2018**, *147*, 1227–1239. [CrossRef]
91. Wang, C.; Lu, I.; Chen, C. Evaluating firm technological innovation capability under uncertainty. *Technovation* **2008**, *28*, 349–363. [CrossRef]
92. Zhang, H.; Gu, C.-L.; Gu, L.; Zhang, Y. The evaluation of tourism destination competitiveness by TOPSIS & information entropy–A case in the Yangtze River Delta of China. *Tour. Manag.* **2011**, *32*, 443–451.
93. Ehrgott, M.; Klamroth, K.; Schwehm, C. An MCDM approach to portfolio optimization. *Eur. J. Oper. Res.* **2004**, *155*, 752–770. [CrossRef]
94. Munda, G. Social multi-criteria evaluation: Methodological foundations and operational consequences. *Eur. J. Oper. Res.* **2004**, *158*, 662–677. [CrossRef]
95. Wątróbski, J.; Jankowski, J.; Ziemba, P.; Karczmarczyk, A.; Zioło, M. Generalised framework for multi-criteria method selection. *Omega* **2019**, *86*, 107–124. [CrossRef]
96. Stewart, T.J. A critical survey on the status of multiple criteria decision making theory and practice. *Omega* **1992**, *20*, 569–586. [CrossRef]
97. Figueira, J.; Roy, B. Determining the weights of criteria in the ELECTRE type methods with a revised Simos' procedure. *Eur. J. Oper. Res.* **2002**, *139*, 317–326. [CrossRef]
98. Mareschal, B.; Brans, J.-P. Geometrical representations for MCDA. *Eur. J. Oper. Res.* **1988**, *34*, 69–77. [CrossRef]
99. Yazdani, M.; Zarate, P.; Zavadskas, E.K.; Turskis, Z. A Combined Compromise Solution (CoCoSo) method for multi-criteria decision-making problems. *Manag. Decis.* **2018**, *57*, 2501–2519. [CrossRef]
100. Kim, S.H.; Ahn, B.S. Interactive group decision making procedure under incomplete information. *Eur. J. Oper. Res.* **1999**, *116*, 498–507. [CrossRef]
101. Mi, X.; Tang, M.; Liao, H.; Shen, W.; Lev, B. The state-of-the-art survey on integrations and applications of the best worst method in decision making: Why, what, what for and what's next? *Omega* **2019**, *87*, 205–225. [CrossRef]
102. Mikhailov, L. Fuzzy analytical approach to partnership selection in formation of virtual enterprises. *Omega* **2002**, *30*, 393–401. [CrossRef]
103. Liesiö, J.; Mild, P.; Salo, A. Preference programming for robust portfolio modeling and project selection. *Eur. J. Oper. Res.* **2007**, *181*, 1488–1505. [CrossRef]
104. Rezaei, J.; van Wulfften Palthe, L.; Tavasszy, L.; Wiegmans, B.; van der Laan, F. Port performance measurement in the context of port choice: An MCDA approach. *Manag. Decis.* **2018**, *57*, 396–417. [CrossRef]
105. Romero, C. A general structure of achievement function for a goal programming model. *Eur. J. Oper. Res.* **2004**, *153*, 675–686. [CrossRef]

106. Romero, C. Extended lexicographic goal programming: A unifying approach. *Omega* **2001**, *29*, 63–71. [CrossRef]
107. Tone, K. A slacks-based measure of super-efficiency in data envelopment analysis. *Eur. J. Oper. Res.* **2002**, *143*, 32–41. [CrossRef]
108. Liu, C.-H.; Tzeng, G.-H.; Lee, M.-H. Improving tourism policy implementation–The use of hybrid MCDM models. *Tour. Manag.* **2012**, *33*, 413–426. [CrossRef]
109. Chen, N.-P.; Shen, K.-Y.; Liang, C.-J. Hybrid Decision Model for Evaluating Blockchain Business Strategy: A Bank's Perspective. *Sustainability* **2021**, *13*, 5809. [CrossRef]
110. Muñoz, P.; Cohen, B. Mapping out the sharing economy: A configurational approach to sharing business modeling. *Technol. Forecast. Soc. Change* **2017**, *125*, 21–37. [CrossRef]
111. Wang, X.; Chen, Q.; Wang, J. Fuzzy rough set based sustainable methods for energy efficient smart city development. *J. Intell. Fuzzy Syst.* **2021**, *40*, 8173–8183. [CrossRef]
112. Abdel-Basset, M.; Mohamed, M. The role of single valued neutrosophic sets and rough sets in smart city: Imperfect and incomplete information systems. *Measurement* **2018**, *124*, 47–55. [CrossRef]
113. Castanho, M.S.; Ferreira, F.A.F.; Carayannis, E.G.; Ferreira, J.J.M. SMART-C: Developing a "smart city" assessment system using cognitive mapping and the Choquet integral. *IEEE Trans. Eng. Manag.* **2019**, *68*, 562–573. [CrossRef]
114. Deveci, M.; Pekaslan, D.; Canıtez, F. The assessment of smart city projects using zSlice type-2 fuzzy sets based Interval Agreement Method. *Sustain. Cities Soc.* **2020**, *53*, 101889. [CrossRef]
115. Awasthi, A.; Omrani, H. A goal-oriented approach based on fuzzy axiomatic design for sustainable mobility project selection. *Int. J. Syst. Sci. Oper. Logist.* **2019**, *6*, 86–98. [CrossRef]
116. Abdelkafi, N.; Hansen, E.G. Ecopreneurs' creation of user business models for green tech: An exploratory study in e-mobility. *Int. J. Entrep. Ventur.* **2018**, *10*, 32–55. [CrossRef]
117. Yuan, J.; Li, C.; Li, W.; Liu, D.; Li, X. Linguistic hesitant fuzzy multi-criterion decision-making for renewable energy: A case study in Jilin. *J. Clean. Prod.* **2018**, *172*, 3201–3214. [CrossRef]
118. Osunmuyiwa, O.; Kalfagianni, A. Transitions in unlikely places: Exploring the conditions for renewable energy adoption in Nigeria. *Environ. Innov. Soc. Transit.* **2017**, *22*, 26–40. [CrossRef]
119. Narayanamoorthy, S.; Annapoorani, V.; Kang, D.; Ramya, L. Sustainable assessment for selecting the best alternative of reclaimed water use under hesitant fuzzy multi-criteria decision making. *IEEE Access* **2019**, *7*, 137217–137231. [CrossRef]
120. Daniel, D.; Marks, S.J.; Pande, S.; Rietveld, L. Socio-environmental drivers of sustainable adoption of household water treatment in developing countries. *NPJ Clean Water* **2018**, *1*, 1–6. [CrossRef]
121. Knieper, C.; Pahl-Wostl, C. A comparative analysis of water governance, water management, and environmental performance in river basins. *Water Resour. Manag.* **2016**, *30*, 2161–2177. [CrossRef]
122. Bohnsack, R. Local niches and firm responses in sustainability transitions: The case of low-emission vehicles in China. *Technovation* **2018**, *70*, 20–32. [CrossRef]
123. Rajiv Mathad, A. Turnaround Management: An Explorative Investigation of the Strategic Leadership Competencies for the Turnaround of Indian IT Firms. Master's Thesis, National College of Ireland, Dublin, Ireland, 2019.
124. Ren, J.Z.; Ren, X.S. Sustainability ranking of energy storage technologies under uncertainties. *J. Clean. Prod.* **2018**, *170*, 1387–1398. [CrossRef]
125. Gumus, S.; Egilmez, G.; Kucukvar, M.; Shin Park, Y. Integrating expert weighting and multi-criteria decision making into eco-efficiency analysis: The case of US manufacturing. *J. Oper. Res. Soc.* **2016**, *67*, 616–628. [CrossRef]
126. McKenna, R.; Bertsch, V.; Mainzer, K.; Fichtner, W. Combining local preferences with multi-criteria decision analysis and linear optimization to develop feasible energy concepts in small communities. *Eur. J. Oper. Res.* **2018**, *268*, 1092–1110. [CrossRef]
127. Baudry, G.; Macharis, C.; Vallée, T. Range-based Multi-Actor Multi-Criteria Analysis: A combined method of Multi-Actor Multi-Criteria Analysis and Monte Carlo simulation to support participatory decision making under uncertainty. *Eur. J. Oper. Res.* **2018**, *264*, 257–269. [CrossRef]
128. Herrera-Viedma, E. Fuzzy sets and fuzzy logic in multi-criteria decision making. The 50th anniversary of Prof. Lotfi Zadeh's theory: Introduction. *Technol. Econ. Dev. Econ.* **2015**, *21*, 677–683. [CrossRef]
129. Geels, F.W. Socio-technical transitions to sustainability: A review of criticisms and elaborations of the Multi-Level Perspective. *Curr. Opin. Environ. Sustain.* **2019**, *39*, 187–201. [CrossRef]
130. Mahmoudi, A.; Deng, X.; Javed, S.A.; Zhang, N. Sustainable supplier selection in megaprojects: Grey ordinal priority approach. *Bus. Strateg. Environ.* **2021**, *30*, 318–339. [CrossRef]
131. Govender, L. Heuristics in Managerial Decision Making during Company Turnaround and Uncertainty. Master's Thesis, University of Pretoria, Pretoria, South Africa, 2016.
132. Bai, C.; Rezaei, J.; Sarkis, J. Multicriteria green supplier segmentation. *IEEE Trans. Eng. Manag.* **2017**, *64*, 515–528. [CrossRef]
133. Greco, S.; Matarazzo, B.; Slowinski, R. Rough sets methodology for sorting problems in presence of multiple attributes and criteria. *Eur. J. Oper. Res.* **2002**, *138*, 247–259. [CrossRef]
134. Rezaei, J. Best-worst multi-criteria decision-making method. *Omega* **2015**, *53*, 49–57. [CrossRef]
135. Yu, S.; Wang, J.; Wang, J. An extended TODIM approach with intuitionistic linguistic numbers. *Int. Trans. Oper. Res.* **2018**, *25*, 781–805. [CrossRef]
136. Yu, L.; Wang, S.; Lai, K.K. An intelligent-agent-based fuzzy group decision making model for financial multicriteria decision support: The case of credit scoring. *Eur. J. Oper. Res.* **2009**, *195*, 942–959. [CrossRef]

137. Kuo, T. A modified TOPSIS with a different ranking index. *Eur. J. Oper. Res.* **2017**, *260*, 152–160. [CrossRef]
138. Liesiö, J.; Mild, P.; Salo, A. Robust portfolio modeling with incomplete cost information and project interdependencies. *Eur. J. Oper. Res.* **2008**, *190*, 679–695. [CrossRef]
139. Miettinen, K.; Mäkelä, M.M. Synchronous approach in interactive multiobjective optimization. *Eur. J. Oper. Res.* **2006**, *170*, 909–922. [CrossRef]
140. Gou, X.; Xu, Z.; Liao, H.; Herrera, F. Probabilistic double hierarchy linguistic term set and its use in designing an improved VIKOR method: The application in smart healthcare. *J. Oper. Res. Soc.* **2021**, *72*, 2611–2630. [CrossRef]
141. Fang, R.; Liao, H.; Yang, J.-B.; Xu, D.-L. Generalised probabilistic linguistic evidential reasoning approach for multi-criteria decision-making under uncertainty. *J. Oper. Res. Soc.* **2021**, *72*, 130–144. [CrossRef]
142. Tian, Z.-P.; Nie, R.-X.; Wang, J.-Q. Probabilistic linguistic multi-criteria decision-making based on evidential reasoning and combined ranking methods considering decision-makers' psychological preferences. *J. Oper. Res. Soc.* **2020**, *71*, 700–717. [CrossRef]
143. Liao, H.; Wu, X.; Mi, X.; Herrera, F. An integrated method for cognitive complex multiple experts multiple criteria decision making based on ELECTRE III with weighted Borda rule. *Omega* **2020**, *93*, 102052. [CrossRef]
144. Simões, J.C.M.; Ferreira, F.A.F.; Peris-Ortiz, M.; Ferreira, J.J.M. A cognition-driven framework for the evaluation of startups in the digital economy: Adding value with cognitive mapping and rule-based expert systems. *Manag. Decis.* **2020**, *58*, 2327–2347. [CrossRef]
145. Silva, A.R.D.; Ferreira, F.A.F.; Carayannis, E.G.; Ferreira, J.J.M. Measuring SMEs' propensity for open innovation using cognitive mapping and MCDA. *IEEE Trans. Eng. Manag.* **2019**, *68*, 396–407. [CrossRef]
146. Zhou, H.; Wang, J.; Zhang, H. Stochastic multicriteria decision-making approach based on SMAA-ELECTRE with extended gray numbers. *Int. Trans. Oper. Res.* **2019**, *26*, 2032–2052. [CrossRef]
147. Yasmin, M.; Tatoglu, E.; Kilic, H.S.; Zaim, S.; Delen, D. Big data analytics capabilities and firm performance: An integrated MCDM approach. *J. Bus. Res.* **2020**, *114*, 1–15. [CrossRef]
148. Liang, R.; Chong, H.-Y. A hybrid group decision model for green supplier selection: A case study of megaprojects. *Eng. Constr. Archit. Manag.* **2019**, *26*, 1712–1734. [CrossRef]
149. Almasi, M.; Khoshfetrat, S.; Galankashi, M.R. Sustainable supplier selection and order allocation under risk and inflation condition. *IEEE Trans. Eng. Manag.* **2019**, *68*, 823–837. [CrossRef]

MDPI
St. Alban-Anlage 66
4052 Basel
Switzerland
Tel. +41 61 683 77 34
Fax +41 61 302 89 18
www.mdpi.com

Axioms Editorial Office
E-mail: axioms@mdpi.com
www.mdpi.com/journal/axioms